This important work is one of the first Marxist studies of the central theoretical problems posed by the nature of the capitalist state. Nicos Poulantzas draws on the classical texts of Marx, Engels, Lenin and Gramsci and aims to provide a systematic political theory by elucidating implicit ideas and axioms in their practical writings. He also, however, confronts the theses of many of the most prominent exponents of Western sociology—from Weber, Parsons or Michels to Easton, Almond and Dahrendorf, Aron or Mills. His book provides a wide-ranging analysis of the position and function of the State within the capitalist mode of production, and offers new concepts for a scientific understanding of class domination and the political oppression assured by it.

Poulantzas criticizes contemporary definitions of power and social class, and seeks to establish a more complex framework for exploring the relationship between the two. He lays great emphasis on the need for a more sophisticated typology of the political 'blocs' and 'fractions' which have histically presided over the different phases and forms of the capitalist state. The roles of ideology and bureaucracy, the relation between regimes and apparatuses of bourgeois rule, and the location of class struggle within the capitalist mode of production, are all surveyed in a fresh light.

Political Power and Social Classes is an essential work for the study of politics today.

Nicos Poulantzas

Verso

Political Power and Social Classes

Translation editor Timothy O'Hagan

First published as
Pouvoir politique et classes sociales, François Maspero, 1968

© François Maspero, 1968

This edition first published by NLB and Sheed & Ward 1973

Translated by Timothy O'Hagan with the assistance of David McLellan, Anna de Casparis, and Brian Grogan

© NLB and Sheed & Ward 1975

Verso Edition 1978

Verso Editions, 7 Carlisle Street, London W1

Typeset in Monotype Ehrhardt
Printed in Great Britain by
Lowe & Brydone Printers Limited, Thetford, Norfolk

ISBN 86091 705 3

Translation editor's note

A number of minor mistakes in the French text have been noted by myself and the author and have been removed. At certain points therefore, this English translation represents a revised version of the original work.

The following short references to works frequently quoted have been used in the footnotes:

The Poverty of Philosophy: Karl Marx, *The Poverty of Philosophy*, Moscow, 1956.

Capital: Karl Marx, *Capital*, Vol. I, London, 1970, Vol. II, Moscow, 1967, Vol. III, Moscow, 1966.

The German Ideology: Karl Marx and Friedrich Engels, *The German Ideology*, Moscow, 1964.

MESW, 1958: Marx-Engels, *Selected Works* in two volumes, Moscow, 1958.

MESW, 1970: Marx-Engels, *Selected Works* in one volume, London, 1970.

Selected Correspondence: Marx-Engels, *Selected Correspondence*, Moscow, 1965.

Anti-Dühring: Friedrich Engels, *Anti-Dühring*, Moscow, 1959.

Pre-capitalist Economic Formations: Karl Marx, *Pre-capitalist Economic Formations*, London, 1964.

Selected Works: Lenin, *Selected Works* in three volumes, Moscow, 1967.

Collected Works: Lenin, *Collected Works*, translation from the fourth Russian edition, 1960.

Prison Notebooks: Antonio Gramsci, *Selections from the Prison Notebooks*, London, 1971.

For Marx: Louis Althusser, *For Marx*, London, 1969.

Reading Capital: Louis Althusser and Etienne Balibar, *Reading Capital*, London, 1970.

T.D.B.O'H.

Introduction

1. Marxism is made up of two united but distinct disciplines, dialectical materialism and historical materialism, distinguished by the difference between their objects.[1]

Historical materialism (the science of history) has as its object the concept of history, through the study of the various modes of production and social formations, their structure, constitution and functioning, and the forms of transition from one social formation to another.

Dialectical materialism (Marxist philosophy) has as its particular object the production of knowledge, that is the structure and functioning of the process of thought. Strictly speaking, the object of dialectical materialism is the theory of the history of scientific production. Indeed, historical materialism founded dialectical materialism as a distinct discipline in one single theoretical movement, in that the constitution of a science of history, i.e. historical materialism, which is a science whose object is defined as the constitution of the concept of history, led to the definition of a theory of science which includes history as a constituent part of its particular object.

These two disciplines are distinct, though there are some interpretations of Marxism which reduce the one to the other. In one interpretation, dialectical materialism is reduced to historical materialism. This is typically so with historicist interpretations (such as those of the young Lukács, Korsch, etc.), which make Marxism into a historical anthropology of which history is an originating and basic category, rather than a concept to be constructed. Reflection on the structures, 'gaining consciousness of their meaning', is a function of the structures themselves, which are interiorized in a process of mediation. In the other interpretation, historical materialism is reduced to dialectical materialism. This is the procedure of positivist-empiricist interpretations, which dilute the

1. See L. Althusser, *For Marx*, London, 1969; *Reading Capital*, London, 1970; 'Matérialisme historique et matérialisme dialectique' in *Cahiers Marxistes-Léninistes*, no. 11; and 'Sur le travail théorique. Difficultés et ressources' in *La Pensée*, April 1967.

proper object of historical materialism, by subsuming all historical objects under the same universally valid 'abstract' law, a 'model' regulating *all historical 'concretization'*.

As Marx demonstrated in the *Introduction of 1857*, in the *Preface to a Contribution to the Critique of Political Economy* and in *Capital,* historical materialism maintains a *general theory* defining the concepts which command its whole field of investigation (the concepts of mode of production, of social formation, of real appropriation and property, of combination, ideology, politics, conjuncture and transition). These concepts allow it to define the concept of its object: the concept of history. The object of historical materialism is the study of different structures and practices (the economy, politics, ideology), which are connected and yet distinct, and whose combination constitutes a mode of production and a social formation. These theories can be characterized as *regional theories.* Historical materialism also includes *particular theories* (theories of the slave, feudal, capitalist and other modes of production). The existence of these particular theories is justified by the diversity of combinations of structures and practices, which define distinct modes of production and social formations. *This order is still only that of an enumeration*: it will be modified and given a foundation below.

We know that the two basic propositions of dialectical and historical materialism are the following:

1. The distinction between real processes and the processes of thought, between being and knowledge.

2. The primacy of being over thought; the primacy of the real over knowledge of the real.

As the second proposition is widely known, the first must be stressed: the unity of the two processes (the real process and the process as thought) is founded on the fact that they are distinct.

Theoretical work then, whatever the degree of its abstraction, is always work bearing on real processes. Yet since this work produces knowledge, it is wholly situated in the process of thought: no concepts are more real than others. Theoretical work proceeds from a *raw material,* which consists not of the 'real-concrete', but of information, notions, etc. about this reality, and deals with it *by means of certain conceptual tools*: the result of this work is the *knowledge* of an object.

It can be said that, in the strong sense of the term, only *real, concrete, singular* objects exist. The final aim of the process of thought is knowledge of these objects: e.g. of France or England at a given moment of their development. Knowledge of these objects does not thus presuppose their existence at the starting-point in the raw material, since, being the concrete knowledge of a concrete object, it is precisely the result of a process which Marx designates in terms of a 'synthesis of a multiplicity of determinations'. In other respects, although the process of thought has knowledge of real-concrete objects as its final purpose and justification, it does not always bear upon these objects: it can also bear upon objects which may be termed *abstract-formal*; such objects (e.g. the mode of production) do not exist in the strong sense of the word, but they are the condition of knowledge of real-concrete objects.

It is possible to distinguish between the various concepts according to their degree of abstraction, from the poorest to the most elaborate and richest in theoretical determinations. This involves determining both their exact place in the process of thought and the object of thought upon which they bear.[2] The most concrete concepts, those which lead to knowledge of a social formation at a definite time in its development, are not, any more than real-concrete objects, the raw material of the process of thought; neither are they *deduced* from the most abstract concepts, nor *subsumed* under these latter, simply particularizing their generality. They are the result of a work of theoretical elaboration which operates on information, notions, etc., by means of the most abstract concepts, in order to produce the most concrete concepts leading to the knowledge of real, concrete, singular objects.

We shall take as an example two fundamental concepts of historical materialism which clearly illustrate the distinction between formal-abstract and real-concrete objects, those of mode of production and of social formation.

By *mode of production* we shall designate not what is generally marked out as the economic (i.e. relations of production in the strict sense), but a specific combination of various structures and practices which, in combination, appear as so many instances or levels, i.e. as so many regional structures of this mode. A mode of production, as Engels stated schematically, is composed of different levels or instances, the economic, political, ideological and theoretical: it is understood that this is merely a schematic picture and that a more exhaustive division can be drawn up. The type of unity which characterizes a mode of production is that of a *complex whole*

2. This precision is necessary in order to avoid falling into the old ambiguity of positivist 'abstraction-concretization'.

dominated, in the last instance, by the economic.[3] The term *determination* will be reserved for this dominance in the last instance. This type of relation between the instances can be distinguished from the one which is proposed in certain interpretations of Marxism. It is not, for example, a circular and expressive totality, founded on a central-subject instance which is the foundation category of the origins and the principle of genesis, and of which the other instances, 'total parts' (*partes totales*),[4] constitute only the phenomenal expression. Nor is it a relation of simple analogy or a correlation of external instances, the one related to the other. This relation is neither one of linear causality, nor of expressive mediation, nor of analogical correlation. It is a type of relation inside which the structure in dominance governs the very constitution (the nature) of the regional structures, by assigning them their place and by distributing functions to them. The relations which thus constitute each level are never simple, but *overdetermined* by the relations of the other levels.

Furthermore, the fact that the structure of the whole is determined in the last instance by the economic does not mean that the economic always holds the *dominant role* in the structure. The unity constituted by the structure in dominance implies that every mode of production has a dominant level or instance; but the economic is in fact determinant only in so far as it attributes the dominant role to one instance or another, in so far as it regulates the shift of dominance which results from the de-

3. For Althusser's use of this terminology, and Ben Brewster's somewhat different translation, see *Reading Capital*, Glossary, p. 319: 'STRUCTURE IN DOMINANCE (*structure à dominante*). The Marxist totality is neither a whole each of whose elements is equivalent as the phenomenon of an essence (Hegelianism), nor are some of its elements epiphenomena of any one of them (economism or mechanism); the elements are asymmetrically related but autonomous (contradictory); one of them is *dominant*. [The economic base "*determines*" ("in the last instance") *which* element is to be *dominant* in a social formation. L.A.] Hence it is a structure in dominance. But the dominant element is not fixed for all time, it varies according to the overdetermination of the contradictions and their uneven development. In the social formation this overdetermination is, in the last instance, determined by the economy (*determiné en dernière instance de l'économie*). This is Althusser's clarification of the classical Marxist assertion that the superstructure is relatively autonomous but the economy is determinant in the last instance. The phrase "in the last instance" does not indicate that there will be some ultimate time or ever was some starting-point when the economy will be or was solely determinant, the other instances preceding it or following it: "the last instance never comes"; the structure is always the co-presence of all its elements and their relations of dominance and subordination – it is an "ever-pre-given structure" (*structure toujours-déjà-donnée*).' [Trans.]

4. For this concept, see below, note 9 to this Introduction.

centration of the instances. Thus Marx shows us how, in the feudal mode of production, it is ideology in its religious form which plays the dominant role, a situation which is strictly determined by the functioning of the economic in this mode. Therefore what distinguishes one mode of production from another and consequently specifies a mode of production is the particular form of articulation maintained by its levels: this articulation is henceforth referred to by the term *matrix* of a mode of production. So to give a strict definition of a mode of production is to lay bare the particular way in which determination in the last instance by the economic is reflected inside that mode of production: this reflection delimits the index of dominance and overdetermination of this mode.

The mode of production constitutes an abstract-formal object which does not exist in the strong sense in reality. Capitalist, feudal and slave modes of production, which equally lack existence in the strong sense, also constitute abstract-formal objects. The only thing which really exists is a historically determined *social formation*, i.e. a social whole, in the widest sense, at a given moment in its historical existence: e.g. France under Louis Bonaparte, England during the Industrial Revolution. But a social formation, which is a real-concrete object and so always original because singular, presents a particular combination, a specific overlapping of several 'pure' modes of production (as Lenin demonstrated in *The Development of Capitalism in Russia*). Bismarck's Germany is characterized by a specific combination of capitalist, feudal and patriarchal modes of production whose combination alone exists in the strong sense of the term; all that exists in this sense is a social formation historically determined as a particular object.

The social formation itself constitutes a complex unity in which a certain mode of production dominates the others which compose it. It is a social formation historically determined by a given mode of production: Bismarck's Germany is a capitalist social formation, that is, one dominated by the capitalist mode of production (the capitalist mode of production will henceforth be designated by the initials CMP). The dominance of one mode of production over the others in a social formation causes the matrix of this mode of production (i.e. the particular reflection of determination by the economic element in the last instance by which it is specified) to mark the whole of the formation. In this way a historically determined social formation is specified by a particular articulation (through an index of dominance and overdetermination) of its different economic, political, ideological and theoretical levels or instances. As a general rule, taking account of the dislocations which will be encountered, this articulation is that of the dominant mode of production. For example, in a social formation dominated by the CMP, as a general rule the dominant role is held by the economic. This is merely the effect of the predominance of the capitalist mode in this formation, a mode which is itself characterized, in its 'purity', by the preponderant role held by the economic.

2. The above data are essential in order to grasp (a) the operation of the constitution of a regional structure as an *object of science*, and (b) the logical order of scientific elaboration, i.e. the necessary order validly linking the various concepts, according to their place in the process of thought. The object of this book is *the political*, in particular the political superstructure of the state in the CMP: that is the production of the concept of this region in this mode, and the production of more concrete concepts dealing with politics in capitalist social formations. The method which will be followed is based on the theory expounded above.

The general theory of historical materialism[5] defines a general type of relation between distinct but united instances (the economic, the political, the ideological), and so defines the relatively abstract concepts of these instances at its own level in a necessary relation with its concepts of mode of production, social formation, dominant structure, etc. Strictly speaking, these are concepts which assign formal parameters to any possible social structure. We are dealing, for example, with the most abstract concept of the political, a concept which functions throughout the field of investigation of the general theory of historical materialism: i.e. in modes of production and social formations in general, and particularly in those modes and formations which are divided into classes. The problem of the relation between the political and history finds its right theoretical place here, and the construction of the concept of this relation is the proper object of historical materialism.

However, the regional theory of the political can advance to concepts richer in theoretical determinations only by locating its object in a given mode of production. According to the principles which led us to construct the concept of mode of production, a regional instance (specifically the political) can constitute an object of regional theory only in so far as it is 'isolated' (*découpée*) in a given mode of production. The possibility of

5. A general theory not to be confused with dialectical materialism, since the latter is not simply the epistemology of historical materialism.

constituting it as an object of science (i.e. constructing its proper concept) does not depend on its nature, but on its *place* and *function* in the particular combination which specifies this mode of production. Localized in this way, this instance may be said to occupy the place strictly assigned to the political by its abstract concept, which depends on the general theory. In particular, it is the articulation of the instances peculiar to this mode of production which defines the *extension* and the *limits* of this regional instance, by assigning the field of the political to the corresponding regional theory. The economic, the political and the ideological are not already constituted essences, which then enter into external relations with each other, according to the schema of base and superstructure – a schema which, if taken literally, is ambiguous. The articulation peculiar to the totality of a mode of production governs the constitution of its regional instances. So to construct the concept of the object of political science, by passing from the poorest theoretical determinations to the richest, presupposes the strict definition of the political as level, instance or region of a given mode of production.

It is here in historical materialism that the junction takes place between what have been defined as regional theories, e.g. the theory of the political, and particular theories, i.e. theories of different modes of production. This junction is not accidental, but takes place according to a valid order, that of the process of thought: the regional theory of the political in the CMP *presupposes* the particular theory of this mode of production. The place assigned to the political in the CMP depends on the particular theory of this mode, on its specific type of articulation, and index of dominance and overdetermination, as expounded by Marx in *Capital*. The particular theory of the CMP possesses its own concepts, which operate throughout its field of investigation, and thus govern the production of the proper concepts of the regional theory of the political in this mode.

Yet at the same time, the CMP and the political in this mode, e.g. the capitalist state or the political forms of class struggle in this mode, constitute abstract-formal objects, since only states of historically determined capitalist formations exist, in the strong sense of the word. The final aim of the process of thought is the production of the most concrete concepts, in other words those richest in theoretical determinations, which allow knowledge of real, concrete, particular objects, namely social formations always original in each case. This logical order, leading from the most abstract to the most concrete concepts, proceeds from the concepts of the general theory of historical materialism to those which (as Lenin says) allow a concrete analysis of a concrete situation.[6]

3. We must also consider two sets of problems, (i) those relating to the information, notions, etc. which constitute the raw material of the theoretical process of this book; and (ii) those relating to the status of the texts of the Marxist classics concerning the political.

The raw material has been collected at source, from the texts of the Marxist classics, from the political texts of the workers' movement, and

---

6. By adopting Althusser's terminology in *For Marx* and by designating by *g.1* (generalities 1) the *raw material* of the process of thought, by *g.2* (generalities 2) the *tools or means of* theoretical *work*, and by *g.3* (generalities 3) *knowledge*, we may schematize in the following way the logical order of the process which goes from the most abstract concepts (bearing on formal-abstract objects) to the most concrete concepts (bearing on real-concrete singular objects), i.e. the various necessary stages in theoretical discourse.

Let our object be the theory of the political in the CMP.

g.3

(Knowledge already obtained by the process of thought on historical materialism: a general theory in which the most abstract concept of the political takes its place as an instance of every structure) from contemporary texts in political science. In this last case, a selection has been made according to their seriousness. It must be said that in the present state of research, and in so far as these works are being considered as the raw material of research, their Marxist or non-Marxist character does not in any way provide a relevant criterion of their seriousness or their lack of seriousness. First of all I have used French political science texts with special reference to the capitalist state. As political science is relatively undeveloped in France, frequent recourse has been made to works in English, whether by British or American authors, and in German. Such works are relatively unknown in France: the characteristic provincialism of French intellectual life is well known, and one of its more important effects is that doors are frequently being broken down which are already open; in other words, there is a calm belief in the originality of a theoretical production, which has already been much more elaborated by foreign authors. However, these works have been considered by means of a critical study bearing on their method and on the often implicit theory underpinning them. In other respects, these works sometimes contain, as scientific elements within an ideological discourse, authentic theoretical concepts which have been purified by this critical work.

Furthermore, in order to use the texts of the Marxist classics as a source of information, particularly on the capitalist state, it has been necessary to complete them and to subject them to a particular critical treatment. Because of the non-systematic character of these texts, the information contained in them sometimes appears incomplete or even inexact, in the light of the historical and political information now at our disposal.

There is another series of problems concerning those texts of the Marxist classics (Marx, Engels, Lenin and Gramsci) which bear on the strictly theoretical treatment of politics. It must first be stated, as a general remark, that these authors did not specifically discuss the region of the political at the level of theoretical *systematicity*. In other words, since they were occupied in the direct exercise of their own political practice, they did not explicitly deal with its theory in the strong sense of the term. What in fact can be found in their works is either (i) a well-ordered body of concepts in the 'practical state', i.e. concepts present in the discourse and destined, through their function, to be a direct guide to political practice in a concrete conjuncture, yet not theoretically elaborated; or (ii) *elements* of theoretical knowledge of political practice and of the superstructure of the state, i.e. concepts elaborated but not inserted in a systematic theoretical discourse; or (iii) an *implicit* conception of the political in general in the Marxist problematic, a conception which rigorously underpins the production of these concepts, but which involves certain risks which beset all thought which is not contemporaneous with itself and therefore cannot be systematically explicit in its principles.

This state of affairs, which we are merely recording at this stage, relates to the real contingent order of development of historical materialism. It must not be confused with the valid logical order of the theoretical process which has just been explained. It involves great difficulties relative to the *status* of the texts which are going to be considered.

a. The first difficulty concerns the location of the original problematic of Marxism in the works of Marx and Engels. This problematic, which represents an epistemological break (*coupure*) from the problematic of the works of the young Marx, is first outlined in *The German Ideology*, a text of the period of the break which still contains numerous ambiguities. This break means that Marx had already become a Marxist. Consequently, it must be pointed out at once that I shall not consider what it has become customary to call the works of the young Marx, except in order to use them for comparison, that is, to use them especially as a point of reference in tracking down ideological 'survivals' of the earlier problematic in the works of the period of maturity. This is particularly important for Marxist political science since the youthful works are principally concerned with political theory. I have used the term 'survivals', but it is fallacious. In fact, the notions of the youthful works which recur in the mature works gain a different meaning in this new context – whether as *signposts* pointing to new problems, as *mere words* illegitimately extended to denote a new way of asking questions, or as *stumbling-blocks* impeding the production of new concepts. Their precise function will have to be elucidated. In other respects, the marking-out of the problematic is also important in considering other authors, notably Gramsci, whose works, despite the epistemological breaks which they contain, reveal a particular permanence of the historicist problematic.

b. Let us now consider the major theoretical work of Marxism, *Capital*. What can be drawn from it concerning, in particular, the study of the political, and notably the political in the capitalist state? Amongst other things which it contains I limit myself to what is of principal interest to us here, namely (i) a scientific treatment of the CMP, of the connection and the combination (matrix) of instances which specify it, and (ii) a systematic theoretical treatment of the economic region of this mode of production. This is not (as has long been believed) because nothing important happens in the other regions and because examination of them is a secondary task, but rather for two reasons: firstly because (as will be seen in a moment) this mode of production is specified by a characteristic autonomy of its instances, which can be subjected to a particular scientific treatment, and secondly because the economic holds the dominant role in this mode, a role over and above determination in the last instance. Thus, the other instances (the political and the ideological) are very definitely *present* in *Capital*, which is not, in this sense, an 'exclusively' economic work, but they are present *implicitly*, that is through their effects in the economic region. No systematic theory of ideology in the CMP is to be found in *Capital*, for the remarks on capitalist fetishism cannot claim this title, nor is there a theory of politics in it. This implicit presence of the political in *Capital* will be very useful to us, without being able to take us very far. It is present both in the strictly theoretical developments of *Capital*, and in the concrete examples which Marx provides as illustrations of these developments, for instance the passages concerning the role of the state in the original accumulation of capital or in factory legislation in England. These remarks illustrate to some extent the implicit presence of the political in the economic, i.e. of the particular theory of the CMP, and are not intended to produce more concrete concepts intended for knowledge of social formations, as is the case in *The Eighteenth Brumaire*.

c. Next, we have at our disposal a series of texts which bear, partly or wholly, upon the object of political science in its abstract-formal form (whether it is the state in general, class struggle in general, or the capitalist state in general), such as Marx's *Critique of the Gotha Programme* or *The Civil War in France*, Engels's *Anti-Dühring*, Lenin's *The State and Revolution* and Gramsci's *Notes on Machiavelli*. However, these are principally texts of ideological struggle. They were conceived as urgent retorts to attacks or distortions of Marxist theory and their authors were frequently forced to place themselves on the same ideological ground as the texts they refute. These texts often contain authentic concepts which are effaced by their insertion in ideology and can be discovered only by a full-scale critical study.

d. We can now consider the political texts in the strict sense of the term. It follows from what has been said that their status is very complex.

As a rule, they bear upon real-concrete objects, i.e. on historically determined social formations, for example France, Germany and England for Marx and Engels, Russia for Lenin or Italy for Gramsci, at a given moment of their development. In particular, these texts comprise a 'concrete analysis of a concrete situation', notably of the conjuncture of these formations. In this sense, they actually contain a whole series of the most concrete concepts concerning the knowledge of this conjuncture. But this is not all: because of the absence of systematic theoretical works in this field, they bear simultaneously on abstract-formal objects, in the same discursive, inexplicit, unanalysed exposition; they depend on a conception of the political element in the general theory, and on a regional theory of the political in the CMP. This is an indisputable and important fact: these political works do in fact contain some of the most abstract concepts, but either in the 'practical state', i.e. in a form which is not theoretically elaborated, or else in a form which is more or less elaborated but only at the level of elements, that is, inserted in a discursive order of exposition which is not their order in the logical order of research.

We can therefore grasp the difficult problems posed by these texts because of their status. When we read them, we must ask them the relevant questions, following the theoretical order of the process of thought defined above. In other words what we must do is use elaboration rather than simple extraction to replace the different concepts contained in these texts in the place which is validly theirs in the process of thought. This process strictly defines their degree of abstraction, i.e. their extension and precise limits. Thus it will sometimes be seen that their field is not at all that which their authors thought was assigned to them. Moreover, it is evident that, through this work, these concepts will undergo some necessary transformations. For example, we shall have to reveal how far certain concepts, which appear in the study of the political in a concrete capitalist social formation, do in fact function (appropriately transformed or not) in the field of the political in the capitalist mode of production; and how they are thus valid for capitalist social formations in general, and indeed for all possible capitalist formations. One example is the concept of 'Bonapartism' produced in connection with Louis Bonaparte's France, whose field of operation is the capitalist type of state. A second question is to what extent concepts propounded in texts concerning other social formations apply to the capitalist mode of production and to capitalist social formations. One example of this is the problem set by Lenin's texts on the united front or bureaucratism in the USSR during the period of transition to socialism. A third question is to what extent certain of these concepts have the political in general as a field. Or, finally, to what extent certain concepts, to which their authors have assigned the political in general as a field, really only have as a field the political in the CMP: an example is Gramsci's concept of hegemony, etc.

Moreover, it is unnecessary to emphasize the fact that under these circumstances we often have to deal (i) with contradictory concepts or (ii) with ordinary words which are taken by their authors for concepts though they can in fact only serve as indicators of problems or (iii) (inevitably) with ideological notions.

4. I shall now make some brief remarks on the *order of exposition*. As emphasized by Marx, the order of exposition of concepts is an integral part of all scientific discourse. Science is a demonstrative discourse, in which the order of exposition and presentation of concepts derives from their necessary relations which should be brought to light. It is this order which connects the concepts and attributes to scientific discursivity its *systematic* character. This order of exposition is distinguished not only from the order of investigation and research, but also, importantly, from the logical, valid order of the process of thought. This latter distinction is the important one: in other words, the systematic nature of the order of exposition, relative to the connection and relations between the concepts in the process of thought, is neither the simple recapitulation nor the simple reduplication of the order of the process of thought. This is clear in Marx's plan of exposition for *Capital*. In our case, the dislocation between the two derives above all from the fact that the system of the process of thought, which is the proper object of dialectical materialism, cannot be explicitly present in the exposition of a text which bears on historical materialism, because of the distinction between the two disciplines.[7]

It is therefore possible to reveal a general order of exposition in my text: the conception of the political in general, the particular theory of the CMP, the regional theory of the political in this mode of production and the examination of concrete capitalist social formations. But its systematicity will have to be considered in the order of its own necessity, and not in the order of its degree of reproduction of the process of thought. Dislocations between the two will appear, notably with regard

7. See A. Badiou, 'Le (re)commencement du matérialisme dialectique' in *Critique*, May 1967.

to the general theory of historical materialism, whose concepts will be introduced progressively, following the necessary order of exposition of a text bearing on the regional theory of the political in the CMP. Dislocations will also appear in the presentation of the particular theory of this mode of production, a theory which, given the object of this text, must already be present in the examination of the general conception of the political. Moreover, it must be admitted that these dislocations are also the result of the present state of research, that is, of the theoretical conjuncture of historical materialism which, at least with regard to the general theory and the particular theories, is still far from a satisfactory systematic elaboration.

5. These difficulties have led me to take *indispensable precautions* in this text. In particular, the analyses bearing on the political in the general theory lay claim only to a relative systematicity, and could not anyway be considered to be exhaustive. In fact I should like to note my reserve towards a currently over-popular tendency to put the cart before the horse, in confusing the order of research and investigation with the logical order of the process of thought, and in systematizing the general theory in the void, before proceeding to a sufficient amount of concrete research: a tendency against which Marx warned us. In the circumstances it seems to me particularly illusory and dangerous (theoretically, of course) to proceed further towards systematizing the political in the general theory, inasmuch as we do not yet have enough systematic regional theories of the political in the different modes of production, nor enough particular systematic theories of the different modes of production.

Although I shall concentrate in this text on the regional theory of the political in the CMP, I shall also take into consideration not simply in research, but also in exposition, concrete capitalist social formations. This 'taking into consideration' in the exposition is used for two distinct purposes: either to illustrate the regional theory, or to produce concrete concepts, which lead to knowledge of the political conjuncture of these formations. The context will make it quite clear which of these, if either, is in question.

We shall consciously leave some *problems open*. Having retained or established the concepts which function over the field of the political of the CMP and consequently of capitalist social formations, or again of the political in concrete capitalist formations, I do not wish to enter into an examination of the possibility of transferring, twisting or transforming these concepts into other modes of production or social formations, notably a formation in transition towards socialism, or the socialist mode of production or socialist formation. In other words, wherever I try to place the concepts exactly in the order of the process of thought, it will always be done in terms of the limits of the object of this text. But the problem is left open not only out of caution due to the state of research; it is also because of the (theoretical) *parti pris* adopted, which consists in locating a theoretical difficulty too often neglected, that of the specificity of the region of the political according to the modes of production and social formations considered.

6. Finally we must define certain supplementary concepts of the general theory of historical materialism, and establish the framework of the particular theory of the CMP. These definitions and remarks will be justified later on in the actual body of the text.

It has been pointed out above that the matrix of a mode of production, the articulation of the instances which specify it, is determined in the last instance by the economic. How does this determination function in general, and in the CMP in particular?

As with all other instances, the economic in general is constituted by certain *elements*, which are invariant, but which in fact exist only in their *combination*, which is variable. Marx points this out clearly when he says:

> Whatever the social form of production, labourers and means of production always remain factors of it. [Marx later adds non-labourers to the factors always present in the social form of production.] But in a state of separation from each other either of these factors can be such only potentially. For production to go on at all they must unite. The specific manner in which this union is accomplished distinguishes the different economic epochs of the structure of society from one another.[8]

We are concerned with a combination (*combinaison*) and not with a combinatory (*combinatoire*),[9] because the relations of the elements

8. *Capital*, Vol. II, pp. 36-7.
9. On the distinction between 'combination' and 'combinatory' see *Reading Capital*, Glossary, p. 310: 'COMBINATION/COMBINATORY (*combination, Verbindung/combinatoire*). The only theory of the totality available to classical philosophy is the Leibnizian conception of an expressive totality in which each part "conspires" in the essence of the totality, so that the whole can be read in each of the parts, which are total parts (*partes*

determine *their very nature*, which is modified according to the combination.[10]

These invariant elements of the economic in general are the following:

1. *The labourer*, the 'direct producer', i.e. *labour-power*.

2. *The means of production*, i.e. the *object* and the *means* of labour.

3. *The non-labourer* who appropriates to himself the surplus labour, i.e. the *product*.

These elements exist in a specific combination which constitutes the economic in a given mode of production, a combination which is itself composed of a double relation of these elements.

a. *A relation of real appropriation* (which Marx sometimes designates by the term 'possession'): it applies to the relation of the labourer to the means of production, i.e. to the labour process, or again to the system of productive forces.

b. *A relation of property*: this relation is distinct from the first, since it makes the non-labourer intervene as owner either of the means of production or of labour-power or of both, and so of the product. This is the relation which defines the relations of production in the strict sense.

These two relations are distinct, and by means of their combination, they can take different forms. With regard to the relation of property, *it should be noted that it belongs strictly to the region of the economic and that it should be clearly distinguished from the juridical forms with which it is invested, i.e. from juridical property.* In societies divided into classes, this

---

totales) homologous with it. Modern structuralism reproduces this ideology in its concept of a *combinatory*, a formal pattern of relations and (arbitrarily occupied) places which recur as homologous patterns with a different content throughout the social formation and its history. Theoretically, the combinatory will produce all the possible structures of the social formation, past, present, and future which are or will be realized or not according to chance or to some kind of principle of natural selection. Marxism has an apparently similar concept, that of *combination* or *Verbindung* (Marx). The *Verbindung*, however, has nothing in common with the formalism of the combinatory: it is a complex structure, doubly articulated (in the mode of production, by the productive forces connexion and the relations of production connexion), and one that specifies its content (its "supports"), which changes with a change in the formation or mode of production analysed.' [Trans.]

10. On this subject, see Balibar, in *Reading Capital*, p. 215 and C. Bettelheim, *La transition vers l'économie socialiste*, Paris, 1967. I must point out, however, that I am here explaining economic relations, and their combination, *in their simplest form*. Bettelheim, in an unpublished lecture, 'Le contenu du économique social', 1967, which he was kind enough to show me, and which is of *decisive* importance, demonstrates the complexity (the double aspect) which these relations and their combination take on.

relation of property always sets up a 'separation' of the labourer from the means of labour, which are the property of the non-labourer who, as owner, appropriates to himself the surplus labour.

On the other hand, the relation of real appropriation, in societies divided into classes, can set up either a union of the labourer with the means of production (this is the case with 'precapitalist' modes of production), or a separation of the labourer from these means: this is the case with the CMP, in which a separation occurs at the stage of heavy industry and which Marx designates by the expression 'separation of the direct producer from his natural conditions of labour'.

These two relations thus belong to a unique and variable combination which constitutes the economic in a mode of production, the combination of the system of productive forces with the system of relations of production. In the combination characteristic of the CMP, the two relations are *homologous*. The separation in the relation of property coincides with the separation in the relation of real appropriation. While that of 'precapitalist' modes of production consists of *non-homology* of the two relations: separation in the relation of property, union in the relation of real appropriation.[11]

The determination of a mode of production by the economic in the last instance, and of the articulation and index of dominance of its instances depends precisely on the forms which the combination in question takes on. This is indicated by Marx in a general way in the following two texts from *Capital*:

The specific economic form, in which unpaid surplus-labour is pumped out of direct producers, determines the relationship of rulers and ruled, as it grows directly out of production itself and, in turn, reacts upon it as a determining element. Upon this, however, is founded the entire formation of the economic community which grows up out of the production relations themselves, thereby simultaneously its specific political form. It is always the direct relationship of the owners of the conditions of production to the direct producers – a relation always naturally corresponding to a definite stage in the development of the methods of labour and thereby its social productivity – which reveals the inner-most secret, the hidden basis of the entire social structure, and with it the

11. *Homology/non-homology* is not to be confused with *correspondence/non-correspondence* (which will be encountered in the case of the *transition*): a combination of non-homology may well consist of a correspondence of the two relations. On the content of the *metaphorical* term *homology*, see Bettelheim, op. cit. I use the term, borrowed from Balibar, for want of a better one.

political form of the relation of sovereignty and dependence, in short, the corresponding specific form of the state.[12]

This combination (of the economic) also determines the instance which adopts the dominant role in a mode of production. Marx replied to the objections made to him:

My view that each special mode of production and the social relations corresponding to it, in short, that the economic structure of society is the real basis on which the juridical and political superstructure is raised, and to which definite social forms of thought correspond; that the mode of production determines the character of the social, political and intellectual life generally, all this is very true for our own times, in which material interests preponderate, but not for the Middle Ages, in which Catholicism, nor for Athens and Rome, where politics, reigned supreme. . . . This much, however, is clear, that the Middle Ages could not live on Catholicism, nor the ancient world on politics. On the contrary, it is the mode in which they gained a livelihood that explains why here politics, and there Catholicism, played the chief part.[13]

He examines these other modes of production only from two precise points of view. Firstly, he considers them as simple *illustrations* of his general thesis, according to which the whole social edifice rests on the differential forms of this combination: from this point of view, his analyses contain only theoretical *indications*. Secondly, he considers them as points of descriptive *comparison* with the CMP, i.e. so as to demonstrate the formal analogies between 'precapitalist' modes of production, resting on a combination of non-homology, and the capitalist mode, resting on a radically different combination, that of homology. We shall return to this important question later. But even at this stage it should be noted that although this treatment by Marx of other modes of production contributes to a clear elucidation of the particular traits of the CMP, it contains serious ambiguities: not only because this treatment has often been considered *for what it is not* (i.e. as a systematic examination of the particular theories of other modes of production), but also because Marx sometimes manages to produce some truly 'mythical' ideas about these modes of production, through this *analogical* and inexplicit treatment of the subject.

7. It is time to take a closer look at the problem. This will be done schematically, by taking only the economic and political instances (in

12. *Capital*, Vol. III, p. 791.   13. *Capital*, Vol. I, p. 82.

particular, that of the state) into consideration; the ideological instance will be left for the moment on one side.

Marx establishes, both in the *Grundrisse zur Kritik der politischen Ökonomie* (especially in that part entitled 'Precapitalist Economic Formations') and also in *Capital*, the following characteristics of the matrix of the CMP:

(i) The articulation of the economic and political in this mode of production is characterized by a relative *autonomy*, *specific* to these two instances.

(ii) In this mode, the economic maintains not only determination in the last instance, but also the *dominant role*.

Marx brings out the first characteristic by opposing the CMP to 'precapitalist' modes. Relative to the CMP, these present what he calls 'mixedness' or 'organic' or 'natural' relations: relations which are sometimes grasped as being 'simultaneous', with reference to the economic and political. It is worth repeating that these remarks should not be interpreted literally, as has often been done, since such an interpretation has led to a whole Marxist mythology concerning for example the feudal mode of production. On the other hand it should be remembered that, on the scientific plane, the CMP is specified by a characteristic autonomy of the economic and the political: this autonomy is the basis of the radical difference between the relations of these instances in the CMP and the relations which they maintain in other modes of production. This does not mean that these instances do not possess a relative autonomy in these other modes, but that that autonomy takes on different forms in them.

This autonomy has theoretical consequences for the object of our study. It makes possible a regional theory (in the very strict sense) of an instance of this mode, e.g. a theory of the capitalist state; it permits us to constitute the political into an autonomous and specific object of science. Marx demonstrated this in *Capital* with regard to the economic and economic science. *Strictly speaking*, this autonomy legitimates the lack of theories concerning other instances of the CMP in the discursive exposition of one instance of that mode.

Let us briefly consider Marx's texts, taking into account these remarks. How does this affect 'precapitalist' modes of production, where the relation of real appropriation is characterized by the union of the direct producer and the means of production?

... in all forms in which the direct labourer remains the 'possessor' of the means of production and labour conditions necessary for the production of his own means of subsistence, the property relationship must *simultaneously* appear as a direct relation of lordship and servitude, so that the direct producer is not free; a lack of freedom which may be reduced from serfdom with enforced labour to mere tributary relationship. . . . Under such conditions the surplus-labour for the nominal owner of the land can only be extorted from them *by other than economic pressure*, whatever the form assumed may be. . . . Thus conditions of personal dependence are requisite, a lack of personal freedom, no matter to what extent, and being tied to the soil as its accessory, bondage in the true sense of the word.[14]

Marx even says that in these cases: '. . . What we see here is, how the [political] *relations of domination and servitude* also enter into this formula of the appropriation of the instruments of production . . .', a relation which belongs to the economic combination.[15]

In the *Grundrisse* and in passages concerning the feudal mode of production in *Capital*, Marx goes still further in giving suggestions about the political in the various 'precapitalist' modes of production. His analyses are interesting for two reasons:

a. Marx relates the different political forms of these modes to the combination which specifies the economic in each mode. Nevertheless, these modes have this in common, that the relation of real appropriation has *essentially* an invariant form, namely the union of the direct producer with the means of production. The specific forms which the labour process takes on in these modes, and which determine the specific forms of property (economic, not juridical), are perceived as variations within the limits of this invariant.

b. Marx attributes the similarity of the economic/political relations in these various modes to this characteristic common to their economic combinations. This similarity is grasped particularly in the following way: as opposed to the CMP, the fact that the labourer and the non-labourer belong to a community (understood here, in the case of societies divided into classes, in the sense of political community, i.e. in the form of political relations), is a *presupposition* of their insertion in the relations of real appropriation ('possession') and of property. The alleged 'mixed-ness' of the economic and the political is catalogued as 'the political "pre-supposed" by the economic'. Thus, in the case of the 'precapitalist' modes:

14. *Capital*, Vol. III, pp. 790–1.
15. Karl Marx, *Pre-capitalist Economic Formations*, London, 1964, p. 102.

The attitude to the land . . . as the property of the working individual, means that a man appears from the start as something more than the abstraction of the 'working individual', but has an *objective mode of existence* in his ownership of the earth, which is *antecedent* to his activity and does not appear as its mere consequence, and is as much a precondition of his activity as his skin, his senses. . . . What immediately mediates his attitude is the . . . existence of the individual as *a member of* a community. . . .[16]

In the case of the Asiatic mode of production, we find in fact ownership of land by small communities (relation of property); but this ownership of land takes the form of hereditary possession by these communities (relation of real appropriation). Marx writes:

The all-embracing unity which stands above all these small common bodies may appear as the higher or sole proprietor, the real communities only as hereditary possessors. . . . It is perfectly possible for the unity to appear as something separate and superior to the numerous real, particular communities. . . . The despot here appears as the father of all the numerous lesser communities, thus realizing the common unity of all.[17]

In the ancient mode of production, we find a coexistence between state property and private property:

To be a member of the community remains the precondition for the appropriation of land, but in his capacity as member of the community the individual is a private proprietor. . . . For the relation of the working subject to the natural conditions of his labour as belonging to him . . . is mediated through his existence as a member of the state – hence through a precondition which is regarded as divine.[18]

In what Marx calls the Germanic form of production and property, a coexistence between communal and private property can be seen:

Among the Germans, where single heads of families settle in the forests, separated by long distances, even on an *external* view the community exists merely by virtue of every act of union of its members, *although their unity existing in itself is embodied in descent* . . . The community therefore appears as an association, not as a union, as an agreement, whose independent subjects are the landowners, and not as a unity. In fact, therefore, the community has no *existence* as a state, a political entity as among the ancients. . . . If the community is to enter upon real existence, the free landowners must hold an assembly, whereas, e.g., in Rome it exists apart from such assemblies.[19]

16. ibid., p. 81.   17. ibid., p. 69.   18. ibid., p. 73.   19. ibid., p. 78.

Finally, in the feudal mode of production:

Here, instead of the independent man, we find everyone dependent, serfs and lords, vassals and suzerains, laymen and clergy. Personal dependence here characterizes the social relations of production just as much as it does the other spheres of life organized on the basis of that production.[20]

In the CMP on the other hand we witness a combination of homology between the relations of property and of real appropriation; a homology which is set up by the separation of the direct producer from the means of production in the relation of real appropriation. Marx designates this as the separation of the direct producer from his natural conditions of labour, a separation which occurs at the stage of heavy industry. The character of the economic in this mode of production, as a process of producing surplus value, results especially from this separation, which converts the labourer himself into an element of capital and his labour into a commodity. This combination determines a specific autonomy of the political and the economic. Marx perceives it in its two manifestations. (i) In its effects on the economic. For example, the process of production in the CMP works in a relatively autonomous way, with no need of the intervention of 'extra-economic factors', as is characteristic of other modes of production. The process of expanded reproduction, as Rosa Luxemburg rightly pointed out, is principally determined by the 'economic factor' of production of surplus value; purely economic crises appear, etc. (ii) He also perceives this autonomy in its effects on the capitalist state.

This specific combination of the economic in the CMP, as determination in the last instance, also attributes the dominant role to the economic in this mode of production. This, we know, has been established by Marx

20. *Capital*, Vol. I, p. 77. If we take account of the fact that: (a) The mode of production is a concept implying the presence of all social instances, (b) the feudal mode of production does not present the same autonomy of instances as the CMP, and (c) the political often, in the feudal mode of production, takes on the dominant role, we can justify Marx's designation of this mode as *feudal*. Indeed, it has often been pointed out that this designation relates especially to the political relations of this 'feudal' mode (see J. Maquet: 'Une hypothèse pour l'étude des sociétés africaines' in *Cahiers d'Études Africaines*, 6, 1961; M. Rodinson, *Islam et Capitalisme*, Paris, 1966, pp. 66 ff., etc.). But what creates a problem is Marx's 'representation' of these feudal political relations: taken literally it would lead to the exclusion from the feudal mode of production of social formations which are based on serfdom, but whose political relations do not correspond to this representation.

both in his analyses of this mode in *Capital*, and also in the passages where he compares other modes of production in which the dominant role falls to the political or the ideological.

In this introduction I have defined the object and the method of this book, as well as the theory which underlies the research and the exposition. I have also defined certain fundamental concepts so as to establish the theoretical framework of the text which follows. These introductory remarks will find their justification in that text.

I
General Questions

1

General Questions

1. The Concept of Politics

We have already established sufficient elements for an attempt to trace out the concept of politics in Marx, Engels and Lenin, and its relations to the problematic of the state. But two preliminary remarks must be made:

1. In this chapter, we shall try to pose the problems of the general Marxist theory of the state and of the political class struggle. This chapter, concerning as it does the general problem of the state, precedes in the order of exposition the chapter on social classes and the class struggle. This is not accidental. It is not, of course, because we can, in a logical order, enter upon an examination of the state without direct and joint reference to the class struggle; nor is it because this order of presentation corresponds to a historical order according to which the state exists prior to the division of society into classes; it is because social classes are the effect (we shall see in what exact sense later) of certain levels of structures, of which the state forms a part.

2. We shall introduce at this stage the distinction between the *juridico-political superstructure of the state*, which can be designated as *the political*, and political class practices (political class struggle) which can be designated as *politics*. But it must be borne in mind that this distinction will become clear in the following chapter on social classes, in which the distinction and relation between (i) structures and (ii) class practices, i.e. the field of class struggle, will be substantiated.

In Marx, Engels and Lenin the problem of the political and politics is linked to the problem of history. The Marxist position on this question derives from Marx's and Engels's two basic propositions in the *Communist Manifesto*, according to which: (a) '*Every class struggle is a political struggle*', and (b) '*The class struggle is the motive force of history*'. A first reading, of a *historicist* type, of the relation between these two propositions is evidently possible. Ultimately, such a reading presupposes the Hegelian type of 'totality' and 'history': this is, firstly, a type of simple and circular totality, composed of equivalent elements, which is radically different from the complex structure in dominance which specifies the Marxist type of unity; secondly, it is a linear type of historicity, whose evolution is here and now contained in the origin of the concept, the historical *process* being identified with the growth (*devenir*)[1] of the self-development of the idea. In this 'totality', the specificity of the various elements in question is reduced to this principle of simple unity: the principle is identical with the concept, of which these elements constitute the objectification. History is reduced to a simple growth whose principle of development is the 'dialectical' passage of the concept from essence to existence.

It is in fact possible to make a historicist reading of the above Marxist propositions. As a result of such a reading, the field of the political would then include *not a particular structural level and a specific practice* but, in general, the 'dynamic/diachronic' aspect of every element, belonging to any level of the structures or practices of a social formation. For the historicist school, Marxism is a 'genetic' science of growth in general and, politics being the motive force of history, it is therefore, in the last analysis, a science of politics, or even a 'science of revolution', identified with this simple unilinear growth. From this the following consequences ensue: (a) an identification of politics with history; (b) what can be called an over-politicization of the various levels of structures and of social practices whose own specificity, relative autonomy and effectiveness is reduced to their dynamic-historical-political aspect (on this interpretation, the political constitutes the *centre*, or the simple common denominator, both of their unity (totality) and of their development. A particularly striking example of (b) is the notorious over-politicization of the theoretical level which ends in the 'bourgeois science/proletarian science' dichotomy); (c) an abolition of the very specificity of the political, which crumbles into all the other elements, not distinguished from one another, and so upsets the balance of the relation between the forces of a formation. These consequences make superfluous the theoretical study of the structures of the political and of political practice and lead to the ideological invariant voluntarism/economism and to the various forms of revisionism, reformism, spontaneism, etc.

In short, the political, in a historicist conception of Marxism, exactly occupies the role finally assumed by the concept in Hegel. I shall not

1. *Devenir* (German *werden*): the Hegelian 'becoming' is translated by the philosophically inaccurate, but stylistically more natural, *growth* in this passage. [Trans.]

consider the concrete forms which this problematic takes on. I shall merely give two quotations in order to locate the problem.

The first quotation is from Gramsci, whose political analyses, though always valuable, are often tainted by the historicism of Croce and Labriola. This quotation illustrates the results already pointed out:

The first question that must be raised and resolved in a study of Machiavelli is the question of politics as an autonomous science, of the place that political science occupies or should occupy in a systematic (coherent and logical) conception of the world, in a philosophy of praxis. The progress brought about by Croce in this respect in the study of Machiavelli and in political science consists mainly . . . in the dissolution of a series of false, non-existent or wrongly formulated problems. Croce based himself on his distinction of the moments of the spirit, and on his affirmation of a moment of practice, of a practical spirit, autonomous and independent though linked in a circle to all reality by the dialectic of distincts. In a philosophy of praxis, the distinction will certainly not be between the moments of the Absolute Spirit, but between the levels of the superstructure. The problem will therefore be that of establishing the dialectical position of political activity (and of the corresponding science) as a particular level of the superstructure. One might say, as a first schematic approximation, that political activity is precisely the first moment or level; the moment in which the superstructure is still in the unmediated phase of mere wishful affirmation, confused and still at an elementary stage. *In what sense can one identify politics with history, and hence all of life with politics? How then could the whole system of superstructures be understood as distinctions within politics,* and the introduction of the concept of distinction into a philosophy of praxis hence be justified? . . . How is the concept of a circle joining the levels of the superstructure to be understood? Concept of 'historical bloc', i.e. unity between nature and spirit (structure and superstructure), unity of opposites and distincts.[2]

In this quotation, the consequences of historicism noted above are already apparent; they lead here, as in the case of Theoretical Leftism of the 1920s, e.g. Lukács, Korsch, etc., to an over-politicization of a voluntarist kind: it provides the counterweight to economism within the same problematic.[3]

2. *Prison Notebooks*, pp. 136–7. For his identification of 'science' and 'philosophy of praxis' with politics, see *Il Materialismo storico e la filosofia di B. Croce*, Turin, 1948, pp. 117 ff., and *Note sul Machiavelli, sulla politica e sullo stato moderno*, Turin, 1949, pp. 79 ff. and 142 ff. For English translations of the more important passages from these works see *Prison Notebooks*.

3. See Althusser's analyses in *Reading Capital*.

My second quotation is taken from Talcott Parsons, the leader of the 'functionalist' school in contemporary sociology. This school will be discussed below at length, since, under the influence of Max Weber's historicism, it has become the dominant tendency in the analyses of modern political science.[4] It is striking that simply by reason of the theoretical principles which it shares with Marxist historicism, it ends up with similar conclusions concerning the political and politics:

> . . . political reality cannot be studied according to a specific conceptual scheme . . . because . . . the political component of the social system is a centre of integration for all the aspects of this system which analysis can separate, and not the sociological scene of a particular class of social phenomena. . . .[5]

In what follows, it will be seen that, on the epistemological plane, there is in fact a direct continuity between the general conceptions of historicism and functionalism. The reduction of the political which results from it is quite plain: in this case the political becomes the simple principle of social totality and the principle of its development, in the synchronic-diachronic perspective which is characteristic of functionalism.

In the anti-historicist conception of the original problematic of Marxism, the political must be located in the structure of a social formation, not only as a *specific* level, but also as a crucial level in which the contradictions of a formation are reflected and condensed. This must be done in order to understand exactly the anti-historicist character of the proposition that it is the political class struggle which constitutes the motive force of history.

Let us begin with this last point which was brought out by Althusser. He showed that for Marxism, the principle by which we understand the process of transformation of societies is not a universal and ontological

4. T. Parsons, *The Social System*, Glencoe, 1951, pp. 126 ff.
5. This functionalist school is directly affiliated to historicism; furthermore, because of the importance which it has gained, it has even been presented as the 'alternative' to Marxism. As W. Runciman puts it in his excellent book *Social Science and Political Theory*, Cambridge, 1963: 'In political science, there is in fact one and only one serious candidate for such a theory . . . apart from Marxism. . . . [Its partisans] would claim . . . that an alternative set of general propositions can be formulated which provide a better explanation of the known facts of political behaviour than Marxism has done' (p. 109). Or again: 'The fact remains, however, that some form of functionalism is the only current alternative to Marxism as the basis for some kind of general theory in political science' (p. 122).

type of history, related to a subject as its originating principle, but rather the theoretically constructed concept of a mode of production as a complex whole in dominance. From this concept, which is presented in historical materialism, can be constructed a concept of history which no longer has any connection with simple linear growth. Just as the levels of structures and practices present their own specificity, relative autonomy and particular effectiveness inside the unity of a mode of production and of a historically determined social formation, so also do their time sequences have different rhythms and metres.[6] The various levels of a social formation are characterized by (i) an uneven development (which is an essential feature of the relation between these differential time sequences in the structure), and (ii) dislocations which are the basis for understanding a formation and its development. To this extent, transformations of a formation and transition are grasped by the concept of a history with differential time sequences.

Let us see the place which the political, and in particular *political practice*, occupies in this context. I use the concept of practice here in the sense of transformation of a definite object (raw material), resulting in the production of something new (the product) which often constitutes, or at the very least can constitue, a break with the given elements of the object. What is the specificity of political practice in this respect? Its *specific object* is the 'present moment'[7] (as Lenin said), i.e. the *nodal point where the contradictions* of the various levels of a formation *are condensed* in the complex relations governed by over-determination and by their dislocation and uneven development. This present moment is therefore a *conjuncture*, the strategic point where the various contradictions fuse in so far as they reflect the articulation specifying a structure in dominance. The object of political practice, as it appears in Lenin's development of Marxism, is the place where relations of different contradictions finally fuse, relations which specify the unity of the structure; it is the starting point from which it is possible in a concrete situation to decipher the unity of the structure and to act upon it in order to transform it. So the object on which political practice bears is dependent on the various social levels: it bears at once on the *economic, ideological, theoretical* and

6. See the Introduction for the distinction between *mode of production* and *social formation*, a distinction which is essential for the *concept* of history.

7. See L. Althusser, 'The Materialist Dialectic', in *For Marx*. It is important to emphasize that given the present state of research, the concept of practice is still only a *practical (technical) concept*.

(in the strict sense) *political*, which, in their interrelation, make up a conjuncture.

The following consequence also ensues concerning the relation of politics to history: political practice is the 'motive force of history' in so far as its *product* finally constitutes the transformation of the unity of a social formation in its various stages and phases. *This, however, must not be taken in an historicist sense*. Political practice is the practice which transforms the unity, to the extent that its *object* constitutes the nodal point of condensation of contradictions of different levels with their own historicities and uneven development.

These analyses are important if we are to locate the concept of the political, and in particular the concept of political practice, in the original problematic of Marxism. In fact, these analyses of *the object and the product of political practice* cannot *in themselves* exactly locate the *specificity of the political*. They need to be completed by an adequate conception of the political superstructure.[8] For if we define the political simply as *practice* with clearly defined objects and products, we risk diluting its specificity and finally identifying everything which 'transforms' a given unity as political. If we neglect the theoretical examination of political *structures*, we also risk losing the concept of the present moment of the conjuncture and collapsing it into the Gramscian notion of the 'moment' (a Hegelian notion). In short, in order finally to supersede a historicist account of the political it is not sufficient to stop at a theoretical analysis of the object of political practice; we must also locate inside a social formation the specific place and function of the level of political structures which are its *objective*: only to this extent will it be possible to bring out the over-determination by the political as related to a differential history.

To approach the heart of the problem: the political structures (what are called the 'political superstructure') of a mode of production and of a social formation consist *of the institutionalized power of the state*. Every time Marx, Engels, Lenin or Gramsci speak of political struggle (practice) by distinguishing it from economic struggle, they are explicitly con-

8. The problem here is what may be termed the *'juridico-political superstructure of the state'*. But this term spans too schematically two distinct realities, two relatively autonomous levels, namely the *juridical structures* (*the law*) *and the political structures* (*the state*). Its use is legitimate in so far as the Marxist classics have effectively established the close relation between these two levels. But we must not forget that this term covers two relatively distinct levels, whose concrete combination depends on the mode of production and the social formation under consideration.

sidering its specificity in relation to its particular *objective*, which is *the state*, as a specific level of structures in a social formation. In this sense, we do indeed find a *general definition of politics* in the Marxist classics: it is precisely the above-mentioned conception of political practice, which has as its object the present moment and which either transforms (or else maintains) the unity of a formation. But this is the case only to the extent that political practice has the political structures of the state as its point of impact and specific strategic 'objective'.[9]

Thus Marx says: 'The political movement of the working class has . . . as its *ultimate objective* (*Endzweck*) the conquest of political power.'[10] It is also precisely in this sense that we must understand Lenin's statement: 'It is not enough that the class struggle becomes real, consistent and developed only when it embraces the sphere of politics. . . . Marxism recognizes a class struggle as fully developed, "nation-wide", only if it does not merely embrace politics but takes in the most significant thing in politics – the organization of state power.'[11] It follows from this quotation that the specificity of political practice *depends on* its having state power as its objective. It is important in this respect to re-emphasize Lenin's position in the texts written in 1917 on the problem of 'dual power', that of the state and that of the soviets. In fact, in these texts also Lenin continues to consider the objective of political practice as linked to the superstructure of the state. In Lenin's thought, the slogan 'all power to the soviets' is linked to the fact that he considers the soviets as a 'second state'. We shall examine later the distinction between state power and state apparatus; what is of interest to us here is that this slogan was not issued because the soviets were under the control of the Bolsheviks (in fact, the soviets at the time of this slogan were under the control of the Mensheviks), but because the soviets, in constituting a state apparatus which assumed some of the functions of the official state, constitute the *real state*. Hence the conclusion that this second state must be strengthened, with the aim of controlling it as a state: '. . . The real essence of the Commune is not where the bourgeois usually looks for it, but in the creation of a *state* of a special type. Such a state has *already* arisen in

9. Thus, Verret's definition of politics is completely acceptable: 'Political practice is the practice of leadership of the class struggle in and for the state', *Théorie et Politique*, Paris, 1967, p. 194. I shall shortly come to the question of the relation between politics and the state as propounded by contemporary political anthropology.

10. Letter to Bolte, 23 November 1871, trans. in *MESW*, 1970, p. 673.

11. *Collected Works*, Vol. 19, pp. 121–2.

Russia, it is the Soviets. . . .'[12] Moreover, these analyses of Lenin's are derived from his theoretical position on the distinction *and relation* between the economic and political struggles. He had already defined this in its essentials in *What is to be done?*: 'Social democracy leads the struggle of the working class . . . not in its relation to a given group of employers alone, but . . . *to the state as an organized political force*. Hence it follows that not only must social democrats not confine themselves exclusively to the economic struggle . . .', or again, 'Political exposures are as much a declaration of war against the *government* as economic exposures are a declaration of war against the factory owners'.[13]

(ii) THE GENERAL FUNCTION OF THE STATE

This thesis, however, poses as many problems as it solves. Why does a practice which has the 'present moment' as its object and which produces transformations of the unity present this specific feature, namely that its result *can be produced only when its objective is state power*? Apparently, this question is not at all obvious, as is demonstrated on the one hand by the economist, trade-unionist tendency, whose objective is the economic; and on the other hand by the utopian-idealist tendency, whose objective is the ideological. To put the same problem another way, what is the difference between a reformist conception and Marx's, Engels's, Lenin's and Gramsci's conception of the passage to socialism, in its demand for a radical change of the state and for the smashing of the previous state apparatus, i.e. its theory of the dictatorship of the proletariat? In short, why, in Lenin's precise terms, is *the basic problem of every revolution that of state power*?

To solve the problem we must return to the scientific Marxist conception of the state superstructure and show that, inside the structure of several levels dislocated by uneven development, *the state has the particular function of constituting the factor of cohesion between the levels of a social formation*. This is precisely the meaning of the Marxist conception of the state as a factor of 'order' or 'organizational principle' of a formation: not in the current sense of political order, but in the sense of the cohesion of the ensemble of the levels of a complex unity, *and as the*

12. 'Letter on tactics', *Collected Works*, Vol. 24, p. 53.
13. *Selected Works*, Vol. I, pp. 144 and 171. On the relation between the economic struggle and the political struggle, see in particular pp. 83 and 92 below.

regulating factor of its global equilibrium as a system. In this way, we can see why political practice, whose objective is the state, brings about transformations of the unity and is thus the 'motive force of history': it is precisely by analysing this role of the state that we can establish the anti-historicist sense of the thesis. There are two possibilities. (a) The result of political practice is the maintenance of the unity of a formation, of one of its stages or phases (i.e. its non-transformation). This is because, in the unstable equilibrium of correspondence/non-correspondence of levels dislocated in their own time sequences, this equilibrium is never *given* by the economic as such, but is maintained by the state. In this case, the objective of political practice is the state as a factor for maintaining the cohesion of this unity. (b) Political practice produces transformations: in this case its objective is the state as the nodal structure in which this unity breaks, in so far as it is its cohesive factor. In this context it is possible to aim at the state as a factor for producing a new unity and new relations of production.

Even at this stage, we can see an indication of this function of the state in the fact that, although it is a factor of cohesion of a formation's unity, it is also the structure in which the contradictions of the various levels of a formation are *condensed*. It is therefore the place in which we find reflected the index of dominance and overdetermination which characterizes a formation or one of its stages or phases. The state is also the place in which we can *decipher* the unity and articulation of a formation's structures. This will become clear when we analyse the relation of structures to the field of class practices. We shall then locate the particular relation of the *state* to the *conjuncture* which itself constitutes the place in which the relation of the structures to the field·of practices can be deciphered. It is from this relation between the state as the cohesive factor of a formation's unity and the state as the place in which the various contradictions of the instances are condensed, that we can decipher the problem of the relation between politics and history. This relation designates the structure of the political both as the *specific level* of a formation and as the *place in which its transformations occur*: it designates the political struggle as the 'motive power of history' having as its objective the state, the place in which contradictions of instances (dislocated in their own time sequences) are condensed.

Certain points must be made more precise. This way of posing the problem of the state allows us to solve a fundamental problem in the Marxist theory of the political. According to a whole Marxist tradition, to construct this sort of theoretical basis for the relation between the political struggle and the state is to fall into a 'Machiavellian' conception of the political. This tradition is based on Marx's condemnation in his youthful works of the conception of the 'exclusively political', i.e. a conception which reduces the political to no more than its relation to the state. According to this tradition, the objective of political practice is not the state, but the transformation of 'civil society', perhaps the relations of production.[14] The mistaken reply to this badly posed problem is called economism: according to it, socio-economic relations are the specific objective of the political struggle. The reformist conception is located precisely in this schema. It is only by turning our attention to the original problematic of the state in the works of the mature Marx that we can grasp the relation between (i) the political struggle and the state and (ii) the relation between these levels and the ensemble of the levels of the social formation.[15]

But this definition of the political as the relation between political practice and the state is still too wide. Even though it is valid in general for social formations divided into classes, this relation can clearly be specified only within the framework of a given mode of production and of a historically determined social formation. In particular, with regard to the function of the state as the cohesive factor in a formation's unity, it is clear that it takes on different forms according to which mode of production and social formation is under consideration. The place of the state in the unity, in so far as it assigns *specifying* and *constitutive* limits to its *regional structure*, depends precisely on the forms which this function of the state takes on. The exact nature of these limits (What is the state?), and also their extension or restriction (Which structures and institutions form part of the state?), are closely related to the differential forms of this function, according to which mode of production and social formation is under consideration. This function of the state, becoming a specific function, specifies the state as such in the formations dominated by the CMP, characterized by the *specific autonomy* of instances and by the particular place which is there allotted to the region of the state. This characteristic autonomy is the basis of the specificity of the political: it

14. e.g. Max Adler, *Die Staatsauffassung des Marxismus*, Darmstadt, 1964, pp. 49 ff. It is regrettable that Adler's work has remained so little known, for he unquestionably possesses one of the liveliest and sharpest minds in the history of Marxist thought.

15. I shall temporarily ignore the problems of the relation between the state (the objective of political practice) and the 'present moment' (the object of political practice).

determines the particular function of the state as the cohesive factor of the levels which have gained autonomy.

The function of the state as the cohesive factor in a formation's unity, which makes it the place in which the contradictions of the instances are condensed, becomes still clearer when we consider that a historically determined social formation is characterized by an overlapping of several modes of production. It must not be forgotten here that even when one of these modes of production succeeds in establishing its dominance by marking the beginning of the phase of expanded reproduction of a formation and the end of the strictly transitory phase, we are in the presence of *a true relation of forces* between the various modes of production present and of permanent dislocations of a formation's instances. The role of the state, the cohesive factor of this complex overlapping of various modes of production, is decisive here. This is particularly clear during the period of transition, characterized by a particular non-correspondence between property and real appropriation of the means of production. As Bettelheim rightly remarks: 'Such a dislocation entails important results with regard to the articulation of the different levels of the social structure. This non-correspondence involves a specific efficacity of the political level.'[16] However, the state's specific efficacity understood precisely as the general cohesive function of a formation's unity, exists permanently in every formation where different modes of production overlap. It is *particularly important* in the capitalist formation where the dominant CMP stamps the domination of its structure on the various modes of production present, and in particular stamps on them relative autonomy of instances, given the dislocations which result from them.[17]

16. Charles Bettelheim: 'Problématique de la période de transition' in *Études de planification socialiste*, no. 3, p. 147.

17. Before tackling the Marxist classics which concern this problem, I should point out that some important works in *contemporary* political science are beginning to emphasize the role of the political as the factor of maintenance of a formation's unity. They are doing this in an attempt to 'define' the political and in some sense to react against Weber, who defined the state exclusively in terms of maintaining the 'monopoly of legitimate force'. In this way, Apter defines the political as a structure which holds 'defined responsibilities for the maintenance of the system of which it is a part' ('A comparative method for the study of politics', *American Journal of Sociology*, LXIV 3, November 1958). Almond insists on the fact that the regional structures of a system are constituted by their 'boundaries', the political having exactly the crucial 'boundary maintenance function' (Almond and Coleman, *The Politics of the Developing Areas*, Princeton, 1960, pp. 12 ff.; see also G. Balandier, *Anthropologie politique*, Paris, 1967,

A good deal of guidance on these questions is found in the Marxist classics. Marxist theory has succeeded in establishing the relation between the *state and the class struggle as political class domination*. And so, before trying to locate the relation of the field of the class struggle (and in particular the political class struggle) to the structures of a formation, it is important to notice that for Marxist theory, this relation of the state to the political class struggle involves the relation of the state to the ensemble of the levels of *structures*: i.e. the relation of the state to the articulation of the instances which characterizes a formation.

This emerges from Engels's analyses, in which he establishes, in sometimes rather paradoxical terms, the relations of the state to 'the ensemble of society'. Engels says:

It [the state] is a product of society at a certain stage of development; it is the admission that this society has become entangled in an insoluble contradiction with itself, that it has split into irreconcilable antagonisms which it is powerless to dispel. But in order that these antagonisms and classes with conflicting economic interests might not consume themselves and society in a fruitless struggle, it became necessary to have a power seemingly standing above society that would alleviate the conflict, and keep it within the bounds of 'order'; and this power, arisen out of society but placing itself above it, and alienating itself more and more from it, is the state.[18]

In order not to multiply quotations, I shall confine myself to this text. What Engels 'says' is that there is a relation between the state and political class domination and the political class struggle. But he also shows that the relation of the state to political class domination reflects (indeed condenses, in our sense of the term) the ensemble of the contradictions of society. What does the term 'society' mean here? For if these terms are not located in the context of the original Marxist problematic, we risk falling into a humanist outlook which relates the institution of the state,

---

p. 43). The same is true of several researchers who use the *cybernetic* model in their analyses, e.g. D. Easton, *A Framework for Political Analysis*, 1965, and K. Deutsch, *The Nerves of Government*, 1966, etc. I shall not discuss the cybernetic model, but it should be noted that it is not to be confused with the functionalist model. I shall simply point out the following: the defining criterion of the state structure as that structure which has the role of cohesive factor of the system, *combined* (as will be seen) with that of monopoly of legitimate force, appears to be a relevant one, but only for the CMP, i.e. in the case of the capitalist state. For these authors' views on the relations between the *political* and the *state*, see below I.1. (iii), note 28.

18. *Origins of the Family*, ch. 9, in *MESW*, 1970, p. 576.

the totality, to the 'vital needs' of a society. The term seems to refer *here* (elsewhere it can be given different meanings) to the rigorously defined concept of a social formation as a complex unity of instances. The state is related to the contradictions peculiar to the various levels of a formation, but only in so far as it represents the place where the articulation of these levels is reflected and where their contradictions are condensed. It is the admission of 'the contradiction of society with itself'.

The state, as Marx puts it, is 'the official résumé of society'.[19] This conception of the state as 'résumé' of contradictions, in the sense of their condensation or fusion, was expressed by Marx, admittedly in a Hegelian perspective, in *The Poverty of Philosophy*. I refer to Marx's analyses of the state in *The Poverty of Philosophy* because of Lenin's use of them in *State and Revolution*. Elsewhere,[20] Lenin quotes Marx's letter to Ruge, in which he says: '. . . the political state represents the table of contents of man's practical conflicts. Thus the political state, within the limits of its form, expresses *sub specie rei publicae* (from the political standpoint) all the social conflicts, needs and interests.' Lenin also characterizes the political (including the state and political class conflict) in epigrammatic terms as 'a concentrated expression of economics'.[21]

In this sense, the state, for Lenin, appears to be the place in which we can decipher the unity of structures and from which we can derive our knowledge of this unity: 'The only field in which this knowledge can be gained is that constituted by the relation of all the classes and strata of the population to the state and the government, i.e. the field constituted by the relation of all classes to each other.'[22] This had already been indicated by Engels, when he called the state the 'official representative' of society: representative here in the sense of the place where the unity of a formation is deciphered. Finally, still in this sense, the state is also the place where the *ruptural situation* (*situation de rupture*) of this unity can be deciphered: the double power characteristic of the state structures constitutes, as Lenin demonstrated, one of the essential elements of the *revolutionary situation*.

19. Marx, *The Poverty of Philosophy*, p. 156 (Appendix: Marx's letter to P. V. Annenkov, 1846).

20. Lenin, 'What the "Friends of the People" are and how they fight the Social-Democrats', *Collected Works*, Vol. 1, p. 162 n.

21. Lenin, 'Once again the Trade Unions, the current situation and the mistakes of Trotsky and Bukharin', *Selected Works*, Vol. 3, p. 527.

22. 'What is to be done?', *Selected Works*, Vol. 1.

This relation between the state and the articulation which specifies a formation originates precisely in the fact that the state has a function of 'order' (political order, of course) in political class conflicts, and also of global order (of organization in the broad sense) as the cohesive factor of unity. The state prevents political class conflict from breaking out in so far as this conflict *reflects* the unity of a formation. (This 'reflection' is not a relation of phenomenon to essence.) The state prevents classes and 'society' from consuming themselves: the use of the term 'society' indicates that it prevents the social formation from bursting apart. It is true that the Marxist classics did not theoretically elaborate this conception of the state but we do find numerous indications of it in their works. Thus Engels precisely characterizes this function of 'order' of the state as the 'organization of the particular class, which was *pro tempore* the exploiting class, for the maintenance of its external conditions of production'.[23] Instead of lingering over the term 'external', which seems to involve a mechanistic conception of the relations of the 'base' to the 'superstructure', we should concentrate on the formulation of the state as the organization for maintaining both the conditions of production and the conditions for the existence and functioning both of the unity of a mode of production and of a formation. That remarkable Marxist theoretician, Bukharin, in his *Theory of Historical Materialism*, formulates very strikingly the conception of a social formation as a system of unstable equilibrium inside which the state plays the role of 'regulator'.[24] And finally, Gramsci's idea of organization, by means of which he analyses the function of the state, has this conception as its basis.

(iii) MODALITIES OF THE FUNCTION OF THE STATE

This function of order or organization of the state presents various *modalities*, related to the levels on which it is exercised in particular cases: i.e. technico-economic function at the economic level, strictly political function at the level of the political class struggle, ideological function at the ideological level. Nevertheless, the technico-economic function and the ideological function of the state are *overdetermined* by its strictly political function (that concerning the political class struggle) *in*

23. *Anti-Dühring*, p. 354.
24. *Theorie des Historischen Materialismus*, Hamburg, 1922, Vol. 2, pp. 162 ff. (English translation, *Historical Materialism*, Ann Arbor, 1961.)

that they constitute modalities of the global role of the state, which is the factor of cohesion in the unity of a formation. *This global role of the state is a political role.* The state is related to a 'society divided into classes' and to political class domination, precisely in so far as it maintains, in the ensemble of structures, that place and role which have the *effect* (in their unity) of dividing a formation into classes and producing political class domination. Strictly speaking, there is no technico-economic, ideological or 'political' function of the state: there is a global function of cohesion which is ascribed to it by its place, and there are modalities of this function overdetermined by the specifically political modality. This is the implication of Engels's statement: 'Here we are only concerned with establishing the fact that the exercise of a social function was everywhere the basis of political supremacy; and further that political supremacy has existed for any length of time only when it discharged its social functions.'[25]

This thesis has been developed in many of the classic texts of Marxism. However, in describing a particular modality not directly related to political class struggle, theorists have frequently interpreted this thesis as a so-called relation of the state to 'society', independent of the struggle between classes. This is a very old thesis, dear to the social democrats and found in works as early as those of Cunow[26] and Renner[27]: it *contrasts* the 'social functions' of the state with its political function, which alone is said to be connected with class struggle and class oppression. The same thesis can be found in most current analyses by the social democrat school of the 'Welfare State'. It is also sketched in outline in certain analyses of the despotic state in the Asiatic mode of production, a state whose existence is said to be related to different technico-economic functions (hydraulic and others) in a mode of production where social classes, in the Marxist sense, are seen as being absent.

Let us look more closely into the problem of these different functions of the state. I shall not yet examine them systematically, but I shall *simply point out* their relation to the political function, in order to elucidate the problem which concerns us.

In describing the forms adopted by this global role of the state the Marxist classics sometimes present it in a *historico-genetic* manner, setting

25. *Anti-Dühring*, p. 248.

26. H. Cunow, *Die Marxische Geschichts-, Gesellschafts-, und Staatstheorie*, 1920–1, Vol. 2, pp. 309 ff.

27. K. Renner, *Marxismus, Krieg und Internationale*, 1917, pp. 28 ff.

out the relations between the state and its various levels as so many factors in the historical creation and birth not only of the state but also of social classes. But this problem of the historical birth of the state, though important, is clearly a separate one. Marx and Engels give outline answers, but we must take into account the inevitably limited nature of the historical information which they possessed.[28] We can however retain these analyses, in so far as they elucidate the functions of the state which are on a par with its place in the complex whole of a given formation divided into classes. The function of the state primarily concerns the economic level, and particularly the labour process, the productivity of labour. On this point we can refer to Marx's analyses of the despotic state in the Asiatic mode of production, in which a centralized power is necessary to carry out hydraulic work needed in order to increase the

28. It may be useful to mention here some problems of *definition* set by *political anthropology*, a subject still in its infancy. Some authors, e.g. G. Balandier (*Anthropologie politique*, 1967), Apter, Easton, Nadel, Pouillon, etc., have questioned the relations established by Marxism between the *political* and *the state*, while at the same time questioning the radical distinction between 'segmentary societies' (without states) and 'societies with a state' and insisting on the possibility of the existence of the political independent from the existence of the state in the strict sense. But the definitions involved must be clarified. These authors are correct, if we accept, as they do, a narrow, juridical (and for a long time preponderant) conception of the state. Indeed, most of these authors (see above, I.1. (ii), note 17) accept a definition of the political *analogous* to the one which I have just shown, but they specify that the political can exist independently from the state, for which they reserve a formal-juridical definition, by accepting for example Weber's criterion of the 'monopoly of legitimate force' or that of 'centralism'. The state is thus identified in a way with the modern state; see Easton, *The Political System*, and Balandier, op. cit. Nevertheless, the problem disappears if we follow Marx and Engels and emphasize that the *political* coincides with the emergence of an autonomized system of government in relation to a specialized and privileged group which monopolizes the state administration. In this sense, we can establish that:

(a) The radical distinction between 'segmentary societies' and 'societies with a state' based on a juridical conception of the state, becomes null and void.

(b) The political as a *particular 'region'* coincides with the minimal emergence of certain state forms, 'embryonic' even, according to Engels. This is the case for example with 'segmentary states'.

(c) The essential point is that the political and the state correspond *to the formation of social classes*: the historical process adopts some extraordinarily complex forms, Marx's analyses of the Asiatic mode of production being by no means an exhaustive list. In particular, the traditional Marxist contrast '*ties of kinship*'/'*class relations*', which overlapped with that of 'segmentary society'/'society with a state', must be revised. See R. Bastide, *Formes élémentaires de la stratification sociale*, Paris, 1965.

productivity of labour. In this context, Engels tells us with regard to the relation between the dominant class and the social division of labour:

It is clear that so long as human labour was so little productive that it provided but a small surplus over and above the necessary means of subsistence, any *increase of the productive forces*, extension of trade, development of the state and of law, or foundation of art and science, was possible only by a greater division of labour. And the necessary basis for this was the great division of labour between the masses discharging simple manual labour and the few privileged persons *directing labour*, conducting trade and public affairs, and, at a later stage, occupying themselves with art and science.[29]

We must remember here the relation between the state (through the agency of the dominant class) and the general direction of the labour process, with particular reference to the productivity of labour. We are faced with this problem again when dealing with the division of labour in capitalist formations: this role of the state corresponds to the twin roles of the capitalist, those of exploitation and of organization-cum-supervision of the labour process. Furthermore we know the importance attached by Lenin to the technico-economic function of the state (including its function of accountancy) in his texts of 1917–20.

This function of the state as organizer of the labour process is only one aspect of its economic function, which also includes, for instance, the function of the judicial system, i.e. the set (*ensemble*) of rules which organizes capitalist exchanges and provides the real framework of cohesion in which commercial encounters can take place. The state's function vis-à-vis the ideological consists of its role of education, teaching, etc. At the strictly political level, that of the political class struggle, this function of the state is the maintenance of political order in political class conflict.

We arrive, then, at two results:

1. The state's global role as the cohesive factor in a social formation can, as such, be distinguished in particular modalities concerning the different levels of a formation, i.e. in functions which are economic, ideological and political in the strict sense of the term (the role in political class conflict).

2. The state's various particular functions, even those which are not directly concerned with the political level in the strict sense (i.e. political class conflict) can only be grasped theoretically in their interrelation, i.e.

29. *Anti-Dühring*, p. 250.

inserted in the state's global political role. This role adopts a *politica,* character, in the sense that it maintains the unity of a formation inside which the contradictions between the different levels condense into a political class domination. It is in fact impossible clearly to establish the political character of the state's technico-economic function, or of its function of allocation of justice, by ascribing them directly to its political function in the strict sense (i.e. to its particular function in political class conflict). These functions are political functions to the extent that they aim primarily at the maintenance of the unity of a social formation based in the last analysis on political class domination.

It is precisely in this context that we can establish the *overdetermination* of the state's economic and ideological functions by its political function, *in the strict sense*, in political class conflict. For example, the state's economic or ideological functions correspond to the political interests of the dominant class and constitute political functions, not simply in those cases where there is a direct and obvious relation between (a) the organization of labour and education and (b) the political domination of a class, but also where the object of these functions is the maintenance of the unity of a formation, inside which this class is the politically dominant class. It is to the extent that the prime object of these functions is the maintenance of this unity that they correspond to the political interests of the dominant class; and this is the precise meaning of the passage quoted from Engels, for whom a 'social function' is always at the root of a 'political function'. This concept of overdetermination, applied here to the functions of the state, thus indicates two things: (i) that the various functions of the state constitute political functions through the global role of the state, which is the cohesive factor in a formation divided into classes, and (ii) that these functions correspond *in this manner* to the political interests of the dominant class.

The displacement of the index of dominance in the structures of a formation is reflected *as a general rule* in the concrete articulation *of the various functions* of the state within its global political role. (The state, as the place where the formation's contradictions are condensed, is the place where this displacement can be deciphered.) Lenin gives us the principles of this analytical model in his texts of 1917 on the state apparatus: in these he distinguishes the state's political function in the strict sense and the 'technical' function of state-administration (of which the function of accountancy forms a part), by showing the subordination (ascribed to the specific articulation of the different levels of the Russian social formation) of this technico-economic function to the political function in the strict sense.[30]

However, the ability to 'read' correctly the articulation of a formation in the articulation of the functions of the state presupposes a principle of reading: namely, a reading of the state's role as the cohesive factor in the unity of a formation. In this sense, in the global role of the state, the dominance of its economic function indicates that, as a general rule, the dominant role in the articulation of a formation's instances reverts to the political; and this is so not simply in the strict sense of the state's direct function in the strictly political class struggle, but rather in the sense indicated here. In this case, the dominance of the state's economic function over its other functions is coupled with its *dominant role*, in that its function of being the cohesive factor necessitates its specific intervention in that instance which maintains the *determinant role* of a formation, namely, the economic. This is clearly the case, for example, in the despotic state in the Asiatic mode of production, where the dominance of the political is reflected in a dominance of the economic function of the state; or again, in capitalist formations, in the case of monopoly state capitalism and of the 'interventionist' form of the capitalist state. Whereas in the case of such a form of the capitalist state as the *'liberal' state* of private capitalism, the dominant role held by the economic is reflected by the dominance of the strictly political function of the state – the state as 'policeman' [*l'état gendarme*] – and by a specific *non-intervention* of the state in the economic. This does not in the least mean that the state has no economic function (as Marx himself shows us in *Capital* in connection with factory legislation) but simply that this function does not have the dominant role. Indeed we shall see later on that it is wrong to consider, as is sometimes done, that the liberal form of state has never held important economic functions. In fact, what allows us to consider these functions of the liberal state as specific non-intervention in the economic, is precisely (i) the non-dominance of the economic function of the liberal state over its other functions (as compared with other forms of state, particularly the one corresponding to monopoly state capitalism); and (ii) what is correlative here, the non-dominance of the instance of the state as the

30. In particular see 'One of the fundamental questions of the Revolution', *Selected Works*, Vol. 2, p. 257. But Lenin distinguishes *stages* and *turning points* of transition, which are marked precisely by permutations in the dominance of the political and economic functions of the state.

cohesive factor in the ensemble of instances of a social formation of private capitalism.

We have therefore to make two additional remarks. Firstly, the state's role as the cohesive factor is not reducible to 'intervention' (in the full sense) by the state at the various levels, and particularly at the economic level. For example, the state's non-intervention in the case of private capitalism in no way means that the state does not maintain this function of cohesion: that function is manifested in this case by a specific non-intervention by the state at the economic level. At this point we need only mention the case of the legal system, which, as Marx and Engels showed, is a condition of the functioning of the economic, in that it not only fixes relations of production in the relations of formal ownership, but it also constitutes a framework of cohesion for commercial encounters, including those for the purchase and sale of labour power. Secondly, we should clearly recognize that though the state has the global function of cohesive factor in the unity, this does not in the least mean that for this reason it always maintains the dominant role in a formation, nor that when this dominant role is held by the economic, the state no longer has this function of cohesive factor.

2. Politics and Social Classes

INTRODUCTION

We now possess enough elements to examine the Marxist concept of social class and class conflict, and its repercussions on the field of the political: here we shall take into especial consideration the political works of Marx, Engels and Lenin. Specific reference to these works in connection with this problem depends both on a principle of reading which concerns their theoretical status, and on the position adopted vis-à-vis the concept of social class.

It must be remembered here that the 'pure' CMP, which has been distinguished from a capitalist social formation, is composed in its pure form of various instances (economic, political and ideological) and is characterized, according to Marx, by a specific autonomy of its instances and by the dominant role taken on by the economic instance in it. This has important repercussions from the theoretical point of view. These various instances, as objects of theoretical research, are subject to a specific scientific treatment. These repercussions are clear as regards the theoretical status of *Capital*, which is a treatment of the CMP. But because of autonomization of the instances which characterize it and because of the dominant place occupied in it by the economic, *this treatment is centred on the regional instance of the economic in this mode*. This does not in any way mean that the other instances are absent from it; they are present, but only, as it were, *implicitly*, through their effects in the region of the economic. This element is in its turn important for the problem of social classes: we find in *Capital* some of the elements necessary for constructing the concept of class, but we must not forget that in it this problem is itself centred on the economic determination of social classes. This by no means implies that this economic determination is sufficient for the construction of the Marxist concept of social class, any more than the specific treatment of the economic instance of the CMP in *Capital* lessens the importance of the other instances for the scientific examination of this mode.

This is why Marx's and Engels's political works are so important in this respect. One remark concerning their theoretical status must be made: the object of most of their works is the study of historically determined capitalist social formations, and in particular the study of their political conjuncture. The problematic of social classes relates chiefly to their presence in these formations. But at the same time the theoretical problem of social classes in a mode of production (in this case the CMP) is posed on the practical level in these texts, in so far as they display the importance of political and ideological determination in the construction of the concept of class. This is very clear in Lenin's political works.

It is important to remember the dates of these texts: accepting the break in Marx's work, we shall only take into consideration those works dating from 1847 (*The Poverty of Philosophy*) up to 1871 (*The Civil War in France*). It is clear that the presentation of the problem of classes underwent further fluctuations during that period, as Marx's original problematic crystallized. Nonetheless, running through all these texts a single question can be deciphered, bearing precisely on the importance of political and ideological determination in constructing the concept of class. It is therefore not surprising that these texts, containing forms of words which are not always transparently clear, have given rise to numerous misinterpretations. Let us then tackle the problem of classes in Marx's political works, and try to understand how it is related to the problem of classes in *Capital*.

(i) THE PROBLEM OF THE THEORETICAL STATUS OF CLASSES

Let us start from some of Marx's texts concerning the distinction between economic struggle and political struggle, between class 'economic interests' and class 'political interests'. In his analyses of this aspect of the relations between the political and the economic, Marx appears to distinguish three levels or three moments. The first two levels relate to 'economic struggle' and 'economic interests'. In the first of these two levels of the economic we find an economic struggle between the capitalist and the worker, in short between 'individuals/agents of production'; but on a literal reading of these quotations, this struggle does not reveal class relations. In the *Communist Manifesto*, Marx says: 'The proletariat goes through various stages of development. With its birth begins its struggle with the bourgeoisie. At first the contest is carried on by individual labourers, then by the workpeople of a factory, then by the operatives of one trade, in one locality, against the bourgeois who directly exploits them. . . . At this stage the labourers still form an incoherent mass' (*MESW*, 1970, p. 42). Progressively and increasingly, these 'individual clashes' between the workers and the bourgeoisie take on the character of collisions between 'two classes'. However, we can distinguish in Marx's texts what appears to be a second level of economic struggle, that of economic interests: this is not manifested at the level of individuals/agents of production, but nor does it express class relations in the strict sense. Nevertheless, Marx sometimes says that we are faced here with a *class-in-itself* as distinct from the *class-for-itself*. He does so in particular in his texts concerning the trade union struggle (i.e. the trade union organization of the working class, as opposed to its strictly political organization): 'In its struggle against the collective power of the possessing classes the proletariat can act as a class only by constituting itself a distinct political party. . . . The coalition of the forces of the working class, already achieved by the economic struggle, must also serve, in the hands of this class, as a lever in its struggle against the political power of its exploiters.'[1] It is unnecessary to add further to Marx's well-known quotations, according to which the proletariat exists as a class only through its organization in a distinct party.[2]

These levels of struggle (the two levels of economic struggle, and the level of political class struggle) are clear in this text from Marx's *The Poverty of Philosophy*:

Economic conditions had at first transformed the mass of the people of the country into workers. The combination of capital has created for this mass a common situation, common interests. This mass is thus already a class as against capital, but not yet for itself. In the struggle, of which we have noted only a few phases, this mass becomes united, and constitutes itself as a class for itself. The interests it defends become class interests. But the struggle of class against class is a political struggle.[3]

We know the importance of these texts of Marx in the elaboration of the Marxist theory of social classes. But it must be pointed out here that these analyses have frequently been misinterpreted; there has been a

1. Article 7a of the General Rules of the First International (1871), *MESW*, 1958, Vol. I, p. 388.
2. Such quotations are to be found in many works, from the *Communist Manifesto* to the letter to Bolte of 1871.
3. *The Poverty of Philosophy*, p. 150. Note that this conception can also be found in the *Grundrisse*, where Marx speaks of the 'mass' of 'free labourers/bare individuals' who constitute themselves progressively into a class.

failure to take into account the demands of a scientific statement of the problem of social classes.

One reading of these texts must be rejected from the start, for it is connected ultimately with the problematic of the 'social group' which has no place in Marx's analyses: this is the *historico-genetic* reading. This reading (a literal and direct reading of Marx's texts) finds in them a historiography of the process of 'genesis' of social classes. On this interpretation, these various theoretical levels of analysis in Marx constitute historical stages in the formation of a class: an undifferentiated mass of individuals at the outset, which comes to organize itself into a class-in-itself, and ends up as a class-for-itself. This reading of Marx's analyses is itself related to a historicist problematic: it must be pointed out here that it is precisely in the theory of classes that its inadequacy is most clearly revealed. We can distinguish two theoretical currents there, though they share the same presuppositions. Both involve importing into Marxism the *ontological-genetic* schema of history (in the Hegelian sense), which is a development of the theme that 'it is men who make their own history'.

(a) In the first current of the historicist problematic, which is a direct continuation of the Hegelian one, the class is conceived as the subject of history, as the factor of genetic production and of transformations of the structures of a social formation. Lukács is the typical representative of this historicist interpretation of class and class-consciousness. From this viewpoint, the theoretical problem of the structures of a social formation is reduced to the problematic of their origin, itself related to the self-development of the class/subject of history. The process of the organization of the class/subject into a political class (class-for-itself) corresponds here very closely to the Hegelian type of historicity of the concept. This same conception of classes can be found in authors like Goldmann and Marcuse.[4]

4. According to this conception, the order of structures and the regulation of their relation are reduced to their 'significant totality' constituted by the centre which is the 'world-view' of the class-for-itself, a subject which produces them. As Lukács expresses it 'for a class to be ripe for hegemony means that its interests and consciousness enable it to organize the whole of society in accordance with those interests. The crucial question in every class struggle is this: . . . how far does the class concerned perform the actions history has imposed on it "consciously" or "unconsciously"? And is that consciousness "true" or "false"?' (*History and Class Consciousness*, London, 1971, pp. 52–3). The problem is even more clearly posed in H. Marcuse, *Kultur und Gesell-*

(b) The second current of historicism is found in certain 'functionalist' interpretations of Marx like those of Geiger, Dahrendorf and, most recently in France, that of Bourdieu.[5] This interpretation has the advantage over the first of bringing out the problem of a social formation as a system of structures, a problem which is not immediately related here to their genesis. However, the synchronic/diachronic dualism adopted by the functionalist school depends in the last analysis on the historicist problematic. This functionalist interpretation defines the social formation as a system of structures only as a framework for reference (the object of a *static* examination) while the *dynamic-diachronic* element of this system is represented by 'class conflict'. On this interpretation, the proper status of the 'group' in Marx's analyses is that of constituting the dynamic element of structures, having the function of being the *principle and the condition of their change*. Social structures and social classes are grasped in a relation of structure to function, of synchrony to diachrony. This diachrony expresses only the historicist conception of 'men who make their own history', of a history founded on social actors, 'the forces capable of changing the elements of the structure',[6] represented by classes as functions. We shall not, therefore, be surprised to see the close relations between Lukács's conception of history and the conception of diachrony in functionalist theories, since both clearly show the influence of Max Weber's historicism. This conception leads to the theoretical division of a *double status* of social class: (i) *class situation*, class in itself determined by its place in the economic structure and (ii) *class function*, classes for themselves, class struggle: the diachronic factor in the change of the structure.[7]

schaft, Frankfurt, 1965, Vol. I, p. 34; and in *One Dimensional Man*, London, 1964, pp. 55 ff. All the themes resulting from this mythology can also be found nearer to home in Touraine's so-called *Sociologie de l'Action*, Paris, 1966.

5. T. Geiger, *Die Klassengesellschaft im Schmelztiegel*, 1949, pp. 37 ff.; R. Dahrendorf, *Class Conflict in Industrial Society*, 1965, passim; A. Bourdieu, 'Situation et position de classe', cyclostyled lecture, and *Travail et travailleurs en Algérie*, 1964. We are speaking here of a functionalist interpretation of Marx, and not of the problem of 'classes' or of the 'group' in the functionalist trend in general.

6. The quotation is from Dahrendorf, for whom classes are the 'variable dynamic elements' which, as 'function', bring about the changes of the synchronic 'structures' (op. cit., pp. 121 ff.).

7. Weber's analyses can be found in *Wirtschaft und Gesellschaft*, Tübingen, 1947, section III, but the results of his analyses appear more clearly in *Gesammelte Aufsätze zur Religionssoziologie* and in *Gesammelte politische Schriften*, Tübingen, 1958. The important point in his theory of classes is his distinction between (a) *'class situation'*, defined principally by incomes: he applies the term 'class' to any group of persons

What we can already see here is that the historicist conception, implicit in the analyses of this school, leads ultimately to the establishment of an ideological relation between individuals/agents-of-production ('men') and social classes; this relation is given a theoretical foundation in the status of the subject. Agents of production are perceived as agents/producers, as subjects which create structures; and social classes are perceived as the subjects of history. The distribution of agents into social classes is itself related to the process (of historicist making) of creation and transformation of social structures by 'men'. However, this conception fails to recognize two essential facts: firstly, that the agents of production, for example the wage-earning labourer and the capitalist, as 'personifications' of Wage-Labour and Capital, are considered by Marx as the *supports* or *bearers* of an ensemble of structures; secondly, that social classes are never *theoretically* conceived by Marx as the genetic origin of structures, inasmuch as the problem concerns the definition of the *concept* of class. We shall see why.

There is another distortion of the Marxist theory of social classes: the 'economist' interpretation, which constitutes the invariable counterpart to the 'voluntarist' school represented by the young Lukács. According to this, the social class is located only at the level of *relations of production* conceived in an economist fashion, i.e. reduced to the position of agents in the labour process and to their relation to the means of production. Now, while it is true that the very concepts of relations of production and mode of production have been interpreted by this school in an

---

located in the same 'class situation'; and (b) *'status group'* (in some sense, a functional term). This distinction leads him to his problematic of the relation of the political classes to the bureaucracy. I shall return to this later, since it seems to me to be the heart of the connection between Marxist historicism and the 'functionalism' of contemporary political science. These two schools of thought have *strictly identical theoretical principles*, and differ only in the opposed conclusions which they draw from them. I merely note here that the *double ideological status* which the 'social group' receives in this problematic is sometimes conceptually marked out, as in the case of Weber's distinction between 'class' (class situation) and 'status group' (function). The task in this problematic is to mark boundaries (a) between social 'classes' (reduced to the economic-class-situation) and (b) between the *different* 'groups', whose relation to the classes always remains mysterious; these groups take part in political-functional relations, while social classes are confined to the economic-class-situation. Here we find the whole of the 'semi-Marxist' school's problem of *political elites*, of groups/functions parallel to classes/situations. The problem is posed with unique clarity by Max Weber's semi-Marxist historicist disciple, R. Michels, in *Political Parties*, Glencoe, 1949.

economist fashion (even using concepts borrowed from pre-Marxist economic theory) it is also true that the problem of the exclusivity or otherwise of the economic determination of classes remains unsolved even in an authentic conception of the relations of production and the mode of production.

Indeed, the 'pure' mode of production (which we have distinguished from a social formation) defines the economic by its *place* and *function* in the complex whole of instances which the concept of mode of production covers. This, however, does not lessen the problem of the specificity of the economic inside this mode. In the case of the 'pure' mode of production, there is always to be found a coexistence of specific levels, in schematic terms, the economic (relations of production), the political and the ideological, which appear as so many regional structures of the 'pure' mode of production. To the extent, then, that the concept of a mode of production not only does not produce the specificity of the instances, but even permits us to locate them as regions in their relation to the region of the economic, the problem of social classes which we have noted cannot be conjured away but remains unsolved. Are they defined solely by their relation to the economic? Our answer to this question will decide the solution to be given to the problem of classes in a social formation.

It can in fact be stated that Marx's analyses of social classes never refer simply to the economic structure (relations of production) but always to *the ensemble of the structures* of a mode of production and social formation, *and to the relations which are maintained there* by the different levels. Let us anticipate and say that everything happens as if social classes were the *result of an ensemble of structures and of their relations*, firstly at the economic level, secondly at the political level and thirdly at the ideological level.[8] A social class can be identified either at the economic level, at the political level, or at the ideological level, and can thus be located with regard to a particular instance. Yet to define a class *as such*

---

8. The delimitation of classes with regard to the 'economic', such as is found in *Capital*, includes for example the following relations:

– relations of production, in the strict sense: producer/owner of the means of production.

– relations of distribution of social labour: producer/producer

– relations of transfer of the social product: producer/producer

These relations are dependent on the combination of two economic relations, real appropriation and property, and so refer to the organization of the labour process *and to the division of labour.*

and to grasp it in its *concept*, we must refer to the ensemble of levels of which it is the effect.

These considerations still remain vague since, although in fact a social class presents itself as the effect of an ensemble of structures, it is nevertheless necessary to demarcate exactly the particular field on which the effects of this ensemble are reflected in taking the form of social class. It must be stated at once that social classes do not present themselves as the effect of one particular structural level on another structural level: i.e., as the effect of the economic structure on the political or ideological structures; hence they do not manifest themselves inside the structure, but entirely as the *global effect of the structures in the field of social relations* which, in class societies, themselves involve the distribution of agents/ supports to social classes: and they do this to the extent that the social classes determine the place of agents/supports in relation to the structures of a mode of production and a social formation. The confusion of these fields has a name in the history of Marxist thought: it is anthropologism of the subject.

It is necessary, therefore, to begin by precisely situating 'social relations' relative to the structures of a mode of production and a social formation. In particular, the confusion between structures and social relations, operated here at the economic level, led economism to reduce social classes to the level of the economic alone; and it is in this distortion that we can discern the impact of anthropologism on the economist tendency. The reduction in fact depends on the confusion of the two terms: the confusion is produced by the use of the terms 'relations of production' and 'social relations of production', *without any distinction*, when in fact they cover different realities. In economism, social classes, as *social* relations of production, are reduced to mere relations of production; the term 'social relations of production' implies the emergence of the social *in the very structure*, and at the privileged point constituted by the 'relations of production/social relations of production'. It is true that Marx himself uses the term relations of production and *social* relations of production without distinction, and it is only by an attentive reading of his texts that we can discover the difference between the realities covered by these concepts.

Let us look more closely. The scientific Marxist conception of social relations of production itself provides the radical critique of any economic anthropology which relates the economy in general to the 'needs' of human 'subjects', and consequently the radical critique of the conception of social relations as intersubjective relations. This is true in two senses: on the one hand, the instance of the economic is composed of the unity between the labour process (concerning the material and technical conditions of labour, and in particular the means of production; in short, the relations 'man/nature' in general) and the relations of production (concerning the relations of the agents of production and the means of labour). Consequently the relations of production do not *denote* simply interrelations between the agents of production, but rather these relations in *specific combinations* between agents and material-technical conditions of labour. On the other hand, social relations of production are relations among agents of production distributed in social classes, i.e. class relations. In other words, the *'social' relations of production*, class relations, manifest themselves, at the economic level, as an effect of this specific combination: agents of production/material-technical conditions of labour constituted by the *relations of production*.

It seems, then, that we can only make a radical critique of any 'anthropologism', whether in its historicist or humanist forms, if we clearly distinguish *structures* and *social relations* (*gesellschaftliche Verhältnisse*), the latter designating the distribution of supports to social classes. These two fields are covered respectively, at the economic level, by the concept of relations of production (*Produktionsverhältnisse*) and by that of social relations of production (*gesellschaftliche Produktionsverhältnisse*). In reality, contrary to the economist conception of social classes, which confuses these two fields and reduces one concept to the other, the economic, which, in the structure, is covered by the concept of relations of production, in no way constitutes any kind of privileged point of emergence from the social. In social relations, the relations of production correspond to the social relations of production: but we can also speak in all strictness of political 'social' relations and of ideological 'social' relations.[9] These social relations, as class relations, isolated here with

9. From another point of view, in the framework of the 'functionalist' conception indicated above, which also ends in the confusion of structures and social relations, it is a matter of establishing a specificity of the 'social' which is not reducible to the 'economic'. Let us take, for example, the case of Bourdieu: 'Weber's antithesis [which Bourdieu accepts] implies the recognition of a strictly social order which owes its relative autonomy in relation to the economic order . . .' ('Situation et position de classe', p. 5). The problem thus posed *is strictly meaningless*. It is as if the economic were not *also* situated in social relations/economic social relations, i.e. in the economic class struggle. But the distinction between 'economic' and 'social' is produced by an

respect to the instances of the political and the ideological, manifest themselves as the effect of the political and ideological structures on social relations. The different instances therefore mark levels and degrees in structures and at the same time in social relations. With respect to the economic instance, let us take the case of the relations of production in the structures: they consist of *specific forms of combination* of the agents of production and the means of production. This structure of relations of production 'determines the places and functions occupied and adopted by the agents of production, who are never anything more than the occupants of these places, in so far as they are supports (*Träger*) of these functions'.[10] The relations of production have as their effect on social relations and in regard to the economic, a distribution of agents of production into social classes which are *at this level* the social relations of production.

Strictly speaking, therefore, relations of production as a structure are not social classes: and here I am not talking about the empirical reality of the 'group', but about the concept of class, meaning that the concept of class cannot cover the structure of the relations of production. These consist of forms of combination, while the relation between the categories of capital and wage-labour is expressed by a particular concept, that of surplus value. Viewed like this, capital and wage-labour are not, of course, the empirical realities of 'capitalists' and 'labourers', but nor can they be designated by a concept (that of social classes) which in fact covers social relations. These remarks are just as valid for the other instances: the structures of the political, notably the juridico-political superstructure of the state, and equally of the ideological, are not social classes. But at and in the level of relations, they do have as their effect juridico-political *social* relations and ideological *social* relations, the distribution of the agents who are their bearers into social classes. In particular, in the case of the law, this effect depends on the formal juridical ownership of the means of production. The importance of these remarks can be understood by considering Godelier's confusion, which results from his leaving these problems unsolved.[11] We can thus try to

---

ideological problematic, whose precise origins are to be found in Max Weber, as is demonstrated by the very title of his major work *Wirtschaft und Gesellschaft* ('Economy and Society').

10. Althusser, in *Reading Capital*, p. 180.

11. The basic error of his analyses is clear in *Rationalité et irrationalité-économie*, 1966 (English translation, *Rationality and Irrationality in Economics*, London, 1972), and

express the relations between the *structures* of a mode of production or a social formation and its *social relations*, the social classes, i.e. we can try to define the theoretical status of social class. Firstly, we are not dealing with a relation of static to dynamic. This is sometimes perceived as relations of synchronic structure to diachronic function, as in a current erroneous trend, which apprehends structures according to their degree of permanence: relations, which are in origin historicist, of subject-producer to his product. Nor is this a simple epistemological relation between the 'group' (the class), i.e. the 'empirical concrete',[12] and its 'theoretical model', in this case the structures: this theory of the model *which identifies structure and concept* depends on an empiricist theory of knowledge. Social classes are not, in fact, an 'empirical thing' of which the structures are the concept. They denote social relations, social ensembles: but they are the concept of them, in the same way as the concepts of capital, of wage-labour, and of surplus value constitute concepts of structures, of relations of production.[13]

More exactly, social class is a concept which shows the effects of the ensemble of structures, of the matrix of a mode of production or of a social formation

in 'Système, structure et contradiction dans *Le Capital*' in *Les Temps Modernes*, November 1966 (translated in Lane, ed., *Structuralism*, London, 1971). According to Godelier, the CMP is characterized by two sets of contradictions situated in the structures: the first and fundamental one operates between *two different structures*, (a) the relations of production (private ownership of the means of production) and (b) the productive forces; while the second, operating between (i) the capitalist and (ii) the wage-earning labourer, operates between *two classes at the heart of the same structure* (i.e., that of the relations of production). This is a double error: (A) the relations of production and the productive forces belong to the same combination-structure of the economic, whereas private (juridical) ownership of the means of production belongs to the superstructure; (B) the contradiction of classes cannot be *inside* the structures and in this way cannot be solely at the level of the relations of production. B is not the same as A, because it is not dependent on the same system, since it concerns social relations: in this sense, it characterizes *all* levels of social relations (of class struggle), and not simply social relations of production. In this respect, we should agree with Lucien Sève's just retort to Godelier that class contradictions are present in all the levels of the social edifice (see *La Pensée*, October 1967).

12. In the sense in which Lévi-Strauss says that 'social relations' are the 'raw material' of the structures. See *Anthropologie structurale*, Paris, 1958, pp. 305 ff.

13. It may be useful to point out this problem. Indeed, a great deal of confusion is evident in this respect in current sociological theory, centred on the problem of knowing whether social 'classes' are a *Realphänomen* (empirical-concrete) or an *Ordnungsphänomen* (a concept in the sense of a model). See Lenski, 'American Social Classes – Statistical Strata or Social Groups?', *American Journal of Sociology*, LIX, 1952; Lipset and Bendix, 'Social Status and Social Structure' in *British Journal of Sociology*, II, 1951.

on the agents which constitute its supports : this concept reveals the effects of the global structure in the field of social relations. In this sense, if class is indeed a concept, it does not designate a reality which can be placed in the structures: it designates the effect of an ensemble of given structures, an ensemble which determines social relations as class relations.[14] This means that social class cannot be perceived theoretically as a regional or partial structure of the global structure, in the way for example that relations of production, the state or ideology do in fact constitute its regional structures. This is so, not because the effect of the structures (namely the class) cannot itself constitute a structure, nor because the class is the 'empirical concrete' (the group) whereas structures are its concept: it is because there is no theoretical homogeneity between the concept of class, denoting social relations, and those concepts denoting structures.[15]

However, though it is true that social classes cannot be considered as a structure in the first field designated, yet they do constitute, as a structural effect, a structure in the particular frame of reference of social relations. This frame of reference is itself structured in so far as it is circumscribed by the limits set by structures, limits which are reflected as effects of the ensemble of one field on the other. This will become clearer when we examine the overlapping of our distinction between structures and social relations with that between structures and practices, class practices.[16]

Marx and Engels give an *indication* of this difference of fields by habitually using two different terms in their works to designate a historically determined social 'whole': these terms are 'social formation' (or

14. We should not, of course, take the term 'effects' in a chronological sense; this would be to make a genesis back to front. *I mean by 'effects' the existence of the determination of structures in social classes.*

15. Several of Lenin's texts on social classes point in the same direction: '. . . the bourgeois class . . . is a product and expression of social "life", which in its turn constitutes the capitalist social formation . . .' (*Collected Works*, Vol. 1, p. 350); or again, 'Note that Marx is speaking here of materialist criticism, which alone he regards as scientific – that is, criticism which compares the political, legal, social, conventional and other facts, with economics, with the system of production relations, with the interests of the classes that inevitably take shape on the basis of all the antagonistic social relations' (ibid., p. 327).

16. This problem is very important and I draw attention to it at this stage. Classes always denote class *practices, and these practices are not structures*: political practice cannot be identified with the superstructure of the state, nor economic practice with relations of production.

more exactly, 'economico-social formation') and 'society' (particularly in the expression 'society divided into classes'). In this sense, the term *'bürgerliche Gesellschaft'* in Marx's mature works, most often means not 'civil society' but 'bourgeois society', used to specify capitalist 'society'. Marx's use of the term 'society' in place of 'social formation' is not merely a theoretical slip or terminological inconsistency, but indicates the problem of a differentiation between structures and social relations. The term 'social formation' refers strictly to structural levels, that of 'society' often points in a descriptive way to the field of social relations.

What concrete results can be inferred from these remarks with respect to the constitution of social classes? Firstly, the constitution of classes is not related to the economic level alone, but consists of an effect of the ensemble of the levels of a mode of production or of a social formation. The organization of instances in economic, political and ideological levels is reflected, in social relations, in economic, political and ideological class practice and in 'struggle' between the practices of the various classes. Since social relations are a field-cum-effect structured from the system of structures, the levels of class struggle are related in the same kind of of way as the instances of the matrix. The determination in the last instance of the economic class struggle in the field of social relations (the relation to the relations of production) may be reflected by a displacement of the dominant role to another level of class struggle – political or ideological struggle. The way in which classes are related to the relations of production and to the economic structure has the determining role in the constitution of social classes: this role provides precise evidence of the constant determination-in-the-last-instance by the economic element in the structures, as reflected in social relations.[17]

That articulation of structures which characterizes a given mode of production or a social formation is as a general rule that of social relations, of levels of class struggle. Let us take as an example the case of the feudal mode of production. It is characterized by a particular articulation of the

---

17. If anyone is still surprised that I conceive of relations of production, in the constitution of classes, as 'economic struggle', he should remember that Lenin claimed that it is *the economic class struggle* which is the base of 'society' and the state. In this he went *too far*, but in the opposite direction from the confusion noted above. i.e., instead of absorbing the 'economic class struggle' (the relation of classes to the relations of production) in the relations of production themselves, Lenin absorbs the relations of production in the 'economic class struggle'.

economic, the political and the ideological; determination in the last instance by the economic is reflected most often by the dominant role of the political (and sometimes even of the ideological), defined according to its place and its function in this mode. Let us now take the case of social relations. The social classes of this mode of production, those classes fixed by their 'public-political' status, show that determination in the last instance by economic class organization is expressed here by the dominant role of its political organization. These classes are firstly determined by the public status of the agents of production, i.e. by their juridico-political organization defined according to the place and function of the political in feudal social relations, which are only the reflection of the place and function of the political in the structures. In numerous texts, especially in the *Grundrisse*, Marx notes (though as we have seen in a descriptive way) this specificity of 'castes' and 'estates' vis-à-vis modern social classes.

(ii) CLASSES IN A MODE OF PRODUCTION
AND IN A SOCIAL FORMATION

Finally, I should make a last remark in connection with social classes as related to a *given mode of production* and a *historically determined social formation*: the problem is that of the 'number' of social classes in Marx and Engels's analyses of a social formation. The variations in the enumeration of classes have often been attributed[18] to the fact that Marx and Engels implicitly admitted a *plurality* of criteria (other than those which are concerned strictly with *structures* of instances) for distinguishing classes.[19]

18. In particular, R. Aron, *La Lutte des Classes*, Paris, 1965; G. Gurvitch, *Le Concept des Classes Sociales* (cyclostyled course), Paris, 1962.

19. This problem of the multiplicity of criteria brought into play in defining classes deserves attention. If we understand by it that social classes are defined not simply by their relation to the economic, but also by their relation to the political and ideological levels, this observation is correct. However, this does not involve any kind of plurality (whether 6, 8 or 14) of criteria, but rather one perfectly defined criterion, which is a complex relation to the levels of structures, levels which are themselves perfectly defined. For example, to enumerate any kind of 'plurality' at the ideological level, e.g. levels of education, class consciousness, 'rationalizing' or 'non-rationalizing' attitude to labour, etc. – I am thinking notably of Bourdieu's well-known works – is erroneous. It is erroneous in the sense that the global relation to the ideological, in its various concrete manifestations, is strictly defined as a relation to the structures of the ideology. The same is true for the problem of the relation between incomes and the relations of production. So, to reject the conception of a plurality of criteria of class is not to reduce classes to their purely economic definition, but is rather to maintain as distinct the

It is clear that such an interpretation is mistaken once we refer to the distinction between mode of production and social formation. In the theoretical examination of a 'pure' mode of production, of the 'pure' CMP for example as it is presented in *Capital*, we see that its effect on the supports is reflected in a distinction between two classes, that of the capitalists and that of the wage-earning labourers. However, a social formation consists of an overlapping of several modes of production, one of which holds the dominant role, and it therefore presents more classes than the 'pure' mode of production. This extension of the number of classes is not due to any variation in the employment of the criteria for distinguishing classes, but is strictly related to (a) the modes of production in this formation and (b) the concrete forms taken on by their combination.

We should, at this point, reject *the conclusion that the analysis of classes in the examination of a 'pure' mode of production should be limited to their relation merely to the economic level* of relations of production, their relation to the other levels of structures being taken into account only in the examination of a social formation. It is important to remember that a 'pure' mode of production consists of an articulation of different instances in which social classes manifest themselves in the examination of this 'pure' mode as the effect of its matrix on its supports: for example, in the theoretical examination of the 'pure' feudal mode of production, the classes of this mode already manifest themselves as particular econ-omico-political 'castes'.

This is also valid for the 'pure' CMP as it is examined in *Capital*. Some remarks already made on this subject should be borne in mind. Because of the specific autonomy of instances characteristic of the CMP, the juridico-political and ideological instances are not analysed there on the same grounds as the economic instance, which is at the centre of its investigation. Yet there is an indication of the immanent presence of these instances in the capitalist relations of production: the effect of the juridico-political or ideological structure on the supports, in their distribution into capitalists and wage-earning labourers, is sketched in but only implicitly. But to show its presence there, it is only necessary to mention the most obvious example, that of formal juridical relations of property, the conditions of the purchase and the sale of labour power. This transaction is strictly dependent on the regional instance of the 'pure' mode of production

relevant effects of structures, in so far as Marxism makes the decipherment of these structures possible.

constituted by the juridical system; and this, in its turn, presupposes the state. Many texts of Marx and Engels are explicit in this respect.[20] It is clear in other respects that there are numerous references in *Capital* (e.g. market fetishism, capitalist fetishism) to the implicit presence of the ideological in the relations of production (the economic) and to their effect on the classes of this mode.

Once this is clear, it is mistaken to claim that in the capitalist (or any other) mode of production, relations of production are alone sufficient to define social classes. This is so not simply in the sense that we must refer also to relations of distribution (i.e. incomes); this is correct, but still concerns the economic structure; but more importantly in the sense that the 'pure' CMP locates relations of production as a regional (economic) structure, by placing them in their relation to the other regional structures, the classes of this mode being the effect of this matrix. Thus the specific autonomy of instances proper to the CMP does not in any way make it possible for classes in that mode of production to be defined solely in terms of relations of production. Feudal classes and capitalist classes (in the respective 'pure' modes of production) do not differ in that the latter, as opposed to the former, can be defined in exclusively economic terms, but in that the effects of the other instances on the capitalist supports are manifested in their specific relation to the relations of production inside this mode.[21]

It can be seen therefore that, in the analysis both of the mode of production and of a social formation, social classes present themselves as an effect of the articulation of the structures either of the mode of production or of the social formation. However it remains the case that, in examining

20. Economism has tried to evade this problem by considering formal juridical relations of property as 'economic' relations: this can be seen clearly in Pashukanis, *General Theory of Law and Marxism*, 1924, 1927 (translation in Babb, *Soviet Legal Philosophy*, Twentieth Century Legal Philosophy Series No. 5, Harvard University Press, 1951). It is unnecessary to point out that this renders the cardinal distinction between real appropriation (i.e. economic property) and formal juridical property in the 'pure' mode of production theoretically impossible.

21. In fact, a whole series of thinkers, attributing to Marx an 'economist' conception of social classes, and also agreeing that the classes of the capitalist mode of production can in fact be defined in exclusively economic terms (thus committing a double theoretical error), reach the following conclusion: they grant the validity of the Marxist theory of social classes thus conceived, but only for the classes of the CMP, and reject it for the others where the exclusively economic definition is particularly clearly insufficient. See T. Bottomore, *Classes in Modern Society*, London, 1966, pp. 16 ff.

social classes inside a social formation, we discover a whole series of *secondary effects* which are the effects, on the supports of this formation, of the *concrete* and in each case original *combination* of the different modes of production constituting that formation. Imagine a social formation composed of a certain number of classes: that does not mean that these classes are going to be found as such in the historical individual form of that formation.

The effects of the concrete combination of the respective instances of the modes of production, effects of combination which are present in the effects of the structures of a *social formation* on its supports (that is to say, in the social classes of a formation) give rise to a whole series of phenomena of splitting, dissolution and fusion of classes, in short of *over-determination* or of *under-determination* of classes, of the appearance of specific categories, etc. These cannot, however, always be located by the examination of pure modes of production entering into the combination. It should be mentioned at this stage that these considerations provide the solution of, for example, the all-important problem of the *great landed proprietors of ground-rent*, whom Marx himself sometimes *wrongly* perceived as a class belonging to the 'pure' CMP.[22] We shall come in a moment to the decisive point in the political problematic of social classes, that of their existence or non-existence as *distinct classes* or *autonomous fractions* of other classes, in short as the *social forces* of a formation. It was necessary to pose the problem, in order to subject some of Marx's political texts on the social classes, quoted above, to a correct reading.

(iii) THE ROLE OF POLITICAL CLASS STRUGGLE IN THE DEFINITION OF CLASSES

In fact, on a first reading, these texts of Marx contain ambiguities resulting from their double theoretical status. They do concern social formations; but it seems clear that they also constitute a parallel effort to pose the problematic of social classes with respect to the 'pure' mode of production.

Let us first of all consider the texts cited above from the point of view of posing the problem of classes in the framework of the examination of *a 'pure' mode of production*. The historicist interpretation of these texts as the genesis of a class must anyway be excluded. But there is one surprising point: it is clear that Marx distinguishes the economic struggle

22. See on this particular subject pp. 231 ff. below.

(which itself appears to be split into two levels) from the political class struggle, and seems to acknowledge the existence of fully constituted classes only at the level of the political struggle; with regard to the economic struggle of the agents of production (i.e. between capitalists and workers) he says that it is not a case of class struggle, and with regard to the economic trade-union struggle he speaks of 'class-in-itself', i.e. he seems to reserve the status of class-for-itself, of class 'as such', for the political struggle alone.

It is easy to explain the first point, concerning the economic struggle of 'individuals' as agents of production. For it was in political works written long before *Capital*, notably in *The Poverty of Philosophy* and the *Manifesto*, that Marx perceived their struggle as not being dependent on class relations. We are dealing therefore with texts from a period when Marx had not yet completely worked out his original problematic, and when the effects of the economic anthropology of his youth were still influential. We know with certainty from *Capital*, and in particular from Volume III, that the relations of individuals as agents of production, the relations between capitalist and wage-earning labourer, as they are presented in Volume I or in the political texts under consideration, are here and now class relations: agents of production are the supports of structures.

The problem however is more difficult with regard to the distinction between economic trade-union struggle and political struggle. The distinction which Marx established in Hegelian terminology in *The Poverty of Philosophy* of 1847 between 'class-in-itself' and 'class-for-itself' remains a *constant* problem in his political works. Why does he continually appear to acknowledge the existence of a class 'as such' only on the political plane, which it is clear from his analyses of the small-holding peasants and from his *subsequent* political analyses of the proletariat, exists as a class only when it is organized in a distinct party?[23] This must be explained.

23. To take only one example, let us quote the first paragraph of article 7a of the rules of the First International, drafted by Marx in 1866: 'In its struggle against the collective power of the possessing classes the proletariat can act *as a class* only by constituting itself a distinct political party . . .' (*MESW*, 1958, Vol. I, p. 388). Also this passage from a letter to Bolte, on 23 November 1871: '. . . every movement in which the working class comes out as a *class* [Marx's emphasis] against the ruling classes . . . is a political movement' (*MESW*, 1970, p. 673). It is in this context that we can clear up the ambiguity of Marx's constant formula, according to which any class struggle (between classes as such) is a political struggle.

Since these political texts from the period up until 1881 constitute also a reflection on classes in a 'pure' mode of production, the different levels of analysis of social relations, described by Marx as moments of historical genesis, ought *here* to be considered as a *theoretical process* of the construction of the *concept* of class. This means that it is an attempt to define the theoretical unity of the field to be covered by the concept of class: i.e. the field of the effects of the unity of the structure either on social relations or (as we shall consider later) on social practices, i.e. class struggles. So, when Marx seems to say that the *existence* of a class at the level of economic struggle is problematic, we should read this as the statement that the concept of class cannot be constituted merely from the relation between social relations and economic structures: the concept of class covers the unity of class practices (class 'struggle'), of social relations as effects of the unity of the *levels* of structures. In short, what is presented in Marx as a type of problematic concerning historical existence is in fact merely a theoretical impossibility.

But a second operation comes in here. Marx is also 'isolating' the levels of class struggle in order to examine them in their specificity, in so far as this is a problem of the CMP, characterized by an autonomization of levels of structures and levels of class practices. This is not only permissible but necessary *on one condition*: that we have at the outset defined the unity of the field in which this theoretical division will be made. In the structures, for example, any 'isolated' theoretical analysis of the regional instance of the economic or the political presupposes the concept of mode of production, which assigns a place to them. In this sense, the isolated examination of economic, political and ideological class practice presupposes the concept of class as covering the unity of these practices ('struggle' between classes) in short the field of social relations. Marx operates this division by directly superimposing it on the process of the theoretical construction of the concept of class. The result of this is that where Marx expresses the impossibility of constructing the concept of class at the sole level of the relations of production he appears at the same time to be making a theoretical division in the void, i.e. marking out an economic struggle which is not a class struggle.[24]

It is in this context that we must locate the particular importance which Marx attributes to the *political* class struggle as a particular level of social

24. I shall return to the implications of Marx's formulae in so far as they concern social formations, and to a more exact definition of class *practice* and of the '*struggle*' of classes.

relations, which consist of economic, political and ideological class struggle. According to an 'over-politicizing' tendency of Marxism, which is linked to the historicist problematic and which presents itself here as the counterweight to economism, the social class, as 'actor-subject' of history, has effective existence at the political level only where it has acquired a class consciousness of its own, etc.: representatives of this tendency are Lukács, Korsch and the Theoretical Leftism of the Third International. The typical schema of this tendency is as follows: the *economic level* in general consists of *structures*; since social classes, the actor-subjects, are absent from it, theoretical analysis of this level does not consequently require the concept of class: we are faced with the famous 'unconscious laws' of the economy. On the other hand, the effective emergence of social classes takes place at political and ideological levels, levels which cannot be analysed in terms of structures, *but solely in terms of class struggle*. The historical process consists, as it were, of economic structures 'set in motion' by a politico-ideological class struggle. This is precisely the conception which Lenin attacked, pointing out that it attributes to politics the role of 'shaking up' the economic 'from above'.[25] This confusion of structures and social relations, i.e. class struggle, has had results which are still felt. In fact, both an economic struggle (i.e. economic class action or economic social relations) *and* political and ideological structures exist. Although Marx insisted on the political class struggle, this by no means shows that classes emerge historically at the political level in a process of essence to existence, and in order to 'set in motion' the economic structures. In this respect, his 1847 formulae of 'class-in-itself' and of 'class-for-itself' are merely Hegelian reminiscences Not only do they fail to explain anything, but they have for years misled Marxist theorists of social classes.

These formulae have in particular played a protective role for the historicist schema, by permitting the conception of an economic structure 'set in motion' by the politico-ideological class struggle, a structure inside which classes are nevertheless to be inserted in the mysterious mode of the 'class-in-itself'. In fact, the role attributed by Marx to political class struggle in social relations is analogous to that attributed to the state in the structures, and is related to the very status of the 'political'. To the extent that the political superstructure is the *over-determining* level of the levels of the structure by *concentrating* their contradictions and by reflecting their relation, the political class struggle is the *over-determining*

25. 'Once again on the Trade Unions . . .', op. cit.

level of the field of class struggles (i.e. of social relations), concentrating their contradictions and reflecting the relations of the other levels of class struggle. This is so to the extent that the political superstructure of the state has the function of being the cohesive factor in a formation, and to the extent that the objective of political class struggle is this state. It is in this context that we can locate an exact meaning for the formula 'the political class struggle is the motive force of history'. Thus, Marx's formulae, which apparently acknowledge the effective existence of classes only at the level of political struggle, therefore relate to the particular character of this level as related to the political superstructure. Political class struggle is the nodal point of the process of transformation, a process which has nothing to do with a diachronic historicist process, 'acted' by an author, the class-subject.

(iv) DISTINCT CLASSES AND AUTONOMOUS FRACTIONS OF CLASSES

The important problem which arises here is that of determining the manner in which classes are present inside a *social formation*. How can the classes in a social formation be determined? In other words, how can we decipher the effects of the concrete combination of the modes of production which constitute a formation, on the supports of that formation? For because of the complexity of these effects, we cannot conclude immediately from the fact that certain classes are present in the 'pure' examination of the formation that they exist concretely as distinct classes in a determinate conjuncture. The most important phenomenon in this respect is that *certain distinct classes*, conceivable in the analysis of 'pure' modes of production which compose a formation, often appear in the social formation *dissolved and fused* with other classes, as groups (autonomous or not) of other classes, or even as specific social categories.[26]

The dominance of one mode of production over the others inside a social formation often has the effect of an *under-determination* of the

26. In fact, the problem of 'fractions' of classes is more complicated, but I am considering here only the case of certain classes which, as a result of combination, become fractions *of other classes*. In the social formation, we can in addition see the appearance of fractions *in the heart of the same class, as effects peculiar to concrete political structures of this formation*. I shall give examples from Marx on pp. 234 ff. below. The splitting-up of a class can also be already present in the 'pure' mode of production and in the economic level of this mode: for example, the commercial, industrial and financial bourgeoisie.

classes of non-dominant modes. We know how this problem is posed according to the historicist view which, *strictly speaking*, does not make any theoretical distinction between mode of production and social formation: a class exists as such, as a *distinct and autonomous class*, only from the moment when it possesses a 'class consciousness' *of its own*, when it is organized in a distinct party, etc. Besides, Marx's texts, considered here as texts concerning determinate social formations, often show the existence of a class as a distinct class in a formation linked to its 'own' political organization.[27] In fact, the specific problem which Marx's political texts pose concerning a social formation is that of the existence in this formation of a distinct class. The answer sometimes given to this problem is however affected by the ambiguities indicated above concerning the theoretical construction of the concept of class. Since a class appears there to have effective existence at the political level alone, a class in a social formation seems to exist as a distinct class when it is organized politically in a 'distinct' party, etc.

In fact, the real problem posed by Marx with regard, this time, to a social formation is that a class can be considered as a distinct and autonomous class, as a social force,[28] inside a social formation, only when its connection with the relations of production, its economic existence, is reflected on the other levels by a specific presence. This anyway follows from the fact that even in the 'pure' mode of production a social class already shows the effect of the ensemble of the structures on the supports. Indeed, strictly speaking, it would not be possible to conclude that it was necessary to refer to the political and ideological levels with respect to the classes in a social formation, if this were not already the case in the 'pure' mode of production. It is this presence that Marx perceives here as the political organization of a class in a distinct party.

How, at the political and ideological levels, should we mark out this presence which constitutes the *distinct character* of the classes (and also the character of an autonomous fraction of a class) in a formation? How can a criterion be defined which will lead us to decipher the existence of a class, or of a fraction, as a *social force* in a determinate formation: that is, a criterion which obviously cannot be supplied exclusively by the economic level? It can be said that this presence exists when the relation to

27. In particular, see his texts concerning the organization of the working class into an autonomous party.

28. Furthermore, this is also valid for the existence of a class fraction as an 'autonomous fraction' or 'social force'.

the relations of production, the place in the process of production, is reflected on the other levels by *pertinent effects*. These 'pertinent effects' can be located in political and ideological structures as well as in social, political and ideological class relations. We shall designate by 'pertinent effects' the fact that the reflection of the place in the process of production on the other levels constitutes a *new element* which cannot be inserted in the typical framework which these levels would present without this element. This element thus transforms the *limits* of the levels of structures or of class struggle at which it is reflected by 'pertinent effects'; and it cannot be inserted in a simple variation of these limits.

I shall take one of the most complex examples, that of the small-holding peasants in *The Eighteenth Brumaire*. In the concrete conjuncture examined by Marx, do they constitute a distinct social class or not? Marx says: 'In so far as millions of [peasant] families live under economic conditions of existence that separate their mode of life, their interests and their culture from those of the other classes, . . . they form a class. In so far as . . . the identity of their interests begets . . . no political organization among them, they do not form a class' (*MESW*, 1970, pp. 170–1). However, we have only to refer to *The Eighteenth Brumaire* and *The Class Struggles in France* in their entirety to see that Marx expressly acknowledges on several occasions the existence, in the concrete conjuncture of Bonapartism, of small-holding peasants as a distinct class, although they possessed, in the Second Empire, neither a political organization 'of their own' nor an ideology 'of their own'. They constitute precisely a distinct class to the extent that their place in the process of production is reflected in this concrete conjuncture, at the level of political structures, by the historical phenomenon of Bonapartism which would not have existed without the small peasant farmers. Louis Bonaparte put himself forward as the representative of the small-holding peasants although he was, in reality, the 'representative' of the interests of the bourgeoisie. Yet it remains the case that the economic existence of the small-holding peasants is reflected, on the political level, by the 'pertinent effects' constituted by *the particular form of state* of Bonapartism as a historical phenomenon. We are faced here with a new but easily located element, i.e. the particular form of state in the Second Empire, a form which cannot be inserted in the framework of the preceding parliamentary state. In this sense, it is, paradoxically, Bonapartism which constitutes the small-holding peasants as a distinct class, i.e. as a *social force* in this formation.

Let us now consider a hypothetical case where the economic existence of the small-holding peasants is not reflected by Bonapartism: in this case, of course, their particular place in the process of production is anyway manifested by a certain presence at the political level, if only in the simple fact that the political organization of the other classes, as well as the institutions of the state, have to take into account the existence of the small-holding peasants, for example, in the case of suffrage.[29] However, in this case, this presence neither constitutes a new element, nor has 'pertinent effects', but is only inserted as a variation into limits circumscribed by the pertinent effects of other elements, for example into the framework of constitutional democracy. It is clear that in this case the small-holding peasants do not constitute a *distinct class*. Indeed, at the economic level alone, owing to the specific under-determination in the French social formation of the patriarchal mode of production, the process of proletarianization of the small-holding peasants was already very advanced; and Marx insists on this point.[30] What, however, makes them function concretely as a distinct class, as a social force, is in fact the historical phenomenon of Bonapartism. On the other hand, the small peasants of Germany (small-holding peasants liberated from the corvée), the feudal tenant-farmers and agricultural workers, never functioned as a social force or as a distinct class, *precisely on account of Bismarckism and the state superstructure*. The problem becomes apparent in Engels. He tends to explain Bonapartism in France as the 'equilibrium' not between the landed nobility and the bourgeoisie, as in the absolutist state, but between these two classes on the one hand and the working class on the other. We shall come back to the inadequacy of this notion of equilibrium for locating Bonapartism in the relations between bourgeoisie and proletariat, but it is noticeable that Engels, unlike Marx, anyway tends to underestimate the role of the peasants. For this reason, he speaks of the *Prussian Bonapartist* phenomenon (Bismarck) and tries to distinguish it from the Second Empire. The small peasants of Germany, undergoing at the economic level the

29. It is evident here that the absence of 'pertinent effects' at the political level does not mean an absence of political practice: suffrage, for example, is a political practice for the person who makes use of it.

30. 'The Eighteenth Brumaire', *MESW*, 1970, pp. 170 ff. Moreover, this functioning of the small-holding peasants in France as a social force depends also on structures of the *ideological*. Marx shows us how Louis Bonaparte managed to put himself forward as the 'representative' of the small-holding peasants, a phenomenon which doubtless goes back to that profoundly ambiguous political ideology of French Jacobinism. See E. Hobsbawn, *The Age of Revolution, 1789-1848*, London, 1962, pp. 109 ff., 149 ff.

domination of the CMP over the patriarchal and feudal mode, do not function in Bismarckism as a social force (as they do in Bonapartism) on account of the feudal structures of the state, which are dislocated relative to the economic level.[31]

Furthermore the case of the small-holding peasants is only one example amongst the many given by Marx. I cite here only his analyses of the period of transition from feudalism to capitalism in Britain. Marx's central objective in his political analyses of this period is to determine the point of time, considering the particularities of this transition in Britain, at which the bourgeoisie constituted itself first as an autonomous fraction and then as a class distinct from the feudal nobility, whilst lacking both ideology and political organization 'of its own': his analyses are conducted from the viewpoint just outlined.[32] This process was carried out by means of their 'representation' by the Whigs, who were in fact the party of a fraction of the landowners.

It is clear that the characterization of 'pertinent effects' and of their novelty relative to the typical form of the levels always depends on the concrete conjuncture of a concrete historical situation. It is only by examining this that we can circumscribe the relations of the limits and variations, and thus characterize the 'pertinent effects'. This pertinence may be reflected in important modifications of political and ideological structures as well as in modifications of the field of the political and ideological class struggle. It may be manifested in an important modification of the relations of class 'representation', in which the economic existence of a class is reflected in important changes of structure or strategy of the party *of another class*, so that the latter can put itself forward also as the representative of the former class, in the case in which its party has an important role in the political class struggle (cf. the case

31. Engels's problem appears most clearly in *The Housing Question* and in the 1874 Preface to *The Peasant War in Germany*. The analysis of the peasants is more searching in *Revolution and Counter-revolution in Germany*, where Engels distinguishes small-holding peasants, agricultural workers and feudal tenant-farmers. But the fact that the greater part of German peasants were from the economic point of view feudal tenant-farmers does not imply that these three classes of peasants did not function as distinct classes in Bismarckism. The feudal tenant-farmers could have worked with the small-holding peasants and the agricultural workers as a social force, precisely because of the abolition of feudal privileges: but there was the state and Bismarck . . . .

32. cf. my article 'Marxist Political Theory in Great Britain', in *New Left Review* 43, and my detailed references to the analyses of Marx.

of the Whigs mentioned above); or again by a displacement of the contradiction in the framework of the political struggle of other classes, etc. It is
important to recognize clearly that the existence of a class in a formation
presupposes its presence at the political level through 'pertinent effects',
which do not however need to extend to its having 'its own' political
organization, strictly speaking, or to its constituting 'its own' class
ideology. In fact, the domination in a social formation of the classes of
the dominant mode of production on the one hand, and the relation
between (i) the political and ideological structures of a formation and
(ii) the dominant class(es) of the dominant mode of production on the
other hand, takes into account the frequent under-determination of the
other classes.[33] These structures, having their effects on the ensemble of
the field of class struggle, often prevent the independent political and
ideological organization of the classes of non-dominant modes of production, and result precisely in *the polarization of these classes* around
classes of the dominant mode. The 'pertinent effects', however, permit the
precise location of the *threshold* from which an *under-determined* class
exists, and indeed functions, as a social force: the same holds for autonomous fractions of a class.

We know the broad lines of this process in which the classes of the
dominated modes of production in a social formation are over-determined
by the classes of the dominant modes. This process depends on the concrete forms of this dominance: transformation of the feudal nobility into
a fraction of the bourgeoisie (due to capitalization of ground rent); of
the petty bourgeois (peasants and craftsmen) into fractions either of the
bourgeoisie (becoming small capitalists) or of the working class; of the
small-holding peasants into wage-labourers. In other words, it depends
on the whole range of *decomposition* of under-determined classes and of
resistance to this decomposition, which exactly controls whether or not a
class or fraction is to exist as a social force, as a distinct class or as an
autonomous fraction.[34]

33. See Poulantzas, op. cit., for a critique of P. Anderson's use of Sartre's concept
of 'detotalized totality' to designate the problem of the under-determination of a class.

34. This problem was systematically discussed by Lenin in *The Development of
Capitalism in Russia*. With regard to the problem of classes in this important work, we
must note that in his preface to the first edition, Lenin emphasizes that he has been
obliged to limit himself *'to the economic aspect of the process'* (*Collected Works*, Vol. 3,
p. 25). The relation of this economic aspect and of the political aspect is however pointed
out in the preface to the second edition, although under the term 'confirmation': 'The

These remarks are important on the political plane. Indeed, the character of a social group as a *distinct class* or *autonomous fraction* (which is not identical with political class practice), has very important consequences with regard both to the role of this class as a social force in its conjuncture and also to its role in the '*declared action*' of social forces. In other words, the presence of a class through 'pertinent effects' at the level of political struggle affects the way in which it is represented on the 'political scene', affects the modalities of its 'declared action' and the constitution of alliances, etc.

In addition, we shall have, in a moment, to go more deeply into the distinction between (i) economic struggle and political class struggle, and (ii) the economic and political levels in the organization of a class. When we speak of dominance by the level of economic organization of a class, as distinct from the level of its strictly political organization, it does not mean that this class is absent in its 'pertinent effects' from the level of political struggle. It means simply that, in the complex organization of a class, it is the economic which holds the dominant role, in addition to determination in the last instance.

Thus, for example, when Lenin clearly distinguishes the economic and political struggles (in *What is to be done?*) by describing and criticizing the trade-unionist stage of the working class as distinct from the political stage (which is characterized by a distinct party, etc.), he does not mean by it that the working class is absent from the political struggle and limited to the economic struggle alone: he clearly means that in this case it is the economic struggle which has the dominant role in the field of the levels of class struggle and class organization. This dominance of the economic struggle is reflected here, not by an absence of 'pertinent effects' at the level of political struggle, but in a certain form of political struggle, which Lenin criticizes by considering it as ineffectual. The importance of the problem is pointed out in a note: 'Trade-unionism does not exclude "politics" altogether, as some imagine. Trade unions have always conducted some political (but not Social-Democratic) agitation and struggle.

---

analysis of the social-economic system and, consequently, of the class structure of Russia given in this work on the basis of an economic investigation and critical analysis of statistics, has now been confirmed by the open political action of all classes in the course of the revolution' (ibid., p. 31). Nevertheless, when we refer to the ensemble of Lenin's analyses of social classes, we see in fact that *open and direct action* does not constitute confirmation at the political level of the economic existence of classes: according to Lenin, *direct, open or declared action* is the reflection in the *conjuncture* of a *social force*.

We shall deal with the difference between trade-union politics and Social-Democratic politics in the next chapter.'[35] This holds, too, *mutatis mutandis*, for the ideological class struggle. We see the appearance here of the distinction between (i) the organization of a class as a condition of its presence by pertinent effects at the political level, i.e. as a condition of its existence as a distinct class, and (ii) its specific organization as a condition of its *political class power*, a distinction which is at the basis of the Leninist theory of *organization*.

(v) FRACTIONS – CATEGORIES – STRATA

A terminological question can, after this analysis, now finally be elucidated: it concerns the terms *category, fraction* and *stratum*, as designating parts of a class.

a. By *social categories*, we mean social ensembles with 'pertinent effects', which, as Lenin demonstrated, may become social forces whose distinguishing feature is based on their *specific and over-determining relation to structures other than economic ones*. Important examples are the bureaucracy, in its relations to the state, and the 'intellectuals' in their relations to the ideological. We shall have to return to the relations between these categories and the classes or fractions of classes to which they belong.

b. We designate as *autonomous fractions of classes* those fractions which constitute the substratum of eventual social forces; and as *fractions*, those social ensembles which are capable of becoming autonomous fractions, according to the criterion of 'pertinent effects'.

c. We can reserve the term of *social strata* for indicating the *secondary* effects of the combination of modes of production in a social formation, (i) on classes; for example, on what Lenin calls the 'working class aristocracy', (ii) on categories; for example, on the 'summits' of bureaucracy and administration mentioned by Lenin, and (iii) on fractions.

It must be borne in mind that Marxist theory has, in general, used the terms category, stratum and fraction in a way that has often been obscure: but it is important to reach agreement on terminology. With regard to the distinction between categories and fractions, particularly autonomous fractions, it should be noted that both are capable of constituting social forces. The problem presents no difficulties for those fractions which can already be located at the level of relations of production, for example, the commercial, industrial and financial fractions of the bourgeoisie: it is

35. *Selected Works*, Vol. 1, p. 122.

this which distinguishes them in this case from categories located at the level of structures other than the economic. However, it becomes more complex in the case of certain fractions described by Marx which are located solely at the political level.[36] What distinguishes them, in this case, from categories is precisely the over-determining relation of the categories to the political and ideological structures of which they are the specific effect. For example with regard to the political level, it is the relation of the bureaucracy to the state apparatus in the strict sense of the term.

The distinction between strata and fractions is especially relevant in so far as it concerns their reflection at the political level: fractions, to the extent that they become autonomous, are capable, unlike strata, of constituting themselves as social forces. This does not in the least mean that the distinction between fractions and strata covers exactly the distinction between the respective effects of the economic and the politico-ideological. We can effectively make out not only fractions dependent on the political level alone, but also simple strata which can already be located in the economic, as is the case with the working-class aristocracy. It would be wrong to believe that such a localization of strata, as distinguished in this way from fractions, is a concession to 'stratificatory' hyper-empiricism. Such a localization is important, in so far as it designates, as products of the secondary effects of the combination of modes of production, certain *fringe-limits* of classes, categories and fractions *which can, without being social forces, exert an influence on the political practice of these forces*. This is the case, for example, with the working-class aristocracy which Lenin designates in *Imperialism* as a social stratum: because of its character as an intermediary fringe, it cannot itself constitute a social force, but it influences the political practice of the working class, functioning politically as the working-class 'agent' of the bourgeoisie.

(vi) CLASS STRUCTURES AND CLASS PRACTICES:
THE CLASS STRUGGLE

The above analyses have established the distinction and relation between two systems of relations, that of structures and that of social relations: the concept of class covers the production of social relations as an effect of

36. This is the case with the 'bourgeois-republican fraction' of the Constituent National Assembly in France: see 'The Eighteenth Brumaire', *MESW*, 1970, pp, 105 ff.

the structures. We now possess the elements necessary for putting forward the two following propositions:

1. This distinction covers the distinction between *structures* and *practices* (i.e. class practices).

2. Social relations consist of class practices, in which social classes are placed in *oppositions*: social classes can be conceived only as class practices, these practices existing in oppositions *which, in their unity, constitute the field of the class struggle*.

Within the scope of this book we can only supply some guidelines. The first proposition summarizes the previous analyses by posing a new problem. Social classes do not cover structural instances but social relations: these social relations consist of class practices, which means that social classes are conceivable only in terms of class practices. In what follows, therefore, we shall insist upon the new form which the distinction between the above fields assumes, and which becomes here a distinction between structures and practices.

The second proposition indicates that social classes are posed only in their *opposition*: class practices can be analysed only as conflicting practices in the field of class struggle, composed of relations of opposition, i.e. of relations of contradiction in the simplest sense of the term. At every level the relation of conflict of the practices of different classes, the 'struggle' between classes, the very existence of classes themselves, are the effect of the relations of the structures, the form assumed by the contradictions of the structures in social relations. They define *at every level* fundamental connections of *domination* and *subordination* of classes (class practices) which exist as particular contradictions.[37] These include, for example, the contradiction between those practices which aim at the realization of profit and those which aim at the increase of wages (economic struggle), and the contradiction between those that aim at the maintenance of existing social relations and those that aim at their transformation (political struggle), etc. Just as the scientific treatment of the contradictions in the relations of the structure requires appropriate concepts, that of the *relations of conflict between the practices of the various classes, of the field of class 'struggle'* demands, whether in the sphere of economic social relations (economic struggle), or of political social relations (political struggle), or of ideological social relations (ideological

37. On class contradictions, see Mao Tse-Tung, 'On Contradiction' and 'On the Correct Handling of Contradictions among the People', both in *Selected Readings*. Peking, 1967.

struggle), concepts *of its own*, that is, concepts not transferable into the examination of structures; and especially it demands those of class 'interests' and of 'power'. We shall not enter into this problem at this point but shall try to come to closer grips with the distinction and relation between structures and practices.

This distinction, when employed in the historicist problematic, has led to a serious confusion: it consists in seeing in structures an 'ossified praxis', the structures being localized, in the last analysis, with respect to the degree of permanence of the practice which is their origin. Althusser, of course, has provided the critique of this conception, by demonstrating the relation between a structural instance and a specific practice; and he has done this by conceiving of practice as a *production*, i.e. a work of transformation. It is important to see that in this sense *a structural instance does not as such directly constitute a practice*: there are two particular systems or series of ordered connections, which possess structures of their own; but their relation is that of structures to practices structured with respect to these structures. To summarize, relations of production are not the same as the economic class struggle, since these relations are not classes, just as the juridico-political state superstructure and the ideological structures are not the same as the political or ideological class struggle, since the state apparatus or ideological language are no more classes than are relations of production. It is very important to insist upon this point, for it is not always clear. A reduction of structures to practices may have serious consequences. These include a failure correctly to locate the relations between the various levels of structures and the various levels of practices, and, thus, the relations between the two systems of relations constituted by structures on the one hand, and by class practices on the other.

I cite a text of Balibar's[38] which is characteristic in this respect: in it, the problem is outlined, and yet at the same time the ambiguity of this confusion makes itself felt. Firstly, Balibar sets the problem in terms of *two forms* of articulation of the various levels, without however making clear that we have here articulations covering two different fields. Concerning the articulation of the various levels of the social structure, he says:

We have already encountered this articulation above *in two forms*: on the one

38. E. Balibar, in *Reading Capital*, pp. 305-6.

hand, in the determination of the determinant 'last instance' in the social structure, which depends on the combination peculiar to the mode of production considered; *on the other* . . . as the determination of the limits within which the effect of one *practice* can modify another practice from which it is relatively autonomous . . . The particular form of correspondence depends on the *structure of the two practices.*

In fact, these two forms of articulation are to be found at one and the same time in the structures and in the practices. They do not in any way relate to a confusion of the two, a confusion in which the structures and practices appear to correspond, as it were, to different simple forms of articulation in one and the same series of relations. We can see the consequences of this confusion in Balibar's next words:

We can generalize this kind of relationship between two relatively autonomous instances; it recurs, for example, in the relationship between *economic practice* and *political practice,* in the forms of *class struggle, law and State.* . . . Here, too, the correspondence is analysed as the *mode of intervention of one practice* within limits determined by another. *This is the case with the intervention of the 'class struggle' within limits determined by the economic structure . . . The same is true of the intervention of law and of the State in economic practice* . . . In this case, too, there is therefore no relationship of simple transposition, translation or expression between the *various instances of the social structure.* Their 'correspondence' can only be thought on the basis of their relative autonomy, of their peculiar structure, as the system of interventions of this type, of one practice in another (here, obviously, I am only locating a theoretical problem, not producing a knowledge).

The consequences of failing to distinguish structures and practices are clear here. In the first place, at the political level the juridico-political superstructure of the state (the state and law) is identified with political class practice. The mode of intervention of the state and the law (structures) in the economic structure is conceived as the intervention of political practice (political class struggle) in economic practice (economic class struggle). The reduction seems to be brought about here by playing upon the term 'intervention' which, in the metaphorical sense, receives the name of 'practice'. Practice, under the name of intervention, is seen as a form of articulation of structures.

In the second place, a still more serious mistake is made. The economic is considered as a structure on which the class struggle 'operates', while this struggle itself is confined to the political and ideological levels alone:

'The same is true of the intervention of the "class struggle" within limits determined by the economic structure . . . .' The confusion of structures and practices seems here, in the last analysis, to take the place of the old misunderstanding which consists in seeing social classes, and the class struggle emerging at the political and ideological levels in order to 'set in motion' the unconscious laws of the economy. The political and ideological are equated with the class struggle, i.e. practice, which results in the disappearance of the juridico-political structure of the state and the ideological; the economic is equated with the structure, which involves the disappearance of the economic class struggle.

I emphasize this ambiguity only because of the consequences which follow from it: its second consequence, indicated above, makes it, in the last analysis, impossible to think Lenin's concept of *conjuncture*.[39] However, I now intend to discuss the first point, namely, the articulation of levels in structures and in class practices. The articulation of the juridico-political superstructure of the state or of the ideological structure on the economic structure, in short, the intervention of one level of structures in the limits imposed by another, can by no means be understood as an intervention of political or ideological practice in economic practice. The relation, for example, between legal contract and exchange is a relation of structures. The same is true with regard to the intervention of the state in the economic; intervention does not here mean practice: it indicates a type of articulation of structures.

Structural levels, presenting a specific rhythm, and characterized by their uneven development, maintain in a formation relations of specific dislocation. The same goes for the relations of the different levels of practices in the field of class struggle. Just as we can discern dislocations between the political and ideological structures of a formation, so can we also discern dislocations between the levels of practice and organization (economic, political, ideological) of a class in its relations, at the various levels of struggle, with those of other classes: e.g. a class's political struggle dislocated in relation to its economic struggle, its ideological struggle dislocated in relation to its political struggle, etc. In short, the decentration which characterizes the relations between the levels of a class's structures also characterizes the relations of its practices, in so far as its practices also constitute a structured system, reflecting the relations

39. I am not of course referring here to Balibar.

of instances on supports.[40] *So what is important is to see that there are in fact two systems of relations here.*

The relations between these two series of relations are themselves relations of dislocation characterized by an unambiguous non-correspondence between the terms of the respective levels of these systems. Let us take Marx's analyses of Britain after 1680. In the relations between levels of structures, there is a dislocation between the economic, the political and the ideological: at the stage when the CMP is in the process of attaining domination, the dominant structures of the state and ideology are still feudal.[41] Then again, let us take the levels of struggle of the bourgeois class, disregarding their internal dislocations, in order to see their dislocations with respect to the structure. In one and the same period the bourgeoisie's political organization and political struggle push ahead, while the class of landed nobility (those 'in charge' of the feudal state) is in reality only the 'representative' of the political interests of the bourgeoisie. We can see clearly, in this example, that the juridico-political superstructure of the state is dislocated not simply in relation to other structures, but also in relation to the level of the political struggle of the bourgeoisie[42] in the field of the class struggle. This is not a feudal

40. One remark must be added here to avoid any confusion. The statement that practices coincide with supports in no way involves a return to a problematic of the subject, of 'concrete men' or social classes, as subjects of practices. In other words, it is impossible to relate practices to an originating subject, not because it is the subjects themselves which practise (the economic struggle is no more the 'action' of relations of production than the political struggle is that of the state or the ideological struggle is that of the ideological level), but because the supports, distributed in classes, cannot theoretically be conceived as subjects.

41. This dominance of the feudal structures of the state persists until 1853, when Marx says of Palmerston: 'To the aristocracy he declared that the constitution would not lose its feudal character . . .' (second article on Palmerston, in *People's Paper*, 29 October 1853). See too all his texts in Marx and Engels, *On Britain* (Moscow, 1962).

42. For a selection of Marx's analyses of political problems in Britain, see K. Marx and F. Engels, *On Britain*, Moscow, 1962. Marx's conception of the landed aristocracy as the 'representative' or 'clerk' of the bourgeoisie is clear (a) in his analyses of the Tories, the declared party of the nobility, which when in power performs the policy of the bourgeoisie. He says of the Tories: 'In a word, the whole aristocracy is convinced of the need to govern in the interests of the bourgeoisie; but at the same time it is determined not to allow the latter to take charge of the matter itself' ('Perspectives for the new coalition government' in *New York Times*, 28 January 1853); and (b) in his analyses of the Whigs, who are the typical representatives of the bourgeoisie vis-à-vis the aristocracy: yet by means of the Whigs, the landed nobility continues to function as

state, dislocated in relation to the economic but corresponding to a politically dominant class of landed aristocracy, which is itself in dislocation relative to an economically dominant bourgeoisie. It is rather a set of relations of dislocation between two systems of relations of dislocation. It is precisely this relation of the two systems which in the concrete conjuncture in question brings it about that the form of reflection of the dominance of the CMP in a feudal state is the political domination of the bourgeoisie in the field of class struggle.

This is equally clear in the case of the *index of dominance* in structures and in practices. For example, if we take the case of monopoly state capitalism and the interventionist state, the dominance of the political in the structures does not necessarily correspond to the dominance of the political class struggle in the field of practices, etc. I do not intend to give further examples here: but the importance of these remarks for any political analysis of a concrete conjuncture is evident.

In the light of these considerations, it is now possible to go more deeply into the question of the forms of intervention of the political struggle in the economic struggle, and of the economic struggle in the political struggle, and to elucidate Lenin's theoretical position concerning the *distinction* and *relation* between the economic and political struggles. This position is found in the basic text *What is to be done?* and in his works up until the time of his controversy with Trotsky and Bukharin over the question of the trade unions in the USSR (1921). It is characterized by the following points:

1. *The distinction* between the economic and political struggles: this emerges from Lenin's critiques of opposing positions. In *What is to be done?*, a critique of the 'economists' who believed that 'the political struggle is only the most developed, broadest and most effective form of the economic struggle'; the point, as Lenin says, is that *it is not only that.* It is also a critique of the economist thesis which holds that 'we must give the economic struggle *itself* a political character'. The texts on the trade-union question are a critique of Bukharin, whose insistence on combining the political *and* the economic approach has landed him in theoretical *eclecticism.*[43] We know that Lenin understands: (a) by economic struggle,

---

the class which is in charge of the state. [This note was reformulated by the author for the English edition.]

43. 'Once again on the Trade Unions . . .', *Selected Works*, Vol. 3, p. 528.

'the "practical economic struggle" which Engels . . . described as "resistance to the capitalists", and which . . . is known as the organized-labour syndical, or trade-union struggle';[44] (b) by political struggle, the struggle whose specific objective is *state power*. The distinction between these struggles is at the basis of their forms of organization: trade unions/parties.

2. This distinction implies a *relation* between the economic and political struggles. The essential character of this relation consists in the fact that the political struggle is the *over-determining* level of the class struggle, in that it *concentrates* the levels of class struggle. From this it follows that:

A. As opposed to an evolutionist conception of 'stages' of struggle (first economic, then political), the political struggle *must always have priority* over the economic struggle; this is the role of the party: 'Politics must take precedence over economics . . . without a correct political approach to the matter, the given class will be unable to stay on top, *and*, *consequently*, will be incapable of solving *its production problem* either';[45] or again: 'The fact that economic interests play a decisive role does not in the least imply that the economic (i.e. trade-union) struggle is of prime importance; for the most essential, the "decisive" interests of classes can be satisfied only by radical *political* changes in general.'[46]

B. A continual intervention of the political struggle in the other levels of struggle, particularly in the economic struggle, and vice versa. For example: (a) An absence of political class struggle does not in the least mean that the economic struggle of this class is not reflected by 'pertinent effects' at the political level. To confine itself to the strictly economic struggle alone may produce wholly positive 'pertinent effects', namely *non-interference* in the opponent's policy. (b) It is possible to conduct a political policy in the strict sense, but one which gives priority to the economic level: this is the policy which, in Lenin's ironical terms, wants to conduct an '*economic* struggle against the *government*!! . . . "Economic struggle against the government" is precisely trade-unionist politics . . . it is precisely the *bourgeois politics* of the working class.'[47]

3. The political struggle, whose *objective* is state power, has as its object the conjuncture. *It therefore bears on*: (a) the economic. Lenin says that '. . . The tactics of the "politicians" and revolutionaries not only do not ignore the trade-union tasks . . . but . . . on the contrary, they alone

---

44. 'What is to be done?', *Selected Works*, Vol. 1, p. 142.
45. 'Once again on the Trade Unions . . .', *Selected Works*, Vol. 3, pp. 527–8.
46. 'What is to be done?', *Selected Works*, Vol. 1, pp. 135–6 n.
47. ibid., pp. 150–1.

can secure their consistent fulfilment';[48] (b) the political, in the strict sense; (c) the ideological. These problems belong to the examination of the concept of conjuncture.

(vii) CONJUNCTURE – SOCIAL FORCES – POLITICAL FORECASTING

This is the theoretical line in which Lenin's political analyses are situated. Against the deviations of the Second International, Lenin returned to the authentic thought of Marx in producing the concept of *conjuncture*, equivalent to that of the 'present moment' which is the specific *object* of political practice.[49] The specific *objective* of political practice is the state, i.e. institutionalized political power, which is the cohesive factor in a determinate social formation and the nodal point of its transformations. But it has as its object the 'present moment', which reflects the always-original (because singular) historical individuality of a formation. By posing the problem rigorously, we make it possible to elucidate a whole series of questions: in particular, those concerning the 'action' of political practice on structures, the list of possibilities which structures offer to political practice, strategic forecasting in political practice, etc.

Lenin's concept of conjuncture is situated *in the field of class practices and class struggle*. The historically individualized originality of a social formation, which is the object of political practice, is constituted primarily by the '*combined action of social forces*'. The field of the conjuncture is homogeneous in that class practices (particularly political class practices) are considered, relative to their 'action' on the structure, as *social forces*.[50] In the texts dating from February–October 1917, Lenin analyses the essential social forces which constitute the reality and originality of the concrete situation in Russia: namely the Tsarist monarchy, the monarchist bourgeoisie, the proletariat and the peasant classes.[51] Amongst these social forces which are distinct classes, Lenin introduces the Tsarist monarchy, an element which seems, at first sight, to designate the political superstructure of the Tsarist state, and therefore

48. 'What is to be done?', *Selected Works*, Vol. 1, p. 145 n.
49. On conjuncture, see Althusser in *Reading Capital* and *Cahiers Marxistes–Léninistes*, Nos. 9–10.
50. The elements of this field are primarily classes, in so far as Lenin's determination of class is not in the least an exclusively economic determination.
51. See 'Two tactics of social democracy in the democratic revolution', *Selected Works*, Vol. 1, pp. 455–566.

an element of the *structure*. However, Lenin is not directly importing an element of the structure as a social force into the conjuncture. Lenin means by Tsarist monarchy 'the feudal ground-landlords and the old corps of officials and generals', to whom, in so far as they constitute *social forces*, he applied the term 'Tsarist monarchy'. In these social forces, while the landowners are a *distinct class*, the 'old corps of officials and generals' constitutes a category. Lenin often speaks of the bureaucracy or the police as social forces, emphasizing that these are not classes. Therefore, if we want to define the *elements* of conjuncture, we can say that: (a) They are *primarily distinct classes and autonomous fractions* which are reflected at the level of *political practice* by 'pertinent effects', and that this characterizes them precisely as social forces. (b) Furthermore they can constitute social forces, *specific categories*, which manage at a concrete moment to have 'pertinent effects', as defined above,[52] at the level of political practice, and may therefore be social forces, without being classes or fractions of classes.

Thus, the conjuncture, which is the object of political practice and the privileged place where the ever-singular historical individuality of a formation is reflected, is the concrete situation of the *political class struggle*. In other words, the articulation and the index of dominance which characterize the *structure* of a social formation are reflected as a conjuncture at the level of political class struggle. How does this reflection operate? Or to put what is simply the other side of the question, how does political practice affect the structure, in so far as the conjuncture is not a simple expression of the structure but sets precise limits on the action of political practice on the structure? What is the mode of determination by the structure of the political practice which acts upon it?

We can find the reply when we see that the interrelations *between* structures and class practices are of the same type as the relations *in* each of these fields. With regard to the relations between the instances, their so-called 'interaction', which is in fact the mode of intervention of one level on another, consists of the *limits* within which one level can modify the other. These limits are the *effect* both of the concrete matrix of a formation and of the respective specific structures of each level, which are themselves determined by their place and function in this matrix. In this

---

52. These categories thus have an 'autonomous' existence which cannot be absorbed by the pertinent effects of the distinct classes and autonomous fractions themselves.

sense, the determination of one structure by another in the relations between structures shows the *limits of the variations* of a regional structure in relation to another (e.g. the state in relation to the economic), these limits themselves being the effects of the matrix. This is also the case for class practices, i.e. for the interrelations between the levels of class struggle.

The relations between class practices and structures, i.e. the relations indicated above between these two systems of relations, are also of the same type. The determination of the practices by the structure and the intervention of the practices in the structure, consist in the production by the structure of limits of variations of the class struggle: it is these limits which are the effects of the structure. But this does not yet exactly delimit the relation of political practice to structure: in fact, at this level *the limits are complex*. Political practice, i.e. the over-determinant practice which concentrates in itself the contradictions of the other levels of class struggle, is itself inscribed in limits which are the effects of the global field of the class struggle and of the various levels of this struggle on political practice. But these limits are raised to the power of two, in that the field of practices is itself circumscribed by the effects of the structures as limits. In this sense, political practice is conducted within the limits set by the other practices and by the global field of class practices (the economic, political and ideological struggle), in so far as this field is itself limited by the effects of the structure as limits. The distinctive character of this series of limits will become clearer in what follows. It should be recalled that the conjuncture appears in the form of the effects of the structures on the field of the practices *concentrated, in their unity, at the level of the political class struggle*. These limits regulate, as such, a play of possible variations of social forces, in short the intervention of political practice, which is here the concentrated intervention of the field of practices on the structures. The effectiveness of the structure on the field of practices is thus itself limited by the intervention of political practice on the structure.

Thus it is important to recognize that the conjuncture, the 'present moment', which is the object of political practice, is produced by the reflection on the practices *of the ensemble of the levels of the structure, in their unity*. The political superstructure of the state is a privileged place which concentrates the contradictions of the levels of the structure and permits the concrete decipherment of their connection; and *the conjuncture allows us to decipher the historical individuality of the ensemble of a formation*, that is, it allows us to decipher the relation between the concrete individuality of the structures and the concrete configuration of the class struggle. In this sense, the political superstructure of the state, which is the *objective* of political practice, is also reflected in the conjuncture as an element of the *object* of this practice. Lenin said that it was necessary to win state power by smashing the state machine; and I need say no more.

Thus, in no case can we see in political practice and conjuncture a field of variations whose limits are produced by the economic structure alone. Such an 'economist-voluntarist' interpretation of Lenin is precisely connected to the mistaken conception of social classes which does not distinguish between structures and the field of class struggle. This conception is still to be found, and it is even theoretically formulated by an author as circumspect as Luporini, who holds that the limits of variations of the action of the forces are constituted by the 'economic structure' alone, covered by the concept of 'socio-economic formation';[53] that this concept of Lenin's covers that level of the 'economic structure' alone in which the social classes 'act', i.e. the political level of the struggle between classes; and that this concept is: 'a model which (as is generally the case for any scientific model) has an interpretative function in relation to the field which it delimits. . . . In fact, this interpretative function permits objective tendencies of development to be located, and forecasts to be carried out in this direction. It is a question of that type of forecasting which relates to the characteristics peculiar to the economic field and to its laws . . . and which permits us to insert into that field the concrete action of a political force or a conscious social group.'[54] Such an inter-

53. This concerns Lenin's formulations in 'What the "Friends of the People" Are', *Collected Works*, Vol. 1, pp. 141 ff., where he seems to identify 'socio-economic formation' and 'relations of production', i.e. the economic level. However, from consideration of Lenin's work as a whole we see clearly that this formulation is the result of a fluctuation of terminology. Besides, in this text, the possibility of political forecasting is said to be due to a process of '*regularity of repetition*' which can be discerned in the 'socio-economic formation', understood as the economic structure. It is not accidental that this 'economist' definition seems here to be paralleled by a conception of unilinear historicism. In fact, the 'mature' Lenin, if we can say this, always saw in political forecasting a reading of conjuncture as reflection of the originality of a social formation according to the authentic Leninist sense of the term: in this sense, the Leninist conception of forecasting is not only based on any 'regularity of repetition', but is entirely based on the constant *originality* and *innovation* of the *present moment*.

54. C. Luporini, 'Realtà e storicità', in *Critica Marxista*, January–February 1966, p. 63.

pretation is in fact only the expression of the historicist conception of social classes, one which sees in these classes the political and ideological level, i.e. class struggle in action on the economic 'structure'. In fact, nothing is further from Lenin's thought. When Lenin saw the Russian conjuncture as the weakest link in the chain of imperialism, he was seeing the effects of the unity of an ensemble of structures on the class struggle, as the limits to the working class's political practice. This ensemble of structures consisted of economic structure, the Tsarist State super-structure and of the ideological structures, all reflected in the conjuncture. Without this conception, Lenin would have remained at the Second International's economist interpretation of Marx, which is ultimately an economist theory of the strongest link.

I shall sum up briefly. The *political practice* of a class or fraction is not identical with the reflection of a class or fraction at the level of political practice in 'pertinent effects'. Only a political practice which has such effects can characterize as a *distinct class* or *autonomous fraction* the con-crete functioning of a class or fraction in a formation. Only these distinct classes or autonomous fractions constitute *social forces*. But Lenin intro-duces a further criterion of the concrete action of the social forces in the *conjuncture*, which is that of their *open or declared action*. He often states that the *only real criterion* of alliances is the open action of social classes, their 'actual participation in the struggle'.[55] Why is this additional criterion needed, when social forces are not simply classes in their econo-mic determination, but are already classes at the political level? In fact, Lenin understands by open or declared action primarily a specific political and ideological organization of a social force, which transcends the simple reflection of that social force at the political level in 'pertinent effects'. At issue is the *organization of a class's power*, which will be analysed in the next chapter. A class or fraction can indeed exist as a social force, without thereby fulfilling the *conditions of organization* which allow it to enter into relations of political power: as a general rule, open action indicates that a social force has its 'own' political *power* and that it is normally associated with its organization as a distinct and autonomous party. Such are the conditions of declared action, which is related to the field of *indetermina-tion* of the conjuncture, of the 'combined action of the social forces'.

55. See 'Two Tactics . . .', *Selected Works*, Vol. 1, pp. 455–566; 'Working-class and Bourgeois Democracy', *Collected Works*, Vol. 8, pp. 72–82.

From a whole list of possible variations within the series of limits indicated, the only criterion which can show the concrete form to be assumed by this combination at a given time is the effective participation in the class struggle of a class which fulfils particular conditions of organization.

3. The Concept of Power

Our previous considerations lead to the problem of power, a problem of supreme importance for political theory. It is all the more important because Marx, Engels, Lenin and Gramsci never produced a theoretical concept of power. It is furthermore one of the most controversial topics in current political theory.

We shall begin by delimiting the field of this concept. In order to do this, we must refer to our previous analyses concerning the distinction between structural levels of a social formation and levels of class struggle (i.e. class practice), in short to the distinction between structures and social relations. The concept of power *is constituted in the field of class practices*. Indeed, every time that Marx or Engels refers to concepts of power or authority, as well as to related concepts such as those of domination, etc., they locate them in the field of class relations. This is even clearer in Lenin, who circumscribes the field of the 'action of social forces', of the 'relations of force' or of *relations of power* as the field of the class struggle.

We can thus already draw certain conclusions regarding the problem of relations between power and social classes. *Class relations are relations of power*. The concepts of class and power are akin, in that the place in which they are constituted is the field bounded by social relations. The kinship between these two concepts does not, however, indicate a relation in which one concept is the foundation of the other, but rather the homogeneity of the field. Class relations are no more the foundation of power relations than power relations are the foundation of class relations. Just as the concept of class points to the effects of the ensemble of the levels of the structure on the supports, so the concept of power specifies the effects of the ensemble of these levels on the relations between social classes in struggle. *It points to the effects of the structure on the relations of conflict between the practices of the various classes in 'struggle'*. In other words, power is not located in the levels of structures, but is an effect of the ensemble of these levels, while at the same time characterizing each of the levels of the class struggle. The concept of power cannot thus be applied to one level of the structure. When we speak for example of *state power*, we cannot mean by it the mode of the state's articulation and intervention at the other levels of the structure; *we can only mean the power of a determinate class* to whose interests (rather than to those of other social classes) the state corresponds.

These preliminary considerations are important because the confusion of relations of power with structures and relations of class practices (i.e. struggle) gives rise to various misinterpretations of Marxism. Let us consider one of the most important contemporary misinterpretations found, for example, in Renner,[1] Schumpeter[2] and Dahrendorf[3] and indeed in Rizzi, Burnham, Djilas, etc. (all of whom are expressly influenced by Marxism), as well as in many 'theorists' of the *ruling class*, whose work will be examined later. The central objective of these theories is an attempt to go beyond an 'economist' conception of social classes, which defines these exclusively at the economic level of relations of production, notably as a function of their relation to the ownership of the means of production: these theories see in the formal ownership of the means of production the immediate expression of the economic level. According to the authors cited, the foundation of classes and class conflict is not in the relations of production, but in the global distribution at every level of *power* inside 'authoritarian' societies: that is to say, inside societies characterized by a global organization of domination and subordination, consisting of an 'inegalitarian' distribution of this power at every level.

So the problem of the relation between (i) relations of production, reduced here to the formal ownership of the means of production, and (ii) the relations of power and class struggle, is formulated by this ideological tendency in the following terms: either relations of production (equivalent, according to this school, to ownership of the means of production) are a *special case* of power, or power is a *special case* of the relations of production.[4] This problem is badly posed in that it involves a confusion between structures and class practices and thus imprisons the reply available to Marxist science in an ideological dilemma. If we tried

1. K. Renner, *Mensch und Gesellschaft*, Vienna, 1952; *Wandlungen der modernen Gesellschaft*, Vienna, 1953.
2. *Capitalism, Socialism and Democracy*, London, 1966.
3. op. cit.
4. On this subject, see the synthetic statement of the question in Dahrendorf, op. cit., p. 21.

to answer that power relations and class relations are a special case of relations of production, what would that mean? It might mean that relations of production are the exclusive foundation of social classes, and that the other levels of class struggle, e.g. political or ideological power, are simply the phenomenon of the economic level; and that power relations are apparently based, in a relation of phenomenon to essence, on relations of production *considered directly* as power relations. Conversely, what would be the consequences implied by the reply that relations of production, as well as formal ownership of the means of production, are a special case of power relations? This would be a reduction both of relations of production and of the juridical system to power relations. Neither relations of production nor relations of formal ownership of the means of production would be perceived as structures, as forms of combination between agents of production and means of production. Instead they would be perceived as originating relations of power between 'capitalists' who, through an exclusive 'control' of these means, impose their 'decisions' on the 'workers', both in the limits of each unit of production and on the social scale.

From a methodological point of view, it is important here to draw attention to the confusion between structures and levels of the class struggle implied by the question as it is posed. In fact, class relations are *at every level relations of power*: power, however, is only a concept indicating the effect of the ensemble of the structures on *the relations of the practices of the various classes in conflict*. In this sense, we can already eliminate one attempt to escape from the ideological dilemma posed above, but one which would involve the same confusion. This would be a refusal to locate power relations at the level of relations of production, in order to introduce them at the other levels of the structure, e.g. at the political level. It would be said that relations of production cannot constitute a special case of power relations, in as much as the economic level, the domain of economic 'laws', does not consist of power relations. Classes defined 'in themselves' at the economic level would be said to be independent at this level from power relations. And power relations would exist only at the political or the ideological levels, where the 'class struggle' (i.e. struggle between classes-for-themselves) would ultimately be situated. Yet this reply should be attributed to a mistaken viewpoint, which defines the 'class situation' at the level of economic structures (relations of production) and the 'class struggle' (relations of power) at the level of political structures. In this way, the economic becomes the field in which politics (i.e. the class struggle) 'operates'. In the same way, levels other than the economic, for example the state structures, would be reduced to relations of power, e.g. to *state power* alone.

What is true in this approach is that the structure of the relations of production (just as the structure of the political and ideological) cannot be directly grasped as relations of classes or relations of power. But on the other hand, it is also correct to say that class relations constitute relations of power at all the levels of practices. Relations of production are not a special case of power relations, but this is not because the 'economic', as opposed to the political, cannot consist of power relations: it is rather because no structural level can be grasped theoretically as power relations. But the economic, viewed as the level of a class's organization or as the specific level of its economic practice in relation to that of the other classes (a level which is located in the above defined field of 'class struggle', i.e. the relation between class practices), does indeed consist of relations of powers.

We are faced here with the problem of 'economic power' and its relations to 'economic laws'. This is a subject which has been discussed many times, and whose proposed solutions present insoluble contradictions because of the identification of the two fields noted above.[5] Can a scientific perspective of economic laws be reconciled with the perspective of economic power? Leaving discussion aside, we can easily see that in the relation of structures to social relations, the economic laws of the *economic-qua-structure* by no means hinder the relations of power at the level of the *economic class struggle*, which shows the effects of the structure of this level on the supports. This is the sense in which Marx often uses the concept of *economic power*, situated at the level of economic class struggle: he often speaks of the economic power of the capitalist class, and it is in this context that the term *economic domination* is quite frequently used, a term which is distinguished both from political and ideological domination. Economic power which can be perceived in the many forms in which it is manifested, is an over-determined effect of relations of production: e.g. the capitalist's authority in the process of production (both the technical and social divisions of labour), in the preliminary negotiations over

5. On the scope of this problem, see e.g. J. Lhomme, *Pouvoir et société économique* Paris, 1965, pp. 70 ff.; F. Perrous, 'Esquisse d'une théorie de l'économie dominante' *AES*, 1948, pp. 243 ff.; Morgenstern, *The Limits of Economics*, 1937, pp. 67 ff.; Boehm-Bawerk, *Gesammelte Schriften*, 1924, pp. 100 ff.

the work contract, etc. On the other hand, we can perceive in the relations of political class practices, in political class *struggle*, relations of political power and political domination, which are themselves effects of the regional structure of the political on political class practice. And the same is true for the ideological.

Therefore to declare that class relations are power relations at every level *is not in the least to admit that social classes are founded on power relations or that they can be derived from them.* Power relations, which have social relations as their field, are class relations; and class relations are power relations, to the extent that the concept of social class shows the effects of the structure on *the relations of the practices of the classes in 'conflict'*.

It is important not to underestimate the importance of these remarks. In fact, the basis of the semi-Marxist theories of *political élites* and *political class*[6] has been the acceptance of a would-be Marxist conception according to which the economic cannot, strictly speaking, consist of power relations: a conception which is merely the counterweight to the economist conception of social classes. Thus from a definition of class from an exclusively economic viewpoint, and from a notion that political relations consist of power relations, the normal conclusion of such theories of élites and political class follows automatically: the groups which take part in political (i.e. power) relations *differ, in their theoretical status,* from economic social classes, whose existence is elsewhere acknowledged. The difference is that these groups are defined by relations of (political) power, according to the definition that each author gives to the term 'power', but their relation to the economic does not, and cannot, acquire a scientific status. We are here exactly at the kernel of the problematic of Weber's *status groups*, of Michel's *political class*, of Wright Mills' power élites, etc.; these are theorists who acknowledge the parallel existence of economic social classes in a distorted Marxist sense, according to which the economic 'class situation' does not call for relations of power.[7] The above-mentioned ideological endeavour to transcend an economist

6. See pp. 326 ff. below.

7. The problem is posed clearly by Wright Mills in his critique of the Marxist concept of 'ruling class', where he explains why he substitutes for it the term 'power élites': ' "Ruling class" is a badly loaded phrase. "Class" is an economic term; "rule" a political one. The phrase "ruling class" thus contains the theory that an economic class rules politically' (C. Wright Mills, *The Power Elite*, New York 1956, p. 277).

definition of social classes by discovering a concept of class based on power relations at every level, but which led to the confusion of structures and the field of practices (i.e. power), differs from this latter one. In the latter case, we are presented with a rupture between the status of the economic 'groups' (classes) and that of the political 'groups', which is the logical conclusion of the 'class-in-itself'/'class-for-itself' perspective. The failures of this school of thought become obvious in the confusions which result when it tries to establish relations between these 'economic classes' and the 'political groups'.

(ii) POWER, CLASSES AND CLASS INTERESTS

Starting with these remarks, we can try to put forward a concept of power. By power, we shall designate *the capacity of a social class to realize its specific objective interests*. This concept is not without difficulties, especially in so far as it introduces the concept of 'interests'; and we know the importance of this concept in Marx and Lenin, for whom the Marxist conception of classes and power is linked to that of 'class interests'. But it is important briefly to locate this definition of power relative to some others which have had important repercussions on political theory.

1. This definition differs from Lasswell's[8] conception of power as 'the fact of taking part in decision-making' and from the definitions common to the whole series of theories of the *decision-making process*. The fundamental defect of this conception, at least in the framework of a society characterized by class conflict, is that (i) it succumbs to a voluntarist conception of the decision-making process, through disregarding the effectiveness of the structures, and it is not able exactly to locate beneath the appearances the effective centres of decision inside which the distribution of power works; and (ii) it takes as a principle the 'integrationist' conception of society, from which the concept of 'participation' in decision-making is derived.

2. This definition of power is different from that of Weber, for whom power (*Herrschaft*) is 'the probability that a command with a given specific content will be obeyed by a given group of persons'.[9] This is because Weber's definition is located in the historicist perspective of a

8. Lasswell and Kaplan, *Power and Society, a framework for Social Enquiry*, 1950, pp. 70 ff.; Lasswell, *Politics: who gets what, when, how*, 1936, pp. 40 ff.

9. M. Weber, *The Theory of Social and Economic Organization*, Glencoe, 1964, p. 152.

society/subject, a product of the normative behaviour of subjects/agents, a view which is at the basis of his conception of 'probability' and of 'specific command'. This command is conceived as being practised inside an 'authoritarian association', a crystallization of the values-ends of these agents. Thus, in the Weberian problematic the concept of power is reduced to that of legitimacy.

3. This definition is distinguished from that of Parsons,[10] for whom power is 'the capacity to carry on certain functions to the profit of the social system considered in its entirety'. Such a definition is expressly bound up with the 'functionalist-integrationist' conception of the social system.

It is, of course, impossible to undertake a detailed critique of the many concepts of power to be found in political science: these few references aim only at showing the complexity of the problem. If the proposed concept of power is accepted, it will be seen to be capable of accounting for the whole range of Marxist analyses of this problem.

A. This concept is related precisely to the field of 'class' practices and of relations of class practices, i.e. to the field of class struggle: its *frame of reference* is the class struggle of a society divided into classes. That means that in these societies the effects of the structure are concentrated in the practices of those particular ensembles constituted by social classes. An initial clarification is necessary here: the concept of power is related to that precise type of social relation which is characterized by class '*conflict*' and struggle; that is, to a field inside which, precisely because of the existence of classes, the capacity of one class to realize its own interests through its practice is in *opposition* to the capacity and interests of other classes. This determines a *specific* relation of *domination* and *subordination* of class practices, which is exactly characterized as a relation of power. Thus, starting from this opposition, the relation of power implies the possibility of demarcating a clear line between the *places* of domination and subordination. In the context of societies where this division into classes is non-existent (and it would be interesting to examine to what extent this is also applicable to non-antagonistic class relations in the transition from socialism to communism) and where therefore these relations cannot be specified by this struggle as relations of domination

10. T. Parsons, *Structure and Process in Modern Societies*, Glencoe, 1960, pp. 199 ff.; 'On the concept of Power', *Proceedings of the American Philosophical Society*, Vol. 107, No. 3, 1963.

or subordination of classes, a different concept should be used, which would ultimately be that of *authority*.[11]

The concept of power cannot be applied to 'inter-individual'[12] relations or to relations whose constitution in given circumstances is presented as independent of their place in the process of production, i.e. in societies divided into classes, as independent of the class struggle: for example, relations of friendship, relations between members of a sports club, etc. In their case the concept of *might* (*puissance*)[13] can be used: this concept has been especially used in political science to indicate the element of 'force', while the concept of power (*pouvoir*) has been used in the case of a *legitimate* force, that is, exercised in a frame of reference of a minimum of 'consent' on the part of those over whom this power is exercised.[14] Yet this distinction, while it can be very useful, is in fact a distinction concerning the *forms of power*, the forms of domination-subordination implied in the relations of power. It should be remembered that the distinction

11. We should note here that the problematic of the concept of 'power' related to that of a specific relation characterized by a demarcation of places of subordination and domination in particular conditions of a 'conflict' was pointed out by M. Weber, op. cit., pp. 152–3 and 130 ff. He designates this relation as a '*Herrschaftsverband*', which produces *legitimacy* capable of engendering relations of 'power'; and he distinguishes it from the general relation 'rulers-ruled', a relation which is found in *every* social organization and which is grasped not by the same concept as the *specific* relation of domination-subordination, but by the concept of '*Macht*'. It is important to add here that that which marks out the domination-subordination relation and locates the 'conflict' is in fact originally situated in a *place exterior* to this relation itself: this 'conflict' is delimited by the structure. In this sense, not every 'rulers-ruled' relation implies by its very intrinsic nature a 'conflict' or, in Marxist terms, a class 'struggle': on the other hand, only a conflict traceable from the structures (in Marxist terms a class struggle) can create a particular relation of domination-subordination grasped by the concept of power.

12. It is unnecessary to point out how mistaken are the different ideologies which locate power as an 'inter-personal' phenomenon; these include the whole range of psycho-sociological-style definitions (see R. Dahl and K. Lewin). These are of the type: 'The power of a person A over a person B is the capacity of A to get B to do something he would not have done without the intervention of A' (See especially R. Dahl, 'The Concept of Power' in *Behavioral Science* 2, 1957, pp. 201–15. F. Bourricaud probably belongs in the same theoretical line).

13. Throughout this section, *pouvoir* is translated *power*; *puissance* is translated *might*. The distinction between the two terms is made clear in the text. [Trans.]

14. Amongst others, see R. Aron, 'Macht, Power, Puissance: Prose démocratique ou poésie démoniaque?' in *AES*, No. 1, 1964; G. Lavau, 'La dissociation du pouvoir' in *Esprit*, June 1953 (special number devoted to the question of 'political power and economic power').

between power and might concerns the frame of reference within which these phenomena are located: that of power is placed in the framework of the class *struggle*, which reflects the effects of the unity of the structures of a formation on the supports. In this sense, we can say that power is a typical phenomenon, traceable from the structures, while that of might is a phenomenon characterized by a sociological amorphy.

B. This concept of power refers to the *capacity* of a class to realize specific objective interests. This element of the concept of power has particular reference to Marx and Lenin's analyses of *class organization*.

As the problem is important, we should stop here in order to introduce some distinctions which will prevent confusion. It has been pointed out in the chapter on classes that a class can exist in a social formation as a *distinct class*, even in the case when it is *under-determined*, i.e. even when it does not possess what it is normally called *its own* political and ideological organization. The condition for this is that its existence at the economic level is expressed at the levels of its political and ideological practices by a specific presence, namely that of 'pertinent effects'. This *presence* of a class as a *social force* in fact presupposes a certain organizational *threshold*, in the broadest sense of the term. For example, in the case of the small-holding peasants, Marx refuses to assign to them in general the character of a distinct class; this is because of their isolation, which excludes any possibilities of organization, in so far as these are conditions of their existence as a distinct class. They were given this organization, in the broad sense of the term, by Louis Bonaparte in the Second Empire. In this broad sense, the term organization covers simply the conditions of a class practice with 'pertinent effects'. However, the theory of organization, in the strict sense of the term found in Marx and especially in Lenin, involves not simply class practices, conditions of existence of a class as a distinct class (social force), *but the conditions of class power, that is, the conditions of a practice leading to class power*. For example, Marx's texts concerning a class's 'own' political and ideological organization do not in fact refer to its functioning as a distinct class. But they are still valuable concerning class power and organization as a condition of this power, which Marx expresses in these terms: '. . . a political movement . . . (is) a movement of the class, *with the object of enforcing its interests* in a general form, *in a form possessing general, socially coercive force*'.[15]

15. Letter to Bolte, 23 November 1871, concerning the Gotha programme, *MESW*, 1970, p. 673.

It is clear that this theoretical line governs Lenin's analyses of organization, and especially his analyses of the organization of the working-class party. The fact that politico-ideological class practice is not identical with an organized practice as a condition of class power was registered by Lenin in his concept of open or declared action, which is not coterminous with that of practice. The *organization of the power* of a class often appears in Lenin *as a condition of its open action*. But the contrary is not necessarily true, since the organization of the power of a class may not lead to a declared action if its power depends on its political eclipse; as is the case of the bourgeoisie under the Second Empire. So we note an essential difference and some important dislocations between class organization in the broad sense, which coincides with the concept of practice-with-'pertinent-effects', and *the organization of power*: for example, the small-holding peasants of *The Eighteenth Brumaire* had, through Louis Bonaparte, an organization which gave them existence as a distinct class, without thereby having any power, since Bonaparte did not satisfy any of their class interests.

On the other hand, though this specific organization of a class is the *necessary condition* of its power, it is not the sufficient condition. This observation allows us better to understand the reasons for distinguishing between a class's practice-with-'pertinent-effects' and the organization of its power. The organization of the power of a class is not a sufficient condition of its power since this power is obtained in the limits (*qua* effects) of the structures in the field of practices: in contrast to the 'voluntarist' conception, the effective realization of interests depends on these limits. But there is also another factor which shows us, in other respects, the basis of the distinction between practice-with-'pertinent-effects' and organization of power: the concept of power specifies as limits the effects of the structure *in the relations between the various practices of the classes in conflict*. In this sense, power reveals relations not directly determined by the structure, and depends on the exact relation of the social forces present in the class struggle. The capacity of a class to realize its interests, of which the organization of its power is the necessary condition, depends on the capacity of other classes to realize their interests. The degree of effective power of a class depends directly on the degree of power of the other classes, in the framework of the determination of class practices in the limits set by the practices of the other classes. Strictly speaking, *power is identical with these limits in the second degree*. It does not show the mode of intervention of the practice of one level of a class directly on the practices of *other* levels of the *same* class; but rather it shows the mode of intervention of the practice of one level of a class on practices of the *same* level of the *other* classes, within the limits which each class practice sets for that of the others. *This precise meaning* of limits is particularly important and has results for problems other than that of power. For example, concerning the political level and the problem of strategy, it shows itself in the specific effects which the political practice of one class has on that of another class, in short, the *strategy of the opponent*.

C. The question of a class's 'interests' and 'objective interests' must now be discussed. Owing to the breadth of this problem, I shall now only give some pointers. My discussion will concentrate on the following theme: what are the relations of class 'interests' to structures and practices? What is the meaning of the term 'objective interests' of a class? My aim will be to arrive at an adequate concept of 'interest'.

At the outset certain mistaken interpretations must be eliminated. Class interests are situated in the field of practices, in the field of the class struggle. We cannot locate interests in the structures without falling into an anthropological interpretation of Marxism, not simply into that of individuals-subjects, but even into that of class-subjects. In fact, though they are in no way a 'psychological' notion, interests can be located only in the proper field of practices and classes. In the structures, for example, wages or profit do not express the interest of the worker, nor of the capitalist with his 'lure of gain', but constitute economic categories related to forms of combination. However, in saying that interests can be conceived only by theoretical reference to a practice, we are not thereby attributing to interests a relation with 'individual behaviour'; as a first step, we are excluding interests from being located in structures.

This exclusion is important. It is true that there are some analyses of the classics of Marxism which, at a first reading, seem to locate class interests in the relations of production. This is the type of reading which identifies structures and practices, and which sees in relations of production the class-in-itself (class interests), as opposed to the political and ideological levels consisting of the practice (i.e. organization) of the class-for-itself. Marx goes so far as to say that class interests, in the class struggle, have an existence somehow prior to the formation itself, to the practice of a class. Concerning the interests of the proletariat he says, in *The German Ideology*, that the German bourgeoisie is in opposition to the proletariat even before the proletariat is organized as a class.

Nevertheless, by reference to the above analyses, it should be possible to see that, in fact, with respect to the relation between class interests and practices, class interests are not identical with the class struggle, in a relation of structures to practices. This leads us to pose the problem of the relations between interests and structures. It might be useful to point out that this preoccupation has been of prime importance in the 'functionalist' school of contemporary sociology: it is one of its merits to have posed the problem. This school goes back in the last analysis to a historicist problematic of the subject, and so leads to a view which defines practice as the behaviour or conduct of agents. It has posed the problem in the following way: the place of agents in relation to structure is determined by *objective interests* which constitute *the agents' role*.[16] The concept of interest is thus at first sight without psychological connotations. However, since the structure is here conceived as the substratum and product of the agents' behaviour or conduct, the interests-structures, the *role*-situation, consist of expectations (probabilities) of certain conducts on the part of agents as a function of their structural role. What is most important for us to note here is that this location of objective interests in the structures (the 'situation') is totally dependent on a problematic of the subject, which sees in the structures the product of agents. These interests are 'objective' to the extent that they are located in the structures, while practices are reduced to conduct or behaviour.

As soon as the functionalist school attempted to pose the problem of structures in a rigorous way, this way of posing the problem of interests led them to an impasse. Since interests cannot effectively be grasped except in the field of supports (agents), the school readily introduces the notions of 'latent interests', determining the agents' structural role, and of 'manifest interests', located, say, in the field of practices.[17] The group has the following theoretical status: latent interests are seen as giving rise to 'quasi-groups' (groups-in-themselves), manifest interests to 'interest groups' (groups-for-themselves).[18] Disregarding the use of the term 'group' (for class), the consequences of this perspective are very precisely the same as for the economist-historicist perspective in Marxism. This latter sees in the economic structure the economic interests (the

16. This general line is found in Parsons, Merton, Dahrendorf, etc.

17. This is particularly clear in R. Merton's application of the concepts of 'manifest functions' and 'latent functions' in his analysis of 'boss-politics' in the United States. See *Social Theory and Social Structures*, 1957, pp. 73 ff.

18. See in particular M. Ginsberg, *Sociology*, London, 1953, pp. 40 ff.

'situation') of the class-in-itself. Similar to the economist-historicist division of social 'class' into two conceptually delimited parts is the functionalist division between (a) class-in-itself: class situation, latent interests, quasi-groups, and (b) groups-for-themselves: status groups, political élites, manifest interests, interest groups.

It is therefore obvious that these attempts to locate class interests in the structures are incompatible with a scientific conception. The concept of interests can only be related to the field of practices, in so far as interests are always interests of a class, of supports distributed in social classes. But this does not mean that interests consist of behavioural motivations, any more than the fact of locating practices in social relations means a return to a problematic of the subject. While the concept of class indicates the effects of the structure on the supports and while the concept of practice covers not behaviour but an operation carried on within the limits imposed by the structure, interests certainly indicate these limits, but at a particular level as the *extension of the field* of the practice of one class in relation to those of the other classes, i.e. the extension of the 'action' of classes in relations of power. This is not any kind of metaphorical play on the terms of limits and field, but a result of the complexity of the relations covered by these terms.

We find an indication of the problem in connection with the political conjuncture in Lenin's analyses. In fact, his concept of the present moment is characterized by: (a) *social classes*, political class practices, the social forces, and (b) *relations of interests*: that which, seen from the viewpoint of the political practice of the working class, is expressed as 'the deeper interest-relationship of the proletariat'.[19] These two terms, social forces and interests, although found in the field of political class practices, *are not identical*. Social forces concern the specific presence of a class, through 'pertinent effects', on the plane of political class practice. In other words, the effects of structures on the field of the class struggle are reflected here as a class's *threshold of existence* as a distinct class, as a social force. But these effects are reflected *also* as an *extension of the ground* which this class can cover according to the stages of specific organization attainable by it (organization of power); and this ground extends as far as its objective interests. If we refer in this way to this double limit of the field (every field having a 'near side' and a 'far side'), a class's objective interests do not appear directly as the *threshold* of its

19. See 'Letters from afar – First Letter', *Selected Works*, Vol. 2, p. 6.

existence as a distinct class, as some kind of 'situation' of the class-'in-itself', but as the *horizon* of its action as a social force. This holds true for all the particular levels of practices in the field of the class struggle. So, just as economic interests do not constitute the 'situation' of a class-in-itself at the economic level, but the horizon of its economic action, so political interests cannot be grasped as the 'finality' of the 'praxis' of a class-for-itself: they are, at the level of political practice, the horizon which delimits the ground of a class's political practice.

Class interests, as limits of extension of a specific class practice, *are displaced* according to the interests of the other classes present. We are dealing always with relations, strictly speaking with strategic oppositions of class interests. It is in this perspective that the strategic distinction (in the proper sense of the term) between *long- and short-term interests* is located. In other words, these limits of extension constitute both limits-effects of the structure, and limits-effects at one remove, imposed by the intervention of the practices of different classes (class struggle) at a particular level of practices. In this sense, the extent or degree to which a class practice actually covers the ground outlined by its class interests also depends on the extent or degree to which it is covered by the opponent. The capacity of a class to realize its objective interests, and so its class power, depends on the capacity, and so on the power, of its opponent.

I have mentioned that class interests are 'objective' interests so as to rule out any question of behavioural motivations. In this sense, Marx says in *The German Ideology*: 'This communal interest . . . (of a class) . . . does not exist merely in the imagination, as the "general interest", but first of all in reality, as the mutual interdependence of the individuals among whom the labour is divided.'[20] But it is obvious that, in the field of practices, owing to the functioning of ideology in this respect, these interests *qua* limits can differ from the *representation* that agents or even classes make of them. This does not mean that when dislocated from (real) interests as limits, these interests as imagined or experienced are 'subjective' limits: because the effectiveness of the ideological (in the present case in the masking of these limits from the agents) cannot be grasped by the category of the 'subjective'. In this respect, the use of the term 'objective' can in fact be considered as superfluous, and it is only retained here in order clearly to show that the concept of interests can and must be stripped of all psychological connotations. However, there is no doubt that in this field of interests, ideology as it functions can give rise

20. *The German Ideology*, p. 44.

to numerous forms of illusion. Power, as capacity to realize interests, refers not to imaginary interests, in a situation where, on account of ideology, they are dislocated from interests-limits, but to these latter themselves.

D. The last element in the concept of power is that of the *specificity* of the class interests to be realized. Indeed, if interests are located not in the structures, as the class 'situation' in the relations of production, but rather as limits of the levels in the field of practices, the possibility of speaking of relatively autonomous interests of a class in the economic, political and ideological spheres is clear. Power is located at the level of the *various* class practices, in so far as there are class interests concerning the economic, the political and the ideological. In particular, in a capitalist formation characterized by the specific autonomy of the levels of structures and practices, and of the respective class interests, we can clearly see the distinction between *economic power, political power, ideological power*, etc., according to the capacity of a class to realize its relatively autonomous interests at each level.[21] In other words, relations of power are not located at the political level alone any more than class interests are located at the economic level alone. The relations of these various powers (their index of effectiveness, etc.) themselves relate to the articulation of the various class practices (class interests) which, in a dislocated manner, reflect the articulation of the various structures of a social formation or of one of its stages or phases.

In short, power relations do not constitute a simple expressive totality, any more than structures or practices do; but they are complex and dislocated relations, determined in the last instance by economic power. Political or ideological power is not the simple expression of economic power. Numerous examples of a class which is economically but not politically dominant,[22] ideologically but not economically or politically

21. It is unnecessary to insist on the clear distinction in Marx, Lenin and Gramsci between economic interests (Lenin), economic-corporate interests (Gramsci), private economic interests (Marx) on the one hand, and political interests on the other. This distinction is connected to the distinction indicated above, between economic struggle and political struggle.

22. The classic case is that of the bourgeoisie in England before 1688. It is the *economically dominant* class, while the landed aristocracy remains the *politically dominant* class despite the revolution of 1640. Yet in 1688 the English bourgeoisie, without becoming the hegemonic class, a subject to which we shall return later, enters the power bloc: its hegemony is confirmed thereafter. The particular case of England is dealt

dominant, etc., can be cited. A class may have the capacity to realize economic interests (the problem of trade-unionism) without having the capacity to realize political interests. It can have an economic power without having a 'corresponding' political power or even a political power without having a 'corresponding' ideological power, etc.

One last remark should be made in connection with the problem of decentration of places of domination at the various levels, places which can be occupied by different classes. This does not mean that we cannot rigorously define which is or are the dominant class(es) in a formation, or, in other words, *which place of domination has dominance over the others*. If we take into account the ensemble of these complex relations, we shall see that in the case of a decentration of this kind, the dominant class(es) in a formation is, in the last analysis, that which occupies the dominant place(s) at that level of the class struggle which maintains the dominant role in the complex whole of that formation. They are therefore that class or those classes which maintain *the dominant power*. For example, in the dissociation of the places of domination in Britain before 1688, the bourgeoisie which has the economically dominant place is often treated as the 'dominant class', although it does not have 'direct domination', in the sense of political domination. This is because, in the concrete case of Britain, the economic appears as maintaining the dominant role. On the other hand, in the dissociation of the places of domination in Prussia at the end of Bismarck's régime, the landed nobility (through its political dominance) is generally treated as the dominant class: it appears that the political there maintains the dominant role.[23]

---

with by Marx, and also by Engels, especially in the 1892 Preface to the first English edition of *Socialism, Utopian and Scientific* (*MESW*, 1970, pp. 385 ff.). On this subject in general, we also possess Engels's numerous texts on the absolutist state, which he sees as reflecting the 'equilibrium' between two classes, the landed nobility and the bourgeoisie. Marx refines this analysis in showing that England during the period in question is characterized not by a political equilibrium between these two classes, as in France during the period preceding the Revolution, but by the fact that 'political power and economic strength are not united in the same hands'. Then again we have the case of Prussia towards the end of the Bismarckian state: on this subject, see Engels, *The Housing Question*, 1872, II.2., concerning economic domination of the bourgeoisie and political domination of the landed nobility. I note in passing that Engels's articles in the *New York Daily Tribune* of 1851–2, which are known under the title *Revolution and Counter-Revolution in Germany*, concern a different phenomenon. On the subject under discussion, see also the remarks of R. Miliband, 'Marx and the State', *Socialist Register, 1964*, pp. 283 ff.

23. See the texts of Marx and Engels cited above.

(iii) STATE POWER – STATE APPARATUS – POWER CENTRES

Accepting this concept of power, it is possible for us to clarify the meaning of such expressions as 'state power', etc., i.e. expressions which seem to attribute power to institutions. The various social institutions, in particular the institutions of the state, do not, strictly speaking, have any power. Institutions, considered from the point of view of power, can be related only to *social classes which hold power*. As it is exercised this power of the social classes is organized in specific institutions which are *power centres*: in this context the state is *the centre of the exercise of political power*. But this does not mean that power centres, the various institutions of an economic, political, military, cultural, etc., character are mere instruments, organs or appendices of the power of social classes. They possess their autonomy and *structural* specificity which is not as such immediately reducible to an analysis in terms of power.[24]

On the other hand, in the context of an examination of the various social institutions with relation to power, these institutions must be considered according to their impact in the field of the class struggle, since the power concentrated in an institution is class power. In other words, the relative autonomy of the various institutions (power centres) in relation to social classes is not due to the fact that they possess a power *of their own* distinct from class power, but to their relation to the structures. In this sense, the various institutions do not, in terms of power, constitute 'organs of power' (instruments of a class power which has an existence prior to them and which creates them with a view to its effective accomplishment) but rather they constitute power centres. In so far as we can distinguish between several forms of power, we can by use of

24. *Structure/Institution*: These two concepts must be clearly distinguished. By *institution* will be meant a system of norms or rules which is socially sanctioned. The concept of institution must not therefore be reserved for juridico-political institutions alone, since the company, school, church, etc., also constitute institutions. (This 'reserved' sense is current and is even often admitted by Marxism, in a notion of superstructural institutions.) On the other hand, the concept of *structure* covers the *organizing matrix* of institutions. Through the functioning of the ideological, the structure always remains *hidden* in and by the institutional system which it organizes. These remarks should be borne in mind in the use which will be made of these concepts. Yet we should add that structure *is not the simple principle of organization which is exterior to* the institution: the structure is present in an allusive and inverted form in the institution itself, and it is in the reiteration of these successive, hidden presences that we can discover the principle of elucidation of the institutions. We shall also have to take this into consideration when using the concept of structure to designate institutional areas.

concrete situations proceed to a concrete examination *of the existing plurality of power centres (institutions at a given moment) and of their relations*: for example companies, the state, cultural institutions, etc. Given the dislocation characterizing the various levels of the class struggle and the various fields of power, it is clear that power relations between classes in a power centre dependent on a given level *cannot be translated in a simple way, just as they are,* into power centres dependent on other instances. It is also clear that the hierarchical organization of these power centres (see for example the characteristic variations of the combination state-church-school/state-school-church) depends both on the articulation of instances and on the relation of forces in the class struggle.

Furthermore it is in this framework that we can establish distinctions such as *formal power* or *real power*, related to institutions (power centres). Lenin, in his texts concerning the 'dual power' of the bourgeois state and of the Soviets in Russia[25] provides us with the model of analysis of such distinctions, with reference to political power. This distinction is not identical with a distinction between institutions *in possession of power, one of which, as opposed to the other, possesses the effective power*. It rather shows that power relations between classes can cause a displacement of gravity among the 'centres' which concentrate this power, in the sense that the real relations of class power are reflected more in one centre than in another. This real displacement depends both on the place of a power centre in relation to the structures of a social formation and on power relations in the field of the class struggle.

It is in this sense that Lenin's distinction between *state power* and *state apparatus* can be precisely interpreted.[26] By *state apparatus*, Lenin means two things: (a) The place of the state in the ensemble of the structures of a social formation, i.e. the state's various technico-economic, strictly political, ideological, etc., functions; (b) The *personnel of the state*, the ranks of the administration, bureaucracy, army, etc., whereas by *state power*, Lenin means *the social class or fraction of a class which holds power*.

In sense (a) of state apparatus, the displacement of real power from one power centre to another (in the case in question, from the official state to

25. 'One of the fundamental questions of the Revolution' and 'On Slogans', *Selected Works*, Vol. 2, pp. 255–62 and 174–80.

26. See 'Political Report of the Central Committee to the 11th Congress of the RCP(B)', 'Five Years of Russian Revolution – Report to the 4th Comintern Congress', and 'Better Fewer, But Better', *Selected Works*, Vol. 3, pp. 671–710, 715–27 and 774–86.

the state of the Soviets) indicates precisely the displacement of the place in which the effective relations of the political class power is concentrated. But this is true in so far as it corresponds to a displacement of the functions of the political superstructure from one institutuon to another,[27] and therefore corresponds to a reorganization of the state in the ensemble of the structures, to a certain *place* of the new institution of 'real power' among the other power centres. The Soviets are the 'real power' in so far as they are a *state* (an important point emphasized by Lenin) to which certain functions of the official state apparatus are transferred and in so far as the effective class power relations are *thus* concentrated in the Soviets. The concept of state apparatus in the sense (b), meaning the personnel of the state, relates at one and the same time to the problem of how the class holding power is related to the personnel who are 'in charge' of the state, and also to the problem of how this personnel is related to the state. This latter relation will be dealt with in greater detail later. The important point to remember here is that Lenin's expression of state apparatus is in no way reducible to an 'instrumentalist' conception of the state as organ or tool of power, but rather has the primary function of locating the political superstructure as to its place and function in an ensemble of structures.

(iv) THE CONCEPTION OF 'ZERO-SUM' POWER

Starting from these remarks, it is now possible to pin down one of the most important, if often implicit, mistaken presuppositions contained in the majority of contemporary theories of power. This will be a useful exercise, since a number of theories have it as their presupposition in their discussion of contemporary capitalist societies. (For example, the theories of 'ruling classes', of 'powers-counterpowers', of 'countervailing powers' etc., are of this kind.) It was clearly formulated by Wright Mills,[28] and consists of the conception of *zero-sum* power. It is a matter of conceiving of power as a *given quantity* inside a society. On this theory, any class or social group *thus has as much power as another does not have*, and any reduction of the power of a given group is directly translated into an increase in the power of another group and so on, in such a way that

---

27. Contrary to an ancient confusion which uses the term 'power' to designate the state's functions.

28. *The Power Elite*, 1956, Introduction; *Power, Politics and People*, pp. 23 ff., 72 ff.

though the distribution of power changes, the amount of power still remains an unvarying quantity. This conception, which is the basis of several contemporary forms of reformism,[29] itself goes back (as will be clearly seen) to the ideological presuppositions of certain analyses of power, which have so far been merely listed. It goes back to a 'functionalist' conception of the social whole, composed of equivalent elements which are related in an integrated equilibrium,[30] and to a misconception of the problem of the structures of a formation. These structures are reabsorbed into the conduct or behaviour of social groups conceived as 'agents' of the social process, with the parallelogram of forces of power relations based on the mutual limitation of this behaviour.

Let us see why this conception of zero-sum power is untenable.

(a) If we consider power as an effect of the structures in the field of the class struggle, we shall see that the capacity of a class to realize its interests, a capacity which depends on the struggle of another class, depends thereby on the structures of a social formation, in so far as they delimit the field of class practices. A reduction of this capacity of a class is not automatically translated into an increase in the capacity of another class, since the eventual redistribution of power is dependent on the structures: e.g. a loss of power by the bourgeoisie does not mean that this power is added to the power of the working class. This is implied by Marx in *The Civil War in France*, when he relates the phenomenon of Bonapartism to the fact that it was the only possible form of government at a moment when the bourgeoisie had lost the capacity of ruling the nation and the working class had not yet acquired it.

(b) This conception of zero-sum power, applied on the *global scale of a social formation*, disregards the specificity and dislocation of different forms of powers at different levels. Loss of power at the economic level, a reduction of a class's capacity to realize its *specific* economic interests, is not translated directly into a loss of political or ideological power or vice versa. On the other hand, an increase of a class's economic power does not directly entail an increase in its political or ideological power. Thus, if the conception of zero-sum power is inaccurate concerning even a specific level of power relations (economic, political, ideological), it is all the more inaccurate concerning power on the global scale of a social

29. See p. 269 below
30. Nothing could be more significant for this subject than Parsons's critique of Mills: 'The distribution of Power in American Society' in *World Politics*, No. 1, October 1957.

formation, because of the characteristic dislocation of the various levels of power.

(c) These objections to the conception of zero-sum power relate to the problem of the reflection of structures as limits of the field of practices. But it must be clearly seen that at the basis of that conception is a conception of the distinctive character of groups or classes being based on power relations. That conception is the one indicated by Weber, according to which societies or organizations of the *authoritarian* type are characterized by a dichotomy between two fundamental groups, the dominant and the dominated. In a functionalist adaptation of this theory, we find the conception of a dichotomy between the two 'roles' of power, that of command and that of obedience. This is the perspective which governs most contemporary theories of the ruling class. According to it, inside organizations or societies of the authoritarian type, the displacement of power consists of an exchange of zero-sum power between *two* groups, any loss of power by one group entailing an increase in the other group's power. But as we know, in a complex social formation, not two but several social classes are to be found related to the overlapping of several modes of production. In this sense, it is impossible to establish a dichotomy of relations of zero-sum power at any level. The loss of power by one class or fraction of a class may or may not indicate a gain in power not of the only other existing 'group' (i.e. the subordinate group), but of a class or fraction of a class among the many classes or fractions contending at every level. A loss of power by one dominant class or fraction of a class may or may not correspond to a gain in power not only by the working class but also by another dominated class; or not only by the various dominated classes but, on occasion, by other dominant classes or groups. In other words, the line demarcating the specific conflict relation between domination and subordination, which effectively characterizes power relations, does not in the least entail the existence of a dichotomy at any level of two groups-subjects exchanging zero-sum power.

(d) Finally, this conception, applied in particular to the level of political power, neglects the problem of the unity of this power in its relations to the state, the cohesive factor of a formation's unity. Political power is conceived as an ensemble of autonomous 'lots', the conquest of one of these lots by the working class meaning that it is torn from the power of the bourgeoisie and added to that of the working class. This problem will be discussed below in Part IV.

II
The Capitalist State

11

The Capitalist State

1. The Problem

We now possess enough elements for examining the capitalist state. Its fundamental distinctive feature seems to be the fact that it contains no determination of subjects (fixed in this state as 'individuals', 'citizens', 'political persons') as *agents of production*; and that this was not the case in the other types of state. At the same time this class state presents a further specific feature: namely, that political class domination is constantly absent from its institutions. It presents itself as a popular-class-state. Its institutions are organized around the principles of the liberty and equality of 'individuals' or 'political persons'. Its legitimacy is no longer founded on the divine will implied by the monarchical principle, but on the ensemble of formally free and equal individuals-citizens and on the popular sovereignty and secular responsibility of the state towards the people. The 'people' is itself erected as a principle of determination of the state, not as composed of agents of production distributed in social classes, but as an accumulation of individuals-citizens, whose mode of participation in a national political community shows itself in universal suffrage, which is the expression of the 'general will'. The modern juridical system, as distinct from the feudal system of rules based on *privileges*, bears a 'normative' character, expressed in a set of systematized laws which starts from the principles of liberty and equality: this is the reign of 'law'. The equality and liberty of the individuals-citizens lie in their relation to abstract and formal laws, which are considered to enunciate this general will inside a 'legal state'. The modern capitalist state thus presents itself as embodying the general interest of the whole of society, i.e. as substantiating the will of that 'body politic' which is the 'nation'.

These fundamental characteristics of the capitalist state cannot be reduced to the *ideological*: they relate to a regional level of the CMP, namely the juridico-political instance of the state, which is made up of institutions such as parliamentary representation, political liberties, universal suffrage, popular sovereignty, etc. It is true that the ideological plays an essential role; but it is a much more complex role which can in no case be identified with the functioning of the structures of the capitalist state.

The principles of explanation of the capitalist state have posed numerous problems for the Marxist science of the state. The central theme of these problems is the following: what are the real characteristics of the economic which imply this capitalist state? In a whole series of replies, running through nearly all the variants, one invariant is revealed: *the reference to the concept of 'civil society' and to its separation from the state.* This is so, even if no break between Marx's youthful and mature works is accepted: as is the case in the works of e.g. Lefebvre, Rubel and Marcuse, who represent the typical historicist tendency; or even if the break is located at the time of the *Critique of Hegel's Philosophy of the State,* as is done by the Italian Marxist school of della Volpe, Cerroni and Rossi.

The invariant theme of these replies is the following: the emergence in the economic level of the CMP, i.e. in capitalist relations of production, of agents of production as *individuals.* Did not Marx, especially in the *Grundrisse,* emphasize the appearance of individuals-agents of production, *bare individuals,* as a real characteristic both of the direct producer (the 'free labourer') and also of the non-producing owner; that is, as a particular form of the two elements which, with the means of production, enter into a combination in those relations which constitute the relations of production? This individualization of the agents of production, *grasped precisely as a real characteristic of capitalist relations of production,* is seen as constituting the substratum of modern state structures; and the ensemble of these individuals-agents as constituting civil society, that is the way in which the economic is somehow present in social relations. Thus, on this theory, separation of civil society and the state indicates the role of a strictly political superstructure relative to these economic individuals, subjects of a society of exchange and competition.

This concept of civil society, borrowed from Hegel and eighteenth-century political theory, refers exactly to the 'world of needs' and implies the anthropological perspective of 'concrete individual' and 'generic man', conceived as subjects of the economy, which is the correlate to the historicist problematic. The examination of the modern state which follows from it starts from the problem of a separation between civil society and the state and is constructed on the schema of *alienation,* i.e. on the schema of a relation of the subject (concrete individuals) to its objectified essence (the state).

Without prolonging our critique of this conception, it will be sufficient to note the following very serious results which follow from it and which make impossible the scientific examination of the capitalist state:

(a) It prevents us from understanding the relation of the state to the class struggle: (i) since agents of production are conceived as originating individuals-subjects and not as supports of structures, it is impossible to constitute social classes from them and (ii) since the state is at the origin related to these economic individuals-agents, it is impossible to relate it to classes and the class struggle.

(b) It results in masking *a whole series of real problems* posed by the capitalist state, by hiding them under the ideological problematic of the separation of civil society and the state. In particular it becomes impossible to conceive the specific autonomy in the CMP of the economic and the political, the effects of the ideological on these instances, the repercussions of this relation between structures on the field of the class struggle, etc.

Let us try to establish the originality of the relations of the capitalist state (i) to the structures of the relations of production, (ii) to the field of the class struggle.

(i) THE CAPITALIST STATE AND RELATIONS OF PRODUCTION

In the first instance, let us examine what Marx means in the *Grundrisse*, especially in the chapter on *Pre-capitalist Economic Formations*,[1] by 'bare individual' as a *theoretical presupposition (Voraussetzung)* and as a *historical condition (historische Bedingung)* of the CMP.

It may usefully be pointed out here that contrary to a historicist conception, this 'bare individual', understood as the historical condition of the CMP, does not mean for Marx the *history of the genesis* of this mode, but the *genealogy of certain of its elements*. In fact the prehistory and the structure of a mode of production must be distinguished, since the effective processes of constituting their elements are different. But once these elements are obtained, the same structure always results from their combination.

1. References to the *Grundrisse zur Kritik der politischen Ökonomie* are from Karl Marx, *Texte zu Methode und Praxis*, Vol. 3, Hamburg, Rowohlt, 1966 (see pp. 40 ff., 47 ff., 65 ff., 127 ff.; and in particular, pp. 132, 138, 150, 154, 157, 167). A complete English translation of the *Grundrisse* will be published, by Penguin Books in association with *New Left Review*, in the course of 1973.

A. What does Marx mean by the appearance of the 'bare individual' (*nacktes Individuum*) as the *historical condition* of the CMP, a term which is linked with that of 'free labourer' (*freier Arbeiter*) in the *Grundrisse* text concerning the direct producer.

This term clearly does not in any way mean the actual appearance in historical reality of agents of production as individuals, in the literal sense of the term. It is being used in a *descriptive* way, so as to show the *dissolution* of a certain relation of *structures*, namely that of the feudal mode of production. In fact, up to and including *Capital*, Marx incorrectly perceives the feudal mode of production as *differing* from the CMP in being characterized by a '*mixedness*' of its instances, a mixedness which is based on a purely mythical conception of their 'organic' relation. We know how this *representation* of Marx's of the feudal mode of production should be assessed.[2] The important point is that 'bare individual' and the 'free labourer' are here only simple words, which exactly describe the *liberation* of the agents of production from feudal 'ties of personal dependence' (*persönliche Herrschafts- und Knechtschaftsverhältnisse*), even called 'natural' (*naturwüchsige Gesellschaft*), conceived as 'mixed' economic-political fetters of the process of production. The dissolution of feudal structures is perceived descriptively as the *stripping* of agents of production, which is only a way of noting a structural transformation, by perceiving it, in an entirely descriptive way, in its *effects*. The term 'bare individual' as a historical condition does not therefore in any way mean that agents, who were previously 'organically' in unities, arise *in reality* as atomized individuals, to be *later* inserted into combinations of capitalist relations of production, and then gradually to constitute social classes.[3] It means that certain relations disintegrate (*sich auflösen*), and that this appears in its effects as a 'bareness', 'liberation' and 'individualization' (*Vereinzelung*) of the agents.

B. However, the term 'bare individual' is also used as a *theoretical presupposition* of the CMP. In an equally descriptive way it here covers a reality which is quite different and very precise. Both in the *Precapitalist Economic Formations* and in *Capital* it denotes *the relation of real appropriation*, as a theoretical characteristic of the CMP: its specific characteristic is the *separation of the direct producer from his 'natural' conditions of*

2. See the Introduction, for this and for what follows.

3. Yet this is in fact what Marx *says* in the *Grundrisse*, in connection with the 'mass' of 'free labourers' who are constituted gradually into classes. I have shown how this should be understood on pp. 57 ff. above.

labour. This separation of the direct producer from the means of production, occurring at the historical stage of large industry, and marking
the beginning of the expanded reproduction of the CMP, is what is
here being descriptively perceived as 'bareness' of the agents of production.

I do not intend to discuss why Marx's terminology fluctuated in this
way. The important point to see clearly here is that the term 'bare
individual' in the second sense (i.e. of the theoretical presuppositions of
the CMP) does not in the least mean the *real emergence* of agents of production as 'individuals'. On the contrary, it is clear that what is really
conveyed by this term, the separation of the direct producer from his
means of production, leads to completely different results. Namely, it
leads to the collectivization of the labour process, that is, to the labourer
as an organ of a collective mechanism of production, which Marx defines
as *socialization* of the productive forces; while from the viewpoint of the
owners of the means of production, it leads to the process of concentration of capital.

So in the scientific Marxist problematic, this famous real existence of
'individuals-subjects', which is ultimately the basis of the problematic of
'civil society' and its separation from the state, cannot be accepted. On the
other hand, by considering the capitalist state as a regional instance of the
CMP, and so in its complex relations with the relations of production, we
can establish its *specific autonomy* relative to the economic. Moreover,
without any doubt, the Italian Marxist school has incorrectly identified
this ideological schema of the *separation* of civil society and the state with
the real problem of the *respective autonomy* in the CMP of the political
and economic structures. This specific autonomy of the political and the
economic in the CMP, descriptively contrasted by Marx with the so-called
'mixedness' of the instances in the feudal mode of production, relates
ultimately to the separation of the direct producer from his means of
production; it relates to the peculiar combination of the relations of real
appropriation and property where, according to Marx, the 'secret' of the
constitution of superstructures is to be found. This separation of the
direct producer from the means of production in the combination which
governs and distributes the specific positions of the economic and the
political, and which sets the limits of intervention by one of the regional
structures at another, has strictly nothing to do with the real appearance
of agents as 'individuals' in the relations of production. On the contrary,

it reveals these agents as supports of structures and thus opens the way to a scientific examination of the relation of the state to the field of the class struggle.

If we consider in this way the function which has been ascribed, in the Marxist theory of the state, to the concept of civil society, we see clearly that it has been at most a *negative* or *critical* function. Civil society has constituted a notion negatively indicating the specific autonomy of the political, but in no way a concept which could cover the structure of the economic, the relations of production.

The juridico-political superstructure of the capitalist state is related to this structure of the relations of production. This becomes clear as soon as we refer to capitalist law. The separation of the direct producer from the means of production is reflected there by the institutionalized fixing of agents of production as juridical subjects, i.e. political individuals-persons. This is as true of the particular transaction constituted by the labour contract (the buying and selling of labour power), as of the relationship of formal juridical ownership of the means of production or of public-political institutionalized relations. This means that agents of production actually appear as 'individuals' only in those superstructural relations which are juridical relations. It is on these juridical relations, and not on relations of production in the strict sense, that the labour contract and the formal ownership of the means of production depend. The fact that this appearance of the 'individual' at the level of juridical reality is due to the separation of the direct producer from his means of production does not mean that this separation engenders 'individuals-agents of production' within those same relations of production. *On the contrary, our task will be to explain how this separation*, which engenders the concentration of capital and the socialization of the labour process within the economic level, jointly sets up agents of production at the juridico-political level, as political and juridical 'individuals-subjects', deprived of their economic determination and, consequently, of their class membership.

It is hardly necessary to emphasize the fact that there is, corresponding to this particular status of the juridico-political instance, a *juridical and political ideology*, which is dependent on the ideological instance. This juridico-political ideology holds a dominant place in the dominant ideology of this mode of production, taking a place analogous to religious ideology in the dominant ideology of the feudal mode of production. Here, the separation of the direct producer from his means of production is expressed, in ideological discourse, in extraordinarily complex forms of individualist personalism, in the setting-up of agents as 'subjects'.

The separation of the direct producer from the means of production in the relation of real appropriation (the labour process), which produces the specific autonomy of the political and the economic, determines the setting-up of agents as juridico-political subjects, *in that it impresses a determinate structure on the labour process*. This is what Marx shows in his analyses of commodity and the law of value: 'Only such products can become commodities with regard to each other, as result from different kinds of labour, each kind being carried on independently and for the account of private individuals.'[4] This, strictly speaking, is a mode of objective articulation of the labour processes, a mode in which the real dependence of the producers introduced by the socialization of labour (social labour) is concealed. These labours are, within certain objective limits, carried out independently one from another (private labours), *that is without the producers having to organize their co-operation to begin with*. It is then that the law of value dominates. This opposition 'dependence/independence', characteristic of the producers but not of the 'private owners' in the relation of real appropriation, is identical to the separation of the producers from the means of production; it therefore indicates that the dependence of the producers poses certain necessary limits to the relative independence of the labour process. This essential question cannot be stressed further here. It must however be emphasized that:

a. It is a matter of an objective structure of the *labour process*. This determines (i) *the relation of property in the economic combination* and thereby a contradiction specific to the economic in the CMP between socialization of the productive forces and private ownership of the means of production; it *thus* determines (ii) the setting up of agents in independent pieces of labour as subjects in the juridico-political superstructure.

b. The agents appear here not as 'individuals/subjects', but as supports of a structure of the labour process, i.e. as agents/producers, maintaining determinate relations with the means of labour.

This structure of the labour process is over-determined by the juridico-political; from its reflection in the juridico-political and from the

---

4. *Capital*, Vol. I, p. 42. Cf. Charles Bettelheim, *Le contenu du calcul économique social*, unpublished lectures kindly communicated to me by the author.

intervention of this latter in the economic, it leads to a whole series of *over-determined effects* in social relations, in the field of the class struggle.

(ii) THE CAPITALIST STATE AND THE CLASS STRUGGLE

We have by no means reached the end of our elucidation of the principles of explanation of the capitalist state. The relation between political structures and relations of production leads on to the problem of the relation *between the state and the field of the class struggle.*

This specific autonomy of the political and economic structures of the CMP in the field of the class struggle (i.e. in the field of social relations) is reflected as an autonomization of socio-economic and socio-political relations, or, as emphasized by Marx, Engels, Lenin and Gramsci, as an autonomization of the economic class struggle and the properly political class struggle. Therefore if we temporarily disregard the ideological, the state's relation to the field of the class struggle can be divided into its relation to (i) the economic class struggle and (ii) the political class struggle.

If we begin by examining the economic class struggle (*the socio-economic relations* of the CMP) we note a *fundamental and original* characteristic, to be defined hereafter as the 'effect of isolation'. It consists of the fact that the *juridical and ideological structures* (determined in the last instance by the structure of the labour process), which set up at their level agents of production distributed in social classes as juridico-ideological subjects, produce the following effect on the economic class struggle: the effect of concealing from these agents in a particular way the fact that their relations are class relations. The socio-economic relations are in actual fact *experienced* by the supports as a specific fragmentation and atomization. The Marxist classics have often indicated this by contrasting the 'individual', 'local', 'partial', 'isolated', etc., economic struggle with the political struggle which tends to present a character of unity, i.e. class unity. So this isolation is the effect on socio-economic relations of (1) the juridical, (2) the juridico-political ideology, (3) the ideological in general. This effect of isolation is *terrifyingly real*: it has a name: *competition* between the wage-earning workers and between the capitalist owners of private property. It is in fact only an ideological conception of the capitalist relations of production which conceives them as commercial encounters between individuals/agents of production on the market. But competition is far from designating the *structure of capitalist relations of production*; it consists precisely in the effect of the juridical and the ideological on *socio-economic relations*.

The fact remains that this effect of isolation is of major importance, particularly in so far as it conceals from the agents of production their class relations in their economic struggle. Furthermore this is undoubtedly one of the reasons why Marx continually locates the constitution of classes *as such* in the CMP at the level of political class struggle. It is not that 'individuals/agents of production' are constituted into classes only in the political struggle. Marx shows, particularly in *Capital*, Volume III, how agents of production, who have already entered the transaction of the labour contract in Volume I, are distributed in social classes. It is because of the effects of the juridical and the ideological on socio-economic relations, on the economic struggle, that this is not experienced as a class struggle.

Further, this 'effect of isolation' on socio-economic relations does not simply appear at the level of each agent of production, i.e. as an effect of 'individualization' of these agents: it appears in a whole series of relations, from relations between wage-earning worker and capitalist owner of private property, between wage-earning worker and wage-earning worker and between private capitalist and private capitalist, to relations between a worker in one factory, branch of industry or locality and workers elsewhere, and between capitalists in one branch of industry or subdivision of capital and the others. This effect of isolation which is designated by the term 'competition' covers the whole ensemble of socio-economic relations.

From another aspect, we can locate an isolation within socio-economic relations among certain classes in a capitalist formation which are dependent on other modes of production coexisting in that formation: this is the case with the small-holding peasants. It must be noted that their isolation is a result of their conditions of economic life, i.e. of their *non-separation* from the means of production, whereas the isolation of the capitalist owners and wage-earning workers is an effect of the juridical and the ideological. Yet the 'effect of isolation' specific to the CMP, by adding itself to the isolation proper to their conditions of economic life, in their relation to the capitalist state, also permeates the classes of the non-dominant modes of production in a capitalist formation, in an *over-determining* way.

The clearest indication that these characteristics of the economic struggle of the CMP are the effects of the juridical and the ideological is the following: when Marx refers to this isolation of the economic struggle and contrasts it with the properly political struggle, he often uses the term *private* in contrast to *public*, the latter term denoting the field of the political struggle. This distinction of private and public depends on the juridico-political, in so far as the agents, set up as individuals/juridico-political subjects (the private sphere), are opposed to the 'representative' political institutions of the unity of these subjects (the public sphere). So the fact that Marx uses the category of private to mean the isolation of the economic struggle in no way implies a distinction between the private sphere of economic individuals/subjects and the political sphere; rather it indicates that the isolation of the whole series of socio-economic relations is an effect of the juridical and the ideological. It is in this sense that we must understand his remarks:

Be that as it may, we could not attain this end (the limitation of the working day) by a *private* compromise between workers and capitalists. The very necessity of a general political action proves indeed that in its purely economic action, capital is the stronger . . .[5]

With this defeat the proletariat passes into the *background* of the revolutionary stage. . . . It throws itself . . . into a movement in which it renounces the revolutionizing of the old world by means of the latter's own great, combined resources, and seeks, rather, to achieve its salvation . . . *in a private fashion*, within its limited conditions of existence, and hence necessarily suffers shipwreck. . . .[6]

In connection with the bourgeoisie:

The struggle to maintain its *public interests*, its own *class interests*, its *political* power only troubled and upset it, as it was a disturbance of *private* business . . . this bourgeoisie, which every moment sacrificed its general class interest, that is, its political interest, to the narrowest and most sordid *private* interests. . . .[7]

These remarks are important if we are to give an exact location to the relation between the capitalist state and the economic class struggle. It must be re-emphasized that this relation is not identical with that of the structures of the capitalist state to the relations of production, in so far

5. Statutes of the First International, 1864. See also the Resolutions of the first Congress of the First International, 5, concerning the trade unions, and moreover the whole range of Marx's texts concerning the trade-union struggle.

6. 'The Eighteenth Brumaire', *MESW*, 1970, p. 102.

7. ibid., pp. 157, 159.

as this latter relation delimits the way in which the state can be related to the field of the class struggle. *The capitalist state is related to socio-economic relations in the form in which they appear in their isolation, i.e. as an effect of the ideological and the juridical.* This is because socio-economic relations are class practices, i.e. the effective and already over-determined action in the economic of agents distributed in social classes: this practice is itself by no means 'pure', but in its concrete reality, it is always over-determined. Thus, the capitalist state is determined by its function with regard to the economic class struggle, in the form in which it appears by reason of its isolation, as indicated above.

In this way the capitalist state constantly appears as the strictly political *unity* of an economic struggle which is in itself a sign of this isolation. It presents itself as the representative of the 'general interest' of competing and divergent economic interests which conceal their class character from the agents, who experience them. As a direct consequence, by means of a whole complex functioning of the ideological, the capitalist state systematically conceals its political class character at the level of its political institutions: it is a popular-national-class state, in the truest sense. This state presents itself as the incarnation of the popular will of the people/ nation. The people/nation is institutionally fixed as the ensemble of 'citizens' or 'individuals' whose unity is represented by the capitalist state: its *real substratum* is precisely this isolating effect manifested by the CMP's socio-economic relations.

A whole series of strictly ideological operations undoubtedly intervenes in this function of the state vis-à-vis the economic class struggle. But we should not under any circumstances reduce these structures of the state resulting from its function vis-à-vis socio-economic relations, to the ideological. These structures give rise to real institutions which form a part of the *regional instance* of the state. The ideological intervenes here *at one and the same time* through its own isolating effect on socio-economic relations *and* in the concrete functioning of the state relative to this effect. This intervention can in no way reduce institutions as real as parliamentary representation, popular sovereignty, universal suffrage, etc. The juridico-political superstructure of the state therefore has *a double function* here, to be clarified under the following two headings:

1. Particularly in its aspect of a normative juridical system (juridical reality), it sets up agents of production distributed in classes as juridico-political subjects and so produces the effect of isolation in socio-economic relations.

2. Relative to the socio-economic relations which show this effect of isolation, its function is to *represent the unity* of isolated relations founded in the body politic of the people/nation. This means that the state *represents the unity of an isolation which, because of the role played by the ideological, is largely its own effect.* This double function of isolating and representing the unity is reflected in internal contradictions in the structure of the state: contradictions between the private and the public, between political individuals/persons and the representative institutions of the unity of the people/nation, even between private and public law, between political liberties and the general interest, etc.

But my chief aim will not be to analyse the organization of these state structures starting from the relations of production or to elucidate their internal contradictions: this would demand a deeper investigation into the relation indicated above between the juridical system and the structure of the labour process. It will rather be to understand their function relative to the field of the class struggle. This entails considering their effect of isolation on the socio-economic relations as *given*, so as to elucidate the state's strictly political role with respect to them and consequently with respect to the political class struggle.

The relation of the capitalist state to socio-economic relations (i.e. to the economic class struggle) has an importance which Marx was at pains to emphasize. Yet his frequent use of terms which are either descriptive (e.g. 'society') or dependent on the youthful problematic (e.g. 'civil society') has led to the misinterpretations indicated above. In fact in his political works, for instance already at the time of *The Eighteenth Brumaire*, Marx uses the term 'society' (which elsewhere is a general term covering social relations and the field of class relations) in order to designate socio-economic relations (the economic class struggle) as a manifestation of the effect of isolation. At times he even goes so far as to re-employ the term 'civil society', thus apparently taking up the problematic of a separation of civil society from the state once again:

Instead of *society* having conquered a new content for itself, it seems that the *state* only returned to its oldest form. . . .[8] The moustache and uniform, which were periodically trumpeted forth as the highest wisdom of society and as its rector were . . . finally bound to hit upon the idea of . . . freeing civil society completely from the trouble of governing itself. . . .[9] It is immediately obvious that in a country like France, . . . where the state enmeshes, controls, regulates,

8. ibid., p. 98.   9. ibid., p. 109.

superintends and tutors civil society . . . the National Assembly forfeits all real influence when it loses command of the ministerial posts, if it does not . . . let civil society and public opinion create organs of their own. . . .'[10] Every common interest was straightway severed from society, counter-opposed to it as a higher, *general* interest, snatched from the activity of society's members themselves, and made an object of government activity. . . . Only under the second Bonaparte does the state seem to have made itself completely independent. . . .'[11] But the parody of the empire was necessary to free the mass of the French nation from the weight of tradition and to work out in pure form the opposition between the state power and society.[12]

These quotations will suffice: we could add many others from *The Class Struggles in France, The Civil War in France, The Critique of the Gotha Programme*, etc.

If we refer back to our earlier remarks, we see clearly that Marx's analyses are not simple echoes or empty reminiscences of a former problematic, nor do they relate to the schema of the separation of civil society and the state. They in fact cover a *new* problem, but in terms borrowed from a former problematic, where they had covered a different problem. In the new problematic, the 'antagonism', 'separation' or 'independence' of the state and civil society (or society) indicates the following fact: that the specific autonomy in the CMP of the capitalist state from the relations of production is reflected in the field of the class struggle by an autonomy of the economic class struggle from the political class struggle. This is expressed by the effect of isolation on socio-economic relations, in which the state assumes a specific autonomy vis-à-vis these relations, in putting itself forward as the representative of the unity of the people/nation, i.e. the body-politic founded on the isolation of socio-economic relations. It is only by disregarding the change of the problematic in Marx's work and by *playing on words*, that this autonomy of structures and practices in Marx's mature works can be interpreted as a separation of civil society and the state.[13]

This has been the interpretation of the Italian Marxist school in particular, whose achievements we should openly acknowledge. In some important works dealing chiefly with the problem of Marxist political

10. ibid., pp. 127-8.   11. ibid., pp. 169-70.   12. ibid., p. 175.

13. In France, this has been the interpretation of e.g. H. Lefebvre, *La Sociologie de Marx*, Paris, 1966 (chapter entitled 'La théorie de l'État') (English translation, *The Sociology of Marx*, London, 1968) and of M. Rubel, *Marx devant le bonapartisme*, Paris-The Hague, 1960.

science, following Galvano della Volpe it has proceeded to attempt to elucidate Marx's thought; and in this has had an important *critical* function. It has radically challenged the vulgarized conception of the state as the simple tool or instrument of the dominant class/subject. Certainly, it has also posed original problems related to the question of the specific autonomy of the structures and the class practices in the CMP. However, it locates Marx's originality relative to Hegel in his critique (in the works on the Hegelian theory of the state) of the speculative empiricism which invariably characterizes Hegel's problematic.[14] But this critique is in fact only Marx's revival of the critique which Feuerbach made of Hegel. The Italian school therefore masks the problems with the theme of the separation of civil society from the state, which leads to a whole series of mistaken results to which we shall have to return when considering concrete problems.[15]

These remarks are also important with regard to the capitalist state's relation to the *political class struggle*. This effect of isolation in the economic struggle has repercussions on the specific functioning of the political class struggle in a capitalist formation. One of the characteristics of this political struggle, which has gained a relative autonomy from the economic struggle, is that (as the Marxist classics continually stress) it tends to

14. In particular Galvano della Volpe, *Rousseau e Marx*, 1964, pp. 22 ff., 46 ff., *Umanesimo positivo e emancipazione marxista*, 1964, pp. 27 ff., 57; Umberto Cerroni, *Marx e il diritto moderno*, 1963, passim; Mario Rossi, *Marx e la dialettica hegeliana*; 1961, Vol. 2, passim.

15. E.g. in *Rousseau e Marx*, della Volpe relates the problem of the autonomy and interrelation of the economic and the political to the young Marx's critique of Hegel's 'speculative empiricism'. Marx criticized Hegel for ending in a confusion, intended as a synthesis, of the economic and the political, a confusion stemming from the fact that his 'speculative' conception, particularly of the state, corresponds to the invasion of unmediated empiricism, 'just as it is', into the concept. Marx perceives the economic as 'the vulgar empirical', whose mediations, which in a bourgeois society turn it into the properly political, must be discovered. According to Marx, Hegel's conception of the state results in a parallel coexistence of the economic and the political in the *estates* which compose his model-state; whereas the real task is to discover their modern separation in the 'universal', abstract character of the bourgeois class (the mediation), and then the transcendence of this separation (the abolition of the political) in the 'universal-concrete' character of the proletariat. This concept of 'universality' is transferred from the anthropological model of 'man as a species-being'. The young Marx's critique of Hegel still retains the conception of the economic/political relation derived from the empirical-concrete/abstract-speculative relation. The young Marx considered the political as the economic 'mediated' in an anthropological 'transcendence' of Hegel's 'speculative empiricism'.

constitute *class unity* out of the isolation of the economic struggle. This has a particular importance *in the relation between the practice (i.e. political struggle) of the dominant classes and the capitalist state*, in so far as this practice is specified by the fact that its objective is the conservation of this state and that it aims through it at the maintenance of existing social relations. Consequently, this political practice of the dominant classes has two functions: (i) to constitute the unity of the dominant class(es) out of the isolation of their economic struggle, (ii) by means of a whole political-ideological operation of its own, to constitute their strictly political interests as representative of the general interest of the people/nation. This is made *necessary* by the particular structures of the capitalist state, in its relation to the economic class struggle, and made *possible* precisely by the isolation of the economic struggle of the dominated classes. It is by analysing this whole complex operation that we can establish the relation between this national-popular-class state and the politically dominant classes in a capitalist formation.

(iii) THE CONCEPT OF HEGEMONY

It is precisely in this context that I shall use the concept of *hegemony*. The field of this concept is the political class struggle in a capitalist formation: in particular it covers the political practices of the dominant classes in these formations. *Thus in locating the relation of the capitalist state to the politically dominant classes, we can say that it is a state with hegemonic class leadership (direzione).*[16]

This concept was produced by Gramsci. It is true that in his works it is a practical (and not truly theoretical) concept and that because of its wide field of application it remains too vague. As a result, a whole series of clarifications and restrictions must be introduced here, as a preliminary step. Because of his particular relation to Lenin's problematic, Gramsci always believed that he had found the concept in Lenin's writings, especially in those concerning the ideological organization of the working class and its role of leadership in the political struggle of the dominated classes. But in reality he had produced a new concept which can account for *the political practices of dominant classes in developed capitalist formations.* Gramsci admittedly does use it in this way, but he also incorrectly extends it so that it covers the structures of the capitalist

16. For the problem of translating Gramsci's concept of *direzione*, see *Prison Notebooks*, p. 55 n.

state. However, if we severely restrict the field of application and constitution of the concept of hegemony, his analyses of this subject are very
interesting. His object is to locate these formations concretely, by applying to them the principles elucidated by Lenin in his analyses of a different concrete object: namely, the situation in Russia.

But Gramsci's analyses pose a major problem, in so far as his thought
is strongly influenced by the historicism of Croce and Labriola.[17] The
problem here is too vast to be gone into deeply. I shall simply point out
that we can locate a clear break between on the one hand the works of
Gramsci's youth (e.g. the articles in *Ordine Nuovo*) and even *Il materialismo storico e la filosofia di Benedetto Croce*, with their typically historicist
approach, and on the other the works of his maturity concerning political
theory (e.g. *Note sul Machiavelli*, etc.), i.e. precisely those works in which
the concept of hegemony is elaborated.[18] This break becomes clear only
if we subject to a symptomatic reading those of his texts in which the
Leninist problematic emerges: it has been hidden by the (mainly historicist) readings which have tried to discover the theoretical links between Lenin and Gramsci.[19] However, even in Gramsci's mature works
we find numerous after-effects of historicism. At a first reading of his
works, the concept of hegemony seems to indicate a historical situation in
which class domination is not reduced to simple domination by force or
violence, but comprises a function of *leadership* and a *particular ideological*
function, by means of which the dominant/dominated relation is founded
on an 'active consent' of the dominated classes.[20] This fairly vague conception seems at first sight to be akin to that of Lukács's class-
consciousness world-view, and to be equally located in the Hegelian problematic of the subject. Transplanted into Marxism, this problematic leads
to the conception of the class-subject of history, a genetic principle which
totalizes the instances of a social formation: it does this by means of class
consciousness which assumes in this problematic the role of the Hegelian
concept. In this context, it is the 'ideology consciousness world-view' of
the class viewed as subject of history, that is of the hegemonic class,

17. On Gramsci's 'historicism', see L. Althusser, *Reading Capital*, pp. 126 ff.

18. On this see L. Paggi, 'Studi e interpretazioni recenti di Gramsci', *Critica Marxista*, May–June 1966, pp. 151 ff.

19. E.g. Togliatti, 'Il leninismo nel pensiero e nell'azione di A. Gramsci' and
'Gramsci e il leninismo' in *Studi Gramsciani*, Rome, 1958; M. Spinella, 'Introduction'
to A. Gramsci, *Elementi di politica*, Rome, 1964; and the typical historicist interpretation
of Gramsci by J. Texier, *Antonio Gramsci*, Paris, 1967.

20. *Prison Notebooks*, pp. 245 and 257 ff.

which founds the unity of a formation, in so far as it determines the adhesion of the dominated classes in a determinate system of domination.[21] It is thus interesting to note that, in this use of the concept of hegemony, Gramsci conceals precisely those real problems which he analyses in the schema of the separation of civil society and the state. These problems, which actually imply the specific autonomy of the instances of the CMP and the effect of isolation in the economic, are masked. In Gramsci, as in the young Marx, this 'separation' *depends on its contrast* with the conception of feudal relations characterized by a 'mixedness' of instances: Gramsci treats this 'mixedness' in his 'economic-corporate' theme. Thus he uses the concept of hegemony in order to distinguish the capitalist social formation from the 'economic-corporate' feudal formation.[22] In particular, the economic-corporate indicates the feudal social relations characterized by a tight overlapping of the political and the economic: what Gramsci calls 'politics *grafted* on to the economy'. Gramsci's analyses of the modern 'national-popular' state are situated in the context of the various Italian Renaissance states' transitions from feudalism to capitalism. It is this context which permits him to analyse the hegemonic function of unity of the modern state, a function related to the 'atomization' of civil society, the substratum of the nation-people. What strikes him in Machiavelli is not simply the fact that he was one of the first theorists of political practice, but above all the fact that he perceived the function of unity assumed by the modern state vis-à-vis the 'popular masses', which are considered here as products of the dissolution of feudal relations. This is particularly clear in his analyses of the initial failure of attempts to form such a state in Italy:

The reason for the failure of the successive attempts to create a national-popular collective will is to be sought in the existence of certain specific social groups which were formed at the dissolution of the Communal bourgeoisie. . . . This function and the position which results from it have brought about an internal situation which may be called 'economic-corporate' – politically, the worst of all forms of feudal society.[23]

But this term 'economic-corporate' has a second meaning for Gramsci. It indicates not only the 'mixed' economic/political relations of the feudal

21. From another point of view, Gramsci also used this concept of hegemony in the field of the political practice of the dominated classes, particularly of the working class: we shall return to this later.

22. *Prison Notebooks*, pp. 12 ff. and p. 56 n.   23. ibid., p. 131.

formation, but also the 'economic' (as distinct from the political) element in capitalist formations. This significant fluctuation of terminology is to be understood as being the result of those historicist influences by which Gramsci's analyses are often tainted. The common characteristic found by him in the 'mixed' economic-corporate relations of feudal formations and the 'economic' (as distinct from political) relations of capitalist formations, is that both are distinguished from the 'strictly political' relations of capitalist formations. Although the after-effects of historicism are thus clearly to be seen in Gramsci's analyses of this subject, it is possible to attempt to purify them. It will be seen that the real problems posed bear no relation to any separation of the capitalist state from civil society, which is held to have been atomized as a result of the dissolution of mixed or organic feudal relations. The real problems are concerned with the specific autonomy of the instances of the CMP, with the effect of isolation in the socio-economic relations of this mode, and with the way in which the state and the political practices of the dominant classes are related to this isolation.

The concept of hegemony, *which we shall apply only to the political practices of the dominant classes* of a capitalist formation, and not to its state, is used in *two senses*:

1. It indicates how in their relation to the capitalist state the political interests of these classes are constituted, as representatives of the 'general interest' of the body politic, i.e. the people/nation which is based on the effect of isolation on the economic. This first sense is for example implied in the following quotation, which should now be considered in the light of the above remarks:

A third moment is that in which one becomes aware that one's own corporate interests, in their present and future development, transcend the corporate limits of the purely economic class, and can and must become the interests of other subordinate groups too. This is the most purely political phase, and marks the decisive passage from the structure to the sphere of the complex superstructures; it is the phase in which previously germinated ideologists become 'party', come into confrontation and conflict, until only one of them, or at least a single combination of them, tends to prevail, to gain the upper hand, to propagate itself throughout society – bringing about not only a unison of economic and political aims, but also intellectual and moral unity, posing all the questions around which the struggle rages not on a corporate but on a 'universal' plane, and thus creating the hegemony of a fundamental social group over a series of subordinate groups. It is true that the state is seen as the organ of one particular group, destined to create favourable conditions for the latter's maximum expansion. But the development and expansion of the particular group are conceived of, and presented, as being the motor force of a universal expansion, of a development of all the 'national' energies. In other words, the dominant group is coordinated concretely with the general interests of the subordinate groups, and the life of the state is conceived of as a continuous process of formation and superseding of unstable equilibria (on the juridical plane) between the interests of the fundamental group and those of the subordinate groups-equilibria in which the interests of the dominant group prevail, but only up to a certain point, i.e. stopping short of narrowly corporate interest.[24]

2. The concept of hegemony is also used in another sense, which is not actually pointed out by Gramsci. The capitalist state and the specific characteristics of the class struggle in a capitalist formation *make it possible* for a 'power bloc', composed of several *politically dominant* classes or fractions to function. Amongst these *dominant* classes and fractions one of them holds a particular *dominant role*, which can be characterized as a *hegemonic role*. In this second sense, the concept of hegemony encompasses the particular domination of one of the dominant classes or fractions vis-à-vis the other dominant classes or fractions in a capitalist social formation.

The concept of hegemony allows us to make out the relation between these two characteristic types of political class domination found in capitalist formations. The hegemonic class is the one which concentrates in itself, at the political level, the *double function* of representing the general interest of the people/nation and of maintaining a specific dominance among the dominant classes and fractions. It does this through its particular relation to the capitalist state.

24. ibid., pp. 181–2.

2. Typology and Type of the Capitalist State

The previous remarks allow us to specify the capitalist type of state. Marxist science of the political has distinguished certain 'types' of state (despotic, slave, feudal, capitalist), corresponding to so many determinate modes of production. Furthermore Marx, Engels and Lenin defined 'forms of state' and 'forms of government' within these specific types of state. The typological problem of determining the state superstructure therefore concerns two things:

a. The task of constituting as an object of theoretical research a *regional instance* of a given mode of production, in this case the juridico-political superstructure of the state. From the point of view of Marxist science, this means that it is first of all a task of grasping the unity and the *specificity* of this 'object', by constituting it as a theoretical object, so that its typical structures, thus defined, allow us to make out its place and function in the complex unity of this mode of production.

b. The task of constituting this typical object out of theoretical principles which will allow us to give an account of what may provisionally be called its *transformations*. For example, in what sense do the forms of capitalist state belong to the type of the capitalist state? To what extent do they refer to 'phases' or 'stages' of a *social formation* dominated by the CMP? The typological problem is here identical with the problem of *periodization*.

As a preliminary remark, we should note that this problem of the typology of an instance of a mode of production cannot be related to a thematic of the historical genesis of this instance. It cannot be reduced to a history of the genesis of the modern capitalist state. Our problem here, in the case of a regional instance of a mode of production, is the same as the one already encountered in the case of the transition from one social formation to another.

In order to grasp the specificity of the regional structures in a given mode of production (e.g. of the capitalist state in the CMP) we must determine its place inside the matrix specifying this mode. That is the only starting-point from which the *concept of this instance* can be constructed.

The specific autonomy of the instances of the CMP, assigning to the state its place in this 'pure' mode, is precisely a specific autonomy of this state in relation to the economic. In particular, it is this autonomy which, as a constant invariant, regulates the variations of intervention and non-intervention of the political in the economic, and of the economic in the political.[1]

Yet it is of major importance to note that these considerations by themselves do not allow us to establish the concept of the capitalist state, in so far as its typical structures must be jointly located *in their relation, or rather their function, vis-à-vis the field of the class struggle* in this mode of production. In fact, the place of the state in the ensemble of structures provides us with a simple schema which cannot be established as a concept before we have examined this state's relation both to the economic class struggle and to the political class struggle. In other words, in order to constitute an adequate concept of the capitalist type of state, this place of the state must be located in the effects produced by that place in delimiting the state's relation to the field of the class struggle.

Thus, the capitalist type of state relates, in the first place, to the specific autonomy of its structures from the economic class struggle, in its relation to the effect of isolation in the socio-economic relations of the CMP. For the sake of clarity, I shall henceforth designate this relation as the state's relation to the isolation of the economic or to the isolation of socio-economic relations. Finally we must confront this type of state with its relation to the political class struggle, especially to the political practices of the dominant classes in this mode. The important point in this case is the state's relation to class hegemony, i.e. to the constitution of one class as hegemonic vis-à-vis the 'people/nation' and the power bloc, whose formation corresponds to the capitalist type of state.

What are the relations between this type of state and a given state of a

---

1. We have seen above, in Part 1, that the construction of the concept of the state in the various modes of production, i.e. the delimitation of the types of state, depends on the differentiated forms assumed by the state in these various modes, in its general function as cohesive factor in the unity of a formation. In that chapter we emphasized with precision that these differentiated forms depend on the state's place in the various modes of production. In this way we established that this function becomes specific for the capitalist state precisely because of the autonomy of the economic and the political characteristic of the CMP. I shall therefore approach the problem of typology by analysing this autonomy, while reserving to Part III an analysis of its repercussions on the concrete forms assumed by the capitalist state in its function as cohesive factor in the unity of a capitalist formation.

social formation? As we know, a historically determined social formation is dependent on the coexistence of several modes of production. In this sense, the state of such a formation results from a combination of several types of state, the product of the different modes of production which come into combination in this formation. In particular, in the case of a concrete social formation dominated by the CMP, the real capitalist state may present several characteristics dependent on types of state corresponding to the other modes of production which coexist in these formations. These characteristics are not simple 'impure residues' in this state; they are a constituent part of it in a given formation. However, I shall use the term capitalist state to designate a state in which the capitalist type of state is dominant (just as the term capitalist social formation denotes a formation in which the CMP is dominant).

Yet because of the dislocations of the various instances and because of the complexity of a social formation, it does not necessarily follow from the fact that the CMP is dominant in this formation that the capitalist type is the dominant type of its state at the level of the political superstructure. We can talk accurately of a capitalist formation or of a formation dominated by the CMP even though its state has a feudal character, i.e. shows the domination of the feudal type of state. This is precisely the meaning of Marx's and Engels's writings on *Bismarckism*, which analyse the existence in a capitalist formation of a state dominated by the feudal type. In this case it is due to the fact that, because of the autonomy of instances characteristic of the CMP and impressed by it on the capitalist formation, this dominant CMP permits the existence, at the level of the political instance, of a state dominated by a type other than that which characterizes the state of this mode. The dominant CMP *impregnates the whole system* and modifies the conditions under which the other subordinate modes of production function. In this case, despite its feudal *structures*, this feudal state can *borrow functions* analogous to those which belong to a capitalist state. This borrowing is the result of the CMP's dominance in the formation and of the place assigned by this dominance to a feudal state. In particular, despite its feudal nature, it can function with the relative autonomy characteristic of the capitalist type of state: in the concrete case of Bismarckism, this makes possible the 'revolution from above' brought about by Bismarck. This functioning of Bismarckism can be characterized as a borrowing, since it cannot be related to a co-existence of characteristics of the feudal and of the capitalist types of state, as these latter are nearly non-existent in the Bismarckian state. Nevertheless, it is obvious that the case in which the connection between the structures and functions of an instance is broken is quite an exceptional one.

(i) MAX WEBER'S TYPOLOGY

We can already conclude from the previous analyses that nothing is further from the Marxist typological problematic and its aim of producing the *concept* of an instance of a mode of production than a typology based on 'schemas', 'models' or 'ideal types'. These models or ideal types are contained in an 'abstract/real' relation, dependent on an empiricist problematic of knowledge. For example, the production of Weber's ideal type consists of locating the differential deviations between several real phenomena belonging to the same 'abstract' type.[2] The operational value of this type is guaranteed by its ability to illuminate concrete reality, i.e. phenomena which are presented as so many deviations from this abstract type.[3] This conception of typology as a schematization of reality and ultimately as a generalization and an abstraction is dependent on an empiricist conception of knowledge which cannot recognize the proper autonomy of theory. It implies that a pre-ordained harmony between the 'abstract' and the 'real' is postulated: typological abstraction is seen as an asymptotic adequation to the concrete reality from which it is drawn. But in the Marxist problematic in this theory, we are attempting rather to produce the concept of a regional instance of a mode of production, not by an abstraction from the concrete real phenomena of a social formation, but by the process of theoretical construction of the concept of this mode of production and of the articulation of the instances which specify it.

2. For French works on Max Weber, whose work is still fairly unknown in France, see J. M. Vincent's fundamental articles, chiefly in *l'Homme et la Société*, Nos. 3 and 4, and J. Freund, *La sociologie de M. Weber*, 1966 (English translation, *The Sociology of Max Weber*, London, 1968). For an excellent critique of ideal types, see R. Establet, *Lire le Capital* (1st edition, Paris, 1965), Vol. 2, p. 338.

3. This important problem is in fact the key one in contemporary discussions concerning methods in the social sciences. As these discussions are at a rudimentary level in France, I refer to an excellent book in which they are presented: E. Topitsch (ed.), *Logik der Sozialwissenschaften*, Cologne/Berlin, 1965. We find in it the text of the famous confrontation between Popper and Adorno concerning these questions (pp. 113 ff., 311 ff.); also a text which illuminates the way in which the problem is posed in political science, by H. Lasswell, *Das qualitative und das quantitative in Politik- und Rechtswissenschaftlichen Untersuchungen*, pp. 464 ff.

The science of models or schemas leads to notions which cannot give an account of the specific object of a particular science: in fact this object cannot be schematized concrete reality, but only a theoretically constructed concept.

The case of Weber's typology is especially interesting, since it unambiguously reveals the relations between the empiricist conception of knowledge and its presuppositions, which are those of the historicist problematic. They are manifest in the Weberian conception of 'understanding' which involves the identity (partial?) of the subject and the object of the knowledge. The epistemological principles, which in Weber's work permit the division into ideal types, are the values proper to the investigator, in so far as he himself is considered to be part of society and history, part of the object of the 'human sciences', which he is helping to 'make'. Concrete reality (the object of science) is the product of the investigator's conduct inserted in a collective praxis and the result of certain values, which are themselves principles for dividing this concrete reality into schemas. And the ontological adequation between the schema and reality is related to this central subject, the subject of society and history and the subject of science, namely the scholar.[4] This conception, whose relations with the Hegelian problematic should be recognized in passing, is particularly interesting when we remember its influence on Lukács's *History and Class Consciousness*, where we find the conception of the class-subject of society and history which is also the subject of knowledge.

Weber proceeds to produce a typology of juridico-political superstructures according to the different combinations (dependent on the order of legitimacy) of mysticism and rationality manifested by them; and amongst types of authority, he distinguishes the rational-legal, the traditional and the charismatic types.[5] These types/objects-of-science are

4. Apart from the general methodological reflections on the 'ideal type' scattered about in Weber's work, for the relation between the conception of 'variables' and the 'ideal type', see *Gesammelte Aufsätze zur Religionssoziologie*, Tübingen, 1922–23, Vol. I, pp. 21 ff., 37 ff., 233 ff. The relation between the 'historicism of values' and the 'model' is clear in the political analyses of e.g. T. Parsons, 'Voting and the equilibrium of the American political system' in *American Voting Behavior*, 1959, edited by Burdick and Brodback. See also Nagel's early critique of functionalism in *Logic Without Metaphysics*, 1956, Part I, Chapter 10, 'A Formalization of Functionalism'. Parsons's line is merely the result of the direct link between Weber and the functionalists.

5. *Wirtschaft und Gesellschaft*, Part II, Ch. 7; and the collection of Weber's texts, *Rechtssoziologie*, edited by J. Winckelmann, Berlin/Neuwied, 1960, passim.

divided up according to the values, ideals, plans, or rather *motives of conduct* in the praxis of the men-subjects who have produced them; in other respects they are appraised in the light of the investigator's own values. The clearest indication of the connection between (i) the epistemological relation ideal-types/real-concrete, and (ii) the historicist problematic is Weber's expressly formulated conception of ideal types as abstract schemas *having the possibility of being realized* in the historical real concrete. These abstract models are simply the values of those who produce the concrete, i.e. the subjects of history, including the scholar, and are thus reducible to the objectification of the essence-subject. Ideal types of authority and state do not cover structures in the strict sense of the term; in the last analysis they cover only the motive of the 'actors'' conduct and behaviour. This Weberian problematic can be found again in Weber's conceptions of power, of the 'capitalist ethos' ('rational' conduct of actors), of bureaucracy (subject of rationality and of the rational type of state), etc.

Nevertheless, the differences established by Weber between traditional, charismatic and rational authority do not cover effectively differential characteristics of types of state. Later it will appear clearly that the capitalist type of state does in fact present, to a certain extent, characteristics *described* by Weber in the notion of 'rational-legal' type of authority: we shall then be able to grasp these characteristics as constitutive traits of the concept of this state.[6]

(ii) TYPES OF STATE, FORMS OF STATE AND PERIODIZATION OF A SOCIAL FORMATION

Let us now turn to the crucial problem of the relations between types of state, forms of state and forms of government (still using the expressions found in Marx, Engels and Lenin). As far as terminology is concerned, the expressions 'forms of state' and 'forms of government' are generally used in the Marxist classics in an identical sense to indicate e.g. 'parliamentary republic', 'constitutional monarchy', etc.[7]

Firstly, let us pose the problem: to what extent can we distinguish between various *forms of state of the same type of state*? This is similar to

6. This empiricist, positivist conception of knowledge, as related to the historicist problematic, is found in another form in Galvano della Volpe and his concept of 'abstract-determinate' model. See *Logica come scienza positiva*, 1947.

7. As in the whole range of Marx's and Engels's political texts and in Lenin's *The Proletarian Revolution and Renegade Kautsky*, *The State and Revolution*, etc.

the theoretical problem posed by the type of the state. We are aiming to establish a typology of *forms of state* which grasps them in such a way that they can both be located in the relations between the instances and the field of the class struggle in a social formation, and also appear as forms of the same type of state. It is, therefore, a double task: (a) to establish a type of the state which can account for the differentiation of forms of state as differentiated forms of this type; and the criteria for this differentiation should be modifications of the relations constituting this type of state and (b) to establish that these modifications do not affect the very matrix of relations, but that they constitute differentiated forms of these relations.

If the capitalist type of state involves in the first place a specific auto-nomy of economic and political structures, which can be located in the autonomy of the state from socio-economic relations, the forms of state of this type will have to be grasped by reference to a modification of the relation of the state to these relations. This modification, however, is situated in the typical framework of their respective autonomy and so cannot basically challenge the terms of this relation: namely, in this case, the structures of the state and the effect of isolation of the economic. These forms of state will be grasped by reference to the *degree* and the *specific forms* of this autonomy. In this way, we can constitute a theory of this type of state and of the forms of this type in its relations with the *economic class struggle*. The problem will be the same concerning the state's relation to the *political class struggle*, in particular to class hege-mony and the power bloc.

The more immediate problem at this stage is that of the *transformations* of the regional instance of a social formation. How can the transforma-tions of the capitalist state be grasped, such that they remain transforma-tions of the same instance? This problem coincides with the major problem of *periodization* at the level of structures and political practices. Is it possible to define typical 'periods' of a social formation, with their own rhythm and scansion, periods to which a particular form of the state corresponds at the political level?

The first necessity is to reject the evolutionist-historicist conception, which posits a unilinear time sequence of the succession either of modes of production or of 'steps'[8] of a social formation or of forms of a regional

8. Poulantzas distinguishes *étape* from *stade*. Both these words are normally trans-lated into English as 'stage'. In order to mark the difference, *étape* has here been trans-lated as 'step', *stade* as 'stage'. [Trans.]

instance of a formation. This conception leads to a method of *chronologi-cal division*, which continues to wreak havoc in the social sciences. In the case of forms of the state, it ends up by seeing a series of successive steps in the transformation of the capitalist state, corresponding to a series of steps in a simple evolution of capitalist formations.

The problem of the transformations of an instance of a formation, in this case of the forms of capitalist state, must be related to the problem of the *phases* and *stages* of the ensemble of a formation. As Bettelheim has pointed out: 'It seems justifiable to reserve the term "phases" to designate the two great moments in the development of a social formation, namely (i) that of its *beginnings*, i.e. the phase of transition in the strict sense . . . (ii) *the phase of expanded reproduction of the structure*. . . . Each of these phases is characterized by a specific articulation of the levels of a social formation and of their contradictions, and therefore by a certain type of unequal development of these contradictions. In the course of one and the same phase, what at a given moment was a chief contradiction becomes a secondary contradiction, or again what was a secondary aspect of the contradiction becomes a chief aspect. These displacements of contradictions provide the rhythm of the different stages of a given phase. . . . They are marked by modifications in the relations between the classes or between the different strata of the same class.'[9] These are the 'typical stages' of a phase.

We can retain this terminology of phases and stages, while making some more precise distinctions. These stages and phases are here those of a *social formation*: the stages of the phases of expanded reproduction of a for-mation are, in our case, those of a formation dominated by a mode of pro-duction, namely a capitalist formation dominated by the CMP. But the stages of this formation relate to the real coexistence of certain differential and specific *forms* of the '*pure*' CMP. These forms cover 'profoundly different economic realities, since they go from simple market production to state monopoly capitalism, passing through private capitalist production, social capitalist production and monopoly capitalism'.[10] These forms of

9. *Cahiers de Planification Socialiste*, no. 3, 1966, pp. 141 ff. The texts quoted from Bettelheim are now reproduced in *La transition vers l'économie socialiste*, Paris, 1968.

10. Bettelheim: 'La construction du socialisme . . .', *La Pensée*, no. 126, April 1966, pp. 58 ff. Bettelheim is speaking here both of the phase of transition and also of the phase of expanded reproduction, i.e. of the whole range of the 'different stages of capitalism'.

capitalism *are forms of the 'pure' CMP* in the very sense which Lenin used in *Imperialism*: 'Imperialism and finance capitalism are superstructures of the former capitalism. Pull down the upper part and the former capitalism will appear. . . .' These forms of the CMP are themselves characterized in theory by certain forms of articulation of the various instances, forms located in the framework of the matrix of this mode of production and involving *tendential combinations* of the CMP towards the other modes in a capitalist formation. These forms have this in common: that they involve the same matrix. But they differ in that the modifications which characterize them bear precisely on the articulations of instances delimited by this matrix. In our case, the CMP involves the specific autonomy of the state from the economic; and this indicates a type of articulation of the political and the economic and a type of effect of one instance within the limits set by the other. Yet though every form of the 'pure' CMP theoretically implies that the political is relatively autonomous from the economic, it is clear that private capitalism involves a non-interventionist state and monopoly capitalism involves an interventionist state. The differences between these forms of state turn precisely on the *specific forms* assumed by the relation between relatively autonomous economic and political instances: *they constitute variables of a specific invariant.*

Let us come back to the problem of the stages of a social formation dominated by the CMP. In addition to the coexistence of various different modes of production, the coexistence *of several 'pure' forms of the CMP* is to be found in this formation: private capitalism, monopoly capitalism, state monopoly capitalism, etc., may exist at one and the same time in it. However, just as the phase of expanded reproduction of a formation relates to the dominance of a mode of production (here the CMP), *the stages of this phase of a formation relate to the dominance of one form of this 'pure' mode of production over the other forms; and this entails a certain concrete combination of the CMP with the other modes of production.* In this sense, we can correctly talk of a stage of private capitalism, a stage of social capitalism, a stage of monopoly capitalism, and a stage of state monopoly capitalism. The forms of state of the different stages of a capitalist formation which is dominated by one of these forms of the CMP are related to the forms of state corresponding to these forms of the CMP.

In this way, these forms of state of a formation are characterized by a specific modification of the relation between the political and the economic. But the relevance here of this modification of relations between structures is the extent to which it can be discovered in its reflection on the field of the class struggle. From this point of view, it concerns precisely:

1. The state's relation *to the isolation of socio-economic* relations, the economic struggle. The modification is cashed in a series of concrete results concerning transformations of legitimacy, differential relations between the executive and the legislative, etc.

2. The state's relation *to class hegemony and the power bloc*, the political struggle. A form of state, located in a stage of a social formation, corresponds to a typical configuration of this power bloc: these various stages, characterized by different forms of state, will be marked by modifications of this bloc.[11]

Finally, a last word should be added on the relations between the economic and the political which mark the various forms of state, and on the various forms of intervention of one of these structures on another in the stages of a capitalist formation. This will be useful for removing certain misunderstandings. A whole tradition of political theory, based on an ideological delimitation of the autonomy of the political from the economic (i.e. the theoretical tradition of the nineteenth century, which involves precisely the theme of the separation of civil society from the state),

11. Since I shall analyse these points later, I simply emphasize here the fact that the modifications of these forms of state, characterized by specific articulations of the economic and political structures within the framework of the same invariant and so by specific forms of intervention and non-intervention of the economic in the political and of the political in the economic, *can only be located in a relevant way in the relations between the state and the field of the class struggle.* Let us take as an example the relations between the legislative and the executive which, according to Marx, characterize in their different modifications, the different forms of the capitalist type of state. The relevance of the criterion of the modifications of the legislative/executive relation cannot be simply determined by the forms of intervention, inside the structures, of one regional structure in the limits set by another. To say, for example, that a form of state which intervenes in a marked way in the economic must be a state where the executive predominates, is not only to take a simple *correlation* for an *explanation*, but is also often incorrect. The problem here is much more complex: the relevance of this criterion of the legislative/executive relation can only be shown, as we shall see, by examining the modifications in the state's relation to the isolation of socio-economic relations (this is the problem of changes in the forms of legitimacy) and in the state's relation to class hegemony in the power bloc.

mistakes this autonomy for that specific non-intervention of the political in the economic which is characteristic of the form of liberal state and of private capitalism. On this interpretation, because of its marked intervention in the economic, the contemporary state in state monopoly capitalism involves an abolition of the respective autonomy of the political and the economic characteristic of the CMP and a capitalist formation: from this it follows that the state form of state monopoly capitalism is a form of transition in that it involves the abolition of this autonomy.

The incorrectness of this conception cannot be over-emphasized. It is of course true that the forms of intervention or non-intervention of the capitalist state in the economic, which mark the forms of this state, presuppose the specific autonomy of the political and the economic. It is the modifications of their relations in the *invariant framework* of this autonomy which precisely regulate the modifications of their respective interventions and lay down their limits. The interventionist state, for example, exercises its intervention precisely by means of the particular forms assumed by its autonomy relative to the economic. In other words, this intervention is exercised in the invariant framework of the matrix of the CMP.

This is the conclusion which emerges clearly from a correct reading of *Capital*. Readers have often seen in it a study of the stage of private capitalism, reading it as the description of the specific non-intervention of the liberal state in the economic. But, in fact, *Capital* gives us the key for constructing the concept of the capitalist state as such: what we find there is not the specific non-intervention of the form of liberal state in the economic, characteristic of the stage of private capitalism, but the respective autonomy of the economic and the political which specifies the CMP in general. What has often been interpreted as a description of the non-intervention of the state (the liberal state) in private capitalism is thus only the analysis of the autonomy of the capitalist *type of state* from the economic, which is a *prior condition* of any form of intervention by the form of state of a stage in the limits of this mode of production.

Once that has been said, a new misunderstanding arises: it is sometimes held that this intervention of the capitalist type of state in the economic is non-existent in *Capital*. This is entirely incorrect. Marx sketches in this intervention, but only implicitly, except in the passage on factory legislation. In other words, he assigns to it a definitely limited place, which is not explicitly studied in *Capital*: and this is precisely because of the specific autonomy of the instances of the CMP and because of the dominant role assumed by the economic in it, as a result of which the interventions of the other instances in the economic are only implicitly sketched in. *Capital* provides neither a study of the capitalist type of state nor a study of its interventions in the economic. Strictly speaking, it is a study of the unity of the structure of the ensemble of the CMP and of the effects of this unity on the regional structure of the economic. We do not find in it a study of the effects of the unity on the other regional structures but rather of the invariant matrix of their specific autonomy; nor, *a fortiori*, do we find a study of the effects of one regional structure on another regional structure, their respective interventions in the framework of the unity, but rather a mere implicit sketch of these interventions in the economic.

A major mistake is to conclude from *Capital*'s analysis of the matrix of the CMP and its implicit sketch of the state's intervention in the economic that it is a description of a mode of production in which the state does not intervene in the economic. This leads to seeing in *Capital* either the description of a simple stage of a capitalist formation, namely private capitalism, or the study of a mode of production 'superseded' (*dépassé*) by current transformations, to which we thus attribute the status of transition. In fact, the limits (i.e. the respective place of the economic and the political), which Marx perceives in *Capital* as characterizing the CMP, *include* both the specific non-intervention of the form of liberal state (non-intervention whose exact meaning I have shown above[12]) and the interventions of the other forms of the capitalist type of state, even of the state in the stage of state monopoly capitalism.

(iii) FORMS OF RÉGIME
AND PERIODIZAION OF THE POLITICAL

These forms of state must however be distinguished from forms of régime (a term which we shall retain in place of the ambiguous term 'forms of government'): this distinction has not been made in the Marxist classics. These various *forms of state* may appear in different *forms of régime*, whose point in common is that they belong to the same form of state. For example, the liberal state can present both the form of régime of constitutional monarchy, e.g. Britain, and that of parliamentary republic, e.g. France. The interventionist state may appear in several forms of régime, e.g. American presidential régime, British two-party

12. See p. 55 above.

parliamentary régime, continental multi-party parliamentary régime. These differences in forms of régime cannot relate directly to the periodization of a formation in stages, since this periodization concerns the relations of the ensemble of the instances: *these differences depend on the particular time-sequence and hence to the specific structures of the political level.* This relatively autonomous level possesses a time-sequence, a rhythm *of its own*, which in articulation with the time-sequence of the other instances, constitutes a historical stage of a social formation. The concrete study of a concrete political *conjuncture* depends precisely on the fusion of this double periodization, concerning respectively the political level and the ensemble of a typical stage. In making a theoretical division between political régimes within a form of state, we depend in the first place on the co-ordinates peculiar to the political level; e.g. if we take the 'power-bloc', we use those co-ordinates which concern the concrete situation of the representation of classes and fractions of class by political parties on the 'political scene'. Political régimes are seen here as variables within the limits set by the form of state of a typical stage. The relations and concrete functioning of the parties, in relation to a régime, are seen as variables within the limits set by the power bloc, corresponding to the form of state of this stage.

Some conclusions concerning the problem of periodization can thus be drawn straight away.

1. The division of a formation into stages cannot be made according to an evolutionist chronological model: it is not a question of stages succeeding one another chronologically, or of forms of an existing state following a unilinear pattern of succession. Because of the coexistence in a capitalist formation of several modes of production and of several forms of the CMP and because of the complex articulation of instances, each with its own time-sequence, the dominance in a capitalist formation of one form of the CMP over another is not expressed in a simple development. In a social formation we may find a stage dominated by monopoly capitalism and the interventionist state before a stage dominated by private capitalism and the liberal state; e.g. the period following the 'war economy' after the First World War in western countries: this period is followed by another, relatively short period, corresponding to a stage dominated by private capitalism and the liberal state. Secondly, we often note the transition from one stage to another without the intermediary of a stage which ought to have been an intermediate stage, if the theoretical law of tendential succession is seen as a path of unilinear historical succession, e.g.

the transition in Britain after the Second World War from a stage of pre-war private capitalism and liberal state to state monopoly capitalism and a 'strong state', without the intermediary of a stage of monopoly capitalism and an interventionist state: the opposite case is that of France. Thirdly, the remarks which were made with regard to types of state can also be made with regard to forms of state. A given state presents the characteristics of several forms of state, due precisely to the coexistence of several forms of the CMP in this stage of the formation. But one form of state shows dominance in the complex unity of a given state, and so attributes its distinctive concrete features to it.

2. Dislocations of relations between structures and of relations between (a) structures (the juridico-political superstructure) and (b) the field of class practices (class struggle) have already been noted. These same dislocations should also be noted with regard to forms of state. These dislocations bring it about that, for example, a stage of monopoly capitalism of a social formation can sometimes have a state dominated by the form of the liberal state: this is because although the form of state continues to constitute one element in the theoretical division of the stage, despite it, the elements and their relations present the characteristics of the *stage typical* of monopoly capitalism, to *such a degree* that the formation can be characterized as such. This dislocation may even produce a torsion of the relation between *structures* and *functions* of this state: e.g. a typically liberal state is called on to perform functions of an interventionist state. This torsion can even go so far as a *rupture* and a situation in which certain structures 'borrow' functions 'corresponding' typically to other structures: an example of this phenomenon was seen in Bismarckism, in the examination of types of state above.

It is in this context that the differences between what may be designated *functional dislocation* and *ruptural dislocation* can most clearly be established. Firstly (as opposed to a 'functionalist' conception), the dislocation between structures (the 'dysfunction') is for Marxism a constitutive element of a unity, e.g. of a typical stage of a social formation: it is the functional dislocation which moves from *homology* between structure and function to *torsion* between them. But yet this dislocation may reach a certain threshold beyond which a regional instance presents a ruptural dislocation with the unity of which it forms a part. This does not mean that this dislocation can be covered by the term 'survival', often used in Marxist popularizations; since the instance dislocated beyond the rupture threshold is not a dead branch or a parasitic excrescence of the unity. It continues to perform functions and so to constitute *one of the elements* which must be considered in the theoretical division of a formation into stages: in addition, it in fact performs *new functions*, though these are in rupture with its structures. In other words, a dislocation beyond the threshold delimited by the unity continues to function in the framework of this unity, but in a ruptural dislocation, which implies that the rupture is always determined inside the unity.[13] These dislocations can also be present in a stage between the structures and the field of class practices: these are the dislocations between forms of state and the concrete configuration of the power blocs inside the stages of a social formation.

I shall not insist further on the concrete problems of a typology of the forms of capitalist state and of the forms of régime: I shall return to them when we possess all the necessary elements and have established the characteristics of the capitalist type of state, by following the theoretical path traced out precisely above. It was necessary at this stage clearly to pose the problem of the relation of the concept of the capitalist state to the forms of state and the forms of régime, within the problematic of *periodization*.

13. I use the term *ruptural dislocation*, which is applied either to an element of the global structure or to a *regional* structure of the unity. It is important not to confuse it with the situation of rupture of the *ensemble* of the unity of a formation, which constitutes a '*ruptural unity*' – the *revolutionary situation*. In this latter case, through the unequal development of the regional structures, the *ensemble* of a formation's contradictions *fuse* at a given moment and thus call forth the transformation of the ensemble of the unity. (See L. Althusser, 'Contradiction and Over-determination' in *For Marx*.) On the other hand, in the case of a ruptural dislocation concerning a regional structure, the unity continues to function in its typical form. In other words, the revolutionary situation of a ruptural unity does not come from a *simple* contradiction between the 'base' and a superstructure which 'no longer corresponds to it'.

3. The Absolutist State, the Transitional State

(i) TYPE OF STATE AND PROBLEMS OF TRANSITION

We can make some observations here about the transition from the feudal to the capitalist type of state. Without enlarging on the question of transition periods in general, we should simply remember that they depend on a specific problematic, which cannot be reduced, in a historicist way, to the genesis of a mode of production. The theory of transition periods is not the theory of a genealogy of elements (i.e. the theory of origins), but that of the beginnings of a new structure. Transition periods present their own typical form, a specific articulation of instances due to a complex coexistence within the transitional formation of the various modes of production, *and to a continuous (often hidden) displacement* of the index of dominance from one mode of production to another.

The absolutist state, perceived here as the state of transition from feudalism to capitalism in western Europe, presents particular problems. The great majority of historians are agreed on the fact that the break between the feudal and capitalist states does not take place at the time of the appearance of that state corresponding to the consolidation of the bourgeoisie's political domination (typified by the state resulting from the French Revolution), but at the time of the appearance of the *absolutist state*. The problem thus appears to be the following: during the period of transition from feudalism to capitalism in western Europe, although the state still presents many of the characteristics of the feudal type of state, it already also presents characteristics which permit us to perceive it from the typological point of view as belonging to the capitalist type of state; and yet the period of transition is characterized by the 'consolidated' non-dominance of the CMP. It follows that the transition from feudalism to capitalism appears to be characterized here in its specificity by a non-correspondence between the political superstructure and the economic instance.

This brings to light the complexity of a problem which we are inclined to over-simplify. One conception sees in the state the appendage and the product of the dominant class. It has often maintained that the transition from feudalism to capitalism is characterized by the fact that the bourgeois class becomes *first* an economically dominant class, and only *later* becomes a politically dominant class, through the tardy institution of the bourgeois state (the paradigm case being the state resulting from the French Revolution). This is correct with respect to the dislocation between the transition state and the field of the class struggle. But it is incorrect with respect to the state superstructure in the structures, since it leads us to consider the absolutist state as a form of feudal state. Yet the absolutist transition state presents, as a general rule, important characteristics of the capitalist type of state, indicative of the break from the feudal state, though the bourgeois class is not yet strictly speaking a politically dominant class. I emphasize the point that this specific presence of the capitalist type of state in the absolutist state is not due to a political alliance between politically dominant landed nobility and economically dominant bourgeoisie. During this phase, the principal contradiction is situated precisely between the nobility and the bourgeoisie.[1]

The structure of the transition in general (of the *ideal passage*, to use Bettelheim's terms again) is specified by a *non-correspondence* between the relation of *property* and the relation of *real appropriation*.[2] In the transition from feudalism to capitalism, this non-correspondence characterizes *manufacture* which is the specific form of the transition from feudalism to capitalism. This is what Marx means when he says: 'At first capital subordinates labour on the basis of the technical conditions in which it historically finds it. It does not, therefore, change immediately the mode of production.'[3] The characteristic feature of manufacture is precisely that its mode of property is already the capitalist form of property: this relation of property establishes that the worker is 'formally subsumed' under capital, and it is expressed in a new (capitalist) form of organization of labour within the very process of manufacture. In the

1. Because of the limited character of these remarks, we shall not be able to distinguish between the various stages of the transition from feudalism to capitalism. To do this, it would be necessary to undertake a concrete analysis of concrete situations in order to locate the break between (i) the unity in a *transitional situation*, presenting certain historical conditions of the transition, which depends on a theory of the *origins* of a mode of production, and (ii) a unity of the *transitional period in the strict sense*, i.e. the period *following upon the break*, which depends on a theory of the *beginnings* of a mode of production. On these problems, see Bettelheim, op. cit.

2. See Balibar in *Reading Capital*, pp. 212 ff. and especially Bettelheim, op. cit.

3. *Capital*, Vol. I, p. 310.

labour process, on the other hand, in the real appropriation of nature by production, manufacture is in no way characterized by the separation of the worker from the means of production, but by their union: this separation enters into real appropriation only at the stage of *large-scale industry* which establishes homology between property and real appropriation.

In the transition from feudalism to capitalism in western Europe, this non-correspondence, which is the specific form of the transition, shows itself in a *chronological* dislocation between the economic structure and the forms both of the law and the political state superstructure. This chronological dislocation between the juridico-political and the economic is in fact the same as the chronological dislocation within the economic combination between the relation of property (distinct from its juridical expression) and the relation of real appropriation. Capital, as an (economic) relation of property, in reality exists *before* the 'real subsumption' of the labourer under capital[4] which, itself, implies the separation of the labourer from the means of production: this is the case both for formal juridical relations of private property and for the transition state. The juridical form of property in the transition period is a capitalist one; the institutional form of political domination (the absolutist transition state) is a form of capitalist state before the separation of the direct producer from his means of production (the *theoretical presupposition* of capitalist relations of production). In fact, during this transition, we encounter certain of the *elements* proper to capitalist relations of production, linked to the formation of the absolutist state, but still as *historical conditions* of the CMP. Thus, if we proceed to analyse the origins of the CMP, we find at the period of manufacture those 'conditions' which Marx covers in the *Grundrisse* with the sign-post terms 'bare individual' or 'free labourer'. However, since a theory of transition is not a genealogy of elements but a theory of beginnings, neither the capitalist structures of the absolutist state nor capitalist formal property can be *theoretically* related to the real existence of these historical conditions. They can be grasped only within the specificity of the transition period, i.e. within the non-correspondence described above.

An important distinction must however be made at this point. The non-correspondence which specifies the transition leads to a common characteristic of *transition in general*, namely the chronological dislocation

4. Noted by Marx in *Capital*, Vol. III, Chapter 47, 'Genesis of Capitalist Ground-Rent'.

between the relation of property and the relation of real appropriation. The economic relation of property and juridical property must always be kept distinct here, in order that we may elucidate the complex forms which this dislocation assumes in the concrete transition from one social formation to another, and thus demarcate the various *stages* of the transition. What specifies the transition from feudalism to capitalism in western Europe, is that the *advance* of property on the labour process concerns *both* economic property (the organization of labour in manufacture) *and* its institutionalized juridical expression. In other words, we are witnessing a certain correspondence, which varies from stage to stage, *between the two relations of property, dislocated, in their relation, from the labour process.* On the other hand, in the transition from capitalism to socialism, the non-correspondence and dislocation assume different forms. This relates, in the last analysis, to that all-important *difference* between the transition from feudalism to capitalism and that from capitalism to socialism, which the Marxist classics have emphasized, though without going deeply into the question: the CMP develops on the territory of private property already established inside the feudal mode of production, private property which is transformed into capitalist private property; whereas socialism establishes the taking over of the means of production by the producers themselves, a process which can in no way be introduced inside the CMP.

So this non-correspondence is important in order to explain *the characteristic presence* of capitalist structures in this transition state, which still contains several feudal traits: these structures in fact impregnate this state. In particular, vis-à-vis the relations of production, it presents the characteristics of a state possessing the specific autonomy of the capitalist state, while the theoretical presuppositions of this autonomy (the separation of the direct producer from the means of production) are not yet actually realized. At the same time, vis-à-vis the social relations of production, it presents the characteristics of a state related to the capitalist isolation of these relations, while the presuppositions of this effect of isolation, *in its capitalist form*, do not yet exist in reality.

It is also possible to decipher this non-correspondence from the function of the transition state: this is the import of Marx's analyses of primary accumulation of capital, although they are intended to present a genealogy of elements rather than a theory of transition. The function of the absolutist state is precisely not to operate within the limits fixed by an *already given* mode of production, *but to produce not-yet-given relations* of production (i.e. capitalist relations) and to put an end to feudal relations of production: its function is to *transform* and to *fix* the limits of the mode of production. The function of this transition state during primary accumulation depends on the specific effectiveness of the political in the initial stage of transition. Thus the degrees and the forms of this intervention of the absolutist state depend chiefly on the concrete existence of the historical conditions of capitalism in the various social formations.

(ii) THE ABSOLUTIST STATE – THE CAPITALIST STATE

In western Europe, the birth of the absolutist state varies according to the uneven development of the various national ensembles, but according to the periodization of the feudal system acknowledged by the historians, it is situated during the period of 'major crisis' of feudalism in the fourteenth and fifteenth centuries. This crisis is characterized by the large-scale collapse of feudal agriculture, by the appearance of manufacturing enterprises, by the development of international commerce, by a decline of population, etc. The absolutist state is strengthened during the new period of expansion, stretching from the middle of the fifteenth century to the middle of the seventeenth century, which creates a 'crisis of the ensemble' of feudal relations of production and indicates (according to Marx) the 'beginning of the capitalist era'.[5] It can be located in an embryonic form in the Italian principalities of the Quattrocento, is found again in France under Louis XIII and Richelieu, and in Spain under the Catholic monarchs Ferdinand and Isabella.[6] In England, because of its different concrete situation, the transition from the feudal to the capitalist state seems to be both more tardy and more direct, allowing only a

5. See M. Dobb and E. Hobsbawm, 'Du féodalisme au capitalisme' in *Recherches internationales à la lumière du marxisme: Le féodalisme*, Paris, 1969, and Paul M. Sweezy, H. K. Takahasi, Maurice Dobb, Christopher Hill, Rodney Hilton, *The Transition from Feudalism to Capitalism: a Symposium*, New York, 1967.

6. Germany is a special case. In fact Germany *never passed* through the absolutist state, as analysed here, despite appearances. Up to and including Bismarck's state, feudal structures (e.g. absence of central power, dissemination of power, etc.) have dominance. It is true that Engels sometimes presents Bismarckism as being *at once* an 'absolutist state' *and* a form of 'Bonapartism' (*The Housing Question*, Part II, § 2). But, as we shall see later, this is due to the fact that Engels's only conception of the relative autonomy of the state is that of an equilibrium between the forces of the classes present.

precarious existence to the absolutist state. Its case resembles that of the Netherlands.[7]

The absolutist state is characterized by the fact that the holder of state power, normally a monarch, concentrates in his hands a power which is not controllable by the other institutions and whose exercise is not curbed by any *limiting law*, whether this be a law of the positive or natural/divine order: the holder of power is *legibus solutus*. In the feudal type of state, state power is limited both by *divine law* (the state being considered as the manifestation of cosmic/divine order) and by the *privileges* of the various medieval *estates*, in that feudal ties mark out a hierarchy of exclusive powers of those in fealty over the land which they own and over the men tied to that land. In contrast to this, the absolutist state appears as a *strongly* centralized state. As the various assemblies held by these *estates* (assemblies whose activity limited the exercise of central power by ·estates general, diets, etc.) are threatened, the state makes its appearance as a centralized institution, as the *source of all* 'political' *power* inside a *territorial-national* domain. It is in this way that the notion of *state sovereignty* gradually takes shape: it expresses the *exclusive, unique*, institutionalized and strictly *public* dominance over a territorial-national ensemble and the effective exercise of central power without the 'extra-political' restrictions of juridical, ecclesiastical or moral order which characterized the feudal state. This sovereignty of the state is also demonstrated in external relations and empowers the monarch to be sole arbiter in relations with other nations: an innovation, when we remember for instance the role held by the Church in relations between feudal states. in short, the fundamental characteristic of the absolutist state is that it represents the strictly political unity of a centralized power over a national ensemble. It contrasts with the division and parcelling out of power into territorial domains, constituting a parallel system of water-tight economico-political cells, related in a hierarchy of exclusive and superimposed powers.

7. On the birth of the modern state in general and on the absolutist state, see: O. Hintze, *Staat und Verfassung*, 1962, pp. 470–96; R. M. MacIver, *The Modern State*, 1926; F. Oppenheimer, *The State: its History and Development viewed Sociologically*, 1914; Kienast, 'Die Anfänge der europäischen Staats-systems im späteren Mittelalter' in *Historische Zeitschrift*, 153 (1936), pp. 229 ff.; R. Mousnier, *Les XVIe. et XVIIe. siècles*, 1954, and 'Quelques problèmes concernant la monarchie absolue' in *Xe Congrès international des sciences historiques*, Vol. 4; G. Lefebvre, 'Le despotisme éclairé' in *Annales historiques de la Révolution Française*, No. 21, 1949. See also the articles in *The New Cambridge Modern History*.

The absolutist state thus presents an autonomy relative to the economic instance. Feudal ties, which in the feudal state are set in the religious key, are replaced by 'strictly political' ties. The central power, whose public character is separated from the sphere of the private, is apparently freed from 'extra-political', religious and moral restrictions and is exercised in an 'absolute' fashion over a 'national/popular' ensemble: thus the barriers to the central power which were constituted by the medieval states collapse. We can see the formation of the concepts of 'people' and 'nation' as constitutive principles of a state which is held to represent the 'general interest'.

From another point of view, we are witnessing a process in which agents are institutionally fixed on the mode of the private as 'subjects of the state'. While it is true that the central and sovereign power is held not to be limited by any 'law', in the feudal sense of the term, it is equally true that a replacement of *medieval privileges* (written and customary) by a *written juridical system* can be dated from the emergence of this power. These are the rules of 'public' law, which already at this stage present the characteristic abstraction, generality and formality of the modern juridical system and which regulate the relations of the subjects of the state to the central power. These subjects are fixed, in the political institutions of the state, on the mode of the private; the central power often respects these laws and only proceeds cautiously to a direct intervention in the private sphere.

The sovereignty of the state, reflected in the works of Bodin, appears to be linked to the problem of the unity of 'strictly political' power: a power which is seen as representing the unity of the subjects of the state in the public sphere. The state is held to embody the general public interest – a new theme on the agenda:[8] this is the essential principle of the concept of *reasons of state*.[9] This concept covers precisely the independence of a state power, unconstrained by any extra-political limit, *inasmuch as* it is the power which represents the general interest. We are witnessing the first formation of the theory of the social contract: in its subsequent form, as elaborated in the eighteenth century, it can be seen as the theoretical expression of the autonomization of the political and economic instances. When it first appeared, the theoretical basis of the

8. See e.g. G. Ritter, *Die Neugestaltung Europas in XVI. Jahrhundert*, pp. 19 ff., Berlin, 1950.

9. cf. F. Meinecke, *Die Idee der Staatsräson in der neueren Geschichte*, 1924 (English translation, *Machiavellism*, London, 1957).

social contract was to be found in the jurists, educated in the universities founded from the thirteenth century onwards. These theorists returned to the sources of the theory of *public contract* (*lex regiae*) of the later Roman Empire, which was embodied in the texts of the Church Fathers and in canon law. On this they laid the foundations of the theory of the *pact of political domination*. Absolute power is founded on the contract by which the 'governed', in their private 'isolation', unite to form a body politic by submitting in this very act to the public power of the 'government'. The parallel problem of the nation seems to hold a central place in the formation of the absolutist state, a sovereign state both inside and outside its 'natural frontiers'.[10]

The important role played by the *army* and the *bureaucracy* in the formation of the *apparatus of the absolutist state* is well known: there have been numerous attempts to show that the importance of this role refutes the Marxist conception of the relations which exist between the state and a determinate mode of production. In fact, in order to analyse this role, we must start from the particular functions of the army and bureaucracy in the period of transition from feudalism to capitalism: i.e. from the *structures* of the absolutist state, which establish the co-ordinates defining the function of the army and bureaucracy and which *assign to them their role in the apparatus of the absolutist state*. The place of the absolutist state's army in the apparatus is determined by the central power. This power maintains an army of its own: military service is no longer founded on the ties of the feudal system, but on a mercenary army in the service of a political power relatively free from the restrictions of feudal ties.[11] This mercenary army, in which the infantry, composed of many social classes (as opposed to the cavalry, composed of the nobility) holds the chief role, can sometimes assume the character of a popular army of a state representing the unity of the people: this is an important element in Machiavelli's analyses.

The situation is yet more obvious concerning the bureaucracy: its function can be traced from many co-ordinates of the period of transition. Its role in the state apparatus is, however, determined by the capitalist *structures* of the absolutist state: this is the birth of bureaucracy in the

10. See H. Hauser, *La modernité du XVIe siècle*, Paris, 1930; and E. Chabod, 'Y a-t-il un État de la Renaissance?' in *Actes du Colloque sur la Renaissance organisé par la société d'histoire moderne*, 1958.

11. See J. Van Doorn, 'The Officer Corps: A fusion of profession and organization' in *European Journal of Sociology*, VI, 1965, pp. 262 ff.

modern sense of the term.[12] The various public offices are no longer directly tied to the quality of their holders as members of 'caste' classes, but gradually assume the character of *political functions* of the state. The content of the jurisdiction of these real organs of power no longer depends on their economico-political ties with a part of the area under jurisdiction, but lies in their exercise of state power. So the exercise of these functions no longer appears as a realization of the economic and political interests of their holders, but as an exercise of the functions of the state representing the general interest. Indeed in the case, e.g. of the *noblesse de robe*, the holder even gains class-membership through exercising this function.[13] The relation between this bureaucracy-function and the emergence of the 'general interest' represented by the absolutist state has been indicated by Weber, in his analyses of the type of rational-legal authority which he sees as characterizing the modern state.

This chronological dislocation between the absolutist state and the

12. See e.g. Santoro, *Gli offici del dominio sforzesco (1450–1500)*, 1948; R. Mousnier, *La vénalité des offices sous Henri IV et Louis XIII*, 1946; K. W. Swart, *Sale of offices in the Seventeenth Century*, 1949. I shall return to Weber's analyses of this question in Part V.

13. One remark must be made here. The dislocation between the absolutist state and the economic instance raises the problem of the way in which the absolutist state functions in favour of the CMP, which is not yet dominant. This problem can neither be explained *directly* as a 'political' *co-domination* or *alliance* of the bourgeois and the landed nobility, nor can it be explained *directly* as a take-over by the bourgeoisie of the absolutist state apparatus. While it is true that the 'summits' of the administration and the bourgeoisie in France were held under the Ancien Régime by the *noblesse de robe*, it must not be forgotten that, as Mathiez showed, they functioned as a class in a way that brought them close to the landed nobility. In his articles in *The New York Daily Tribune*, and particularly in his texts on the Whigs, Marx showed with unparalleled clarity that in Britain the summits of the state apparatus were occupied by a fraction of the landed nobility. The same is true, according to Marx, of Spain. Thus the way that the absolutist state functions in favour of the CMP is not due *directly* either to the position of the bourgeoisie in the field of the class struggle or to the class membership of the state apparatus. We must also take into account the structures of the absolutist state and their role in the transition period. Furthermore, it is the absolutist state's relative autonomy in its structures from the economic instance which allows the state apparatus to function in a way that is autonomous from, indeed contrary to, its class membership. In short, the relation between the bourgeoisie's still unconsolidated economic domination (I am talking exclusively of *economic* domination) and the functioning of the absolutist state can be established only by means of an elucidation of a whole series of dislocations, firstly between the various instances and secondly between (i) the instances and (ii) the field of the class struggle.

economic instance in the period of transition from feudalism to capitalism, related to the non-correspondence indicated above, can be *explained* by the functions of the state during primary accumulation of capital. In fact, these functions of the state (expropriating small landowners, financing, supplying funds for starting industrialization, attacking seigneurial power, breaking down commercial barriers within the national boundaries, etc.) *can be performed only by a state with a capitalist character*, by a centralized public power of a strictly political character. These are precisely its 'national/popular' institutions which, to a large extent, permit it to function against the interest of the nobility, at a time when it still cannot *clearly rely* on the bourgeoisie. This role of the 'force' of the state in favour of the 'emergent bourgeoisie', as Marx describes it, can only be analysed as the *intervention* of the absolutist transition state. In other words, it is not any state which could have had this role of 'force' in fixing the limits of a not-yet-given mode of production. The transition, which assigns these functions to the state, allows them to be performed only by a state with a capitalist character.

I shall conclude this section with a last remark on the relation of this transition state to the class struggle. Can the characteristic autonomy of the absolutist state relative both to the economic instance and to the field of the class struggle, which was precisely what allowed it to function in favour of primary accumulation of capital, be related purely and simply to an equilibrium of forces (as Engels says) between the nobility and the bourgeoisie? We shall see later that the general explanatory schema in which the relative autonomy of the state is related to an 'equilibrium' between the social forces present cannot provide an exhaustive account of a state presenting pronounced capitalist features. In particular, the absolutist transition state does not correspond (not at least at every stage of the transition) to an equilibrium of forces between the politically dominant nobility and the economically dominant bourgeoisie: the bourgeoisie's economic dominance becomes established only gradually, and only in exceptional circumstances does it manage to outweigh the political dominance of the nobility, e.g. in France towards the end of the Ancien Régime.[14] The fact that, during these stages, the principal aspect of the contradiction, and even the principal contradiction are sometimes displaced and operate not between the bourgeoisie and the landed nobility, but between the latter and the independent small-scale producers, does not automatically indicate that there is an equilibrium of forces between

14. See M. Dobb, *Studies in the Development of Capitalism*, London, 1963, pp. 83 ff.

these two classes. The class alliance between the nobility and the bourgeoisie is frequently marked by a very clear predominance of the nobility. The 'relative autonomy' of the absolutist state is due both to its capitalist character and its function in the transition period and also to its *complex* relation to the field of the class struggle.

Thus, from the point of view of the state, the initial stage of transition from feudalism to capitalism involves a state with pronounced capitalist features, while the bourgeoisie is not the politically dominant class and often not even the economically dominant class: this *initial* stage rarely corresponds to an equilibrium of forces between the bourgeoisie and the nobility. After the bourgeoisie's accession to political power, which does not necessarily involve its political hegemony, the transition continues up to the consolidation of the CMP and up to the beginning of the phase of expanded reproduction: the first stage of this phase corresponds (always through the medium of uneven developments) to the liberal state found in western Europe in the second half of the nineteenth century.[15]

15. We must therefore distinguish clearly between 'Bonapartism', which is not dependent on the transition phase strictly speaking, and absolutist monarchy. I note this because Engels sometimes tends to short-circuit, in historical terms, the theoretical difference between the two phenomena (particularly in *The Housing Question*, Part II, § 2), by somehow seeing in Bonapartism the continuation of the absolutist state. This follows from the two facts indicated above: (a) in Bismarckism, Engels tends to see a Bonapartist phenomenon. (b) He sees in Bismarckism a function similar to that of the absolutist state, and so assimilates it to that state. This is doubly incorrect: (i) Bismarckism is not a transitory form of state, if we continue to use the term *transition* in its strict sense; and (ii) the beginnings of Bismarckism are characterized by a feudal 'type' of state which, however (and herein lies the whole problem), has a side similar to that of the capitalist transition state. This double incorrectness allows him to see in Bonapartism, which he assimilates to Bismarckism, a continuation of the absolutist state, Bismarckism being equated with the absolutist state.

4. The Models of
the Bourgeois Revolution

INTRODUCTION

I have just brought to light some general *tendential* features of the transition from feudalism to capitalism in western Europe, while indicating that this transition shows particular features according to the national ensembles under consideration: we can now begin to identify these national ensembles with concrete social formations. One important problem which arises is: can we speak of a *typical model* of the 'bourgeois revolution'? Contrary to a widespread view which takes the French Revolution as the *example* of the bourgeois revolution, I shall examine the particular cases of Britain, France and Prussia in order to show that such a 'model' does not exist. In fact, though the transition in general (*the ideal passage*) presents common features, related to a theoretical tendential form, the problem of the bourgeois revolution, when we relate it to the concrete form assumed by the transition, depends on the conjuncture of a formation in its historical individuality, original in every case. It should be added that the problematic of models of the bourgeois revolution can only be located from the perspective of dislocations and uneven developments (noted above) between two systems of relations between dislocations: that of structures and that of the field of the class struggle.

In the following sections, I shall follow, but at the same time carry through, *the lines which emerge from Marx and Engels's political analyses*. I shall give no references here, since I am now synthesizing their exact statements which I analyse elsewhere in the book.

(i) THE BRITISH CASE

In Britain, the two dates 1640 and 1688 mark the bourgeois revolution, but 1688 appears as a turning-point in the revolutionary process begun in 1640. This process clearly poses the problem of the relations between industry and agriculture; this is a problem which has often been underestimated as a result of misinterpretations of Marx's theoretical analyses of the genesis of ground-rent in *Capital*, misinterpretations which have taken them to be simple historical analyses. The class character of this revolutionary process, particularly of the 1640 revolution, is that it clearly marks the beginning of the process of the establishment of the CMP through the capitalization of ground rent.[1] This is a characteristic case in which the concrete functioning of landed proprietors can be established. The 1640 revolution and its turning-point in 1688 mark the start of the transformation of part of the class of the feudal nobility into a capitalist class. This revolution, which is a bourgeois revolution in the strict sense of the term, appears to be of ambiguous character: it has the form of a principal contradiction between fractions of the feudal nobility, since although the commercial bourgeoisie is already in existence, it plays only a secondary role. The ambiguity in this case arises from the character of the class which directs the revolutionary process: leadership passes from the feudal nobility to the bourgeoisie, which becomes the nucleus of the industrial bourgeoisie as the process of the capitalization of ground-rent proceeds.

Since the commercial bourgeoisie was insufficiently developed and the industrial bourgeoisie was almost non-existent, neither could take over the leadership of the process. This revolution might therefore appear *premature*, when regarded from an exclusively political point of view. But if we consider the ensemble of the relations of the formation, the revolution happened *at the right time*, since it made it possible to dispose of the problem of the dominance of the CMP over the other modes in agriculture; i.e., to liquidate small-scale production. In fact, the revolution in Britain impressed a particularly swift and radical rhythm on the process of the dominance of the CMP in the countryside, i.e. on the process of dissolution and destruction of the patriarchal mode of production. In the transition from feudalism to capitalism in Britain, this problem could be solved only by initiating the revolutionary process in an apparently *impure* form under the leadership of a fraction of the landowning bourgeoisie which was already on the way to establishing its independence from the feudal nobility. In other words, the revolutionary process had to be initiated on the political plane and under the leadership of a fraction which, politically speaking, was still a fraction of the nobility.[2] In

1. See M. Dobb, *Studies in the Development of Capitalism*, 1963, pp. 177 ff.; and P. Anderson, 'Origins of the present crisis' in *New Left Review* 23, January/February 1964 and E. P. Thompson, *The Making of the English Working Class*, London, 1963.

2. This is what Lenin designated as *one of the ways* in which the CMP is established in the countryside under the political leadership of the aristocracy or bourgeoisie; it is

Bismarck's Prussia, the process of establishing the dominance of the CMP also began in order to profit a fraction of the nobility, which suggests a formal similarity to the case in Britain. But in Prussia, the fraction had not reached the turning-point of its passage into the bourgeoisie by means of ground-rent. And while in Britain the large-scale ownership of ground-rent was attained by a fraction of the nobility which was to become the nucleus of the industrial bourgeoisie, in France it was attained by an already existing bourgeoisie which expropriated the aristocracy.

In Britain, the revolution's most important effect on relations of production was the constitution of a capitalist agriculture. This consisted of three elements: (i) large-scale owners of ground-rent, an infinitesimal minority which monopolized the ownership of land; (ii) tenant-farmers; and (iii) agricultural workers, who constituted the immense majority. It is clear that from now on there are no feudal tenants (of whom traces can be found in East Prussia), no medium landowners and, above all, no small landowners. That is to say, there are no small-holding peasants of the sort who were the typical product of the French Revolution and who made their mark on all of France's subsequent development. The British 'peasantry' as a social force will henceforth play no part in its country's political development. This particular process in which the dominance of the CMP was established by destroying the possibility of small-scale agricultural production gave the commercial, industrial and, later, financial bourgeoisie an opportunity for an exceptional development. But these results were not confined to the countryside: small-scale production in general lost its opportunity for good and all, and this includes the petty bourgeoisie, which has never been a social force in Britain and which has never made its bow on the political stage by an open action such as forming a party of its own.

However, the establishment of this open and particularly successful dominance of the CMP is reflected at the political level in a manner which might appear paradoxical if we failed to take into account the peculiar nature of the process in Britain and its resultant dislocations. The 1640 revolution laid the foundations for the bourgeoisie's political domination

---

the way of transition from feudalism to capitalism, initiated principally by means of the large-scale ownership of ground-rent. The second way is the *American way*, in which the absence of feudalism made it possible to initiate the process by means of small or medium land ownership. See 'The Agrarian Programme of Social Democracy in the First Russian Revolution, 1905–7', *Collected Works*, Vol. 13, pp. 217–431. On the theoretical question of the big landowners, see p. 231 below.

but it did not give it political power. The bourgeoisie's economic domination (and I mean here the commercial bourgeoisie and the owners of ground-rent) developed at the start under the political domination of the landed nobility: and in this respect, exactly the same happened in France *before* the revolution. Afterwards, by a number of steps and as a result of a number of turning-points, the commercial and ground-rent owning bourgeoisie obtained power under the hegemony of the nobility; and then as a result of the 1832 Reform Act, it obtained hegemony of the power bloc. However, the ensemble of the process meant that the bourgeoisie first gained an appearance on the political scene by obtaining power through the intermediary of the nobility, who represented the owners of ground-rent and the commercial bourgeoisie. Later on, when the bourgeoisie obtained hegemony and the industrial and financial bourgeoisie began to predominate, it was represented by the Whigs, the owners of ground-rent who acted as the bourgeoisie's intermediary. As a result of this process, the Whigs functioned for a long time as an autonomous fraction of the bourgeoisie, i.e. as a social force. In this way, the very hegemony of the industrial and financial bourgeoisie on the political scene continued to be hidden; and this has posed numerous problems for historians of the social formation in Britain.

The peculiarities on the plane of the juridico-political instance are equally striking. The 1640 revolution transformed the *juridical status of property* and the functioning of the monarchy, but it left the feudal type dominant over the capitalist type in the state. This is clear from the importance attributed to the House of Lords, the importance of local magistrates as centres of local power, etc. This indicates a dislocation between *the juridical system and the state*, which is frequently encountered in the transition from feudalism to capitalism. This dislocation, in which the capitalist legal system is prior to the state, reveals itself in the fact that the British legal system, unlike the Continental systems, will continue to be unwritten and uncodified. Further, the dominance of the feudal type in the state continues even after the bourgeoisie have obtained political power, providing a characteristic example of the dislocation between the state's structures and its political power. This dislocation exists in the continuity of feudal characteristics, even after the bourgeoisie has obtained hegemony: and it also combines with the continued functioning of the owners of ground-rent as a social force and with the masked hegemony of the bourgeoisie. Unlike France, the 'heights' of the state apparatus itself (the army and administration) continue to show a class membership of the nobility. A relative change takes place later on, to the profit of the owners of ground-rent.

As a result of the peculiarity of the process, the actual functions of the state,[3] in performing its role to the profit of the large-scale landowners in private accumulation, can exactly be fulfilled by means of the dominance of feudal structures; there is then no need for it to pass through the stage of the absolutist state. Unlike France, we could even say that the vital part of this accumulation happens *after* the revolution; and anyway, its economic function is limited to its general function of accumulation. The transition did not necessitate a subsequent intervention by the state into the process of industrialization: this, on the other hand, was the case in France (with the absolutist state) and in Prussia (with the Bismarckian state). In the last stage of its transition, the British state, with its feudal and capitalist structures in equilibrium, was replaced by the form of the liberal state whose non-intervention in the economic is particularly pronounced. But this allowed feudal characteristics to continue late into the liberal form of the British state. In France, on the other hand, the liberal state intervenes in a far more important way into the economic, to the profit of the bourgeoisie: but these interventions are the successors of those of the absolutist state. Moreover, the peculiar functioning of the state, combined with the destruction of the small-holding peasants' and the petty bourgeoisie's small-scale production, brought it about that the British state apparatus (the army and the administrative bureaucracy) never took on the role which it was later to play in France and Germany: and this was so, despite its class membership.

Some conclusions can now be drawn. The British revolution was *particularly successful* in that it allows the open dominance of the CMP over the other modes of production in the social formation. This open dominance brings it about that the matrix of this mode of production decisively permeates this formation. In the historical individuality of this formation, this domination is expressed in the fact that up to the stage of monopoly state capitalism, the economic instance almost constantly possesses (i) determination in the last instance, and (ii) the dominant role. This, in turn, is expressed in the dominance of economic power over political power: in the case of the decentration of the places of economic and political domination held by different classes or fractions, those which occupy the place of economic determination are those which in the final

3. See E. Hobsbawm, *The Age of Revolution*, op. cit., pp. 175 ff., 192 ff.; M. Dobb, op. cit., pp. 25 ff.

analysis appear as hegemonic classes or fractions. On the political plane, the success of this revolutionary process in this formation's conjuncture means that it operates at first for the benefit of the nobility. In obtaining political power and later in obtaining hegemony of the power bloc, the bourgeoisie is tardy and operates in a masked manner. The same is true of the transformation of the state's structures and the state apparatus, in their dislocations from the economic instance and from the field of the class struggle (i.e. state power). The result of all this is that the success of the revolution in Britain is characteristically masked and appears to have miscarried on the political plane.

(ii) THE FRENCH CASE

The French Revolution has often been presented as *the example* of a 'typically' successful bourgeois revolution. On this theory, the revolution happened at the moment when the particular transition produced by the absolutist state put the commercial and industrial bourgeoisie in a position where they could take over the leadership of the process; i.e. it occurred at the moment when feudal society had deliberately matured all its possibilities within itself. According to this, the revolution had the following results: (i) the bourgeoisie openly obtained political power; (ii) the state's structures were radically transformed, which was to the benefit of the bourgeoisie, since the state which emerged from the revolution was a state of the capitalist 'type'; and (iii) Jacobinism, a 'typically' bourgeois political ideology, dominated the French formation. In other words, the bourgeoisie as the subject of history was able to expand its essence fully on the political plane in France. Amongst Marxist theorists, this theory has been remarkably strong: Gramsci was by no means its last perpetrator; and its success in the theory of the working class is exceptionally suspect.[4]

The subject is extremely broad, and so I shall merely give sufficient indications to show that this interpretation is *mythical*.

1. What is the truth about the CMP establishing dominance over the

4. It is also interesting to see how the various political currents of the working-class movement have interpreted the French Revolution: Trotsky's view is undoubtedly one of the most revealing. In the rest of this section, I refer the reader to the classic works, such as those of Mathiez and Lefebvre, and also to the history by Albert Soboul, *Précis d'histoire de la Révolution Française*, Paris, 1962 (English translation, *The French Revolution*, London, 1973 [forthcoming]).

other modes? In fact, globally this was much less open and decisive in France than it was in Britain or in Germany where under Bismarck the Prussian revolution was managed *from above*. Above all, this dominance radically failed to cut the knot which in this transition concentrated the relation between the CMP and the other modes of production in the relations of production. It was unable to cut the thread of small-scale production in France; in fact the French Revolution laid a firm foundation for small-scale production, both in agriculture and in the petty bourgeoisie. (i) *Agriculture (the peasants)*: because of the absolutist state and the role of the nobility, and therefore (as it were) because of the non-existence of a premature revolution during the phase of primitive accumulation, the process of establishing the CMP in the ensemble of the formation was not initiated by the ground-rent landowners. Rather it was initiated by the commercial and industrial bourgeoisie which, with the aim of taking over large-scale landed property by expropriating the nobility, sought to use the 'peasantry' as a support against this nobility. As a corollary, the decisive result of the revolution in agriculture is not the expropriation of agricultural producers, but the attribution of a status of ownership to and an expansion of small-scale agricultural exploitation. This was confirmed by the Jacobin dictatorship after the peasant revolt against feudal agricultural structures.[5] From this results the typically French case of the small-holding peasants, who, for a long time in the future, continue to play a very important role on the political scene. (ii) *The petty bourgeoisie*: the remarkable victory of small-scale production is equally clear in the case of the petty bourgeoisie. This sector of the bourgeoisie developed side by side with the stealthy advance of the commercial and industrial bourgeoisie in the absolutist noble state and was to establish itself with a firm base as a result of the policy of the Convention. This petty bourgeoisie did not (like its German counterpart) throw in its lot with capital from the start: while it opted for the bourgeoisie in 1848, it took the side of the proletariat during the Paris Commune. It remains nonetheless an extremely important social force in France, as we can see from the phenomenon of radicalism.

The result of all this was, as Hobsbawm remarks, that the economic development of the nineteenth century

. . . contains one *gigantic paradox*: France. On paper, no country should have advanced more rapidly. It possessed institutions ideally suited to capitalist

5. See G. Lefebvre, *Questions agraires au temps de la terreur*, Paris, 1932.

development. . . . Yet in fact French economic development at the base was distinctly slower than that of other countries . . . This was because . . . the capitalist part of the French economy was a superstructure erected on the immovable base of the peasantry and petty bourgeoisie. . . .[6]

This situation was subsequently protracted in various forms: e.g. (i) the rhythm of technological development, the rhythm of the process of capitalist concentration, which is much slower in France than in either Britain or Germany; and (ii) the peculiar manner in which small- and medium-scale enterprises continue to operate.

2. What is the truth about political power? The French bourgeoisie did of course obtain political power, unlike their equivalents in Britain, *but at what a price*! It obtained it only at the price of depending widely on the small-scale peasantry and the petty bourgeoisie and even sometimes on the manufacturing workers, found mainly amongst the Parisian *sans-culottes*.[7] The bourgeoisie obtained power openly this time, but only in so far as it fairly clearly eliminated the nobility. In fact, everything happened as if the French Revolution had failed to coincide with itself, as if it were simultaneously *early* and *late* for itself; late, in that it failed to smother small-scale production at birth; early, in that it had to drop back in order to win back the small-scale producers who had been polarized around the proletariat which was now in process of being constituted. The petty bourgeoisie and the small-holding peasants were related to the bourgeoisie by a whole range of relations, ranging from antagonistic contradiction to support or even alliance. This prevented the French bourgeoisie from forming a state alliance with the nobility, as was the case in Britain and, later, in Prussia. Because of the presence of these classes, any alliance with the aristocracy (as was attempted in fact under Charles X) could only have been *a highly retrograde step*, since it would not only have contradicted the most elementary interests of the bourgeoisie, but it would also have completely disregarded those classes which would have checked such a retrogression in order to maintain the *status quo*. The particular forms taken on by the contradiction between the bourgeoisie and these classes led straight to the historical phenomena of the First and Second Empires. There we are faced with those particular forms of the capitalist state in which the bourgeoisie apparently

6. E. Hobsbawm, op. cit., pp. 177 ff.

7. Labrousse and Soboul have shown (i) against Mathiez, that Robespierre *was led* to 'depend' on the small-scale producers; and (ii) against Guérin, that the industrial proletariat did not function as a social force during the revolution.

resigns its political power to benefit a state apparatus which manages public business by depending on the small-holding peasants and the petty bourgeoisie.

Thus, on the political level, this 'model' revolution creates an almost constant situation of *crisis* in the bourgeoisie's political power. This produced a constant disequilibrium (until 1848) between the bourgeoisie and (i) the nobility, and (ii) the small-scale producers; and it thus made the bourgeoisie incapable of consolidating its hegemony. In 1848, the bourgeoisie finally rid itself of the nobility and turned towards the small-scale producers; and after the fall of Louis Bonaparte, it made an effort to stabilize its position; *but it was much too late*. For the industrial proletariat, which had emerged in 1848, was waiting for it at the turning-point of the Commune in 1870. This event led the bourgeoisie to confirm its dependence on the small-holding peasantry by its subsequent agricultural policy.

3. What is the truth about the 'model' character of the French Revolution on the plane of the juridico-political instance of the state? Ought we to estimate its success in the fact that (unlike the British Revolution) it founded a typical capitalist state? But this is untrue. It is true that the state resulting from the revolution was more successful than the British state in ridding itself of feudal characteristics. The conception of the state as 'typically' capitalist is the result of superficial observations on (i) the establishment of universal suffrage after the rising of August 1792 and on (ii) the institutional policy of the Montagne Convention, considered as a prefiguration of the capitalist state. But to see matters in this way is to make the mistake of neglecting the division of a formation into phases and stages and the distinction between the capitalist *type* of a state and the *forms of state* corresponding to these phases and stages; it is to make the mistake of considering a theoretical concept (the capitalist state) to be something directly identifiable with social reality as its historical essence. In fact, the state in question is considerably in advance of the transition stage in which it is located. In this sense, we can rigorously declare that this is not the state of a bourgeois revolution which is politically successful at this moment and in this conjuncture, but rather the state of a bourgeois revolution which is politically *held in check*. At this precise moment it is not in fact the state of a hegemonic bourgeoisie, but that of the peasantry and the petty-bourgeoisie, as Tocqueville rightly saw. This state anyway failed to last. In fact, the state of the First and Second Empires is the state of the bourgeoisie, a bourgeoisie which is now

breathless to catch up with the peasantry and the petty-bourgeoisie and to put the machine into reverse against the developing proletariat; it continues to bear the marks of the ambiguous support of the small-scale producers.

Unlike the situation in Britain, the French situation involves a frequent and lasting reflection of the dominance of the CMP in *the dominant role of the state instance.*

Firstly, the state's economic functions already existed in the absolutist state and were by no means confined to primary accumulation; they gained new life during the Jacobin dictatorship and were taken up again during the two Empires, especially that of Louis Bonaparte; and they even continue in the context of the French liberal state of the Third Republic, where they are much more important than the British liberal state.

Secondly, because of the role played by the peasantry and the petty bourgeoisie as social forces, and by the working class (which establishes itself on the political scene in a particular fashion), the strictly political function of the state in the class struggle is much more important than in Britain. Thus this second phenomenon (that of the state's strictly political function) has some bearing on the constant political crisis from which the bourgeoisie's particular contradiction with the peasantry and petty bourgeoisie stems. Between these two latter classes the working class has been able to carve its path across easy terrain, a fact which explains the *ambiguous* relations which it has always had with these two classes as well as the unique snare (to be considered later) into which the French working class has always been led.

It is precisely from this dominant role of the state instance in France, combined with the particular presence of various classes on the political scene, that Engels derives his conception of France as the most representative country in Europe, from the political point of view (*The Eighteenth Brumaire*, Preface to the third edition). But he is wrong in thinking that this results from the fact that the bourgeois 'political' revolution was typically successful there. On the contrary, his conception relates strictly to the fact of its *failure*: the resultant dominant role of the juridico-political instance makes France a country in which this instance can most suitably be studied as it functions relative to the various classes thrown on to the political stage.

Finally, this particular role of the state combined with the frequen functioning of the small-holding peasantry and the petty bourgeoisie a social forces explains both the political importance attached to the state apparatus (the army and the administrative bureaucracy) and to its class membership, bourgeois and petty-bourgeois. It cannot be over-emphasized that this French state apparatus which is so often considered to be the last word in the 'typical' capitalist state is the result of the French bourgeoisie's political failures rather than of its political successes.

4. Finally, what is the truth about the political ideology of the French bourgeoisie? This has frequently been contrasted with the impurity of the British bourgeoisie's ideology, tainted with numerous aristocratic characteristics. It has been presented as the 'typical' though contradictory ideology of the bourgeoisie, in short as the ideology of *Jacobinism*. This interpretation belongs to an over-politicizing historicist conception of ideologies which relates the unity of the dominant ideology in a formation to its level of purity as the product of the dominant class-subject. But precision is necessary here. It is true of the universe of bourgeois political ideology, in which the citizens' formal political liberty and equality vis-à-vis a state founded on the general interest of the people-nation is extolled. But while this is true of bourgeois political ideology, it is not entirely true of Jacobinism. It is one aspect of Jacobin ideology from Robespierre to Saint-Just, but only, as it were, its bourgeois aspect. It is however a complete misunderstanding of Jacobinism not to recognize that it has a *particular social content*, combined with the ideological phenomenon of 'sans-culottism'. This social content is present, for instance, in an obscure form in Saint-Just's demands for *social* equality (equality of opportunity), his attacks on 'wealth' and his orations on the social 'happiness' of the citizens.

Marxist authors, and Gramsci above all, have often noted this social content of Jacobinism; but it is frequently interpreted from a historicist viewpoint, as the *contradiction which is somehow immanent* in the 'typical' political ideology of the *bourgeoisie-subject*. On this interpretation, the *social* content of Jacobinism is the maggot hidden in the fruit of the 'pure' *political* ideology of the bourgeoisie: it is its other side, the hidden but true seed of that social universalism to be realized by the proletariat when they set Jacobinism back on its feet. But it is important not to conceal the repercussions of this interpretation according to which (a) *bourgeois political democracy* already contains within itself *proletarian social democracy*; (b) the final and consistent conclusions to be drawn from the very principles of political democracy lead to social democracy; and (c) social democracy, in the form of the social content of Jacobinism, is the authentic vocation of the working class. This is, of course, the young Marx's conception. But it is also found in the Italian Marxist school, in particular in della Volpe's famous study of Rousseau and Marx, where he follows Max Adler in seeing the 'Jacobin' Rousseau as the apostle of social democracy.[8]

Nothing could be falser than interpretations of this kind: however much we squeeze the ideology of bourgeois political democracy and the social content of Jacobinism, we shall never extract a hint of the principles of the *socialist democracy of the dictatorship of the proletariat.*[9] Jacobinism does indeed have a social content, but it is a particular one connected with the images and aspirations of the small peasants and the petty bourgeois; i.e. in its 'social' content, it is basically the ideology of the *smallholders.* Jacobinism projected as its social ideal a society made up of small-scale independent producers (both peasants and artisans), a society in which each man owns his own field, his own shop or stall and is able to support his family without recourse to wage-labour and without being exploited by 'the very rich'. In particular, 'sans-culottism' corresponds to the manufacturing workers' old utopian vision of a harmonious corporatist guild society. The social content of Jacobinism is a direct contradiction of bourgeois political democracy. This contradiction can be schematized as that between Rousseau's ideology and the political ideology of Montesquieu and Constant; but it must be noticed that this social content is due to the insertion into bourgeois political ideology of ideological elements stemming from different classes (namely the small-scale producers) whose interests are contradictory to those of the bourgeoisie.[10]

8. Within the limits of this book, it is not possible to go further into the influence of Jacobinism on the working-class movement. Its most remarkable feature (though we should not be surprised by it) is the way in which two interpretations of Jacobinism merge: (i) the interpretation of the 'theoretical leftists' of the 1920s (Gramsci's notion of the proletariat's 'inversion' of Jacobinism) and (ii) the social-democratic interpretation, exemplified by Jaurès, for whom 'socialism emerges from the republican movement . . . So socialism will not be a rupture from the French Revolution, but its consummation.'

9. The same can be said for the Jacobin/*enragiste* conception of *revolutionary dictatorship.* This conception, of which traces can be found in Marat, Babeuf and Blanqui, is more closely related to *social Caesarism,* combined with small-scale producers' anarchist aspirations for 'direct democracy' (see Proudhon) than to the Marxist conception of the dictatorship of the proletariat. See Max Adler on 'workers' councils'.

10. This social aspect of Jacobinism also affects its political aspect, which, in turn, corresponds to its bourgeois class character. From the bourgeois viewpoint, Jacobinism is essentially no different from political democracy as advocated by Montesquieu and Robespierre, since it is in this sense merely a representative of the bourgeoisie. But this

For us the most significant feature of Jacobinism is the highly ambiguous way in which (i) it was received throughout the rest of Europe, (ii) it was taken over by the two Bonapartes, with their reliance on the small-scale producers, (iii) it found its direct continuation in French 'radicalism'. In its various later forms, the French working-class movement was imbued with Jacobinism, in particular by means of *utopian socialism*, represented by Louis Blanc and Proudhon; it was with good reason that Louis Bonaparte cut the ground from under its feet, as Karl Marx showed in *The Eighteenth Brumaire*. To conclude, Jacobinism is profoundly ambiguous not because it has a contradictory purity stemming from its role as the typical political ideology of the (contradictory) bourgeoisie, but because of the particular character of the bourgeois revolution in France.

(iii) THE GERMAN CASE

I shall now consider the case of Germany, in particular Prussia.[11] My remarks will be brief, since I shall have to return to the subject later because of its major importance for the modern reformist movement. We note at the outset that the bourgeois revolution in Prussia (and generally in Germany) *simply did not take place*. The 1848 movement and the issuing of a constitution by the king did not mark an important turning-point in the process of the transformation of relations of production; and they did nothing to alter the state's superstructure or the occupier of political power. Despite the customs-union (*Zollverein*) which had already been accomplished by the time of this movement, the landed nobility still retained political power and the Prussian state was to remain for a long time dominated by feudal structures. It was in fact this state which under Bismarck undertook to bring the bourgeoisie to political domination, a process characterized exactly by Marx and Engels as 'revolution from above'. Under Bismarck, this state transformed itself from within, as it were, in the direction of the capitalist state.

'bourgeois' political aspect of Jacobinism is masked by the fact that it uses an ethical (and not a political) language. Even its bourgeois aspect is expressed in a classical (ethical) manner; and the small-scale producers experience their aspirations in the same manner. This becomes clear if we compare the senses in which Montesquieu and Robespierre use the notion of 'vertu', Montesquieu using it in a political sense close to Machiavelli's 'virtus'. The notion is identical in both, being dependent in the last analysis on the bourgeois aspect of Jacobinism, but the different sense given to it by Rousseau reveals the petty-bourgeois mask of that aspect.

11. In particular, see A. Rosenberg, *Sozialismus und Demokratie*, 1966 (reprint).

The reason is that the German bourgeoisie waited until *too late in attempting to bring about its revolution*. The bourgeoisie's economic development (the process of industrialization) had already made a decisive start at the beginning of the nineteenth century. As in France, it was organized *without* capitalizing ground-rent; but unlike France, it was organized *alongside* the nobility's undisputed political domination and in the framework of a state which had not reached the turning-point of the absolutist state. This is why the transition went forward at a particularly slow pace during the initial stage, and why, when the bourgeoisie finally woke up, it found itself confronted by the emerging organization of the working class – a traumatizing experience from which it never recovered. By one of those errors of judgement which stemmed from the fact that ideology was at that time infiltrating unevenly into developing national formations, the German bourgeoisie could not make up its mind to break with the nobility: this was because it was obsessed by the French revolution of 1848 and by memories of the Jacobinism of the Great Revolution. It therefore left to the state the task of establishing its own political domination. This domination was expressed in:

a. the continuity of feudal structures almost until the First World War and the continuity of the nobility's characteristic hegemony in political power, a hegemony which was however countered by the specific autonomy of the Bismarckian state.

b. the particularly important role assumed by the state, after the phase of primary accumulation and during the process of industrialization. The role played by the state was much more important in Germany than in Britain or even France: it foreshadowed the state of 'war capitalism' of the First World War and even the Nazi state's particular intervention into the economic in the period between the two world wars.

Another sign of this transition process is a characteristic dislocation between the juridical system and state institutions. We have also noted the existence of this dislocation in Britain, where it took on different forms. In Germany in the first half of the nineteenth century, despite the state's feudal structures, the juridical system already contained forms of formal capitalist ownership, albeit in a masked way; it took these forms under the cover of a revival of Roman law (as opposed to the Napoleonic Code), whose lasting imprint continued even after the promulgation of the German civil code at the beginning of the twentieth century.

What does this dominance of the CMP over the other modes in the domain of German agriculture mean? It was established by expropriating small-scale producers, by concentrating landed property in the hands of the squireens and by transforming vast numbers of peasants into agricultural labourers. However, this process was *very slow* and traces of serfdom existed for a long time in East Prussia; on the other hand, because of the peculiarities of the ensemble of this formation, which distinguishes it from Britain, the squireens (the Prussian Junkers) remained characteristically ground-rent nobility, failing to seize the turning-point at which ground-rent could be capitalized. This establishment of the dominance of the CMP ended small-scale agricultural ownership, but it benefited the nobility to some extent. This was a heavy burden on the political and ideological level of the German peasantry. The German peasantry has never been a social force, as it was in France, and it functioned differently from the British peasantry; it was permeated by memories of Münzer-type peasant risings and yet it was terrified by its equivocal proletarianization, which it could not assimilate into its ideology. As a result, especially in the eastern provinces, it became, without any doubt, an element which contributed to the rise of Nazism.

The bourgeoisie developed so cautiously, by means of a strong state dominance and within the *enclaves* of a feudal formation, that the petty bourgeoisie was able to exist and develop. But the petty bourgeoisie took on a different role from its French counterpart. In Germany, the petty bourgeoisie originally co-operated with the bourgeoisie and was its constant ally in the struggle against the nobility's permanent political hegemony. The contradiction between them rarely went so far as open action; the German petty bourgeoisie, untouched by Jacobin ideology, shared the bourgeoisie's attitude to the working class, as is clear from its constant mistrust of the proletariat. As we know only too well, the relation between the bourgeoisie and the petty bourgeoisie was of major importance for Nazism.

This role of the state, this growth of the bourgeoisie and the presence of the petty bourgeoisie explain why the state apparatus (the army and bureaucracy) was so important in German political development. The German state apparatus, unlike the French, depends on the fact not that the bourgeoisie is constantly outstripping itself but that it is constantly lagging behind. This state apparatus belongs generally to the noble, bourgeois and petty-bourgeois classes, but renders service to the particular relation between the bourgeoisie and the petty bourgeoisie, a service which was previously masked and distorted by the nobility; and it is this which allows it to function in the framework of Nazism and which distinguishes it so radically from Bonapartism.

In conclusion, it can be seen that though the transition from feudalism to capitalism throughout western Europe presents common tendential characteristics, no paradigm case of the bourgeois revolution can be found. However, one very striking point common to every case should perhaps be noted: namely *the bourgeoisie's lack of political capacity (because of its class constitution) successfully to lead its own revolution in open action*. The characteristic feature of the bourgeois revolutions reviewed above is precisely the absence of political organization capable of producing a consistent leadership for the revolutionary process. In short, we note the bourgeoisie's characteristic incapacity to lead politically its revolution of political democracy, i.e. the bourgeois/democratic revolution. The all-important factor here is the *non-typical* character in their conjunctural originality of the various bourgeois revolutions. It was the bourgeoisie's political incapacity which struck Marx, Engels and Lenin so strongly.

It is also important to observe that the particular features of the transition in these various formations as well as of the respective bourgeois revolutions have had serious repercussions *on the working-class movements in these countries*. The major point here is the *ideological* influence of the models of these revolutions on the working-class movements. The working class can so rarely escape having to live according to the mode imposed by the dominant ideology, that even its revolt against the existing system is conducted according to it. In this case, these models of the bourgeois revolution and their attendant ideological forms are manifested in their effects on the working class's ideology as a number of *dangers of specific deformations* lying in wait for revolutionary theory; as a number of *temptations*, as it were, to the working class to *imitate* the revolutions of its national bourgeois class. Bearing in mind the analyses made above, we can explain the characteristic dangers which lie permanently in wait for the British, French and German working-class movements.

1. For the British working-class movement, the danger is '*trade-unionism*' which is already to be seen in the corporatist conceptions of the Chartists and Robert Owen. According to it, priority is given to class struggle at the economic level, i.e. to the trade-union struggle, at the expense of the political struggle aimed at seizing state power.

2. For the French working-class movement, the danger is *Jacobinism*, which is already present in utopian socialism. In its general form this is a contamination of working-class ideology and revolutionary theory by the ideology peculiar to the small-scale producers (i.e. the French small-holding peasantry and petty bourgeoisie) under the vague cover of a democratic radicalism in the ambiguous sense adopted by Jacobinism. Clearly, 'working-class' Jacobinism permits a whole series of variations within itself, from Blanquism to classical social-reformism, *via* anarchism. But the important point is that this is a deformation of the ideology and revolutionary theory of the working class in its relations with the small-scale producers.

3. For the German working-class movement, the danger is *Lassallism*. As opposed to the economist reformism characteristic of trade unionism, it considers the state as a factor in the socialist revolution 'from above'. The aim is not to smash the state's apparatus and structures and gain control of them, but rather to force its hand, as though it were a third party mediating between the classes in conflict.

III
Fundamental Characteristics
of the Capitalist State

INTRODUCTION

We shall now attempt to grasp some basic characteristics of the capitalist state. But first it is important to restate certain points vital for what follows.

A. The characteristics of the capitalist type of state are contained in the concept of that state which can be constructed from the 'pure' CMP as elaborated in *Capital*. However, owing to the specific autonomy of the instances proper to this mode of production the characteristics of the capitalist state are only sketched in implicitly in *Capital*. Consequently I shall refer mainly to the political works of Marx, Engels, Gramsci and Lenin, whose *double status* has already been pointed out (particularly in the case of Marx and Engels): as well as containing a study of historically given capitalist states, they contain at the same time a theory of the capitalist type of state. So as to indicate, in this way, the theoretical construction of the capitalist type of state, I shall refer to formations dominated by the CMP, in order to study the capitalist state in operation.

B. The state in its role as cohesive factor in the unity of a formation (a role which is especially important in the capitalist formation) has several functions: economic, ideological and political. These functions are the particular modalities of the globally political role of the state: *they are over-determined by, and condensed in, its strictly political function, its function in relation to the field of the political class struggle*. It is around this function and this relation that the following analyses will be grouped.

C. The nature of the relation between the state and the field of the class struggle belongs to the type of relations which hold between the structures and this field. The capitalist state, in which the specific autonomy of instances is located by its relation to the relations of production, *sets the limits* which circumscribe the relation of the field of the class struggle to its own regional structures. In other words, these state structures, as they appear in the relation of the instances, *carry inscribed within them a set of variations* which in delimiting the class struggle achieve concrete reality according to the effects which this struggle has on the state within the limits thus set. Henceforth, when we say that in a capitalist formation certain characteristics of the class struggle are related to the capitalist state, it must not be understood as meaning that these characteristics are a simple phenomenon derived from its structures or that they are exhaustively determined by them. It must be understood as meaning that the field of the class struggle has fundamental effects on this state, effects which are realized within the limits set by its structures to the extent that they control a set of variations.

The line of demarcation between the relations of the state to the dominant classes and its relation to the dominated classes can give a guide to our study of this state. The capitalist state presents this peculiar feature, that nowhere in its actual institutions does strictly political domination take the form of a political *relation* between the dominant *classes* and the dominated classes.[1] In its institutions everything takes place as if the class 'struggle' did not exist. This state is organized as a political unity of a society of divergent economic interests and these are presented not as class interests but as the interests of 'private individuals', economic subjects: this is connected to the way in which the state is related to the isolation of socio-economic relations, an isolation which is partly the state's own effect. Because of this isolation, in performing its political function the state presents a characteristic ambivalence, depending on whether it is dealing with the dominant or the dominated classes.

1. With regard to the dominated classes, the function of the capitalist state is to prevent their political organization which would overcome their economic isolation: it does this by maintaining them in this isolation which is partly its own effect. The state assumes this function in a very particular form which allows a radical distinction to be drawn between this state and other states, such as slave or feudal states. These latter limit the political organization of the dominated classes by institutionally fixing the classes of slaves or serfs in their very structures by means of *public statutes*, that is to say, by institutionalizing political class subordination in the form of estates or castes. On the other hand, by virtue of its isolating effect on the socio-economic relations and by also taking advantage of this effect, the capitalist state maintains the political disorganization of the

1. Structure/Institution: see p. 115n above.

dominated classes, by presenting itself as the unity of the people-nation, composed of political-persons/private-individuals. The capitalist state thus fulfils its function both by concealing their own class character from the dominated classes and also by specifically excluding them from the state institutions, in so far as they are the dominated classes.

2. On the other hand, with regard to the dominant classes, the capitalist state is permanently working on their organization at the political level, by cancelling out their economic isolation which, in this case too, is the effect both of the state and of the ideological.

The capitalist 'popular-class' state's principal contradiction, i.e. the effective (class) aspect of its internal contradiction (that between private and public), could be described as follows: its function is to disorganize the dominated classes politically, and at the same time to organize the dominant classes politically; to prevent the dominated classes from being present in its centre as classes, whilst introducing the dominant classes there as classes; by relating itself to the dominated classes as representative of the unity of the people-nation, whilst at the same time relating itself to the dominant classes *qua* politically organized classes. In short, this state exists as a state of the dominant *classes* whilst excluding from its centre the class 'struggle'. Its principal contradiction is not so much that it 'calls' itself the state of all the people, although it is in fact a class state, but that, strictly speaking, it presents itself in its very institutions as a 'class' state (i.e. the state of the dominant classes which it helps to organize politically), of a society which is institutionally fixed as one not-divided-into-classes; in that it presents itself as a state of the bourgeois class, implying that all the 'people' are part of this class.

1. The Capitalist State and the Interests of the Dominated Classes

This first characteristic of the capitalist state depends on the specific autonomy of the political and economic struggle, of political and economic power and of political and economic class interests in capitalist formations. The capitalist state, characterized by hegemonic class leadership, does not *directly* represent the dominant classes' economic interests, but their *political interests*: it is the dominant classes' political power centre, as the organizing agent of their political struggle. Gramsci expressed this excellently when he remarked that:

The life of the state is conceived of as a continuous process of formation and superseding of unstable equilibria ... between the interests of the fundamental group and those of the subordinate groups – equilibria in which the interests of the dominant group prevail, but only up to a certain point, i.e. stopping short of narrowly corporate interest (*Prison Notebooks*, p. 182).

In this sense, the capitalist state has inscribed in its very structures a flexibility which concedes a certain guarantee to the economic interests of certain dominated classes, within the limits of the system. To the extent that this guarantee is in accordance with the hegemonic domination of the dominant classes, i.e. with their political constitution vis-à-vis this state, as representatives of the general interest of the people, this concession is part of this state's very function. The concept of the capitalist state of course involves a specific function for *political ideology*, a form of power based on 'consent', which is organized and directed in a specific manner for the dominated classes. However, the aspect of the capitalist state under discussion here is not simply that of ideological conditioning. The notion of the general interest of the 'people', an ideological notion covering an institutional operation of the capitalist state, expresses a *real fact*: namely that this state, by its very structure, gives to the economic interests of certain dominated classes guarantees which may even be contrary to the short-term economic interests of the dominant classes, but which are compatible with their political interests and their hegemonic domination.

This brings us to a very simple conclusion but one which cannot be too often repeated. This guarantee given by the capitalist state to the economic interests of certain dominated classes cannot be seen *per se* as a restraint on the *political power* of the dominant classes. It is true that the *political and economic struggles of the dominated classes* impose this on the capitalist state. However, this simply shows that the state is not a class instrument, but rather the state of a society divided into classes. The class struggle in capitalist formations entails that this guarantee of the economic interests of certain dominated classes is inscribed *as a possibility*, within the very limits imposed by the state on the struggle for hegemonic class leadership. But in making this guarantee, the state aims precisely at the political disorganization of the dominated classes; in a formation where the strictly political struggle of the dominated classes is possible, it is the sometimes indispensable means of maintaining the dominant classes' hegemony. In other words, according to the concrete conjuncture, a *line of demarcation* can always be drawn within which the guarantee given by the capitalist state to the dominated classes' economic interests not only fails to threaten the political relation of class domination but even constitutes an element of this relation.

In fact, this is a *particular* characteristic of the capitalist state stemming from the specific autonomy of the political superstructure from the economic instance, of political power from economic power. In the 'pre-capitalist' formations where the relation between the instances does not take this form, an 'economic' demand from the dominated classes (e.g. the repeal of a law, obligation or privilege) is most often a political demand directly challenging the system of 'public power'. Rosa Luxemburg correctly pointed out that the economic struggle is to some extent a directly political struggle, according to the content of these concepts in these 'preceding' formations.[1] These demands of the dominated classes can be satisfied only to the limited extent that they are compatible with the definite economico-political interests of the dominant classes and do not challenge the state's power. In the case of the capitalist state, the autonomy of the political can allow the satisfaction of the economic interests of certain dominated classes, even to the extent of occasionally

1. R. Luxemburg, 'The Mass Strike', and 'The Political Party and the Trade Unions', *Rosa Luxemburg Speaks*, New York, 1970, pp. 207 ff.

limiting the economic power of the dominant classes, restraining, where
necessary, their capacity to realize their short-term economic interests;
but on the one condition, which has become *possible* in the case of capitalist states, that their political power and the state apparatus remain intact.
Hence, in every concrete conjuncture, the dominant classes' political
power, which has become autonomous, represents in its relations with
the capitalist state *a limit within which the restrictions of the economic power
of these classes has no effect.*

Thus the capitalist state's particular characteristic feature of representing the general interest of a national-popular ensemble is not simply
a mendacious mystification, because within these limits it can effectively
satisfy some of the economic interests of certain dominated classes. Furthermore, it can do this without however allowing its political power to be
affected. It is obviously impossible to delineate once and for all the limit
of this hegemonic domination: it depends equally on the relation between
the forces in the struggle, on the forms of the state, on the articulation of
its functions, on the relations of economic power to political power and on
the functioning of the state apparatus.

In this state, political power is thus apparently founded on an *unstable
equilibrium of compromise.* These terms should be understood as follows:
   1. *Compromise,* in the sense that this power corresponds to a hegemonic
class domination and can take into account the economic interests of certain dominated classes even where those could be contrary to the short-
term economic interests of the dominant classes, without this affecting
the configuration of political interests;
   2. *Equilibrium,* in the sense that while these economic 'sacrifices' are
real and so provide the ground for an equilibrium, they do not as such
challenge the political power which sets precise limits to this equilibrium;
   3. *Unstable,* in the sense that these limits of the equilibrium are set by
the political conjuncture.

So this equilibrium clearly does not indicate (as with a pair of scales)
any sort of *equivalence* of power amongst the forces present. This latter
meaning of equilibrium must not be confused with that attributed to it by
Marx and Engels when they speak of the state's autonomy in the situation
where, in the political struggle or in the relation between the political and
economic struggle, the classes are close to a state of equilibrium. The
equilibrium which is at issue here indicates the complexity and dislocation of relations of power in the framework of the capitalist state, and the

relations of force in the field of the economic struggle within the limits set by political power. In this sense, Gramsci pointed out:

Undoubtedly the fact of hegemony presupposes account be taken of the interests and the tendencies of the groups over which hegemony is to be exercised, and that a certain compromise equilibrium should be formed – in other words, that the leading group should make sacrifices of an economic-corporate kind. But there also is no doubt that such sacrifices and such a compromise cannot touch the essential.[2]

The capitalist state is therefore characterized by a *two-sided* feature: on the one hand, its autonomy vis-à-vis the economic involves the possibility of a social policy (according to the concrete relation of forces), i.e. of economic sacrifices to the profit of certain dominated classes; on the other hand, this very same autonomy of institutionalized political power sometimes makes it possible to cut into the dominant classes' economic power without ever threatening their political power. It is in this context that we should locate, for example, the whole problem of the so-called 'Welfare State', a term which in fact merely disguises the form of the 'social policy' of a capitalist state at the stage of state monopoly capitalism. The political strategy of the working class depends on adequately deciphering in the concrete conjuncture this limit which fixes the equilibrium of compromises and which is the demarcation line between economic and political power.

Now this 'social policy' of the capitalist state is sketched in implicitly in *Capital*, especially in the texts of Volume I concerning *factory legislation*, even though these deal only with false sacrifices which in fact correspond to the precise economic interests of capital.[3] It is elaborated more clearly both in *The Class Struggles in France* – on the subject of the February Republic, which is a historical example of a capitalist state which had to present itself as a 'republic surrounded by social institutions' – and in *The Eighteenth Brumaire* with regard to Louis Bonaparte's 'social Caesarism'.[4] Moreover, it is obvious that this 'social policy' of the state has nothing to do with state *intervention* in the relations of production in the strict sense of the term, which is an entirely different problem. I mean that the type of capitalist state, sketched in implicity in *Capital*, involves the possibility inscribed within the limits of its structures of a 'social

2. *Prison Notebooks*, p. 161.
3. See P. Sweezy, *The Theory of Capitalist Development*, New York, 1962, pp. 239 ff.
4. *MESW*, 1970, pp. 97 ff.

policy' whose realization and modalities (variations) obviously depend on the concrete relation of forces in the class struggle. So this 'social policy', though it may happen to contain real economic sacrifices *imposed on* the dominant class *by the struggle of the dominated classes*, cannot under any circumstances call into question the capitalist type of state, so long as it operates within these *limits*.

2. The Capitalist State and Ideologies

(i) THE HISTORICIST CONCEPTION OF IDEOLOGIES

The particular relation between the capitalist type of state and the dominated classes also manifests itself at the ideological level. In fact hegemonic class domination, as a particular type of class domination, marks the particular place and function of the ideological in its relations to the political in capitalist formations: in short, it marks the particular way in which '*bourgeois ideology*' functions politically. In fact, this particular feature of bourgeois ideology is merely the political aspect vis-à-vis the state of the specific operation of ideology as such, which Marx saw in *Capital* as the condition of existence of the CMP. The question is all the more important in that it concerns one of the crucial problems of political science, that of *legitimacy*.

On this subject, Gramsci's analyses of class hegemony are very enlightening, especially on this point: on the one hand Gramsci, with amazing acuteness, perceived the problems posed by the political functioning of bourgeois ideology in a capitalist formation; on the other hand, though his analyses are distinct from the typical historicist conception of ideologies as presented for example by Lukács, because of the historicist problematic which essentially governs his work, they demonstrate very clearly the impasses and errors to which this problematic of ideology leads. This is why a radical critique of the historicist conception of ideologies is so important as a prior condition to the scientific posing of the question.

To do this we must first of all briefly mention the problematic of ideology as found in the young Marx, which was centred on the subject. Marx's conception of ideology, as well as of the superstructures in general, was based on the model: '*the subject/the real/alienation*'. The subject is deprived of its concrete essence in the 'real', this concept of the 'real' being constructed theoretically from the ontological objectification of the subject. Ideology is a projection in an imaginary world of the subject's mystified essence, i.e. the alienating 'ideal' reconstitution of its essence, objectified-alienated in the socio-economic real. Ideology, modelled according to the schema of alienation-abstraction, is identified with 'false consciousness'. Thus in the young Marx's elaboration of the concept of ideology there are the following oppositions characteristic of the historicist problematic: state/civil society, superstructures/base, ideology/real, alienation/essence, abstract/concrete.

This conception of ideology has remained alive in the historicist school of Marxism whose problematic is centred on the subject. It has had numerous consequences, including in the first place an inadequate analysis of ideologies in capitalist formations and of their current transformations. In fact, whether the subject is seen as the social class, the concrete individual, social work, praxis, etc., this problematic inevitably identifies *ideology* with *alienation* and results in an inadequate theoretical status being granted to ideologies: these are considered as the 'products' of consciousness (i.e. class consciousness) or of freedom (i.e. freedom of praxis), alienated from the subject. Hence this status of ideologies presupposes that the 'subject' is at once both alienated and not-totally-alienated in the 'real'. For example, in the case of a communist society where the subject is supposed to have recovered his essence, ideologies have disappeared and given way to a 'scientific' transparency of consciousness to its objectified existence. But what is more interesting here is the fact that this perspective dominates the contemporary theme of the 'end of ideology' which, according to some ideologists inspired by Marxism, characterizes contemporary 'industrial societies'. In fact, in the case of a total alienation of the subject in the real, ideologies are seen as having swung 'into reality'; they have done this precisely in so far as consciousness has been entirely ensnared in, and the subject entirely lost in the real, and so any possibility of a projection of the essence on to an ideal world, a projection which is 'alienating' yet in the sole case of the proletariat (the privileged class in the real) 'liberating' and relatively coherent, has disappeared. It is this precise invariant relation 'ideology/the real/ alienation' which governs the often implicit theme of the 'end of ideology' in numerous authors from Marcuse[1] to Adorno[2] and Goldmann.[3] They interpret contemporary developments of the capitalist formation closely in accordance with the schema of a total reification-alienation of

1. *One-Dimensional Man*, Boston, 1964, and 'Über das Ideologieproblem in der Hochentwickelten Industriegesellschaft' in Kurt Lenk (ed.), *Ideologie*, Neuwied, 1961, pp. 334 ff.

2. *Prisms*, London, 1967.

3. *Pour une sociologie du roman*, Paris, 1964.

the subject in the real in the industrial-technological society. Although there are notable differences between these authors, the common conclusion which they reach is, as Marcuse puts it, the 'absorption of ideology into reality',[4] a claim that contemporary capitalist formations have been de-ideologized, indeed, de-politicized.

However, the historicist conception of ideologies is even more clearly expressed in the typical example of Lukács's theory of 'class consciousness' and 'world-view' (*Weltanschauung*). It is important to dwell on this theory for it poses clearly the whole problem of the epistemological presuppositions of a historicist ideological perspective. More important still, because of Gramsci's historicism as expressed in his views on dialectical materialism and in particular in his concept of the 'historical bloc', the majority of Marxist theorists use the concept of hegemony in a sense relating it to Lukács's problematic. The most important part of my following remarks is an exposition of the erroneous relation established by this problematic between the politically dominant class and the dominant ideology in a formation; and consequently, the relation between the dominant ideology and the politically dominated classes: more specifically, it is in this latter context that the extremely debatable consequences of Gramsci's analysis are located.

In the Lukácsian problematic of the subject, the unity characterizing a mode of production and a social formation is not that of a complex ensemble with several specific levels and determined in the last instance by the economic. In it this unity is reduced to a totality of the functionalist type, composed of *gestalt* interactions, of which Hegel's concept of the concrete-universal is a good example: in other words it is an *expressive totality*. In this case, the unity of a formation is related to a central instance, originating and giving meaning to this unity. In Lukács, this 'totalizing' instance is represented by the class-subject of history: the unity of a social formation is referred back to the political organization of this class (itself reduced to the role of founding a 'world-view') which erects this world-view into a central principle in the unity of a determined formation. This world-view which encompasses *both ideology and science*,[5] expresses the unity of a formation within a linear and circular

4. op. cit., p. 11. It should be noticed that Marcuse refuses, explicitly, to reach the conclusion of the 'end of ideologies'.

5. This identification of ideology and science, or the conception of ideology as encompassing science, itself goes back to the relation between the subjective and the

totality, in so far as it is related to the central principle of unity, the class-subject. This latter, through its world-view, constitutes the conscious-ness-will of the 'totality' of men 'who make their own history' through praxis. Thus the role assigned to ideology through the medium of the class-subject is that of the principle of totalizing a social formation, which is precisely the young Marx's position when he held that it is ideas that rule the world and the weapons of criticism that can change it.

This relation between ideology and the unity of a social formation is the more interesting because it governs the contemporary problematic of the 'functionalist' sociological school. It is implicit, as we shall see when discussing legitimacy, in many of the analyses of contemporary political science. In order to bring to light the links between Lukács's Hegelian totality and the functionalist totality, we need only refer to the direct filiation between Lukács and Max Weber. What links the theories of Weber to those of functionalism (as Parsons noted) is that the global structure is, in the last analysis, considered as the *product* of a society-subject which in its teleological becoming creates certain social values or ends. In functionalism, these determine the formal framework for an *integration* of the various particular and 'equivalent' structures in the social 'whole'. This integration is related to an 'equilibrium' based on certain regular and recurrent processes of *normative* elements, e.g., motivations of conduct,[6] which govern social 'action'. For Weber,[7] these

---

objective within the framework of a problematic of the subject. In fact, the subjective character of ideology as the expression of the subject encompasses the objectivity of science in the case in which a 'rising class's' subjective consciousness of the world takes in the totality of a social formation. This side of the argument, as applied by Lukács, Korsch, etc. to the proletariat and 'proletarian science' is well known. According to it, the proletariat is in essence a universal class, so its subjectivity is universal; but a universal subjectivity can only be objective, therefore scientific. The consequence of this conception is also well known – spontaneism.

6. Motivations of conduct in the strict sense of the term. This leads exactly to Adorno's notion of 'political temperament' (see Adorno and Horkheimer, *The Authoritarian Personality*, New York, 1950).

7. On the connections between Weber's and Lukács's theories of classes, which have been almost ignored in France, see Weber, *Gesammelte politische Schriften*, Tübingen, 1958, pp. 294–431, especially 'Parlament und Regierung im neugeordneten Deutschland', written in 1918. As to the connections between Weber and Parsons, Parsons certainly misinterprets Weber's work in some respects: see *The Social System*, New York, 1964, pp. 100 ff., 519 ff., etc. However, the relation between Weber and functionalism which he establishes is in the last analysis correct. On the problem of Weber's historicism, it should be noted that Weber himself made an explicit critique of the historicist 'totality', particularly in his analyses of Eduard Meyer's work (see

social values are the crystallization of social actors' projects and are the elements out of which his ideal types are formed. In the case of the state, his conception leads to a typology exclusively of types of legitimacy, these types being constituted exactly out of the values of the agents-actors. Weber frequently relates the creation of these social values or ends to the action of social groups (the well-known 'status-groups' which he distinguishes from class situations, i.e., classes-in-themselves), which are the subjects of society and history: these considerations are at the basis of his conception of bureaucracy. But the theory of class consciousness of Lukács, whose explicit links with Weber are well known, looks like an attempt at a heavy-handed Marxization of Weber. It presupposes an expressive totality,[8] within which there is simply no role for a dominant factor (as Weber himself quite correctly saw), yet at the same time it attributes to ideology the role of dominant factor in the social whole.[9] Gramsci's historicist conception of dialectical materialism, coupled with the ambiguity of his formulations, has led several theorists to reduce his analyses of class hegemony to the Lukácsian problematic.[10] On such an interpretation, a hegemonic class becomes the class-subject of history which through its world-view manages to permeate a social formation with its unity and to lead, rather than dominate, by bringing about the 'active consent' of the dominated classes. This interpretation of Gramsci

Gesammelte Aufsätze zur Wissenschaftslehre). However, despite his warnings, his theory may be considered as a 'typical' historicist theory. On the relations between Weber's 'ideal type' and Hegel's 'concrete-universal' concept, see especially K. Larenz, *Methodenlehre der Rechtswissenschaft*, 1960.

8. Weber's historicism goes hand in hand with the conception of an expressive totality of the social whole without a dominant instance, as is clear in his theory of *'factors'* and *'variables'*. It is also found in *The Protestant Ethic and the Spirit of Capitalism*, London, 1930, and particularly in *Gesammelte Aufsätze zur Religionssoziologie*.

9. There is no better example of this perspective, applied to political analysis, than the work of Marcuse, although it leads him to different results. As long ago as 1935, for instance, he admitted that the unity of a social formation (as opposed to a purely 'functionalist' conception) lay in the 'dominance' of a certain element of this formation over the others. However, he saw this element as the consciousness-cum-world-view of a class which was ideologically dominant in this formation (*Kultur und Gesellschaft*, Frankfurt, 1965, pp. 34 ff.). Marcuse now argues that a global de-ideologization characterizes industrial societies; from this he concludes that a social formation is an integrated Hegelian-functionalist 'totality', in the absence of an ideologically dominant class and in the absence of a proletarian 'class consciousness' which would 'countervail the whole' (*One Dimensional Man*, op. cit., pp. 51 ff.).

10. A characteristic example is L. Magri, 'Problems of the Marxist theory of the revolutionary party' in *New Left Review* 60, March/April 1970.

is for example very clear in the Marxist school of *New Left Review* which I have had the occasion to criticize elsewhere.[11] It appears in embryo in the following definition of hegemonic class by Perry Anderson, one of the most important representatives of this school: 'If a hegemonic class can be defined as one which imposes its own ends and its own vision on society as a whole, a corporate class is conversely one which pursues its own ends within a social totality whose global determination lies outside it.'[12] It is clear that the unity of a social formation, the social 'totality', is here related to a hegemonic class; its hegemony would consist in constituting a world-view which would establish that class as the unifying principle of a determinate formation: 'A hegemonic class seeks to transform society in its own image, inventing afresh its economic system, its political institutions, its cultural values, its whole "mode of insertion" into the world.'[13]

Moreover, Gramsci undeniably lays himself open to a misinterpretation of his analyses of historical materialism, particularly of his analyses of political domination, i.e. hegemonic class domination, because of his historicist conception of dialectical materialism. This historicism becomes clear in his treatment of the status of ideology, in Gramsci's concept of the 'historical bloc'. This concept allows Gramsci to think the unity of theory and practice, the unity of ideology, encompassing science ('organic intellectuals') and structure; i.e. the unity of a social formation in its ensemble at a historically determined instant. But this unity is precisely the expressive totality of the historicist type, which conflates the ideological and theoretical instances in the ensemble of the social structure. 'The analysis of these propositions tends to reinforce the conception of "historical bloc" in which precisely material forces are the content and ideologies are the form, though this distinction between form and content has purely didactic value.'[14] In this context the historical bloc is merely the theoretical formulation of the Hegelian historical 'present', the co-presence of instances in the expressive totality of linear becoming, with ideology conceived as the mere expression of history. This role of central principle of unity of a formation attributed to ideology/world-view is also manifest in the somewhat ambiguous metaphor, in Gramsci's context of ideology

11. N. Poulantzas, 'Marxist Political Theory in Great Britain' in *New Left Review* 43, May/June 1967. I must however point out that this school's theoretical conceptions have in the meantime developed considerably.

12. P. Anderson, 'Origins of the Present Crisis' in *New Left Review* 23, January/February 1964, p. 41.

13. ibid.   14. *Prison Notebooks*, p. 377.

as the 'cement' of a formation: 'This problem is that of preserving the ideological unity of the entire social bloc which that ideology serves to cement and to unify . . .' Or again: 'One might say "ideology" here, but on condition that the word is used in its highest sense of a conception of the world that is implicitly manifest in art, in law, in economic activity and in all manifestations of individual and collective life.'[15]

However, it is also true that we find several theoretical breaks in Gramsci's work, particularly in his analyses of dialectical and historical materialism: a *symptomal reading* of Gramsci, which is outside the scope of this work, would certainly reveal the scientific and original features contained (under the polemical cover of 'absolute historicism') in his conception of ideology. We may simply mention two of them here:

a. Gramsci's metaphor of ideology as the 'cement' of a society poses the major problem of the relation between the dominant ideology and the unity of a social formation in an original manner.

b. In the history of Marxist thought Gramsci is the first to break with the conception of ideology as a conceptual system, in the strict sense of these two terms.

(ii) DOMINANT IDEOLOGY, DOMINANT CLASS
AND SOCIAL FORMATION

How can the Lukácsian problematic explain the Marxist tenet that the dominant ideology in a social formation is generally that of the dominant class? In other words, how does it explain the fact that the dominant ideology, possessing a unity of its own and thus reflecting in a relatively coherent universe the ensemble of the social formation which it permeates, is that of the dominant class? This is, in fact, *three series* of questions concerning the relation between the dominant ideology and the unity of a social formation:

1. Concerning that specific unity and relative coherence (what the Lukácsian problematic happily terms 'totality of meaning') belonging to the ideological universe, i.e. to a formation's dominant ideology considered as a *regional structure* of instances.

2. Concerning the fact that this coherent universe is a dominant ideology precisely in so far as it also permeates the dominated classes, and becomes their world-view also, i.e. in so far as its internal coherence corresponds to the ensemble of classes engaged in struggle in a formation.

15. ibid., p. 328.

3. Concerning the fact that this dominant ideology is that of the dominant class.

It is useful to separate these three series of questions since their Lukácsian explanation depends precisely on conflating them, by reference to the generic principle of the class-subject of society and history. Once the unity of a formation is attributed to a class-subject and hence to the 'consciousness' of this class, the role of central determinant instance of the social whole will be attributed to that global world-view, which is the direct product of this class. So the answer to these questions will reside in the genetic relation between the dominant ideology and the class 'for itself', the subject of history. As Lukács says: 'For a class to be ripe for hegemony means that its interests and consciousness enable it to organize the whole of society in accordance with those interests. The crucial question in every class struggle is this: which class possesses this capacity and this consciousness at the decisive moment? . . . The question then becomes: how far does the class concerned perform the action history has imposed on it "consciously" or "unconsciously"? And is that consciousness "true" or "false"?'[16] The dominant ideology both presents a unity and constitutes a characteristic world-view of the ensemble of a formation in so far as it is genetically related to the dominant class – or rather, to the rising class. This class, which is the subject of a historical becoming, progresses through broader and broader totalizations until it reaches the final coincidence of objectification and essence; it is always pregnant with the meaning of history and concretely incarnates the totality of meaning and unity of a social formation.

This conception of ideology leads to a whole series of errors of which I shall indicate only the more important.

A. In general it leads to what can be termed an *over-politicization* of ideologies, the latter being considered as if they were political number-plates worn by social classes on their backs. The ideological structure is reduced to the political organization of a class and this political organization is constituted by its *own* world-view which establishes it as a class-for-itself, the subject of history. In this way, political class consciousness is identified with the function performed by the world-view. Consequently no specific autonomy can be attributed to the ideological instance. In particular, it is impossible in this conception to decipher the concrete relation between the dominant ideology and the politically dominant

16. *History and Class Consciousness*, London, 1971, pp. 52–3.

class or fraction. It leads to errors when we try to locate precisely the dominant class or fraction in a historically determined situation. In fact, one of the indices permitting this location is to be found precisely in the relation between the dominant class or fraction and the structures of the dominant ideology: but this relation cannot be admitted in the Lukácsian problematic, except in the very rare cases in which the dominant ideology appears in the 'purity' of its relation to the dominant class or fraction. But in reality, the dominant ideology does not simply reflect the conditions of existence of the dominant class, the 'pure and simple' subject, but rather the concrete political relation between the dominant and the dominated classes in a social formation. It is often permeated by elements stemming from the 'way of life' of classes or fractions other than the dominant class or fraction. We have, for example, the classic case in which the dominant bourgeois ideology of capitalist formations receives 'elements' of petty-bourgeois ideology ('Jacobinism' and its successor 'radicalism'), and even of working-class ideology – the 'bourgeois social-ism' described by Engels (e.g. Saint-Simonism during the Second Empire in France).[17]

Furthermore, owing to the specific autonomy of the ideological instance, and to the very status of the ideological in the structures, the relations between the dominant ideology and the dominant class or fraction are always masked. In the complex constitution of the ideological level, this ideology which (like all ideologies) hides its own principles from itself may appear closer to the way in which a class or fraction other than the dominant class or fraction experiences its conditions of existence. In short we can establish the possibility of a whole series of dislocations between the dominant ideology and the politically hegemonic class or fraction. These can be due to several factors: for example, to the concrete function of the caste of 'intellectuals'; or again to the uneven development of the various levels of the structures due to their specific rhythm and to their dislocation from the field of class practices. For example, a dominant ideology profoundly impregnated by the way of life of a class or fraction can continue to remain the dominant ideology even if this class or fraction is no longer dominant; in the latter case the ideology is not a mere 'survival' but is subject to a whole series of modifications with regard to its concrete political functioning. We can decipher these however only on condition that we break with the historicist problematic of ideology. The typical example of this case is Britain, where the displacement of the index

17. See C. Willard, *Socialisme et communisme français*, 1967, pp. 18 ff.

of political dominance from the aristocracy to the bourgeoisie is characterized by the permanence of a dominant, though modified, aristocratic
ideology. The Lukácsian problematic will mask the way in which this
index has changed, since from the permanence of aristocratic ideology it
will deduce the continuity of the domination of the feudal class.[18] In short,
this problematic cannot establish an adequate relation between the series
of questions indicated above; it only poses the question of the relation
between the dominant ideology and the politically dominant class.

B. Moreover it can lead to errors on the question of the relations between
the dominant ideology and the *dominated classes*. This is demonstrated by
one of Gramsci's own theses in which he incorrectly extends the concept
of hegemony to the strategy of the working class. Though this thesis may
appear to contradict the explicit conclusions of this problematic, it does
however stem from the same theoretical principles and has to a large
extent contributed to the falsification of the scientific content of the concept of hegemony, in the sense that hegemony is no longer considered
as a type of class domination. Gramsci introduces a theoretical break
between *hegemony* and *domination*. According to him, a class can and must
become the leading[19] class *before* it becomes a politically dominant class;
and it can win hegemony before the conquest of political power. In this
context, the concept of hegemony effectively indicates the fact that a class
imposes its own world-view on a formation and so (in this sense) gains
ideological domination *before* the conquest of political power. But
Gramsci applied this theoretical analysis to working-class strategy in
opposition to Leninist theses. On many occasions Lenin insisted on the
fact that in the case of a concrete conjuncture of transition from capitalism
to socialism (as opposed to certain cases of transition from feudalism to
capitalism, e.g. the case of the bourgeoisie in France), the working class
cannot gain ideological domination before conquering political power.
This analysis is at the root of Lenin's texts on the necessity of the ideological organization of the working class by its party. Gramsci's thesis is
on the face of it opposed to the Lukácsian problematic in so far as it
advocates a dislocation between the dominant ideology (which for Gramsci
could be that of the dominated class) and the politically dominant class.
Nevertheless, it flows from the same principles: the problem of the politi-

18. See my 'Marxist Political Theory in Great Britain', op. cit.

19. Following the English translation of Gramsci's *Prison Notebooks* (see p. 55 n. 5),
dirigente is translated 'leading', in contrast to 'dominant'. [Trans.]

cal organization of a class is apparently related to the elaboration of a world-view which it imposes on the ensemble of society.

In this case it is, however, impossible for a class not only to be politically dominant but even to have a strictly political organization without having gained the position of dominant ideology, since its ideological organization coincides with its emergence as class-subject of society and of history. Here we recognize Lukács's analyses of the proletariat's class consciousness, modelled on the general theme of the 'rising class', the bearer of the meaning of history. It is in this light that we can see in Gramsci's thesis the logical consequence of the Lukácsian thesis. Gramsci's dislocation between the ideologically dominant class (the hegemonic proletariat) and the politically dominant class (the bourgeoisie), i.e. the *historical* dislocation (which takes on the appearance of a *theoretical* dislocation in this thesis) between hegemony and domination, simply enables him to explain the facts by an inadequate theory, which provides an apparent contradiction to the Lukácsian conception. This also explains why Gramsci always thought that he had found this usage of the concept of hegemony in Lenin: Lenin indeed stressed the necessity for the autonomous ideological organization of the working class, but only as one of the aspects of its political organization. His theory differs importantly from Gramsci's in that according to it, (i) ideological organization has nothing to do with the proletariat's conquest of ideological domination before the taking of power, and (ii) ideological organization is even systematically conceived as being directed against the dominant ideology: even after the conquest of power this dominant ideology continues for a long time to remain bourgeois and petty bourgeois.

C. Finally, if ideologies were seen as number-plates carried on the backs of class-subjects (as in the historicist picture), it would be impossible (i) to establish the existence within the dominant ideology of elements belonging to the ideologies of classes other than the politically dominant class and (ii) *to account for the permanent possibility of contamination of working class ideology by the dominant and petty-bourgeois ideologies.* According to this conception of ideology there can be no *world over and beyond* the ideology of each class: these various ideologies each function as it were in a vacuum. Hence it is impossible to see the effects of ideological domination by the dominant ideology on working-class ideology. This leads directly to various forms of *spontaneism* and to its practical consequences: simply because it is the ideology of the proletariat-universal class, working class ideology is considered to possess the keys to Marxist science. Yet numerous texts of Marx, Engels and Lenin show that the spontaneous ideology of the working class was at the root of anarcho-syndicalism and later of trade-unionism and of reformism: this is merely the effect of the permanent domination of working-class ideology by the dominant bourgeois and petty-bourgeois ideology. This conception is also at the base of Lenin's acceptance of the famous Kautskyist thesis according to which revolutionary ideology must be imported into the working class from outside. Whereas amongst the representatives of the leftist movement of the 1920s, some (Lukács, Korsch, etc.) propounded the thesis according to which the intellectuals should be rejected since the proletariat was its own intellectual, others (Rosa Luxemburg, etc.) failed to recognize the ideological role of the party. In short, the revolutionary ideology of the working class can exist only on the basis of a permanent critique of its spontaneous ideology by Marxist science. Such a critique presupposes a radical distinction between *ideology* and *science*, which cannot be made within the historicist conception.[20]

(iii) THE MARXIST CONCEPTION OF IDEOLOGIES

In order to reveal the particular political function of ideologies in the case of hegemonic class domination, it is necessary to establish a scientific link between the three series of questions noted above, concerning the relation between the dominant ideology and the politically dominant class. To do this we must return to the status of the ideological.

Ideology consists of a specific objective level, of a *relatively coherent* ensemble of representations, values and beliefs: just as 'men', the agents within a formation, participate in an economic and political activity, they also participate in religious, moral, aesthetic and philosophical activities.[21] Ideology concerns the world in which men live, their relations to nature, to society, to other men and to their own activity including their own economic and political activity. The status of the ideological derives from the fact that it reflects the manner in which the agents of a formation, the bearers of its structures, live their conditions of existence; i.e. it reflects their relation to these conditions as it is 'lived' by them. Ideology is

20. The fact that Gramsci always combated 'spontaneism' can be explained by the theoretical breaks in his own work.

21. See L. Althusser, 'Marxism and Humanism', *For Marx*.

present to such an extent in all the agents' activities that it becomes indistinguishable from their *lived experience*. To this extent ideologies fix in a relatively coherent universe not only a real but also an *imaginary relation*: i.e. men's real relation to their conditions of existence in the form of an imaginary relation. This means that in the last analysis ideologies are related to human experience without being thereby reduced to a problematic of the subject-consciousness. This social-imaginary relation, which performs a real practical-social function, cannot be reduced to the problematic of alienation and false consciousness.

It follows that through its constitution ideology is involved in the functioning of this social-imaginary relation, and is therefore *necessarily* false; its social function is not to give agents a *true knowledge* of the social structure but simply to insert them as it were into their practical activities supporting this structure. Precisely because it is determined by its structure, at the level of experience the social whole remains *opaque* to the agents. In class-divided societies this opacity is over-determined by class exploitation and by the forms which this exploitation takes in order to be able to function in the social whole. Hence, even if it includes *elements* of knowledge, ideology necessarily manifests an adequation/inadequation vis-à-vis the real; it was this which Marx grasped under the term 'inversion'. It also follows that ideology is not itself visible to the agents in its internal action; like all levels of social reality ideology is determined by its own structure which remains opaque to the agents on the level of experience. This brings us to the problem of the specific unity of the ideological, i.e. of its *structure* and its relation to the dominant class. This unity of the ideological is not derived from some kind of genetic relation to a class-subject and its class consciousness. It is derived fundamentally from the relation between ideology and human experience in a formation, and to the imaginary form which this relation takes on. As opposed to science ideology has the precise function of hiding the real contradictions and of *reconstituting* on an imaginary level a relatively coherent discourse which serves as the horizon of agents' experience; it does this by moulding their representations of their real relations and inserting these in the overall unity of the relations of a formation. This is certainly the fundamental meaning of the ambiguous metaphor of '*cement*' used by Gramsci to designate the social function of ideology. Ideology, which slides into every level of the social structure, has the particular function of *cohesion*. It fulfils this function by establishing at the level of agents' experience relations which are obvious but false, and which allow their practical activities (division of labour, etc.) to function within the unity of a formation. Consequently this coherence specific to the ideological differs from that of science precisely because of their different social functions. As opposed to the scientific notion of system, ideology refuses to allow a contradiction within it, but attempts to resolve any contradiction by excluding it.[22] In other words the structures of ideological and scientific discourse are fundamentally different.

In this sense, if we abandon the conception of ideology as a *conceptual system* (in the strict sense of both of these terms) we can say that it encompasses what is often described as the 'culture' of a formation: provided, of course, that we do not fall into the mistake of ethnological culturalism which generally uses this term to cover a 'social formation' in its ensemble.[23] As Gramsci clearly realized, ideology encompasses not merely scattered elements of knowledge, notions etc., but also the whole process of symbolization, of mythical transposition, of 'taste', 'style', 'fashion', i.e. of the 'way of life' in general.

But the limits of this ambiguous metaphor of 'cement' must be pointed out. It must under no circumstances be applied to the agents of a formation, the bearers of structures, as the origin and central subject of these structures; nor must it be applied at the level of 'experience' to men as the producers of the unity of the ideology. This is because the coherence (unity) specific to ideological discourse, which is necessarily involved both in the imaginary form taken on by agents' experience and also in its function of masking real contradictions from scientific investigation, does not cause but rather presupposes the decentration of the subject at the level of supports. In fact the above considerations have demonstrated that it is necessary for the coherence of ideological discourse to be related to its social function, but they have not yet determined the principles of this coherence, i.e. of the *hidden structure* of the dominant ideology. Ideology, as a specific instance of a mode of production and social formation, is constituted within the limits fixed by this mode and this formation in that it offers an *imaginary coherence* to the unity governing the real contradictions of the ensemble of this formation. The structure of the ideological depends on the fact that it *reflects* the unity of a social formation. From this point of view, its specific, real role as unifier is not that of constituting the unity of a formation (as the historicist conception would have it) but

22. cf. Macherey, 'Lénine, Critique de Tolstoi', *Pour une théorie de la production littéraire*, Paris, 1966.
23. cf. R. Establet in *Démocratie Nouvelle*, June 1966.

that of reflecting that unity by *reconstituting* it on an imaginary plane. Hence, the dominant ideology of a social formation encompasses the 'totality' of this formation not because it constitutes the 'class consciousness' of a historico-social subject, but because it reflects (with those biases of *inversion* and *mystification* which are specific to it) the index of articulation of the instances which specifies the unity of this formation. As in the case of every other instance, the region of the ideological is fixed in its limits by the global structure of a mode of production and social formation.

We can thus determine the precise meaning of the relation between dominant ideology and politically dominant class in class-divided societies. In these societies the original function of ideology is over-determined by the class relations in which the structures distribute their agents. The correspondence between the dominant ideology and the politically dominant class is not due (any more than the specific internal coherence of the ideology is) to some kind of historico-genetic relation. It is due to the fact that the ideological (i.e. a given ideology) is constituted as regional instance within the unity of the structure; and this structure has the domination of a given class as its effect in the field of the class struggle. The dominant ideology, by assuring the practical insertion of agents in the social structure, aims at the maintenance (the cohesion) of this structure, and this means *above all* class domination and exploitation. It is precisely in this way that within a social formation ideology is dominated by the ensemble of representations, values, notions, beliefs, etc. by means of which class domination is perpetuated: in other words, it is dominated by what can be called the ideology of the dominant class.

In this way it can easily be understood that the structure (unity) of the dominant ideology cannot be deciphered from its relations with a class consciousness/world-view, considered in a vacuum, *but from the starting-point of the field of the class struggle*, i.e. from the concrete relation between the various classes in struggle, the relation within which class domination functions. Hence we can understand not only why the dominated classes necessarily experience their relation to their conditions of existence within the discourse of the dominant ideology, but also why this discourse often presents elements borrowed from ways of life other than that of the dominant class. Lenin points this out in an enlightening way: 'The *elements* of democratic and socialist culture are present, if only in a rudimentary form, in every national culture . . . But *every* nation also possesses a bourgeois culture, in the form, not merely of "elements" but of the dominant culture.'[24]

The dominant ideology contains features from ideologies other than that of the dominant class, incorporated as 'elements' in its own structure; but we also find in capitalist formations true *ideological sub-ensembles* which function with a relative autonomy vis-à-vis the dominant ideology within a formation: e.g. feudal and petty-bourgeois sub-ensembles. These sub-ensembles are dominated by the ideologies of the corresponding classes – feudal, petty bourgeois – but only to the extent that these ideologies which dominate the ideological sub-ensembles *are themselves dominated* by the dominant ideology; we shall see below the form in which this happens. Furthermore these ideological sub-ensembles themselves contain elements stemming from ideologies other than those which dominate them, or other than the dominant ideology of a formation. This is characteristically the case in the recurring relations between the ideologies of the petty bourgeoisie and the working class.

(iv) BOURGEOIS POLITICAL IDEOLOGY AND THE CLASS STRUGGLE

Before a further examination of political ideologies in capitalist formations, it is necessary to point out one more important fact. Ideology itself is divided into various *regions* which can be characterized, for example, as moral, juridical and political, aesthetic, religious, economic, philosophical ideologies. Without going more deeply into this problem, it must also be said that in the *dominant ideology* of a social formation it is generally possible to decipher *the dominance of one region of ideology over the others*. This dominance is itself very complex and is manifested in the fact that the other regions of the ideology function by borrowing from the dominant region the notions and representations peculiar to that region; it can even be seen in the fact that the first steps of science are based on such borrowings.

It is not accidental that one ideological region dominates the others within the limits of the dominant ideology. The specific coherence of the dominant ideology which from this point of view is guaranteed by the domination of one ideological region over the others results from the fact that it reflects the unity of the structure, i.e. its index of dominance and over-determination, with the characteristic ideological effects of inversion and masking. *It could be said that the role of ideology here is not simply that*

24. 'Critical Notes on the National Question', *Collected Works*, Vol. 20, p. 24.

of hiding the economic level which is always determinant, but that of hiding the level which has the dominant role and hiding the very fact of its dominance. The dominant region of ideology is precisely that one which for various reasons best fulfils this particular function of masking.

I shall briefly illustrate this. In a feudal formation the dominant role often falls to the political; but the dominant region of the ideological is not the juridico-political ideology but the religious ideology. Furthermore, as Marx stressed, the dominant role is often held by the ideological level itself. It could doubtless be shown that the religious ideology is precisely that region of ideology which, because of its specific structure, is best suited to mask the dominant role of the ideological itself, i.e. the direct class function specific to the ideological. The particularly 'mythical', 'obscurantist' and 'mystifying' function which the medieval Catholic religious ideology took on was due to a large extent to the fact that it often held the dominant role and that it had to hide its true function from itself. In the CMP and in a capitalist formation, where the economic generally plays the dominant role, we see the dominance of the *juridico-political region* in the ideological. But in particular at the stage of state monopoly capitalism, in which the dominant role is held by the political, it is the economic ideology (of which 'technocratism' is only one aspect) which tends to become the dominant region of the dominant ideology. *In short, everything takes place as if the centre of the dominant ideology is never in the place where real knowledge is to be sought; as if it carried out its masking role by altering the position, i.e. by deforming the object, of science.*

Before seeking the reasons why the juridico-political ideology is best suited to fulfil the role of masking the dominance of the economic in the CMP and the capitalist formation, we should provide some examples which demonstrate the dominance of this region. Let us first consider its direct dominance: the dominant form under which the bourgeois class experienced its first protests against the feudal order and experienced its subsequent conditions of existence, and which has permeated the ensemble of capitalist formations is the form of juridico-political discourse. Liberty, equality, rights, duties, the rule of the law, the legal state, the nation, individuals/persons, the general will, in short all the catchwords under which bourgeois class exploitation entered and ruled in history were directly borrowed from the juridico-political sense of these notions, as formulated for the first time by medieval legal theorists of the social contract in the Italian universities. There is no better analysis of this dominance of the juridico-political in capitalist ideology than Max Weber's: he also showed how it was related to the formation of a caste of 'legal specialists'. We can sum up as follows: in western Europe the dominant ideology of the slave class was moral and philosophical, that of the feudal class was religious, and that of the bourgeois class juridico-political: it is not accidental that Marx, Engels and Lenin (especially Marx in *The German Ideology*, *The Poverty of Philosophy*, *The Communist Manifesto*, *The Eighteenth Brumaire* and *Capital*) studied this ideological region as the focal point and privileged object of their critiques.

Secondly, the dominance of the juridico-political region over the others is manifested not only by the fact that it is *distinct* from philosophical, moral and religious ideologies, but also by the fact that these latter ideologies borrow notions from the juridico-political, notions which enable them to think themselves or which they use as a reference point to establish their own notions.

a. Philosophical ideology: we need only mention the particular importance conferred on 'philosophy of right' and on 'political philosophy' by Spinoza, Kant, Hegel, etc. and the formation of the philosophical notions of 'nature', 'liberty', etc., in the French social contract theorists and also in Locke, Mill, Bentham, etc.[25]

b. Religious ideology: we need only mention Weber's analyses of the impact of the juridico-political ideology on Protestantism, as related to what he calls 'rational-legal' legitimacy.

c. Moral ideology: we need only mention how the domination of the juridico-political ideology transformed the notions of 'individual' and 'person', of 'right' and 'duty', of 'virtue' (in e.g. Machiavelli and Montesquieu) and of 'love', which it turned into a true 'contract' of mutual recognition. In this case the moral is not simply subordinated to the political, but above all moral notions are constituted from a point of reference (often a point of *contrasting reference*) provided by the political. But furthermore, when a science is constituted, its notions are often formulated in or strongly influenced by the juridico-political ideology, such as the modern notion of 'law' as found in Montesquieu. The classical case of this is economic science, in which Marx criticizes the very name of '*political*' economy. Finally, the privileged discourse within which the

25. See M. Villey, 'Cours d'histoire de la philosophie du droit' in *Cours de droit*, Nos. 3 and 4.

dominated classes 'spontaneously' live their revolt against the bourgeois class is dominated by the juridico-political region of the dominant ideology: 'social justice', 'equality', etc.[26]

These examples are intentionally simple and very schematic; by means of them I claim to do no more than indicate the problem. On the other hand, I shall dwell at greater length on the reasons for the dominance of the juridico-political region in the dominant ideology, linking that problem directly to the problem of its particular mode of functioning within the framework of hegemonic class domination.

It is apparent that the juridico-political ideology is the dominant region in bourgeois ideology because it is in the best position to fulfil the particular role of ideology in the CMP and in a capitalist formation. This is also closely linked to the specific role played by the real juridico-political level, i.e. the state and law. The 'cement' of ideology permeates every layer of the social structure, *including economic and political practice*. It has been seen above that in the CMP and in a capitalist formation, ideology manifests itself vis-à-vis *economic* practice in a particular effect, namely the *effect of isolation*: this effect of isolation can also be seen in the impact of the juridico-political level on socio-economic relations. In its various aspects, this effect of isolation is an indispensable condition for the existence and functioning of the CMP and of a capitalist formation. This is the real meaning of Marx's analyses of capitalist fetishism, as distinct from simple market fetishism, in the 'pure' CMP. The phenomena covered by the term 'fetishism', as well as the generalization of exchange, competition, etc., presuppose this particular isolation effect ascribable to ideology as the condition of their existence. Marx grasped this effect in a descriptive way in opposing it to what he called the 'natural ties' of pre-capitalist social formations.

In the case of capitalism, this effect of isolation is the privileged product of the juridico-political ideology, and more specifically of the juridical ideology. We could say that if the sacred and religious *bind together*, the first step of the juridico-political ideology is to *separate and untie* (in the

26. It is true that this dominance of the juridico-political region in the dominant bourgeois ideology takes on *different forms* depending on the social *formations* in question. This is what Marx meant when he said that: 'The Germans have a head for philosophy, the English for economics, the French for politics.' But in the context, this remark also indicates that this dominance of the juridico-political region of ideology is only a general rule and that it can be threatened in a given capitalist formation.

sense in which Marx says that it 'frees') the agents from 'natural ties'. Its functions include setting up political 'individuals-persons', 'subjects of law', who are 'free' and 'equal' one to the other; this allows the functioning of those juridico-political structures which permit the labour contract (buying and selling of labour power), capitalist private property (N.B. the role of this ideology as the *condition of existence* of the juridical relation of property), the generalization of exchange, competition, etc. Alongside this, in the various forms which it takes on in economic reality and by its retroactive effects on the ideological, this effect of isolation is the very basis which masks from the agents the real structures of the economic, its dominance in the CMP, class structures, etc. This is in fact the meaning of Marx's analyses of fetishism, of the role of competition in class relations, of the impact of ideology on classical 'political' economy, etc.

However, this is only one aspect of ideology's function in a capitalist formation. Although it plays the role of cohesion and liaison which belongs to ideology in general, it also in the capitalist formation has a *particularly important* role at the level of the agents. This importance is due primarily to the specific autonomy of the instances in a CMP and in a capitalist formation, reflected in a specific autonomy of the economic, political and ideological practices. It is also due to the effect of isolation produced by the ideological and to the cohesive role accruing to it from this isolation which, since the juridico-political level plays a part in it, is largely its own effect. The political role of the dominant bourgeois ideology, dominated by the juridico-political region, is to attempt to impose upon the ensemble of society a 'way of life' through which the state can be experienced as representing society's 'general interest', and as the guardian of the universal vis-à-vis 'private individuals'. These latter are a creation of the dominant ideology, which presents them as unified by an 'equal' and 'free' participation in the 'national' community, under the protection of the dominant classes who are held to embody the 'popular will'.

One of the particular characteristics of dominant bourgeois ideology is, in fact, that it conceals class exploitation in a specific manner, *to the extent that all trace of class domination is systematically absent from its language.* It is true that its very status forbids any ideology to present itself as the ideology of class-domination. However, in 'pre-capitalist' ideologies, class operations are always *present* in their *principles*, although they are justified as 'natural' or 'sacred'. Such is the typical case of feudal religious ideology, where the 'difference' between 'men' is present in the structure, although it is justified by reference to the 'sacred' order.[27] Similarly in the moral or philosophical ideologies of social formations based on slavery, this difference is justified by reference to the 'natural' order. On the other hand the dominance of the juridico-political region in the dominant bourgeois ideology corresponds precisely to this particular masking of class domination. It is clear that the ideological region is thus especially suited to play this role, particularly when we recall the analogous absence of class domination in the institutions of the capitalist state and in modern law. Thus the impact of this region on the other regions of the ideological and the political role of the dominant bourgeois ideology consists not only in the fact that it justifies the direct economic interests of the dominant class but that above all it presupposes, composes or imposes the image of an 'equality' of 'identical', 'disparate', and 'isolated' individuals, unified in the political universality of the state/nation. It is in this context that we recognize the political implications of the ideologies of 'mass society', 'consumer society', etc. It is precisely by this specific masking of class domination that the juridico-political ideology best fulfils its particular cohesive role, which accrues to the ideological in the CMP and capitalist formations. In short, everything occurs here as if the region of ideology which is *the best placed* to hide the real index of determination and dominance of the structure is also in the best place to cement the cohesion of social relations by reconstituting their unity on an imaginary plane.

This specific masking of class domination, combined with the particular role of cohesion which accrues to bourgeois ideology, under the dominance of the juridico-political region of ideology, is precisely reflected in the close relation between ideology and the capitalist state. This is what Gramsci called the 'ethico-political' function of the state; it is seen in the capitalist state's take-over of education and in its regimentation of the cultural domain in general. The capitalist state's role relative to ideology is presented as 'organizational': this is merely the result of inserting the capitalist state's specific unifying role into the discourse which is itself constructed according to the particular role of the dominant bourgeois ideology.

Hence the specific efficacity of this ideology is constantly present in the

27. The constitution of classes as 'estates/castes' must be related *both* to the dominance of the ideological *and* to the dominance within ideology of the region of religious ideology. On this subject and on the 'desacralization' of politics in the 'modern state', see R. Balandier, *Anthropologie politique*, 1967, pp. 103 ff., 191 ff.

functioning of the capitalist state itself. Let us take the case of bureaucracy, the state apparatus, without however anticipating the specific problem of bureaucracy which will be discussed later. In his mature works, notably in *The Eighteenth Brumaire*, Marx drew attention to this role of ideology in the modern bureaucratic apparatus. This apparatus does not present itself directly as an apparatus of class domination, but rather as the 'unity', the organizing principle and incarnation of the 'general interest' of society. This manner of presentation has crucial effects on the concrete functioning of the bureaucratic apparatus: it produces a permanent masking of knowledge within this apparatus by relaying hierarchical and formal rules of jurisdiction, something which is only possible with the advent of the juridico-political bourgeois ideology. The 'formal rationality' of the bureaucratic apparatus is in fact possible only where political class domination in particular is absent from it, being supplanted by this ideology of organization.[28]

Ideology plays a similar role in the concrete functioning of the *political scene* (an area specific to the capitalist state), the place in which political representation in the capitalist state is conducted: Marx, Engels and Lenin frequently characterize this area as the modern representative state. In it, parliament is seen as the 'representative' of the public will, the parties as the representatives of public opinion, etc. Ideology intervenes in the functioning of the state in order to provide the class actors with the veneer of representation by means of which they can insinuate themselves into the institutions of the general popular-class-state and under cover of which they can mask the divergences inevitable in the capitalist state between the actions of these actors and the classes which they represent. In his mature works Marx stresses this role of ideology in his analyses of the relations (i) between parties and classes and (ii) between the state and those classes which in the capitalist state have the specific function of being 'supporting classes' (as distinct from dominant classes): see his analyses of the role of ideology in the fetishism of power by the petty bourgeoisie, the small-holding peasantry, etc.

Bourgeois juridico-political ideologies therefore conceal their political significance in a very specific manner, which means that they have the

28. It is in this sense that we accept the relations established by Weber between bureaucratic 'rationality' and the 'rational-legal' type of authority, based on the 'general interest' of the nation.

following remarkable characteristic: they achieve this concealment by explicitly presenting themselves as science. Contrary to superficial analyses of this subject, we can see that the theme of the '*end of ideologies*' (to use the current expression) is in fact the theoretical basis of all such ideologies. This is clear in the constitution of the political categories of '*public opinion*' and '*consensus*': they are related to the specific way in which the dominated classes accept these ideologies. In fact, the specific characteristic of these ideologies is not at all, as Gramsci believed, that they procure a more or less active 'consent' from the dominated classes towards political domination, since this is a general characteristic of *any* dominant ideology. What specifically defines the ideologies in question is that they do not aim to be accepted by the dominated classes according to the principle of participation in the sacred: they explicitly declare themselves and are accepted as scientific techniques. It is, in fact, in capitalist formations that the political category of public opinion[29] and the related category of consent, first mentioned by the physiocrats, make an appearance: in the discourse of the dominant ideology they are linked to the conceptualization of the relative autonomy of the political and of the economic in a capitalist formation. Hence they are related to a whole theoretical revolution concerning the concept of the political, which, until then, had remained faithful to the Aristotelian ethical tradition.[30]

The theoretical break which appeared in Machiavelli and Morus, is carried on by the school which constitutes politics according to the model of apodictic *knowledge* (*episteme*) as exhibited in the concept of public opinion. This concept covers the field of the strictly political – of the public as opposed to the private; in the various forms into which it has evolved, it points to the need for the 'citizens' to have a 'rational knowledge' of the laws of the functioning of the political order, which was already deemed to be an 'artificial' order by Hobbes. The knowledge in question is knowledge of the conditions of their specific 'practice' (*techne*) which is henceforth seen as strictly political practice. Political ideology, in the form of public opinion, presents itself as a body of practical rules, as technical knowledge, as the citizens' 'enlightened consciousness' of a specific practice, as the 'Reason' of this practice. This is the underlying conception of the whole series of political liberties: of the freedom of

29. On this subject, see J. Habermas, *Strukturwandel der Öffentlichkeit*, 1965, pp. 65 ff.

30. On the concept of the political and of politics in the Greek philosophical tradition, see F. Chatelet, *Platon*, 1966, and J. P. Vernant, *Mythe et Pensée chez les Grecs*, 1966.

speech, freedom of the press, etc. Public opinion, which is a necessary factor in the functioning of the capitalist state and which is the modern form of political consent (consensus) cannot in fact function unless it manages to present itself and to be accepted in terms of 'rational' scientific technique, i.e. *in so far as it sets itself up in its principles in opposition to that which it designates and marks out as utopian.*[31] It thus designates as utopian any representation in which the class struggle is present in any form whatsoever. We can also clearly locate in the same theoretical line those contemporary ideologies of 'mass society', of 'communication techniques', etc. which have created the ideological myth of the 'end of ideologies', the term ideology here being identified with 'utopia'. In fact in its political functioning bourgeois ideology has always presented itself as a scientific technique. It has done this by defining science by reference to a 'beyond' which it has termed 'utopian'.

The particular function of bourgeois ideology dominated by the juridico-political region, can also account for what has wrongly been called its 'totalitarian' nature. Modern political science has used this term in order to contrast contemporary political ideologies with 'liberal' political ideologies. In this usage, totalitarian political ideologies are characterized firstly by the fact that they destroy the barriers accepted by liberal ideology between the individual and the state, in advocating the 'total' assimilation of the individual by the state; and secondly by the fact that they are now invading every aspect of social practice. This is in contrast with liberal ideology which carries within itself its own limits, in that, for example, it recognizes domains exterior to itself (the economic) and insists on the non-intervention of the state in the economic and the ideological.

I shall return to my critique of these theories of totalitarianism, in so far as they also concern the way in which the contemporary capitalist state functions.[32] For the moment I shall simply note that these theories grasp (in an ideological form) certain real problems posed by bourgeois

31. The link between this operation of public opinion and the specific ideology in which class domination is present by its very absence is described as follows by Habermas: 'Class interest is the basis of public opinion. This interest must however correspond at a certain stage to the general interest, in so far as this opinion must be able to be valued as "public", i.e. as mediated by public reasoning and thus as rational', op. cit., p. 100. See also on this subject, J. Touchard, *Histoire des idées politiques*, 1967.

32. See p. 290 n below for a bibliography of 'totalitarianism'.

ideology; these problems relate however to the particular function of ideologies in capitalist formations, and liberal political ideology is in no way an exceptional case.

A. Bourgeois political ideology's particular function of isolation and cohesion leads to a totally remarkable internal contradiction, sometimes thematized in the theories of the social contract by the distinction and relation between the *pact of civil association* and the *pact of political domination*. This ideology sets agents up as individuals/subjects, free and equal, and presents them as it were in a pre-social state, and so defines the specific isolation of social relations. This aspect which has been described as 'bourgeois individualism' is well known. But it is important to point out the other, perhaps right, side of the coin. These individuals/persons, who are individualized in this way, do not seem able in one and the same theoretical movement to be unified and attain their social existence except by means of gaining political existence in the state. The result is that the private individual's freedom suddenly appears to vanish before the authority of the state which embodies the general will. Indeed, for bourgeois political ideology *there can be no limit based on law or principle to the activity and encroachment of the state* in the so-called sphere of the individual/private. In the last analysis, this sphere appears to have no other function but that of providing a reference point, which is also a *vanishing point*, for the omnipresence and omniscience of the political instance. In this sense Hobbes appears to be the true anticipation of the theories of social contract and Hegel of their culmination: this is a complex case, but so are all theoretical cases. Rousseau's characteristic position should be noted: 'Man must be as independent as possible from other men and as dependent as possible on the state.' It is even clearer in the classic example of the physiocrats, fierce partisans of *laissez-faire* in the economic and equally fierce partisans of political authoritarianism: they called for the absolute monarch to embody the general will and interest. All this is also characteristic of liberal political ideology:[33] the best example is the clear but often misunderstood influence of Hobbes on Locke and on the classical British Liberal political school of 'utilitarianism', on Bentham, on Mill and, above all, on Stuart Mill.

In short, to use two equally ideological terms, the individualism of bourgeois political ideology inevitably goes hand in hand with (and only

33. See the important work of C. B. Macpherson, *The Political Theory of Possessive Individualism*, Oxford, 1964.

with) its totalitarianism.[34] We are concerned with the contradiction specific to the very *type* of bourgeois political ideology, the contradiction which stems from the particular character of the function which it performs. (We are not concerned with any particular form of that ideology, e.g. that of the present day.) In fact this juridico-political ideology operates as if in one stroke it has both founded that specific isolation which is individualization, and has also gained the means of maintaining its specific cohesion, thanks to the role it attributes to the political instance.

B. Bourgeois juridico-political ideology does not carry in its own structures limits to the intervention of the political instance in the economic or ideological, based on *principle* or *right*. This is the point being made when it is said that this ideology fundamentally recognizes only one plane of existence, the political plane, that it extends the domain of the political to encompass the whole of human life, that it believes that all thoughts and actions have a political significance and that consequently they fall within the sphere of political action.

What is exactly correct in this statement is that bourgeois political ideology, the dominant region of the dominant ideology, does not recognize *worlds which are by right outside* the intervention (to be distinguished from the place of constitution) of the political: this, *mutatis mutandis*, was not at all the case for the moral and philosophical ideology of slave society nor with the religious ideology of feudalism. We need only consider that advocacy of state interventions in the economic not only by the theorists of the French Revolution, but also by the classical liberal theorists, from Locke to the utilitarians (this advocacy must of course be distinguished from the real functioning of the state). This aspect of bourgeois juridico-political ideology in fact concerns the particular role of agent of unity devolving on the capitalist state, a role which here is invested in the discourse of the dominant ideology.

On the other hand, although it is true that the discourse of bourgeois juridico-political ideology penetrates and invades all social activities, including the economic, it is incorrect to consider this trait as specifying this ideology. In fact, it characterizes any dominant region of a dominant ideology. For example, economic activity is here *invaded* by juridico-political ideology just as it was by philosophical and moral discourse in

---

34. In spite of his general theoretical line and his very disputable conclusions, see on this J. L. Talmon, *The Origins of Totalitarian Democracy*, London, 1966.

formations based on slavery, or by religious discourse in feudal formations.

To conclude: the concept of *hegemony* as applied to the domination under hegemonic class leadership in capitalist formations here covers the above-mentioned specific characteristics of the dominant capitalist ideology, by means of which a class or a fraction manages to present itself as incarnating the general interest of the people-nation and thereby to condition the dominated classes to a specific political acceptance of its domination.

(v) THE PROBLEM OF LEGITIMACY

These remarks on ideologies provide the indispensable background for the question of the *legitimacy* of a political system, a vital question in modern political science. *By legitimacy of political structures and institutions we can designate their relation to the dominant ideology in a formation. In particular legitimacy covers the specifically political impact of the dominant ideology.*

This definition is important when we compare it to the meaning modern political science gives to this notion. According to it legitimacy (or 'political culture') generally indicates the way in which political structures are *accepted* by the agents of the system. After Max Weber, this notion was however incorporated into the functionalist problematic which is wedded to the conception of the historical subject and so discovers in the ideological language of a formation the aims or ends of the practice of the social actors. In this context, the ideological (i.e. the values, symbols and predominant styles of a formation) is given the sense and the theoretical function of the central instance of a social system: this is the conception of anthropological culturalism. Normative political models establish the framework for integration which specifies the expressive and circular form of the relations between the elements of a system, in the functionalist sense of the term. The legitimacy of political structures thus signifies their integration into the functionality of the system governed by its social ends, aims and values; it indicates their acceptance by the actors, integrated by means of this acceptance, into a social ensemble.[35] In the case where the

35. See G. Almond and S. Verba, *The Civic Culture*, 1963, pp. 3–78, where legitimacy is defined as 'orientation of political action'; and also the introduction to the important work of Almond and Coleman, *The Politics of Developing Areas*, 1960, pp. 3–64; Mitchell, *The American Polity*, 1962; Shils, *Political Development in New States*, 1962, and

political structures do not coincide with the normative models of a society, they are conceived as being dysfunctional, i.e. as constituting a badly integrated ensemble which specifies their illegitimacy.[36] Then by applying the general functionalist conception of the political system as the central integrating factor of a social system, the political system can be specified as the 'authoritarian distribution of values for the social ensemble' and the study of the political can be seen as the study of a process of legitimization of the relations of a social system.[37]

I shall not go into a detailed analysis of the consequences of this theory: I shall point out only the more important ones which, incidentally, are often identical to those which stem from the historicist conception of ideologies:

a. An over-estimation of the ideological, in particular of the proper function of legitimacy. The dislocation between the political structures and the dominant ideology is not given a scientific status but is apprehended under the category of the dysfunctional which is evidently meaningless in the theoretical context of functionalism.[38] However, this dislocation (i.e. the possibility that illegitimate political structures may function) is perfectly well explicable by Marxist theory, the theory of a unity comprising levels which are dislocated up to the point of rupture. That is because, (i) this dislocation between the ideological and the political does not necessarily reflect a dislocation between the political and the economic or, in its complexity, a situation of rupture of the ensemble of the formation, and (ii) because the state apparatus of force and repression operates.

b. From this conception there follows a typology of political structures based principally on the types of legitimacy – a non-operational typology of these types; this was already the case with Weber's types of authority.

c. It makes it impossible to conceive in a rigorous manner, the co-

Towards a General Theory of Action, 1951; J. H. Kautsky, Political Change in Under-developed Countries, 1962.

36. e.g. L. Binder, in his important study, Iran: Political Development in a Changing Society, Berkeley, 1962, pp. 7 ff.

37. See especially D. Easton, in his two very important works already mentioned: A Framework for Political Analysis, 1965, and A Systems Analysis of Political Life, 1965. I have pointed out the relation in Weber's work between the concepts of authority and legitimacy.

38. e.g. Binder, who is more conscious than anyone else of these difficulties, introduces the notion of efficacity or effectiveness of political structures, alongside that of legitimacy.

existence within a formation of several types of legitimacy and the participation of various concrete institutional structures characterized by such
different types of legitimacy.

After saying this, it still remains true that the differentiation of political
structures and institutions according to types of legitimacy is brought out
in Marxist theory, by reference to the relations between the political and
the dominant ideology. It is in fact correct to say that as a general rule
political domination corresponds to a particular mode of acceptance and
consent from the unity of a formation, *including the dominated classes*: this
is clearly demonstrated by the relations indicated above between the
dominant ideology and the unity of a formation. This does not, of course,
mean that these classes are in some way integrated in this formation, that
there is no class struggle: this fact is related to the very status of the
ideological and *to the complex form in which the dominant ideology dominates
the ideological sub-ensembles within a formation.*

   The dominance of this ideology is shown by the fact that the dominated
classes live their conditions of political existence through the forms of
dominant political discourse: this means that often they live *even their
revolt* against the domination of the system within the frame of reference
of the dominant legitimacy. These remarks are of great importance since
they not only indicate the possibility of a lack of a 'class consciousness' in
the dominated classes, but they imply even that these classes' 'own'
political ideology is often modelled on the discourse of the dominant
legitimacy. This domination of the dominant ideology may present itself
in various forms:[39] often it does not show itself simply by imposing the
very content of its discourse upon the dominated classes; rather it is that
this dominant discourse appears to these classes as a *counter-point*, as
something which by its absence defines the difference between their
ideology and the dominant ideology. For example, the attitude of the
dominated classes towards 'political democracy' often takes the form of a
demand opposed to 'other forms of political democracy'. This is still a
way of participating in the dominant legitimacy which in this case is
dominant precisely in that it constitutes a *referential model* for opposing it.
In other cases the opposition sometimes manifests itself simply in a
different *manner* of conduct vis-à-vis the signs and symbols imposed by
the dominant legitimacy. Thus it is not at all surprising that in the working

39. See Pierre Bourdieu's work. Despite the reservations one must have concerning
his conception of social classes, they are of major importance.

class we can sometimes observe not merely a classical reformist ideology which openly accepts the dominant legitimacy, but even the coexistence of a strongly articulated revolutionary ideology with an ideology subject to the basic frameworks of the dominant legitimacy. Besides, it should be unnecessary to stress that even when the revolutionary ideology of the working class extends to those classes which are sometimes supports of the state (e.g. the small-scale producers) it is received only in a complex relation to the dominant ideology.

Hence we can see that, just as in a concrete formation the structures of the state, under the dominance of one type of state, present structures depending on other types, these structures often, under the dominance of one type of legitimacy, participate in different types of legitimacy.[40] They participate for instance in ideologies which were previously dominant and corresponding to classes which are no longer politically dominant. For example, feudal legitimacy has not only often characterized feudal structures coexisting in capitalist states (a simple case) but even structures typical of capitalist states; this is the case with the modern executive body which frequently participates in monarchical legitimacy. In a concrete state, the relation of coexistence of structures depending on several types and of legitimacies depending on several types engenders a whole complex series of combinations of their relations. Lastly, in dealing with a concrete capitalist state we should not underestimate the existence of legitimacies which depend mainly on particular class ideologies such as those of the petty bourgeoisie or the small-holding peasantry.

This analysis could undoubtedly be extended. However, the above remarks on bourgeois political ideologies which correspond to a domination with hegemonic class leadership are sufficient to pinpoint what may be described as the bourgeois type of legitimacy, characteristic of the CMP and of a formation dominated by this mode. I shall simply have to return to the question of the distinction between the various forms of this type of legitimacy according to the forms of the capitalist type of state.

40. See M. Duverger, *Institutions politiques*, 1966, pp. 32 ff. The dislocation between the type of state and the dominant legitimacy in a formation (corresponding to different political forms) is particularly striking in countries in the process of de-colonization and development (e.g. in Africa), where the setting up of 'modern' states is constantly dominated by traditional ideologies; on this subject see, e.g. D. Apter, *The Politics of Modernization*, 1955, and R. Balandier, *Anthropologie politique*, 1967, pp. 186 ff.

3. The Capitalist State and Force

The particular place and function of the capitalist state also allow us to determine the way in which 'force', 'repression' or 'violence' function in the framework of this state. The state can in no way be reduced to a mere apparatus or instrument of force in the hands of the dominant class. This element of force appears as a *general* characteristic of the functioning of the class state. It is, however, unnecessary to insist on the fact that the institutions of class domination, far from being derived from any kind of psycho-social relation of force, are in fact what assign to this repressive force its concrete functioning in a determinate formation.

What is to be understood by repressive force and violence, which are vague notions and useless until they are made specific? *The term force in fact covers the functioning of certain institutions of organized physical repression, such as the army, the police, the penitentiary system, etc.* This repression is socially organized and is one characteristic of *all power relations*. Thus the notion of force cannot be theoretically isolated from power relations (in the notion of *might*, for example[1]); nor can it be extended to represent in a general way (e.g. in the notion of violence) the positions of domination and subordination occupied by social classes in the relations of class domination. It is important therefore to grasp the concrete way in which organized physical repression functions in the case of the state corresponding to a hegemonic class domination. Gramsci pointed out this problem when he characterized this way of functioning as 'consent reinforced by coercion', seeing hegemony (consent to state 'leadership') as a 'complement' to state force, given that he wrongly included state structures in his concept of hegemony. These remarks indicate a question, but are far from providing an answer, since in fact, this 'consent reinforced by coercion' is a general characteristic of power relations. Because of the state's position in a formation (its ideological function, etc.), the political relations of domination present an aspect of legitimacy, which is precisely what allows the functioning of organized

1. See p. 107 above.

physical repression. What is often described as a *police state*, a term which indicates the particularly intense action of repressive institutions in certain conjunctures, does not in fact constitute a type of distinct domination corresponding to hegemonic class domination: when this sort of action appears within this framework, it must be related to the historically determined situation in which it functions.

Furthermore, these remarks of Gramsci's stem from a frequent conceptual confusion in his analyses. In them hegemony is not even on the practical level a concept locating a specific theoretical object (i.e. a type of political class domination) in its unity, but serves only to isolate the 'moment' of consent, of 'intellectual and moral leadership' and of 'organization' from the moment of 'force' and 'coercion', notions which remain vague and imprecise throughout his work. To grasp the relation between these two 'moments' he uses the significant term *'complementarity'*. From this stems a confusion of the areas in which hegemony is exercised, a confusion frequently encountered in his works, according to which, force is exercised by the state in 'political society', hegemony in 'civil society' by means of organizations usually considered to be 'private': the church, cultural institutions, etc. But the status of the distinction between hegemony and force, in so far as these cover respectively the economic and the political spheres, depends on the historicist conception of their relation. This distinction is the key to the model with which historicism apprehended the relations between the economic and the political: it saw the political (the class struggle) as the motor, *the force*, of the 'economic laws' conceived in a mechanistic fashion; in other words, politics is conceived as the motor of economic 'automatism' – an automatism which is indicated here by the 'moment of consent'.

In fact, the scientific examination of the capitalist state can mark out the place occupied by this element of 'force' in its form of organized physical repression. In this respect, this state's characteristic is *that it holds the monopoly of organized physical repression*, as opposed to other social formations in which institutions such as the church, seigneurial power, etc. have, parallel to the state, the privilege of exercising this power. Organized physical repression thus takes on a strictly political character. It becomes the exclusive prerogative of political power, and its legitimacy is henceforth derived from that of the state: it presents itself as a 'constitutionalized violence' and is subject to the normative regulation of the 'state based on right' (*l'état de droit*). In this sense the capitalist state holds the monopoly of *legitimate* force, taking account of the transformations under-gone by legitimacy in that state.[2]

This concentration of force in the hands of the state hence appears to correspond to (i) the autonomy of the instances in the CMP, (ii) the attribu-tion of a public character to the state's political institutions, and (iii) the assigning, by the state itself, of a private character to the institutions exercising this force in other formations. The exercise of physical repres-sion is henceforth legitimized in that it is presented as corresponding to the general interest of the nation-people; here legitimacy is related exclu-sively to the state. The repressive organization is deemed to be subject to the control of public opinion (see e.g. the institution of tribunals, juries, etc.) and it is not accidental that the first theoretical works on police organization are those which manufacture the concept of the 'state based on right'.[3] In short, in the capitalist state, organized physical repression appears (in Marx's phrase) 'naked', stripped of its extra-political justifica-tions and also inserted in the institutions of the popular-class-state.[4] So the capitalist state's possession of the legitimate monopoly of organized physical repression is apparently linked to that specific autonomy of the instances characteristic of a formation dominated by the CMP which assigns its place to the state. Further, this characteristic of the capitalist state is *implied in the actual functioning of the CMP as described by Marx in* Capital. I say 'implied' because this characteristic of the capitalist state is also only sketched in implicitly. This 'pure' mode of production can function only so long as organized physical repression is not directly organized by the agents in the domain of the social relations of production, but is left to the state. It is in this sense that we should understand Marx's analyses of the CMP, in particular the 'absence of *violence*' in the economic

2. Thus we can accept Weber's thesis that one of the characteristics of the state is that it holds a monopoly of legitimate force, provided that the object of the thesis is seen to be the *capitalist state*.

3. See the work of R. Mohl, published in 1832, with the following illuminating title: *Polizeiwissenschaft nach den Grundsätzen des Rechtsstaates*.

4. I shall spend no more time on the relation between political structures and force, because this relation is brought out clearly in the Marxist conception of the political. It seems more important to attack the 'Sorelian' distortion which sees in force (in the vague sense of violence) the factor which creates political structures. It is, however, useful to point out that contemporary political science, in the main, allows that the characteristic of organized and legitimate physical force is a constitutive feature of political structures in general. On this, see Weber; also R. Dahl, *Modern Political Analysis*, 1963, pp. 12 ff.; Easton, Coleman and Apter, op. cit.; Balandier, op. cit., pp. 32 ff. and 144 ff.

level of this mode, and not, as is often believed, in the sense of the non-intervention of state repression in this mode's *social relations of production*. Such repression is in fact constantly present: it should not be confused with the state's intervention or non-intervention in the *structure of the relations of production*. This characteristic of the capitalist state does not itself therefore indicate any kind of lessening of repression: rather it indicates the real and important fact that in exercising the monopoly of repression, the state attempts to present itself as conforming constantly to the general interest of the people. Its repression is moreover frequently exercised within the limits of the constitution and the law, in the modern sense of the term.

4. The Capitalist State and the Dominant Classes

In its specific structure and relations with the dominant classes and fractions the capitalist state presents a further particular feature, compared with other types of states. This is the problem of the 'power bloc'. The concept of hegemony may help us to study the functioning of the political practices of the dominant classes or fractions in the power bloc and to locate the relations between the state and this bloc.

In the case of this type of state, we note a specific interrelation between these classes or fractions to whose political interests this state corresponds. This fact permits us to locate the relations which hold between the forms of this type of state and the typical configuration presented by this interrelation between dominant classes and fractions in a stage of a capitalist formation.

I should first of all re-emphasize that the line of political demarcation between domination and subordination cannot be marked out from the viewpoint of a 'dualist' struggle between dominant and dominated classes, i.e. from a relation between the state and a dominant class: this is the instrumentalist and historicist conception of the state. A social formation is formed by an overlapping of several modes of production, which implies the coexistence in the field of the class struggle of several classes or fractions of classes and therefore, possibly, of several dominant classes or fractions.

But this characteristic is not in itself sufficient to explain the phenomenon of the power bloc which appears to be a phenomenon entirely peculiar to capitalist formations. At any rate, though this coexistence of several classes is a general characteristic of every social formation, it takes on specific forms in capitalist formations. In these formations we can establish the *relation* between (a) a specific institutional operation inscribed in the capitalist state's structures and (b) a particular configuration of the interrelations between the dominant classes: these relations, as related to the state, function within a specific political unity, covered by the concept of the power bloc.

A. The reasons for the appearance of the power bloc can already be found in the structure of the capitalist state. This structure presents the following particular feature: namely that it has as an effect the coexistence of the political domination of several classes and fractions of classes. Strictly speaking, by the internal play of its institutions, the capitalist state (in its relation to the field of the political class struggle, a relation conceived of as that which provides the limits to that struggle) makes the constitution of a power bloc *possible*.

Marx makes this point repeatedly. We shall take as our example of these institutions universal suffrage, the typical institution of a state which has gained autonomy from the economic and which presents itself as the incarnation of the general interest of the people: 'The *bourgeois monarchy* of Louis Philippe can be followed only by a *bourgeois republic*, that is to say, whereas a *limited section* of the bourgeoisie ruled in the name of the king, the whole bourgeoisie will now rule *on behalf of the people*.'[1] Marx presents universal suffrage as an institution which extends the relation between the capitalist state and the *particular simultaneous domination of several dominant classes and fractions of classes*: 'The first thing that the February Republic had to do was . . . *to complete the rule* of the bourgeoisie by allowing, beside the finance aristocracy, *all the propertied classes* to enter the orbit of political power. The majority of the great landowners . . . were emancipated from the political nullity to which they had been condemned by the July Monarchy.'[2] According to Marx, the function of universal suffrage is to circumscribe a particular space which he describes as the *political scene, sphere or orbit*, a class's presence in this scene being separate from its participation in the power bloc. But parallel to this, he conceives universal suffrage as that which locates a particular relation existing between (a) the state and (b) the relations which hold between the various classes or fractions in *power*. To grasp this relation, Marx uses the expression 'participation' in, or 'possession' of, political power, and thereby distinguishes this type of state from that which sanctions the 'exclusive domination' of one class or fraction. Universal suffrage is only one example amongst many, but it is one which illustrates especially clearly those characteristics of the capitalist state which permit the phenomenon of the power bloc to arise.

1. 'The Eighteenth Brumaire', *MESW*, 1970, p. 102.
2. 'The Class Struggles in France', *MESW*, 1958, Vol. I, p. 146.

B. The phenomenon of the power bloc is thus related to the field of the political practices of the ruling classes in a capitalist formation: it depends on the existence of a 'plurality' of dominant classes (and fractions) char- acteristic of this formation. This in turn depends on the general fact that in every formation several modes of production and hence several classes and fractions coexist. However, in the capitalist formations with which we are concerned this general fact takes on an *utterly particular* form, which goes back to the specific way in which the domination of the CMP was estab- lished in agriculture: this is the problem of the *big ground-rent landlords.* In *Capital*, Marx sometimes sees these big landlords as a separate class belonging to the pure CMP. But though his remarks here indicate the existence of a specific problem, they are inexact. Lenin clearly showed that landed property, private ownership of land, does not belong to the rela- tions of combination of the 'pure' CMP. 'The assumption of the capitalist organization of agriculture necessarily includes the assumption that all the land is occupied by separate private enterprises; but it in no way includes the assumption that the whole of the land is the private property of those farmers, or of other persons, or that it is, in general, private property.'[3] However, in the establishment of the CMP in agriculture under the politi- cal leadership of the 'nobility' or 'bourgeoisie' we can establish the follow- ing characteristics:

a. This establishment of the dominance of the CMP is *in fact* executed *(for mainly political and ideological reasons)* by the private ownership of land.

b. It is established through the concentration of big landed property. Here Lenin distinguishes *two paths*. In the case of a transition from *feudalism* to capitalism (despite certain major differences in the various examples) the big landowner always intervenes at the beginning of the process of capitalization of agriculture. This is for political reasons con- cerning the relations in the feudal mode of production between the feudal class of landed proprietors and the bourgeoisie. In that case in which feudalism in the strict sense is absent, the 'American path' prevails. The process is initiated by the middle and small independent landholders but leads eventually to big landed property.[4]

What then is the class of big ground-rent landowners which Marx incorrectly described as a distinct class of the pure CMP? In characterizing

3. 'The Agrarian Question and the "Critics of Marx" ', *Collected Works*, Vol. 5, p. 121.

4. Lenin, 'The Agrarian Programme of Social Democracy in the First Russian Revolution, 1905–7', *Collected Works*, Vol. 13, pp. 217–431.

it, politico-ideological determinations are decisive. It functions as a separate class in the transition from feudalism to capitalism and belongs to the feudal mode of production as transformed by the establishment of the dominance of the CMP: this was the case with Prussia. Or else it can function as a fraction of the nobility: as, for example, Great Britain. However, at the end of the process, precisely because of the *capitalization of ground-rent*, it is absorbed into the bourgeoisie and for a whole period forms part of this class as an *autonomous fraction* of it. In this case, its character as an autonomous fraction is dependent on: (a) politico-ideological factors going back to its tradition of belonging to the feudal nobility, (b) economic factors which stem from the fact that ground-rent is a particular mode of transfer of the social product and distribution of surplus value. It is this last factor which won the day, e.g. in France, where the bourgeoisie bought up big landed property and expropriated the nobility. Two principal factors led Marx to consider the big ground-rent landowners to be a class of the pure CMP: (i) the fact that the necessary transition from feudalism to capitalism was effected under the politico-ideological leadership of the nobility or the bourgeoisie by means of them, and (ii) the fact that they maintained their autonomy even after absorption into the bourgeoisie.

I have already pointed out the *decisive importance* of the ground-rent landowners as a separate class or autonomous fraction in capitalist formations. Its importance is related to the particular aspect taken on by the complex coexistence of several modes of production in a *capitalist formation*: it is in this way related to the plurality of dominant classes or fractions which is a characteristic feature of the power bloc. This plurality corresponds to the structures of the capitalist state which allow a characteristic 'participation' in power, either by the dominant classes of the dominated modes of production or by those fractions of the bourgeoisie whose autonomy depends on their relation to these modes.

C. Further, in the CMP, the class of the bourgeoisie appears as constitutively divided into fractions. The problem of fractions of a class is in fact rather complicated in Marx. It is important to point out that certain fractions of the bourgeois class, such as the commercial, industrial and financial, are not (as is often the case with fractions of classes in a formation) related simply to the concrete combination of the various modes of production, or to the particular effects of the political instance alone. In this latter case, the effects of the political instance (i.e. the classes which result from the effects of the ensemble of instances on social relations) may produce fractions of a class in the field of political class practice alone. For example in *The Eighteenth Brumaire*, Marx says of the republican bourgeois fraction:

> It was not a faction of the bourgeoisie held together by great common interests and marked off by specific conditions of production. It was a clique of republican-minded bourgeois, writers, lawyers . . . that owed its influence to the personal antipathies of the country against Louis Philippe, to memories of the the old republic . . . but above all to French nationalism.[5]

The commercial, industrial and financial fractions are, however, related to the very constitution of capital in the process of expanded reproduction, as a relation of production. Marx, of course, does not in *Capital* explicitly use the term fraction to designate mercantile, industrial and financial capital. These are grasped as 'forms of existence', though 'separated', of the same capital: 'The existence of capital as commodity capital [commercial capital] . . . forms a phase in the reproduction process of industrial capital, hence in its process of production as a whole . . . These are two different and separate forms of existence of the same capital.'[6] Commercial capital, producing surplus-value in the form of interest, thus does not constitute an autonomous form of industrial capital, producing surplus-value in the form of profit. However: 'Whether the industrial capitalist operates on his own or on borrowed capital does not alter the fact that the class of money-capitalists confronts him as a special kind of capitalist, money-capital as an independent kind of capital, and interest as an independent form of surplus-value peculiar to this specific capital.'[7] In short, this fractioning of the bourgeois class is related to the place occupied by these fractions in the process of production: the same is true of the big land-owners once they become a fraction of the bourgeois class: 'What kept the two factions apart [the big landowners and capital], was not any so-called principles, it was their material conditions of existence . . . the old contrast between town and country, the rivalry between capital and landed property.'[8]

This presence of big landowners, the bourgeoisie and various fractions of the bourgeois class in a formation dominated by the CMP is one of the

5. 'The Eighteenth Brumaire', *MESW*, 1970, p. 104.
6. *Capital*, Vol. III, p. 268.   7. ibid., pp. 376–7.
8. 'The Eighteenth Brumaire', *MESW*, 1970, p. 117.

important causes of the power bloc. The structures of the capitalist state and the existence of these classes and fractions, i.e. *the particular participation of several classes and class fractions in political domination*, enable us to discern the relations which hold between this state and the political organization of these classes and fractions in the power bloc.[9]

(ii) POWER BLOC, HEGEMONY AND PERIODIZATION OF A FORMATION: MARX'S POLITICAL ANALYSES

The concept of power bloc is not then introduced expressly by Marx or Engels; *it indicates the particular contradictory unity of the politically dominant classes or fractions of classes as related to a particular form of the capitalist state*. The power bloc is related to the periodization of the capitalist formation in typical stages.[10] The concept of power bloc covers both the concrete configuration of the unity of these classes or fractions in stages characterized by a specific mode of articulation and also a specific rhythm of the ensemble of the instances. In this sense, the concept of power bloc is related to the political level and covers the field of *political practices*, in so far as this field concentrates within itself and reflects the articulation of the ensemble of instances and levels of class struggle in a determinate stage. The function of the concept of power bloc is here analogous to that of the concept of the form of state in connection with the juridico-political superstructure.

9. Engels describes the concrete consequences of this situation in the following words: 'It seems a law of historical development that the bourgeoisie can in no European country get hold of political power – at least for any length of time – in the same exclusive way in which the feudal aristocracy kept hold of it during the Middle Ages' ('Socialism, Utopian and Scientific', Preface to the English edition, 1892; *MESW*, 1970, p. 389): or again, in the preface to 'The Peasant War in Germany' (1850): 'It is a peculiarity of the bourgeoisie, in contrast to all former ruling classes, that there is a turning point in its development after which every further expansion of its agencies . . . only tends to make it more and more unfit for political rule. . . . From that moment on, it loses the strength required for exclusive political rule . . . it looks around for allies with whom to share its rule, or to whom it can cede the whole of its rule, as circumstances may require' (ibid., pp. 238–9). It will be seen however that (i) this term 'alliance' is inadequate to mark off this particular feature of the bourgeoisie, since, as Engels frequently noted, the feudal class also enters into alliances, and (ii) this is in fact a power bloc, within which the bourgeoisie neither 'shares' nor 'completely gives up' political power.

10. See pp. 147 and 153 above.

But this periodization is distinct from that periodization of the rhythm specific to the political level, in that the latter is particularly related to the co-ordinates of class *representation by the political parties*. Through a whole series of dislocations, this representation reflects the displacements of class contradictions (principal and secondary contradictions, aspects of the contradictions, etc.), displacements which are, however, situated within the limits of the power bloc characteristic of a stage. Concerning the state, this second periodization is covered by the concept of form of régime; concerning the political class struggle it is covered by a series of concepts which indicate class relations in parties, situated in that particular space generally described by Marx as the *political scene*, in which the direct action of classes operates. In this space we can precisely delimit the dislocation between (i) the field of political class practices (the power bloc) in a form of state and (ii) the representation of classes by parties in a form of régime.

Marx and Engels studied these problems in their political works: they are dealt with particularly in Marx's *The Class Struggles in France* and *The Eighteenth Brumaire of Louis Bonaparte*. Because of the limited period considered in these works, the problems of periodization are not always clear, nor are the concepts implied in them always precise. But even so, as Lenin points out, the particular character of the period studied by Marx should not be overlooked: it presents in a concentrated way the stages of transformation of a capitalist formation: 'There is not the slightest doubt that these features are common to the whole of the modern evolution of all capitalist states in general. In the three years 1848–51 France displayed, in a swift, sharp and concentrated form, the very same processes of development which are peculiar to the whole capitalist world.'[11] It is in this sense that general indications can be extracted from these works, as well as some scientific concepts which, though refracted by the limited scope of their analysis, are valuable in the study of these problems.

In fact Marx's analyses of the *first* of these two periodizations (i.e. the periodization into stages) point out the following constant element: the specific contradictory unity of several dominant classes or class fractions, a unity which corresponds to a particular form of state. But what is lacking in Marx in order to grasp this unity theoretically, are precisely the concepts of power bloc and of hegemony applied to this bloc. This is what leads him to talk often of an 'exclusive domination' or of a 'monopoly of

11. 'The State and Revolution', *Selected Works*, Vol. 2, p. 290.

power' by a class or fraction, although his analyses constantly demonstrate the political domination of several classes and fractions.

We shall take the case of the Restoration of the Bourbons, of the constitutional monarchy of Louis Philippe, and of the parliamentary Republic from the fall of Louis Philippe to the Bonapartist coup d'état, all of which Marx, despite certain reservations, takes to represent particular forms of the capitalist state. The Restoration is portrayed as the 'exclusive domination' or the 'monopoly of power' by the big landowners,[12] the constitutional monarchy as that of the financial aristocracy.[13] However, Marx elsewhere says of this monarchy that it constitutes the 'exclusive domination' or the 'monopoly of power' by *two fractions*, that of the financial bourgeoisie and that of the industrial bourgeoisie.[14] It is, in fact, their particular political unity which corresponds to the constitutional monarchy, here seen as a form of state. Let us now consider the parliamentary Republic: this latter corresponds, as a form of state, to the particular political unity between fractions of big landowners (the legitimists) and the financial bourgeoisie and the industrial bourgeoisie:

In the bourgeois republic . . . they had found the form of state in which they could rule conjointly.[15]

The parliamentary republic was more than the neutral territory on which the two factions of the French bourgeoisie, Legitimists and Orleanists, large landed property and industry, could dwell side by side with equality of rights. It was the unavoidable condition of their common rule, the sole form of state in which their general class interest subjected to itself at the same time both claims of their particular factions and all the remaining classes of society.[16]

It is at this point that the problems are posed. Marx does in fact establish the relation between a form of state and the concrete configuration of unity of several dominant fractions and, though he does not utilize the concept of power bloc to think this unity theoretically, he nevertheless assigns to it a particular place. *He does this by replacing the term 'alliance' by 'coalition', 'union' and above all 'fusion'.* The results of the lack of this concept of power bloc are the following: (i) Marx is sometimes unable to reveal the coexistence of several fractions in political domination; he thus makes one of them appear as the 'exclusively dominant' fraction while in

12. 'The Class Struggles in France', *MESW*, 1958, Vol. I, p. 189.
13. ibid., p. 142.
14. 'The Eighteenth Brumaire', *MESW*, 1970, pp. 110–11.
15. ibid., p. 110.   16. ibid., pp. 151–2.

reality he is dealing with a unity of several dominant fractions, and (ii) when he locates and gives this unity a name the term which he uses is the totally inadequate one of 'fusion'. This frequently used term was openly borrowed by Marx and Engels from physics and chemistry, and it can, if employed incautiously, indicate an expressive totality composed of 'equivalent' elements. Thus this term can imply simultaneously both the conception according to which these elements *share* state power (i.e. a negation of the unity of the capitalist state's power) and also the conception of a circular unity of these elements, without a dominant instance, a unity in which they lose their specific autonomy:

> The nameless reign of the republic was the only one in which both factions could maintain with equal power the common class interest without giving up their mutual rivalry. If the bourgeois republic could not be anything but the perfected and clearly expressed rule of the whole bourgeois class, could it be anything but the rule of the Legitimists *supplemented* by the Orleanists, the *synthesis* of the restoration and the July monarchy? . . . They did not comprehend that if each of their factions, regarded separately, by itself, was royalist, the *product of their chemical combination* had necessarily to be republican.[17]

Here we see the notions of complementarity and synthesis, both typical of the problematic of an expressive totality.[18]

The phenomenon of the power bloc cannot be thought by means of the notion of fusion: this is because the power bloc does not constitute an expressive totality of equivalent elements, but a complex contradictory unity in dominance. This is how the *concept of hegemony* can be applied to *one* class or fraction within the power bloc. This hegemonic class or fraction is in fact the *dominant* element of the contradictory unity of politically *'dominant'* classes or fractions, forming part of the power bloc. When Marx speaks of the 'exclusively dominant' fraction, while at the same time admitting the political domination of several fractions, he precisely attempts to isolate, within the power bloc, the hegemonic fraction. Thus in describing the Restoration and Louis Philippe's monarchy, Marx says that both of these gave the 'monopoly of power' to one of the

17. 'The Class Struggles in France', *MESW*, 1958, Vol. I, pp. 189–90.
18. In the chapter on social classes, in dealing with the under-determination of the classes of non-dominant modes of production, I described their dissolution and fusion with the classes of the dominant mode of production. However, the term 'fusion' was there being used to indicate that certain classes or fractions do not function in a formation as 'distinct classes' or 'autonomous fractions' with pertinent effects at the level of

fractions, but he adds immediately afterwards: 'Bourbon was the royal name for the predominant influence of the interests of the one faction. Orleans was the royal name for the predominant interests of the other faction – the nameless realm of the republic was the only one in which both powers could maintain with equal power the common class interest.'[19] In fact, both the Restoration and Louis Philippe's monarchy corresponded to a power bloc of the *three* fractions in question (big landowners, financial bourgeoisie and industrial bourgeoisie), the power bloc of the Restoration being realized under the protection of the hegemonic fraction of the financial bourgeoisie.

The power bloc of the parliamentary Republic is in this respect typical. Does it, as Marx tells us throughout his analyses, constitute a domination with *equality of power*, a 'fusion', of these fractions? Not at all:

Our whole exposition has shown how the Republic, from the first day of its existence, did not overthrow, but consolidated the finance aristocracy. . . . The question will be asked, how the coalesced bourgeoisie could bear and suffer the rule [i.e. hegemony – N.P.] of finance, which under Louis Philippe depended on the exclusion or subordination [i.e. power bloc – N.P.] of the remaining bourgeois factions. The answer is simple. First of all, the finance aristocracy itself *forms a weighty, authoritative part* of the royalist coalition, whose common governmental power is denominated republic.[20]

Here we see clearly that far from the power bloc of the Republic representing an *equal share-out* of power between the fractions constituting it, it rests on the hegemony of the financial fraction. In relation to the republican form of state this hegemony takes on a different form from the hegemony of the same fraction in the power bloc of constitutional monarchy.[21]

---

the political, i.e. they do not function as 'social forces'. Here, however, the term 'fusion' is used to grasp a type of unity amongst social forces.

19. 'The Class Struggles in France', *MESW*, 1958, Vol. I, p. 189.
20. ibid., p. 209.
21. We can see the implications and consequences of using the notion of fusion in several contemporary works in Marxist political science. My article 'Marxist Political Theory in Great Britain', op. cit., provides a critique of this concept as employed by authors such as P. Anderson and T. Nairn in their analyses of the evolution of capitalism in Britain. In this article I draw attention to Marx and Engels's concrete analyses of the 'power bloc' in Britain; these follow the same *theoretical* lines as Marx's analyses of the French case. We should note in passing that the particular *historical* feature of France in this respect was the almost constant hegemony of *financial capital* from the time of Louis Philippe onwards. Britain and Germany differ from France in that in them this hegemonic place is frequently taken over by commercial and industrial

In conclusion: (i) the power bloc constitutes a contradictory unity of *politically dominant* classes and fractions *under the protection of the hegemonic fraction*; (ii) the class struggle, the rivalry between the interests of these social forces, is *constantly present*, since these interests retain their specific character of antagonism. These are the two reasons why the notion of 'fusion' cannot give a proper account of this unity. The hegemony of a class or fraction within this bloc is not accidental; it is made possible (as we shall see) by that unity which is the particular mark of the institutionalized power of the capitalist state. As this latter unity corresponds to the particular unity of dominant classes or fractions (i.e. is related to the phenomenon of the power bloc), it precisely prevents the relations between the dominant classes or fractions from consisting of a '*sharing*' of state power, with 'equality of power'. (This could however be the case in other types of state.) The relation between the capitalist state and the dominant classes or fractions pushes them towards *their political unity under the protection of a hegemonic class or fraction*. The hegemonic class or fraction *polarizes* the specific contradictory interests of the various classes or fractions in the power bloc by making its own economic interests into political interests and by representing the general common interest of the classes or fractions in the power bloc: this general interest consists of economic exploitation and political domination. In an illuminating passage on the hegemony of the financial fraction in the parliamentary Republic, Marx indicates how this hegemony is constituted:

In a country like France, . . . a countless number of people from all bourgeois or semi-bourgeois classes must have an interest in the state debt, in the Bourse gamblings, in finance. Do not all these interested subalterns find their natural mainstays and commanders in the faction which represents this interest in its vastest outlines, which represents it as a whole?[22]

Another important fact must be pointed out. The process whereby the hegemony of a class or fraction is constituted differs according to whether this hegemony is brought to bear only on the other dominant classes or fractions (the power bloc) or on the ensemble of a formation, including the dominated classes. This difference coincides with the line of demarcation between the places of domination and subordination occupied by the social

---

capital. On the reasons for this situation in France, see G. Dupeux, *La société française, 1789-1960*, 1964, pp. 39 ff., 132 ff.

22. 'The Class Struggles in France', *MESW*, 1958, Vol. I, pp. 209–10.

classes of a formation. The general interest represented vis-à-vis the dominant classes by this hegemonic fraction depends in the last analysis on the place of exploitation which they hold in the process of production. The general interest represented vis-à-vis the ensemble of society (and therefore vis-à-vis the dominated classes) by this fraction depends on the ideological function of the hegemonic fraction. We note however that the function of hegemony in the power bloc and the function of hegemony vis-à-vis the dominated classes *are generally concentrated within the same class or fraction.* This latter sets itself up in the place of hegemony in the power bloc, by constituting itself politically as the hegemonic class or fraction of the ensemble of society. On the parliamentary Republic and the hegemony of the financial aristocracy in the power bloc, Marx says that it was the only form of state 'in which their general class interest subjected to itself at the same time both claims of their particular factions *and all the remaining classes of* society';[23] and again: '. . . the old powers of society had *grouped themselves, assembled, reflected and found unexpected support in the mass of the nation,* the peasants and petty bourgeois. . . .'[24] Marx also provides a whole series of concrete analyses of the process whereby the financial bourgeoisie is constituted as the hegemonic fraction of both the power bloc and the ensemble of society.

However, though this *concentration* of the double function of hegemony within one class or fraction is inscribed in the operation of the capitalist state's institutions, it is still only a general rule whose realization depends on the conjuncture of the social forces. Thus we may note the possibility of dislocation, dissociation and displacement of these functions of hegemony to different classes or fractions, one representing the hegemonic fraction of the ensemble of society, the other representing the specific hegemonic fraction of the power bloc: this has important consequences at the political level.

(iii) POWER BLOC, ALLIANCES, SUPPORTING CLASSES

The concept of power bloc must be distinguished from that of *alliance.*[25]

23. 'The Eighteenth Brumaire', *MESW*, 1970, pp. 151–2.
24. ibid., p. 101 (my emphasis).
25. On the concept of alliance, see Linhart's article on the NEP in *Cahiers de planification socialiste*, Paris, 1966. It is worth pointing out here that Lenin (as well as Mao) often stressed the limits of the concept of alliance by trying to mark off from it such specific concepts as that of the *united front.* I shall not discuss their analyses

The latter also implies a *unity* and a *contradiction* of the interests of the allied classes or of fractions of class in the alliance. The two concepts are distinguished by:

1. The *nature of this contradiction* relative to a 'form' of capitalist state within a stage. In the case of the power bloc we can make out *a threshold* beyond which the contradictions between the classes and fractions composing it can be clearly distinguished (relative to *a form of state and within a particular stage*) from the contradictions which exist between those classes and fractions and the other allied classes or fractions. An alliance can function either between the classes or fractions of the power bloc, or between one of those classes or fractions and another class or fraction outside the power bloc: see e.g. the frequent relation between the petty bourgeoisie and the power bloc.

2. The fact that the nature of the contradictions amongst the members of the power bloc and amongst the members of an alliance determines the *different characters of their respective unities*: an alliance generally functions only at a determinate level of the field of the class struggle and is often combined with an intense struggle at the other levels. For example, a political alliance between the power bloc and the petty bourgeoisie is often combined with an intense economic struggle against the latter; or again, an economic alliance with the petty bourgeoisie is often combined with an intense political struggle against its political representation.[26] On the other hand, in the case of the power bloc, there is a *relative extension of the unity* (and so of mutual sacrifices) at all levels of the class struggle: economic unity, political unity, and often also ideological unity. This, of course, does not prevent the existence of contradictions between the members of the power bloc: there is simply a relative homogeneity between their relations at all levels.

These differences between power bloc and alliance become very clear in the case of an important reversal of the relation of forces, or in the case in which either the power bloc or an alliance is dissolved. In the framework of the power bloc, such reversals correspond *as a general rule to a transformation in the form of state*. Marx, for instance, shows how the

---

because they centre on the dictatorship of the proletariat and the transition from capitalism to socialism and cannot therefore be directly applied to the capitalist formation. However, the fact that they find it necessary to employ the concept of the united front, as distinct from that of alliance, makes my recourse to the concept of power bloc legitimate.

26. 'The Class Struggles in France', *MESW*, 1958, Vol. I, p. 164.

power bloc of the parliamentary Republic was transformed relative to the advent of Louis Bonaparte.[27] On the other hand, in the framework of alliances such reversals do *not* coincide with a transformation of the form of state. Thus Marx shows how the dissolution of the alliance with the petty bourgeoisie (who exchanged the status of *ally* for that of *satellite*) occurring at the end of the first period of the parliamentary Republic, did not at all lead to this form of state being replaced by another, but (in the case in point) led to a transformation of the form of régime.[28]

Thus the distinction between power bloc and alliance should not be confused with a *chronological* distinction (between long and short duration) which would, as it were, see the power bloc as a long-term alliance. In fact, class alliances can be observed which outlast the transformations of the power bloc: a characteristic example is the *permanent* alliance in Germany between the petty bourgeoisie (allied) and the financial bourgeoisie (member of the power bloc); Engels focused attention on this in *Revolution and Counter-Revolution in Germany*.

To generalize these remarks: the typical configuration characterizing a power bloc corresponding to a form of state in a stage rests upon the concrete combination of three important factors:

1. the class or fraction which conçretely holds hegemony,
2. the classes or fractions which participate in this, and
3. the forms assumed by this hegemony, i.e. the nature of the contradic-·· tions and concrete relation of forces in the power bloc. A displacement of the index of hegemony of the bloc from one class or fraction to another; an important modification of its composition (the exit or entry of a class or fraction); a displacement of the principal class contradiction or of the principal aspect of the class contradiction either between the power bloc and the other classes and fractions, or within the very power bloc; any of these can, depending on the concrete effect of their *combination*, correspond to a transformation of the form of state. It is clear that the *typical configuration* of a determinate power bloc depends on the conjuncture, i.e. on the *concrete combination* of the factors outlined above: in any case it offers us a framework for deciphering the class relations typical of a *stage* of a determinate formation, by setting the *limits* of its typical form. Within the limits posed by this stage there is a series of variations of class relations

---

27. 'The Eighteenth Brumaire', *MESW*, 1970, pp. 151 ff.
28. 'The Class Struggles in France', *MESW*, 1958, Vol. I, p. 164; 'The Eighteenth Brumaire', *MESW*, 1970, p. 114.

and modifications of the power bloc, which do not however threaten its typical configuration and the form of the corresponding state.[29]

Thus because of the complexity of the power bloc we can more easily locate its relation to alliance. In fact, its typical configuration, which corresponds to a form of state, allows a series of *variations* to manifest themselves in e.g. *displacements of the threshold* of demarcation between alliance and power bloc within the very limits of its typical configuration. According to these displacements, for example, an allied class may cross this threshold and become part of the power bloc, or, vice versa, a member of the power bloc may alter its status and become an allied class or fraction. When the displacements of this threshold are situated within the above-mentioned limits they do not as a general rule entail a transformation of the form of state. But when these displacements are due to a *combined* transformation of the factors producing the power bloc they do entail such a transformation.

To supplement these concepts of power bloc and alliance (still vis-à-vis the variations of the limits of a form of state and power bloc in a determinate stage), Marx employs another concept which covers a particular category of relations between the classes of the power bloc and other classes: these are the classes by which a form of capitalist state is 'supported'. Typical examples of these *'supporting classes'* are the small-holding peasantry and the *Lumpenproletariat* in the framework of Bonapartism, and the petty bourgeoisie at the end of the first period of the parliamentary Republic.

The support is differentiated from the power bloc, as well as from the alliance, (i) by the nature of the contradictions between the power bloc and (a) the allied classes and (b) the supporting classes and, (ii) by the nature of the unity between the power bloc and (a) the allied classes and (b) the supporting classes. The particular status of supporting classes or supporting fractions of classes has the following characteristics:

1. The support which they give to a determinate class's domination is generally not based *on any real political sacrifice* of the interests of the power bloc and of the allied classes in their favour. Their support, which is indispensable to this class domination, is based primarily on a process of *ideological illusions*. Marx demonstrates this in the case of the small-holding peasantry whose vital support for the Bonapartist state is based on a whole ideological context relying on 'tradition' and on the origins of

29. Concrete examples of this will be dealt with later.

Louis Bonaparte. The Bonapartist state, supported by these peasants, did not take any appreciable political measure in favour of their particular interests. It simply took certain measures of a *compromise* sort so as to continue to feed this ideological illusion at the base of this political support.

2. The particular support of the supporting classes is due *to the fear, whether real or imaginary, of the power of the working class*. In this case the support is, of course, based neither on a community of interests stemming from real mutual sacrifices, nor on an ideological illusion concerning this sacrifice, but on the political factor of the struggle of the working class. This factor is an essential element in the unity of the power bloc or in the unity of alliances of class domination; and it also becomes essential in the case of the supporting classes. It is the *exclusive* factor in their support for classes which eventually attack their interests, although to a lesser degree, real or supposed, than the working class would have done. The ideological illusion is not here concerned principally with the attitude of the state or of the dominant classes, but with the proletariat's attitude towards them. A typical case is the status of the petty bourgeoisie in certain conjunctures.

These factors which produce the support of the supporting classes and the nature of the contradictions which separate them from the classes of the power bloc and allied classes influence the nature of their unity with these latter. This unity does not as a general rule manifest itself in immediate class relations *but operates through the intermediary of the state*. The supporting classes' relation to the power bloc and to the allied classes manifests itself less as a relation of political class unity than as support for a determinate form of state. Ideological illusion, which is all-important in the case of the supporting classes, takes on the particular political form of *power fetishism* of which Lenin spoke. This is (i) the belief in a state above the class struggle which could serve their interests against those in the power bloc and allied classes; and (ii) the belief in a state as guardian of the *status quo*, as a barrier to the conquest of power by the working class. In both these cases, the particular ideological masking of the nature and function of the state, as well as of its role as mediator between (a) the supporting classes and (b) the power bloc and the allied classes, depends *on the degree of political under-determination, characteristic of the supporting classes*, and on their incapacity to achieve an autonomous political organization because of their specific place in the process of production. Their political organization goes through the direct mediation of the state, as in the classical case of the small-holding peasantry, and often of the petty bourgeoisie. In other words, the cleavage between (a) the power bloc and the alliance and (b) the support, is also exhibited in the supporting classes' incapacity to achieve autonomous political organization. In this sense Marx said of the classes of small producers that:

They cannot represent themselves, they must be represented. Their representative must at the same time appear as their master, as an authority over them, as an unlimited governmental power that protects them against other classes and sends them rain and sunshine from above ('The Eighteenth Brumaire', *MESW*, 1970, p. 171).

Thus we can observe a whole series of *complex* relations depending on the concrete conjuncture between the classes and fractions of the power bloc, the allied classes or fractions and the supporting classes or fractions. The modifications of alliances and supports do not however generally correspond to a modification of the form of state in the framework of the periodization into stages, except when they are combined with modifications of constituent factors of the configuration of the power bloc.

(iv) POLITICAL PERIODIZATION, THE POLITICAL SCENE,
RULING CLASSES, CLASSES IN CHARGE OF THE STATE

It is evident that these pointers provided by Marx are of vital importance for any concrete study of the relations between the political state superstructure and the field of the class struggle. However, the concepts just clarified must be supplemented by a series of other concepts which refer to a different periodization and space. The concept of the power bloc will emerge more clearly in this way.

In fact this concept is related to the general periodization of a formation into stages. Along with the concept of form of state, it covers the political level as related to the ensemble of the instances of a formation in a determinate stage and as characterized by a particular articulation of these instances. This periodization, marked by the relation between the time-sequences peculiar to each level, is distinct from the periodization concerning the specific time-sequence of the political level. The first periodization defines a stage's limits, as fixed at a determinate level of structures and practices; the second marks the particular rhythm of this level within these limits. But the time-sequence of a level depends on its own particular structures: this second periodization, particular to the political level, depends on the specific structures of this level in a determinate formation.

In *The Eighteenth Brumaire* Marx himself clearly brings out the distinction between these two periodizations. On the first he says:

> Three main periods are unmistakable: *the February period;* May 4, 1848, to May 28, 1849: *the period of the constitution of the republic,* or *of the Constituent National Assembly*; May 28, 1849, to December 2, 1851: *the period of the constitutional republic or of the Legislative National Assembly.*[30]

This is the precise periodization covered in the structures by the concept of the form of state, and in the field of the practices of the dominant classes, by the concept of the power bloc.

This general periodization is however to be distinguished from another one, as Marx shows in the following remarks on the period of the constitutional Republic, which naturally divides into three main periods, namely:

1. May 28, 1849, to June 13, 1849. Struggle of the petty bourgeoisie with the bourgeoisie and with Bonaparte. Defeat of the petty bourgeois democracy.

2. June 13, 1849, to May 31, 1850. Parliamentary dictatorship of the Party of Order. It completes its rule by abolishing universal suffrage, but loses the parliamentary ministry.

3. May 31, 1850, to December 2, 1851. Struggle between the parliamentary bourgeoisie and Bonaparte. . . . Passing of the parliamentary régime and of bourgeois rule. . . .[31]

In the structures, this periodization is covered by the concept of forms of régime, whose transformations cannot be directly related to those modifications of the relation between the political and economic which mark the transformations of forms of state. They relate rather to the structures peculiar to the capitalist state, to the coordinates of the system of party representation, to the institution of suffrage, etc.

More important here, however, are the concepts applied by Marx to the study of the specifically political periodization in the field of the practices of the dominant classes. It should be noted that Marx circumscribes the *particular space* of the field assigned to this second periodization; he calls this space the '*political scene*'. This expression covers a particular space at the level of political class practices in the formations studied by him: from a study of the whole range of his political texts it is apparent that this

30. 'The Eighteenth Brumaire', *MESW*, 1970, p. 100.
31. ibid., p. 166.

space precisely contains *the struggle between social forces organized in political parties.* The metaphors of presence in the political scene, of the place of a class in this scene (whether in the forefront or not), etc. *are constantly related to the modalities of class representation by parties and to the relations between the political parties.* The entry and the exit of a class in the political scene depend on the concrete conjuncture which determines its *organization of power* and its relations to the parties. It is moreover precisely in this context that the relations which Marx establishes between the political scene and universal suffrage must be situated. This suffrage precipitates the formation of numerous classes in the political scene, precisely because, in the concrete circumstances studied by Marx, it constitutes one of the factors contributing to the organization of certain classes into parties.

However, in marking off this new space of the political scene, we pose certain theoretical problems, notably that of its relation to the space of political practices in general. In fact, the existence of a class or fraction as a *distinct class or autonomous fraction, i.e. as a social force,* presupposes its presence at the political level in *'pertinent effects'.* However, this presence at the level of political practices is distinct from presence on the political scene: this latter presupposes a class's *organizational power,* as distinct from its political practice. Lenin makes this distinction in his concept of open or declared action and this concept also existed in the practical state for Marx, who termed it 'true action'. Although the open action of social forces is not identical with the concept of political practice, we can say that in capitalist formations the political scene is a privileged place in which the open action of social forces can take place by means of their representation by parties.

So the space of the political scene has a very precise function for Marx: *it is the place in which we can observe a series of dislocations between (a) the classes' political interests and practices, and (b) their representation by parties and the political parties themselves.* The political scene, as the particular field of the political parties' action, is often dislocated in relation to the political practices and to the terrain of political interests of the classes, represented by the parties in the political scene: this dislocation is thought by Marx through his problematic of 'representation'.

The exact delimitation of the political scene (i.e. the field of the second periodization) has numerous consequences. For example, it allows us to establish the fundamental relations between the forms of régime and the field of action of the parties. We shall see later that the principal factor of a typology of forms of régime (as certain contemporary theorists have shown)[32] is the relation of these forms of régime to the concrete action of the political parties in the field of the political scene. As was the case with the relations between the forms of state and the power bloc, the forms of régime (a concept covering the specific periodization of political structures) are related to a concrete configuration of relations between parties of the dominant classes in the political scene (a concept covering the specific periodization of the political class struggle).[33] At this point we can show the usefulness of the concept of power bloc in the relations between (a) the dominant classes and (b) the action of these classes' parties on the political scene. The power bloc of a stage sets the limits of the various relations of the parties, relations which mark the rhythm of that stage in the political scene. These relations correspond to a form of régime, itself situated within the limits posed by the form of state corresponding to the power bloc. The power bloc and the relations determined by it between the dominant classes and fractions thus allows us to locate and decipher the real (class) significance of the strictly party relations within a stage, and after that to decipher their dislocation from political class relations.

In fact, anyone who restricts himself to the field of the political scene in order to determine class relations, reduces them to party relations alone and is inevitably led to errors which derive from a misunderstanding of these dislocations. For example, we often have to deal with situations in which a political class disappears from the political scene, although it remains in the power bloc. This can be due to its party's electoral defeat, to the disintegration (for various reasons) of this party in the field of the

32. See in particular Duverger, pp. 318 ff.

33. We shall deal more fully later with concrete analyses of this relation between the political scene (the place in which party representation takes place) and the typology of political régimes. Marx indicated this relation, and it was emphasized by Gramsci in his analyses of *The Eighteenth Brumaire*, particularly in his text 'Observations on certain aspects of the structure of political parties in periods of organic crisis', in which he uses the term 'terrain of the parties' instead of 'political scene': 'At a certain point in their historical lives, social classes become detached from their traditional parties. In other words the traditional parties, in that particular organizational form, with the particular men who constitute, represent and lead them, are no longer recognized by their class (or fraction of a class) as its expression . . . *These situations of conflict between "represented and representatives" reverberate out from the terrain of the parties . . . throughout the State organism. How are they created in the first place?*' (*Prison Notebooks*, p. 210). Given that Gramsci is here only examining the case of a crisis of the political scene, the important point to note is the relation which he points out between the 'state organism' and the concrete functioning of party representation.

political scene or to its exclusion from having party-type relations with the other parties of the dominant classes. However, this absence of a class or fraction from the political scene does not directly mean that it is excluded from the power bloc. There are many cases in which a class or fraction is absent from the periodization of the political scene, but continues to be present in the periodization of the power bloc. Such examples are plentiful in Marx's political works, the most characteristic being that of the industrial bourgeoisie under Louis Philippe.

Marx emphasized the importance of this case by clearly distinguishing between *politically dominant* classes or fractions, which are part of the power bloc, and *ruling* classes or fractions, whose political parties occupy the dominant places on the political scene. This dislocation between the place of a class or fraction in the field of political practices and its place in the political scene is of course accompanied by a series of transformations with respect to its party representation: these transformations relate to the composition of the parties, to the relations between them, to their degree of representativity, etc. The class or fraction's political interests are represented, certainly in a distorted way, by the parties of other ruling classes or fractions, so the above-mentioned transformations can be revealed only by elucidating the dislocations between political practice and the political scene. In this dislocation, the role of ideology becomes decisive. Furthermore, *the displacements* within the field of political practices are not the same as those within the political scene. A displacement of the index of hegemony from one class or fraction to another in the power bloc does not necessarily involve displacements of party representation in the political scene: it does not, for example, necessarily correspond to a movement from the background to the foreground of the scene. Further, it is possible for the *hegemonic* class or fraction in the power bloc *to be absent* from the political scene. The dislocation between politically dominant classes or fractions and ruling classes or fractions is here translated by a distinction between the actual hegemonic class or fraction and the ruling class or fraction: this is so, for example, in the bourgeoisie towards the end of the Bismarckian régime.

The hegemonic class or fraction which in the last analysis holds political power should also not be confused with the class or fraction which is '*in charge*' *of the state apparatus.* According to Marx, this latter class or fraction is the one from which the political, bureaucratic, military, etc., personnel is recruited and which occupies the 'heights' of the state. This analysis is schematically presented in Marx's texts on the landed aristocracy in Britain, in which he states:

The Whigs are the aristocratic representatives of the bourgeoisie, of the industrial and commercial middle class. Under the condition that the bourgeoisie should abandon to them, to an oligarchy of aristocratic families, the monopoly of government and the exclusive possession of office, they make to the middle class, and assist it in conquering, all those concessions, which in the course of social and political development have shown themselves to have become unavoidable and undelayable. . . . The interests and principles which they represent besides, from time to time, do not belong to the Whigs: they are forced upon them by the development of the industrial and commercial class, the bourgeoisie.[34]

It is sufficient for the moment to remark that these hegemonic classes or fractions, ruling classes or fractions, and classes or fractions in charge are sometimes identical and sometimes distinct. The hegemonic class or fraction may be both ruling and in charge of the state; but the ruling class or fraction may be in charge of the state without thereby being hegemonic. This was so in Britain after 1832, where the landed aristocracy occupied the political scene and provided the top bureaucratic-military personnel, whereas the bourgeoisie held hegemony. In this case, the landed aristocracy is the ruling class in the form of the Tory party; here Marx even uses the term 'governing' class instead of 'ruling' class, in stating that in England the governing class did not at all coincide with the class directing the state. The governing class was also the class in charge of the state, in the form of the Whig party: in fact Marx is here talking about different fractions of the landed aristocracy.

The concrete combination which is not a simple combinatory may go as far as a complete decentration of these three positions, each of which can be occupied by a different class or fraction. The ruling class or fraction (and *a fortiori* the classes or fractions in charge) may not only not be hegemonic, *but even on occasion may not be part of the power bloc*: a class whose status is merely that of being allied to this bloc may for a brief period be the ruling class. The clearest example of this is provided by the *radical* governments of the Third Republic in France before the 1914 war; the

34. See *On Britain*, Moscow, 1962, pp. 112–13. See also the texts on Palmerston, ibid., pp. 204–11, 309–14. Engels's important analyses of this subject are found in the Preface to the first English edition of *Socialism, Utopian and Scientific*, 1892 (*MESW*, 1970, pp. 385 ff.) which also contains his incisive remarks on the periodization of the 'power bloc' in Britain.

financial fraction was hegemonic and shared with the industrial fraction the place of the class in charge, while the petty bourgeoisie, in a complex alliance with the middle bourgeoisie, appeared as the ruling class.[35] This sometimes occurs, although always with the *petty bourgeoisie*, in certain cases of *social democrat* governments, especially in France. In this case a characteristic dislocation between this class and its party representation is generally found: its party plays the role of 'clerk' for the hegemonic class or fraction or even for another class or fraction in the power bloc. The same holds for the class in charge of the state.

At a later stage we shall go more deeply into the numerous problems posed by this dislocation between political practice and the political scene. I shall here summarize the preceding analyses by pointing out that it is vital to mark the limits between political class practices and the political scene: in making this distinction we are opposing a *double confusion* in contemporary political science which reduces class relations to party relations and party relations to class relations. In following this distinction through logically, all relevant concepts must be specified so as to designate the relations between the elements on both these terrains. Thus the concept of power bloc (like the concept of hegemony) has as its object the field of political class practices: so it enables us to elucidate the relations between the dominant classes which underlie and set the limits to the relations between the parties (their effects) on the political scene; these class relations are often masked by the numerous variables of party relations. It is true that we sometimes use specific concepts which cover the two terrains. This is the case with the concept of ruling class or fraction, which covers (though only as a general rule) the role of the hegemonic class or fraction in the political scene. We can note once again the case of the concept of *bloc of parties* which often covers the relations between the parties of the classes and fractions of the power bloc in the political scene. Sometimes however we encounter non-specified concepts, such as that of *alliance*. In using such a concept, it is useful to make clear whether we are talking of a class alliance or a party alliance: otherwise we can agree to use different terms, e.g. to reserve the term alliance for class relations and to speak of an '*entente*' to indicate party relations. In fact, the dislocation between these two terrains constantly appears in all the concrete relations

35. See G. Dupeux, *La société française, 1789–1960*, 1964, pp. 182 ff. It should however be noted that since Dupeux does not employ the distinctions indicated above, he grasps this situation (though with some reservations) as a 'loss of political power' by the big bourgeoisie.

of their elements. For example on the political scene the power bloc can give rise to a bloc of parties, to an alliance of parties, or even to an open and declared struggle between the parties: see e.g. the frequently encountered case of a *parliamentary opposition party* (during a 'step' [*étape*] of the periodization of the political scene) which in fact represents a class or fraction of the power bloc (of a stage of a formation in which this 'step' is situated). Conversely, a party *entente* may mask an intense struggle in the field of political practices: see the frequently encountered case of certain exclusively electoral *ententes*.

A final remark should be made concerning the relations between the two periodizations which cover respectively the political and the political scene. The distinction between them cannot be reduced to a question of *chronology*, e.g. to considering the periodization of the political as a periodization of long duration, and that of the political scene as one of short duration. The distinction between them in fact depends on a difference *of field*, and it is only by starting from the theoretical distinction between these periodizations that we can understand the chronological divergences: for example, a party *entente* may last longer than a class alliance, in so far as a class may maintain its agreement with another through the intermediary of its party (or parties) on the political scene, even though they have effectively broken their alliance in the field of the class struggle. This is equally clear with respect to political structures: a form of régime (e.g. the two-party system in Britain) may effectively outlast a form of state.

IV

The Unity of Power
and the Relative Autonomy
of the Capitalist State

I. The Problem as Theoretically Posed by the Marxist Classics

In this section I shall deal with one of the most important characteristics of the capitalist type of state, one which has given rise to numerous controversies and misinterpretations. This is the question of the *unity proper to* institutionalized political power and its *relative autonomy*.

These notions of unity and autonomy do not of course as such appear to be sufficiently rigorous for use in the treatment of scientific problems. Though they are habitually employed in Marxist theory, they have often only had the function of preventing theorists from making a deeper analysis of these questions. In fact, no one should be allowed to use these notions unless their meaning is precisely specified: this is what I shall attempt to do throughout this chapter. In order to pin down these ideas, I shall start by making some preliminary working definitions, indicating the problems covered by them in Marxist theory.[1]

a. By the *unity proper to* institutionalized political power I mean that particular feature of the capitalist state which makes the institutions of state power (which have gained a relative autonomy from the economic) present a *specific* internal cohesion: this cohesion can be perceived in its effects. As an approximate statement at this stage, we can say that it is that which prevents the relations, (a) between the classes or fractions of a power bloc and (b) *a fortiori* between these latter and the allied or supporting classes and fractions, from being based on a '*parcellization*', *division* or *sharing* of the institutionalized power of the state. This feature appears to be peculiar to the capitalist state. The 'preceding' types of state, whose

---

1. I use these terms because they are already established and *must be taken into account*. On this subject, I cannot resist the temptation of mentioning Lenin's answer to Parvus who accused him of using the 'figurative' term of 'active boycott': 'Of course, Parvus may object that conventional terms are not binding on him. Formally, such an objection would be justified, but it is worthless in essence. One must surely know what is under discussion. We are not going to quibble about words, but here we are dealing with political terms which have already taken root in Russia' (*Collected Works*, Vol. 9, p. 268).

relation to the economic is radically different from that of the capitalist state, did not present this specific coherence of an autonomized juridico-political superstructure. Their institutions consisted of a compartmentalized plurality of power centres of a politico-economic kind; and in them class relations were often based on a sharing of these centres.

b. Nor by *relative autonomy* of this type of state do I mean a direct relation between its structures and the relations of production. I mean rather the state's relation to the field of the class struggle, in particular its relative autonomy vis-à-vis the classes and fractions of the power bloc, and by extension vis-à-vis its allies or supports. The expression is found in the Marxist classics: it covers the general functioning of the state in the case in which the political forces present are 'prepared to balance each other'. I use it here in a sense which is at once both wider and narrower than this, in order to denote a functioning which is *specific* to the capitalist state. By this usage, I hope clearly to mark the gap which separates this conception of the state from a simplistic and vulgarized conception which sees in the state the tool or instrument of the dominant class. Our task therefore is to grasp the specific functioning of the capitalist type of state relative to preceding types of state, and to show that the conception of the state in general as a simple tool or instrument of the dominant class, erroneous even in its generality, is particularly useless for grasping the functioning of the capitalist state.

I shall also add (and this is an important point) that in what follows a *correlation* between these two characteristics of the capitalist type of state is observable. It presents a relative autonomy vis-à-vis the dominant classes and fractions, but it does this exactly to the extent that it possesses its own peculiar unity (unity of class power) as a specific level of the CMP and of a capitalist formation. At the same time it possesses this institutionalized unity in so far as it is relatively autonomous from these classes or fractions, i.e. because of the function which devolves upon it vis-à-vis these classes or fractions.

These remarks are even more important because the whole historicist school of Marxism, with its invariable duo 'voluntarism/economism', has firmly established this relation between the unity of institutionalized political power and its function vis-à-vis the dominant classes and fractions, but it has interpreted this relation wrongly. This school ultimately sees in the state the product of a subject, usually of the dominant-class/subject, whose mere tool of domination, manipulable at will, it is. The unity of this state is hence related to a presupposed unity of the 'will' of the dominant class with regard to which the state presents no autonomy. The state, unified by this class's single will for domination is merely its inert tool. This immediately entails the following conclusion: as soon as one admits a relative autonomy of the state from the dominant class this is immediately interpreted as a rupture of the unity of institutionalized political power, as a fragmentation and division of this power of which the working class could conquer an autonomous 'part'. Another conclusion, based on a flagrant theoretical inconsistency, is that the capitalist state is at once the simple 'clerk' of the dominant class and also a conglomeration of lots which are waiting only to become the prey of the working class.

To conclude these introductory remarks: I have already indicated the relation which exists between the capitalist state and the ensemble of the levels of *structures* of the CMP by pointing out the capitalist state's particular function of being the factor of unity in a capitalist formation, composed of specific and relatively autonomous levels. I shall approach the problem here not by directly examining the state's relations to the other instances but rather its relations to the *field of the class struggle, in particular, the field of the political class struggle*. It must never be forgotten that this latter relation reflects the relation between the instances, for it is its effect, and that the state's relation to the political class struggle concentrates within it the relation of the structural levels to the field of class practices. In other words, the unity of power characteristic of the state, related to its role in the class struggle, is the reflection of its role of unity vis-à-vis the instances; and its relative autonomy vis-à-vis the politically dominant classes or fractions is the reflection of the relative autonomy of the instances of a capitalist formation. In short, this unity and autonomy of the capitalist type of state is related to the *specificity* of its structures (relatively autonomous vis-à-vis the economic) in their relation to the political class struggle, which is relatively autonomous vis-à-vis the economic class struggle.

Marx and Engels studied and analysed these characteristics of the capitalist state in their political works. But two preliminary remarks should be made concerning these works:

a. On these problems at least, these texts are not always explicit. Moreover, as was the case with the power bloc, Marx and Engels often analyse historical realities by explicitly referring to notions insufficient for their explanation. These texts contain valuable guidelines, so long as the necessary scientific concepts contained in them are deciphered, concepts which are either absent, or, as is more commonly the case, are present in the practical state;

b. The ambiguities of these texts must be recalled: despite appearances, they are not simply historical analyses of concrete phenomena in a determinate formation, but (in a duplication complex and hard to decipher) they also contain a theoretical reflection on the political forms of the CMP.

If we refer for example to Marx's texts on the 1848–52 period in France, we find that Lenin already saw them as representing, in a concentrated form, the transformations undergone by the capitalist state. By this, Lenin meant that these texts are an attempt at the *theoretical construction of the concept* of the capitalist state. Reading the texts from this angle, we can decipher in the concrete historical forms of the French social formation studied by Marx and in the various 'steps' of transformation of the political forms, the constitutive characteristics of the concept of the capitalist state. In this reading we are not aiming to construct a type of state by making a generalization from historical data, i.e. from the concrete political forms described by Marx. We are aiming rather to relate ourselves to the concept of the capitalist state, which is quite a different enterprise. It is by means of this concept that we can understand the historical transformations analysed by Marx in a 'concentrated' form. In doing this we must never forget the fragmentary and schematic character of these analyses which provide us only with *theoretical indications*. In short, if *Capital* provides us implicitly with the conceptual characteristics of the capitalist state as analysed above, the political works provide us with those of the unity and relative autonomy of this type of state.

Having said this we shall approach the problem of *Bonapartism*, which is all-important in this respect. Marx and Engels's texts concerning Bonapartism contain in the first place the analysis of a concrete political phenomenon in a determinate formation. However, parallel to this, Marx and Engels *systematically conceive* Bonapartism not simply as a concrete form of the capitalist state, *but as a constitutive theoretical characteristic of the very type of capitalist state*. This was expressed in a letter by Engels to Marx, on 13 April 1866:

Bonapartism is after all *the real religion of the modern bourgeoisie*. It is becoming ever clearer to me that the bourgeoisie has not the stuff in it for ruling directly itself, and that therefore . . . a Bonapartist semi-dictatorship is the normal form; it upholds the big material interests of the bourgeoisie (even against the will of the bourgeoisie) but allows the bourgeoisie no part in the power of government.[2]

Engels returns to this point in the famous foreword to the third edition of *The Eighteenth Brumaire* (*MESW*, 1970, pp. 94–5) in which he considers France to be equally representative of the CMP, with respect to political forms, as Britain is with respect to the economic. This conception is also contained implicitly in Marx's own 1869 Preface to *The Eighteenth Brumaire* where he opposes Bonapartism *as the political form of the modern class struggle in general* to the political forms of formations dominated by modes of production other than the capitalist mode:

> Lastly, I hope that my work will contribute towards eliminating the school-taught phrase, now current, particularly in Germany, of so-called Caesarism. In this superficial historical analogy the main point is forgotten, namely, that in ancient Rome the class struggle took place only within a privileged minority, between the free rich and the free poor, while the great productive mass of the population, slaves, formed the purely passive pedestal for these combatants. . . . With so complete a difference between the material, economic conditions of the ancient and modern class struggles, the political figures produced by them can likewise have no more in common with one another than the Archbishop of Canterbury has with the high priest Samuel.[3]

So, in referring to these texts we must always sort out the two readings which are possible of them and distinguish between that which relates to the concrete historical phenomenon of Bonapartism in France and that which relates to Bonapartism as a constitutive characteristic of the capitalist type of state.

One of the essential characteristics of Bonapartism in the second sense is *the relative autonomy of the state vis-à-vis the dominant classes or fractions*, and it is precisely from this angle that Marx and Engels consider it. But what is this schema used by Marx and Engels to explain Bonapartism? They most frequently have recourse to a *general explanation* of the state's relative autonomy when the classes in struggle are 'close to equilibrium'. In this sense, Marx says in *The Civil War in France* that Bonapartism is explained by that moment 'when the bourgeoisie had already lost, the working class had not yet gained, the ability to govern the nation'. This is even clearer in Engels's works: on the question of Bonapartism, he himself resorts to the general explanation admitted by Marxism of the relative autonomy of the state in the case of an equilibrium of social forces present,

2. *Selected Correspondence*, p. 214. 3. *MESW*, 1958, Vol. I, pp. 244–5.

and because of this he has a tendency *to assimilate* such different phenomena as the absolutist state, Bismarckism and Bonapartism. It is
however important to point out that Bonapartism, as a historical phenomenon, concerns the state of a social formation in which the dominance
of the CMP is already consolidated. So, as opposed to the absolutist state
of the transition period, we are concerned here with a political form belonging to the phase of expanded reproduction: and Bismarckism is a different
phenomenon again. And it is because of this that in making his concrete
study of Bonapartism, Marx initiates a reflection on the capitalist type of
state.

It is clear that to explain the relative autonomy of the Bonapartist state
(considered as the 'religion of the bourgeoisie') as a constituent characteristic of the capitalist type of state, by reference to a situation of equilibrium
between the social forces in struggle, is *totally insufficient*. What is more, it
is even insufficient to explain the concrete phenomenon of Bonapartism
in France. It somehow looks as though Marx and Engels refer to their only
theoretically elaborated conception of the relative autonomy of the state
in order to explain facts for which this conception proves insufficient.
But in fact a deeper reading of the texts shows that in the case of Bonapartism in France, Marx in no way admits an equilibrium between the bourgeois and the working classes in the sense, for example, in which we can
speak of an equilibrium between the feudal and the bourgeois classes in
the very last period of the Ancien Régime: the working class, disorganized
by the events of 1848, not only does not maintain a situation of equilibrium
of forces with the bourgeoisie, but 'even disappears from the scene'. The
principal contradiction is displaced and is concentrated between (a) the
bourgeoisie and (b) the petty bourgeoisie and the peasantry: but this does
not mean that we can speak of an equilibrium between these forces either.

In his texts on French Bonapartism, Lenin also follows this schema of
explanation.[4] Gramsci's position alone is more advanced on this point,
although he fails to reach the root of the problem. In his important text
on 'Caesarism', he attempts to mark out this specific political phenomenon
by situating it in relation to *the various types of state*. In this way, he sees
in Napoleon III's Bonapartism a particular form of Caesarism, situated in
the framework of the capitalist state. He does not attempt to consider
Bonapartism, from the theoretical point of view, as characteristic of the
capitalist type of state: the fact that Bonapartism belongs to this state

4. Notably in *Collected Works*, Vol. 25, pp. 219 ff ('The Beginnings of Bonapartism').

enables him to concretize that phenomenon as a particular form of Caesarism. He relates Caesarism, as a specific political phenomenon, not just to any equilibrium of the social forces present, but to a *particular equilibrium* grasped by his concept of *'catastrophic equilibrium'*, which produces *political crises*: 'Caesarism can be said to express a situation in which the forces in conflict balance each other in a catastrophic manner; that is to say . . . in such a way that a continuation of the conflict can only terminate in their reciprocal destruction.'[5] These important remarks are close to those of Marx, who relates French Bonapartism to that particular equilibrium of forces when the bourgeoisie had already lost the opportunity of governing the nation, while the working class had not yet acquired it.

However, while it is true that this particular catastrophic equilibrium (which we must distinguish, as Gramsci does, from general equilibrium as manifested in the case of the absolutist state) leads to the specific phenomenon of Caesarism, it is equally true that it cannot (any more than general equilibrium) explain the *concrete historical phenomenon of French Bonapartism*. That Gramsci is in fact very aware of this is evident from the precautions which he takes in explaining French Bonapartism, which is in no way reducible to this political crisis of catastrophic equilibrium:

. . . the catastrophic phase may be brought about by a 'momentary' political deficiency of the traditional dominant force, and not by any necessarily insuperable organic deficiency. This was true in the case of Napoleon III . . . [in which] the existing social form had not yet exhausted its possibilities for development, as subsequent history abundantly demonstrated. Napoleon III represented . . . these latent and immanent possibilities: his Caesarism therefore has a particular coloration . . . [in it] there was no passage from one type of state to another, but only 'evolution' of the same type along unbroken lines[6]

The French Bonapartist state's relative autonomy vis-à-vis the dominant classes or fractions can be understood only from the fact that this concrete form belongs to the capitalist type of state – a state which presents this relative autonomy as a constitutive feature of its concept. So this feature stems from the relation between this state and the specific characteristics of the class struggle in the CMP and in a capitalist social formation: this relation sets the limits which circumscribe the concrete action of this struggle on the state. This autonomy exists even in the situation where there is neither an equilibrium in the general sense nor a catastrophic

5. *Prison Notebooks*, p. 219.   6. ibid., pp. 221–2.

equilibrium of social forces, the source of the principal contradiction. That means that this autonomy, which is *inscribed as a possibility within the institutional play of the capitalist state, and whose variations and modalities of realization depend on the concrete conjuncture of the social forces*, can neither be reduced to the general schema of equilibrium of these forces, nor to the catastrophic schema which underlies the particular phenomenon of Caesarism.

In this chapter I shall examine the reasons for, and the precise meaning of this autonomy, of which Marx gives some indications in his political works. This is not to say that the autonomy of the capitalist type of state excludes the possibility that, in a historical form of this type, autonomy due to the general or catastrophic equilibrium of forces may function. It should be clearly seen that in the relation of the state to the field of the class struggle these autonomies are not of the same order: in the case of an equilibrium of the social forces present, as Engels says, the state can effectively perform the role of *arbitrating* (in the objective sense) between these forces. On the other hand, that autonomy which is constitutive of the capitalist type of state, in its limiting relation to the specific characteristics of the class struggle in the CMP, cannot as such be understood in terms of arbitration. While these modes of relative autonomy can be *combined* (*conjugués*) in a concrete form of the capitalist state, they can also be contradictory. As we shall see, the relative autonomy of a form of this state, resulting from an equilibrium between the social forces present, may threaten its function vis-à-vis the dominant classes and fractions and hence the mode of relative autonomy which devolves upon it because it belongs to the capitalist type of state.

2. Some Misinterpretations and their Consequences

Before getting to the root of the problem, it is useful to stress its importance, by noting the confusions issuing from certain contemporary conceptions of the state and political power. These currents of thought have been formulated mainly outside or on the fringe of Marxist thought, but through the medium of European Social Democracy, they have often influenced working-class strategy in Europe. They often have implicit repercussions on the Marxist theory of the state. I shall also point out certain distortions of Marxist theory which take the opposite view from these currents although they continue to admit the same theoretical principles; they thereby move away from the scientific standard of the Marxist theory of the state, in particular concerning the problem of the state's own unity and relative autonomy.

While it is difficult systematically to classify such apparently diverse theories currently presented in an edifyingly syncretic form, it is at least possible to establish a *common thematic*. To do this it is sufficient to read a series of very revealing correlations across the variants. These correlations appear to be:

a. *Underestimation of the political*: it loses its specificity as the relatively autonomous level of social structures and practices. In other words, there is no scientific concept of the relation between the economic and political, which, as the invariable matrix of the CMP and of a capitalist formation, governs the variations of this relation in the various stages and phases of this formation. The failure to recognize this relation appears theoretically *in two forms*, (i) *the dissolution* of the political into the economic and (ii) *the absorption* of the economic into the political.

b. *Lack of a conception of the unity of state power and of political power in general*: instead we find a series of conceptions of a parcelling-out of institutionalized political power into a 'pluralism' of *powers/counter-powers, of veto-groups, of decision-making, centres, etc.*

c. *Either lack of a conception of the relative autonomy* of political power, which is seen as the booty which the many bearers of these parcelled-out powers (e.g. the groups, the ensembles, etc.) share out amongst themselves, or the *misinterpretation of this autonomy*, as, for instance, the conception of the strong state as arbitrator or of the state as susceptible to a socialist revolution from above.

d. *Lack of the conception of the class struggle or the misinterpretation of the theory of the political class struggle.* In addition, we may refer to the epistemological principles of these theories which are apparently of somewhat diverse origins. Formulated in their modern shape, they go back to Veblen's and Commons' original conceptions of 'institutionalism' and to the 'neo-corporatist' conceptions of the state which took shape in Germany after the Weimar Republic. Afterwards, of course, they assumed very diverse forms and were more or less modernized by being channelled into several theoretical and political currents. They were most often inserted into the various contemporary conceptions of the so-called transformations of capitalist society. In this way their origins have been obscured with time. I make this relatively precise reference to their origins for the two following reasons:

a. To show that a very old ideological function is hidden underneath their 'modern' form, which stems from the so-called transformations (contemporary transformations, naturally) of society; this function consists of the masking of the class characteristics of institutionalized political power. Thus, it is not accidental that these 'contemporary' theoretical and political forms blend with the principles and conclusions of their decrepit origins. These ancient forms had identical repercussions on the European Social Democratic current before the Second World War as they have on present-day Social Democracy.

b. To show how they pose with particular clarity the problems of the capitalist state's own unity and relative autonomy.

The characteristics common to these theoretical principles can be traced back to the Hegelian origin of German neo-corporatist conceptions. These have been continued in the contemporary corporatist current, resulting in profound repercussions on the functionalist school, as can be seen clearly in most contemporary theories of the Welfare State.[1] I shall spend no further time on this point: it will be sufficient to recall the relation between

1. On the functionalist presuppositions underlying these conceptions of the 'Welfare State' and on their decisive impact on the British Labour Party's conception of power, see D. Wedderburn, 'Facts and Theories of the Welfare State', *The Socialist Register 1965*, pp. 127 ff.

the historicist problematic and functionalism. In dealing with the problem of the unity and relative autonomy of the capitalist state, these currents ultimately relate to the problematic of the central subject and cannot therefore admit the structuring of a social ensemble into specific levels each with its own efficacy. All unity, whether of a particular level or of the ensemble of the social system, is related to a totality of the *Gestalt* type; i.e. to a simple and circular totality consisting of homogeneous and equivalent elements. The unity and relation of these elements are based on the originating subject, the centre of totalization.

The series of above-mentioned correlations can be located within this problematic in the various forms subsequently assumed by these theories:

a. Lack of the scientific concept of the class struggle. Instead there are relations of 'integration' between certain 'groups', 'ensembles', 'constellations of interest', etc. in a social-subject system.

b. In this context, the state's institutionalized political power cannot be grasped according to its status as a specific level of the social system. The notion of institution accepted by these currents makes this apparent. Moreover, this notion presents a characteristic confusion and is replaced indiscriminately by the terms structure, organization, association or corporation. It covers both the domain of the economic (meaning by this the economic 'groups' or 'ensembles' like the large enterprises, the unions, the lobbies, the pressure groups, etc.) and the specific structures of political power. The state-institution is seen as one element of the social system-ensemble, an element homogeneous and equivalent to the others, as a product of the originating subject, integrated in its circular equilibrium. It participates in the diffuse and vague function – devolving on all its total parts [see Introduction, note 9 above] – of welding the social whole; a typical example is Parsons' conception of the political, which was discussed above.

c. The state itself, as a particular element of the social-system-ensemble, does not present an internal unity in the strict sense. Institutionalized political power is conceived as being composed of a 'totality' of 'powers/ countervailing powers', of 'compensatory-powers', of 'veto-groups', i.e. of equivalent parts. These parts are themselves shared out among the various ensembles or groups in equilibrium in this circular system. There is thus a circular equilibrium, which governs both the social ensemble and all its specific elements, both at the economic, and at the political level. The equilibrium and share-out of political power are here modelled on the equilibrium which is hypothesized in the economic domain between the 'ensembles-groups' which compose it. In this schema these ensembles share the political power out between them, *and the class struggle of course is absent.*

It is possible to fine down these general statements by concretely considering their current formulations and the consequences entailed by the absence of specificity of the political level, the dissolution of the political into the economic and the absorption of the economic into the political.

a. The first tendency appears today in the 'neo-liberal' school, which is attached to the classic liberal concepts of 'equilibrium' and 'pluralism'.[2] Thus, the state is here encapsulated as an 'institution' and does not constitute a particular level or an institutionalized political power with its own unity and specificity. On this theory, this political power is watered down into a 'pluralist' multiplicity of new decision centres, between which equilibrium is 'automatically' realized by the 'concertation' of the various 'power-groupings' or 'pressure-groups' or 'de facto powers' (enterprises, trade unions, consumer organizations) representing the 'economic forces' of an integrated society.[3] The unity of institutionalized political power seems to have been disintegrated to the advantage of these institutions. Its specificity is watered down through the various 'elements', powers/countervailing powers, compensating powers, veto-groups, etc., to the benefit of those forces whose equilibrium is realized by a 'mutual limitation', by a 'respective control' in the social process of the ensemble.[4]

2. The literature on this subject is vast. The two theoretical currents which confuse the political and the economic often overlap. But in A. A. Berle, for instance, the 'neo-liberal' tendency is clearly dominant: see *The Twentieth-Century Capitalist Revolution*, 1955; 'Corporations and the Modern State' in Arnold (ed.), *The Future of Democratic Capitalism*, 1961; Berle and G. Means, *The Modern Corporation and Private Property*, 1933. See also J. K. Galbraith, *The Affluent Society*, London, 1958.

3. This conception is already found in H. Laski, 'The Pluralist State' in *Foundations of Sovereignty*, 1931; also *A Grammar of Politics*, 1948; and H. J. Kaiser, *Die Repräsentation organisierter Interessen*, 1956. On the concept of 'pluralism', it is necessary to remember that it does not merely serve to designate a 'multiparty' political system as opposed to a one-party system, but that it is also extended to a whole 'integrationist' conception of the social system in its ensemble. R. Aron's popularizations are interesting: see *Démocratie et totalitarisme*, pp. 25 ff. and 101 ff.

4. See H. Pross, 'Zum Begriff der pluralistischen Gesellschaft' in *Zeugnisse Theodor Adorno*, 1963, pp. 441 ff. In their neo-liberal form, these concepts of 'control', 'equilibrium' and 'pluralism' also underpin J. A. Schumpeter's analyses in *Capitalism, Socialism and Democracy*; their influence on European Social Democracy is well known.

According to this current (as opposed to classical liberalism) the 'automatic' and natural equilibrium of the market (which presupposes an autonomous political power without any intervention in the economic process) is here transposed into an equilibrium of 'mixed' powers in the 'technological-industrial' society. This 'planned' equilibrium is achieved by the concerted efforts of the economico-political forces, whose 'decision-making powers' share out the institutionalized political power.[5]

In addition to the problem of the unity of this power, the problem of its autonomy from these 'forces-groups' cannot be posed in this context, precisely because it does not possess its own specificity. It takes on a 'technical' function of 'organization' which furnishes this 'pluralist' society which is already institutionalized and integrated with a framework of formal cohesion. Its role, defined by the principle of '*subsidiarity*', is limited to being the simple executor of the concerted decisions of the various economico-political 'powers' which share the state power. But the basis of the equilibirum between these powers is principally the domain of the economic process. The existence of state autonomy may exceptionally be admitted grudgingly according to the mode of dysfunction of the state-institution vis-à-vis the society-subject. Leaving aside the supposed transformations of the capitalist process of production acknowledged by the contemporary school, let us retain only the lack of specificity of the political level, which is diluted into the economic level.

b. The inverse case is found today in the continuations of the institutionalist 'neo-corporatist' conception of the state. Its proponents, while theoretically presupposing the same integrationist relation between the various 'ensembles' or 'constellations of interests' of the economic level, admit the worrying existence of certain antagonisms between them, without of course going so far as to talk of class struggle. They are therefore forced to conceive of an institutionalized political power functioning as the central factor of 'enlightened direction' (*dirigisme éclairé*) in the dynamic harmonization of these ensembles.[6] There is no question of

5. See Macpherson's critique of this point, in 'Post-liberal democracy?' in *New Left Review*, September/October 1963.

6. The ancestors of the confusion between the political and the economic and of the neo-corporatist conception of the state are German theorists such as Schmidt, Spann and Larentz (with their forerunner Gierke). The confusion characterizes Catholic doctrine, as expressed in Pius XI's 'Quadragesimo anno' encyclical and more recently

abandoning the general conceptions of functionalist institutionalism: the harmonized pluralism of equivalent elements is still compulsory. However, while in this second version, these various powers/countervailing powers, etc., present themselves as 'institutionalized', not in so far as they constitute 'economico-social' institutions outside the shadow-state, but in so far as they are directly institutionalized by the strong state. These various interest groups and pressure groups are seen as directly receiving a public status, being officially recognized and directly enrolled by the state which realizes their unity. The instance of the state-institution makes its reappearance: centres of political power and various public commissions or organisms belonging to the state are created, in which these 'institutionalized' groups cooperate under the leadership and neutral arbitration of the technico-bureaucratic administration with a view to a 'directed orchestration' of the society. This is the modern form of the conception under the term '*the institutionalization of the class struggle*'.[7]

This neo-corporatist conception of the state obviously raises the problem of the unity peculiar to political power and of its autonomy: yet it presents this unity precisely as being disintegrated to the advantage of the institutionalized powers. Whereas the neo-liberal theory of a global dissolution of the political level to the advantage of a pluralism of '*de facto* economico-social' powers (i.e. a dissolution of the specifically political level into a virtually self-managed society) is presented in the opposite form. This theory sees a multi-centred dissemination of political power, inside the state-institution, to the various politically institutionalized pluralist interest-ensembles. The dissolution of political power into the economic domain is here translated by an absorption of the economic into the political.

These two currents are, however, in correlation in that they both lead to a failure rigorously to delimit the economic and the political. The state autonomy is effectively a problem in the second corporatist current since the political instance is recognized in the necessity for 'directed' arbitra-

---

in the 'Mater et Magistra' encyclical (on which see U. Cerroni in *Politica ed Economia*, August–September 1961). The American turning-point from neo-liberalism to a neo-corporatist conception is clear in the *Reports of the 66th Congress of the American Economic Association*, 1953. The confusion is still to be found today in Ehrmann, *Interest Groups on Four Continents*, 1959; T. Eschenburg, *Herrschaft der Verbände?*, 1955; W. Weber, *Spannungen und Kräfte im westdeutschen Verfassungssystem*, 1951.

7. Thematized by Dahrendorf, op. cit.; see also T. Parsons, *The Social System*, pp. 127 ff.

tion. But it is related to the classic conception of bureaucracy, of which the theory of élites and of the ruling class is but the latest offspring.

(ii) MARXIST POLITICAL THEORY

These theoretical currents have often *implicit* repercussions on the contemporary theory of the working-class movement. We too often underestimate the extent to which the Marxist theory of political power is contaminated by these ideological currents. It must be repeated that these conceptions, in their contemporary form, are true to their old ideological function in invoking the so-called transformations of the 'classical' capitalist mode of production. In fact, faced with the vacillations of Marxist theory on the nature of state monopoly capitalism and with the lack of a scientific theory of its transformations, they have had a powerful impact. It is sufficient to note, for example, the importance attributed by the contemporary social democratic current to conceptions of countervailing-powers, of compensatory powers, etc. In this way, it finds its bearings on the line of all reformism: this line is connected precisely with the problems of class unity and the relative autonomy of the power of the capitalist state.[8] Hence, to indicate the permanent existence of the ideological function of these theories, it is very useful to recall their influence on the history of the working-class movement. Let us take two notable and characteristic examples:

A. The most cogent example is undoubtedly that of the disastrous influence of the 'institutionalist-corporatist' conception of the state on the German social democratic current.[9] These theories crystallized after the setting up of the Weimar Republic,[10] and their 'pluralist' character

8. These themes of the social-democratic ideological conception of power are found (in a paradigm case of confusion) in the writings of several French socialists See, for example, L. Blum's preface to the French edition of Burnham's *Managerial Revolution*; L. Laurat, *Problèmes actuels du socialisme*, 1955; G. Mollet (taking up Schumpeter's themes) in his preface to Weille-Raynal, *Déclin et succession du capitalisme*, 1944; A. Philip, *Le socialisme trahi*, 1957. See also A. Gorz's critique of these conceptions in *Stratégie ouvrière et néocapitalisme*, 1964, pp. 5 ff.

9. This was pointed out at the time by F. Neumann, in an article reproduced in *The Democratic and Authoritarian State*, pp. 65 ff.; also by H. Marcuse, 'The Struggle against Liberation in the Totalitarian view of the State', reproduced in *Negations*, 1968, pp. 3 ff.

10. This is a particularly significant case: for given the relative equilibrium of forces of the capitalist and working classes at the moment of the constitution of the Weimar

brought forth a plentiful flow of ink from the pens of political theorists of the period: they had already had direct repercussions on Kautsky's and Bernstein's writings.[11] The state's unitary political power appears to be diluted to the advantage of 'corporative' ensembles directly institutionalized in the state. This appears in ideological political theory through a *critique* of classical liberal theories, which founded the unity and sovereignty of the state on its 'moral personality' and 'superior will', this being in fact the direct ideological explanation of the unity of the class state. Henceforth, this unity was based on a 'constellation of interests', on institutionalized corporations, balanced and harmonized inside the state through a confusion of the economic and the political: this theme was on the agenda after *the state of war capitalism*. State power thus appears to be disseminated and shared between these corporatist ensembles. The consequences of such a conception can easily be guessed. The working class appears able to constitute one of these ensembles and, by its integration into the state institution, to hold an autonomous 'parcel' of pluralist political power.

We know the rest: these 'pluralist' theories were extolled by several liberal and social-democratic theorists of the period and were the direct predecessors, through Schmitt and Larenz, of the 'corporatist-institutionalist' conception of the Nazi state (see D. Guérin's excellent analyses of the problem of the 'corporatist state' as a whole in *Fascisme et Grand Capital*). The 'institutionalization' of the working class did in fact take place in the Nazi state but (one suspects) without a sharing of power with the dominant classes. This is a clear and characteristic example from the theoretical viewpoint: in fact, it makes plain the at first sight *worrying* relation which holds between certain social democratic conceptions of the state and the corporatist conceptions of the fascist state. This current moreover extended its influence so as to touch the development of the British Labour Party's Fabian theory in the twenties.

B. The problem of the relative autonomy of the capitalist type of state is equally important. In their contemporary forms, these theories have had a decisive influence on the modern forms adopted by the ancient current of 'revolution from above' attached to Lassallism:[12] they have done this

---

Republic, it seemed to indicate the *appearance* of pluralism. See P. Sweezy, *The Theory of Capitalist Development*, pp. 329 ff.

11. This is particularly clear in Bernstein's *Evolutionary Socialism*, New York, 1911.

12. I refer to Lassalle here because he was the first to produce a theoretical formulation of this current in Marxist terms. It should, however, not be forgotten that 'social

mainly through the current which emphasizes the state's 'enlightened direction' and the role of the administration in this domain. Like its predecessor, this contemporary current does not present itself as the partisan of a conception of the state as neutral arbitrator and conciliator of the classes. The question is more complicated because this current invokes Marx's and above all Engels's analyses of Bismarckism. It is particularly interesting in so far as it concentrates on the question of the relative autonomy of the capitalist state.

The problem is the following: can the state have such an autonomy vis-à-vis the dominant classes that it can accomplish the passage to socialism without the state apparatus being broken by conquest of a class power? Let us recall the characteristics of Bismarckism: in Prussia during the particular period of transition from the feudal mode of production to the capitalist mode of production, the Bismarckian state took on a totally particular autonomy, because of the dislocations introduced by the complex overlapping of these modes in this formation, dislocations (i) between the instances, and (ii) between these instances and the field of the class struggle. The autonomy of the state's structures allowed it to accomplish the passage from feudalism to capitalism against the politically dominant feudal class, by consolidating the emerging economic domination of the bourgeois class and by elevating it to political domination. The Prussian state thus had an autonomy vis-à-vis the politically dominant feudal class and this autonomy cannot be reduced to an equilibrium of force between the landed nobility and the bourgeoisie.

What then are the presuppositions admitted by the contemporary formulation of the theory of revolution from above? It finds a *historic analogy* between the present situation and the Bismarckian phenomenon. On this theory, we are today in a period of transition from capitalism to socialism, which constitutes the phase of state monopoly capitalism. This transition is characterized by a specific non-correspondence between the state's juridico-political superstructure and the economic, in the sense that (just as in the transition from feudalism to capitalism) the juridico-political superstructure (i.e. nationalization planning, etc.) is somehow in advance of the economic and already exhibiting the features of the socialist state. Owing to this fundamental characteristic, there is a particular autono-

Caesarism' has tenacious traditions in the French working-class movement where it has assumed totally original forms; it goes back to Blanc and Proudhon (remember the latter's attitude to Louis Bonaparte) and undoubtedly has its roots in the Jacobin current.

mization of the contemporary state from the economic. This is reflected in a particular autonomization of the state apparatus from the monopolist bourgeoisie, the contemporary technico-bureaucratic category playing a role analogous to that of the Bismarckian bureaucracy. To this is frequently added the hypothesis that there is now an equilibrium of forces between the bourgeoisie and the working class. This hypothesis reveals the impact of the conceptions of a postulated equilibrium between official powers and the countervailing-powers possessed by the working class. This supposed equilibrium of the social forces present is thought to furnish one more analogy with the Bismarckian phenomenon, itself explained by means of a supposed equilibrium between the feudal nobility and the bourgeoisie.

These conceptions are undoubtedly radically wrong both in their analyses of the Bismarckian phenomenon and in their explanation of the transformations of the CMP on the model of a transition from capitalism to socialism. *In fact it is just a repetition of a typical form of revisionism, that of 'state socialism', which invariably appears whenever the capitalist state undertakes massive interventions in order to adapt and adjust the system in the face of the socialization of productive forces*: 'Lassallism' for Bismarck; Proudhon's 'social Caesarism' for Louis Bonaparte; 'social capitalism' for Roosevelt's New Deal; the 'Welfare State' for state capitalism under imperialism. But I do not intend to enter into this debate. It is another point which interests us here; namely the *real problem* of the relative autonomy of the capitalist state vis-à-vis the dominant classes and fractions posed by these contemporary conceptions. This autonomy, which they effectively establish, appears to them to be explicable only according to the mode of an equilibrium of social forces, coupled with the autonomization of non-corresponding structures in a transitory phase in the strict sense of the term.[13] This leads them to misinterpret the autonomy of the state *under imperialism*: this is only the concrete form currently assumed by the relative autonomy constitutive of the *capitalist type of state*. This precise mode of relative autonomy is to be radically distinguished (a) from the autonomy of the superstructure of a formation in

13. The problem appears very clearly in what is, however, a very shrewd article by L. Barca: 'Sviluppo dell'analisi teorica sul capitalismo monopolistico di Stato' in *Critica Marxista*, September/December 1966, pp. 55 and 62, where he refers to precisely this explanation in order to criticize the schematic conception of the state as agent of the monopolies, of the state and the monopolies making up a single and 'unique mechanism'.

transition, and (b) from the autonomy resulting from an equilibrium between the social forces present: in no way can it function with a view to effecting a revolution from above.

In the face of these ideological conceptions, although Marxism has sometimes allowed itself to be taken over surreptitiously by them, it has as a general rule repeated the schema of the state as the tool or instrument of the dominant classes. This schema appears to take the opposite course to these conceptions, but, in fact, it does so only by admitting the same theoretical principles. So it is not at all surprising that it is exactly this schematic phraseology, radical only in appearance, which under its cover allows Marxist theory to be contaminated by ideology. In particular, the theoretical continuation of this schema leads to the conception of the *state as agent of the monopolies* in *state monopoly capitalism*. There is, of course, no doubt that in the development of imperialism, the transformations of the CMP entail a whole specific, complex articulation of the economic and of the political. But the schema of the state as the agent of the monopolies wrongly involves a confusion of the economic and political, and thereby comes close to the above-mentioned contemporary ideologies of the state; it is, in fact, only a term which covers the absence of a scientific theory in this domain.

This is demonstrated by numerous contradictions: in particular we find a notion of state autonomy similar to that admitted by the advocates of revolution from above, grafted non-critically on to this schema. The state is related to the monopoly fraction as its agent/tool: this relation is understood as a conspiracy which uses personal contacts to place the state (still, however, capable of conducting the revolution from above) in the hands of a small group of monopolists. Let the people as a whole drive out these usurpers and the state will do the rest![14] But the problem is even more complicated than it appears: for while this conception can lead to a

14. In fact, the thesis – which dominated the colloquium at Choisy-le-Roi on 'state monopoly capitalism' – of the fusion of the powers of the monopolies and of the state in a 'unique mechanism' in order to save capitalist society, runs the risk of having this conclusion drawn from it. Although this thesis appears to be ultra-revolutionary, it nevertheless admits quite clearly that this famous 'unique mechanism' has no effect on the state's structures. The report of F. Lazard at this same colloquium makes this clear: for him, this loudly proclaimed unique mechanism affects only 'the content of the state's intervention, the forms in which it manifests itself'. See *Économie et politique*, special issue, Vol. I, p. 19. What is implied here is that this state, if it were 'utilized' in a different way, could operate the passage to socialism.

right-wing opportunism, it has also led to a *left-wing extremism*, as shown in the Third International's analyses of the state in the Social Democracies (the notion of 'social fascism' as the agent of the monopolies). This extremism was later corrected at the Seventh Congress of the International.[15]

I shall not deal with the consequences of such a conception of the state. I shall point out simply that the relative autonomy of the contemporary state vis-à-vis the dominant classes or fractions is only the concrete form taken on by this autonomy, constitutive of the capitalist type of state, in so far as it reflects a new articulation of the political and the economic in the relations between the structures and the field of the class struggle. This articulation *presupposes*, however, *that type of relation* between the political and the economic which occurs in the CMP: it constitutes a *variable* within *invariant limits*. This relative autonomy has nothing to do with a state in transition or with a state with an equilibrium of forces. In other words, it does not call into question the profound relations between the contemporary state and the hegemonic fraction of the monopolies: on the contrary, it presupposes them.

15. See, in particular, G. Dimitrov's report to the Seventh Congress of the Communist International, in *Inprecorr*.

3. The Capitalist State and the Field of the Class Struggle

(i) THE GENERAL PROBLEM

The specific unity and relative autonomy of the capitalist type of state vis-à-vis the dominant classes and fractions depends on the position of this state in the structures of the CMP and on its particular relation to the field of the class struggle in this mode. We must remember here our prior analyses of this subject.[1]

a. Capitalist relations of production (i.e. separation of the direct producer from his means of production in the framework of the relation of real appropriation) assign to the state's juridico-political superstructure a specific autonomy vis-à-vis the relations of production. In the field of the class struggle, this autonomization is reflected in an autonomy of the economic class struggle (socio-economic class relations) from the political class struggle (socio-political class relations). The *juridical* structures of the capitalist state, combined with the juridical ideology and the ideological in general in this mode of production have as *their effect* on the economic class struggle (on the socio-economic relations) the *isolation* of the agents in a mode of production in which, nonetheless, the real structure of the relations of production (separation of the direct producer from the means of production) leads to a remarkable *socialization* of the labour process. This isolation, which is an over-determined but real effect, is experienced by the agents according to the mode of competition; it ends by concealing from these agents the fact that their relations are class relations. This isolation applies just as much to the capitalists/private owners as to the wage-labourers, although it clearly does not appear in the same way in the socio-economic relations of these two classes. Marx and Lenin showed how important they thought these characteristics of the economic struggle of the working class to be, when they emphasized the necessity for a political party: one of the functions of such a party is to constitute the revolutionary *political unity* of the working class, which is constantly ravaged by 'individual', 'local', 'partial', 'isolated' economic struggle.

b. In the framework of a *capitalist formation* dominated by the CMP,

1. See p. 123 ff. above.

we must take into consideration the isolation of the socio-economic relations of those classes which belong to other modes of production coexisting in this formation: for instance, the *petty bourgeoisie* and the *small-holding peasantry*. Their isolation (on which Marx, Engels and Lenin laid so much stress) is not identical with that of the classes of the CMP: it depends in particular on the very relations of production of these classes, relations which are precisely characterized by a non-separation of the direct producer from the means of production. However, in so far as these classes are present in a *capitalist* formation, this real isolation peculiar to them is *over-determined* by the *effect of isolation* imposed by the CMP.

c. There is a twofold relation between the capitalist state and the field of the class struggle: it bears on (i) the political class struggle and on (ii) the economic class struggle. On this subject we have already noted this state's relation to the socio-economic relations, as they present themselves through the effect of isolation produced by the state itself together with the ideological. This state possesses institutions inside which the economic existence of classes and the political class struggle are absent. By its effect of isolation on the socio-economic relations, this state presents itself as the strictly political, public *unity* of the particular, private, economic antagonisms of the ensemble of 'society'. The institutionalized power of the capitalist state presents *its own unity* in its relations to socio-economic relations (the economic class struggle), in so far as it represents the unity of the people-nation, composed of agents set up as subjects, as 'individuals/political persons', i.e. in so far as it represents the political unity of an economic isolation which is its own effect. On the level of the relations of the state to the political class struggle, this leads to a result which seems *paradoxical*, but which in fact constitutes the 'secret' of this national-popular-class-state: the institutionalized power of the capitalist class state presents *its own class unity*, precisely in so far as it can pose as a national-popular state, i.e. as a state which does not represent the power of one or several determinate classes, but which represents the power of the political unity of private agents, given over to economic antagonisms which the state claims to have the function of surmounting by unifying these agents within a 'popular-national' body.

d. This characteristic of the capitalist state is related to a precise *ideological function*: given the specific efficacity of the ideological and its role in the framework of the capitalist state, it would be wrong to underestimate the importance of this function, which in fact concerns the complex problem of the *legitimacy* of this state. The ideological function must not be conflated with the intervention of the ideological in the actual organization of this state, i.e. in the setting-up of the agents as juridico-political subjects and in the constitution of the national-popular body.

However, one remark needs to be added: the fact that the state's juridico-political superstructure is related to its ideological function does not in itself mean that the former is *reduced* to the ideological. In short, the state as 'representative' of the political unity of the nation-people, is nevertheless reflected in a *whole real institutional framework which tends to function effectively* according to the concrete situation of the forces present, *in the direction* of a specific unity of the state's power and of a relative autonomy vis-à-vis the dominant classes. Although it is truly impossible to over-estimate the institutional framework and although we must always keep what it hides in view, it is equally impossible to ignore the specific efficacy which it presents, coupled with the ideological function of legitimizing the state, vis-à-vis its own unity and its relative autonomy.

In effect, this state is supposed to represent the general interest, the general will and the political unity of the people and the nation. In the characteristic forms of the principle of representation, the general interest, public opinion, universal suffrage, public liberties, it presents the normative institutional ensemble of *political democracy*. However, in order to examine the problem of the state's unity, I shall refer in particular to the concept of popular sovereignty and to the formation of the concept of the people.

In political theory, this concept of popular sovereignty, which covers that of the capitalist state, is linked to the problem of the *unity peculiar* to institutionalized political power. The problem of sovereignty had already been forged in connection with the absolutist state, where it indicated (still in a fairly confused way) the unitary structure of political power which had gained autonomy from the economic. In the sense of popular sovereignty, it designates an ensemble of citizens, of formally and abstractly free and equal individuals set up as political persons, as a source of the state's legitimacy. This ensemble is conceived as the body politic of society, as the people. However it is more important for us to note here that *the state's sovereignty and popular sovereignty are identical*. This people, composed of citizens, is supposed to acquire its existence as the body politic, as the source of legitimacy, only in so far as it takes on a unity directly embodied in the unity of state power. In the political theories of the social contract and of political democracy this is expressed in the ambiguous relation between the *pact of civil association* and the *pact of government*: the truth of this is seen in the fact that, excepting Rousseau, whose conclusions smash the framework of political democracy, it is Hobbes who appears as the true embodiment of the theories of social contract. See for instance the problem of the general will and the principle of representation in the institutions of the state resulting from the French Revolution: *representation* of the people through various elected assemblies is not strictly speaking the mere expression of the body politic as a pre-constituted unity; it actually constitutes the unity (even the existence) of this body politic. Popular sovereignty is identified with state sovereignty since the people are identified with the state only if they are *represented*. The role of the people's representatives is not that of expressing *the will of the nation* but, to use the expression which constantly recurs in the theorists of liberal democracy, that of expressing *the will for nationhood*; that is to say, it is the role of constituting the body politic, which is the people, by attributing unity to the members of the 'society'.[2]

It is possible to ascertain the repercussions on the state's institutions of this relation between state sovereignty and popular sovereignty, i.e. of the relation established by means of this conception of representation. The state's power constitutes unity of its own in so far as its institutions are organized so as to constitute the people's and the nation's unity. The state, which is established as the place of the 'universal', of the general will, of the general interest and of the public, supposedly represents not this or that private interest and socio-economic constellation (nor even their sun), but the unitary political ensemble of the people-nation. The state's sovereignty thus appears to be linked to the state's 'moral personality', one and undivided. Each part of the state's power and each particular state organ *is institutionally fixed as representing simultaneously the unity of the body politic and the unity of the state's power*: it is in this way that each representative in the elected assemblies is supposed to represent not the private interests of his electors, but the whole of the electoral body. (Note that the opposite is the case in the 'estates general'.) Moreover, it is because of this that the possibility of the *imperative mandate* is excluded from the framework of political democracy. The administrative organs themselves represent the unity of the state's power: this is a characteristic of modern bureaucracy which functions within a hierarchy of competence, delegated

2. Useful works on this subject are G. Burdeau, *Traité de Science Politique*, Vols. V, VI and VII; and Leibholz, *Das Wesen der Repräsentation und der Gestaltwandel der Demokratie in 20. Jahrhundert*, 2nd edn., 1960.

from the central power. The actual relation of the state's institutional powers, which is conceived as a 'separation' of these powers, is in fact fixed in the capitalist state as a mere *distribution* of power, out of the undivided unity of state sovereignty: this is precisely how Montesquieu gave it theoretical expression.[3] This feature of the unity of the capitalist state governs its *centralized* organization: the decline of local powers is directly related to the unitary organization of the state based on the central point of popular sovereignty. Moreover, the state's unity is found, under other forms, in the *modern juridical system* in the strict sense: this specific normative ensemble, made up of 'legal subjects' (*'sujets du droit'*) modelled according to the image of citizens, presents a *systematic unity* of the highest degree, in that it regulates the unity of these 'subjects' by means of laws.[4]

I have no intention of multiplying examples adduced here simply by way of explanation. I shall merely remark that the juridico-political region of the capitalist state is effectively *organized* as an *institutional unity* of strictly political power (public) in so far as it constitutes the unity of an ensemble of elements (citizens) whose economic determination and therefore class memberhsip is systematically absent from its institutions.

We are now able to proceed with the second stage of the investigation: that is, to show how this unitary institutional framework, coupled with the ideological function peculiar to this state, allows the state to function, in its relations to the class struggle, as the *unambiguous* (*univoque*) political power *of the dominant classes or fractions*; and also to show in what precise sense the unambiguous functioning of this state implies its relative autonomy from these classes and fractions. I shall start with what Marx says on this subject in his political works.

(ii) MARX'S ANALYSES

The first and most striking point in Marx's political works on the theoretical type of capitalist state is that he grasps these distinctive features of the state precisely according to the mode of an 'opposition between state and

---

3. On this subject, see C. Eisenmann, 'L'Esprit des lois et la séparation des pouvoirs' in *Mélanges Malberg*, Paris, 1933.

4. I have given some indication of this in my articles: 'L'examen marxiste de l'État et du droit actuels' in *Les Temps Modernes*, August/September 1964, and 'À propos de la théorie marxiste du Droit' in *Archives de Philosophie du Droit*, XII, 1967; this volume is entitled *Marx et le droit moderne*.

society'. Thus he says: 'Only under the second Bonaparte does the state seem to have made itself completely independent. As against civil society, the state machine has consolidated its position so thoroughly . . .';[5] and 'the parody of the Empire [the cult of the emperor] was necessary to free the mass of the French nation from the weight of tradition, and to work out in pure form the opposition between the state power and society'.[6] This opposition was also described as follows: 'Every *common* interest was straightaway severed from society, counterposed to it as a higher, *general* interest, snatched from the activity of society's members themselves and made an object of government activity. . . .'[7] The state is thus understood as 'freeing civil society completely from the trouble of governing itself', from the trouble of 'self-government',[8] under the second Empire, 'before the executive power, it [the nation] renounces all will of its own and submits to the superior command of an alien will, to authority'. The Bonapartist State 'expresses the heteronomy of a nation, in contrast to its autonomy'.[9]

These remarks are vital to Marx's analyses of the capitalist type of state but they may seem strange at first sight. They have misled numerous interpreters into the error of seeing them as a late return by Marx to his early works, to the conception of the state as alienation from civil society, in the sense which this concept ('concrete individuals-generic man') has for the young Marx. Consequently, these anlayses of Marx appear to contradict his mature conception of the *class state*. Thus, in his introduction to *The Eighteenth Brumaire*, Nora writes: 'But Marx made two sorts of judgement on this apparatus of the centralized state: on the one hand he affirms that it is the instrument of oppression of the dominant class . . . on the other, he feels that this centralized apparatus, by perfecting its mechanism, becomes increasingly independent from society and is the place of the general interest.'[10] Or again, as Rubel says: 'It does not seem at first sight that Bonapartism corresponds to the idea which Marx himself had of the state as the instrument of the power and domination of the exploiting class. . . . He traces out an ideal picture, in which Bonapartism is a "relation of forces" in which state and society are at the extremes, confronting each other in an absolute antagonism.'[11]

But even if these interpretations are incorrect they nevertheless accentu-

---

5. 'The Eighteenth Brumaire', *MESW*, 1970, p. 171.   6. ibid., p. 176.
7. ibid., pp. 170–1.   8. ibid., p. 110.   9. ibid., p. 170.
10. P. Nora, Introduction to *18 Brumaire*, Paris, 1963, p. 15.
11. M. Rubel, *K. Marx devant le bonapartisme*, Paris–The Hague, 1960, p. 155.

ate the importance of our problem. In fact, in the rigorous scientific perspective of his mature works, Marx *constantly* and *systematically* establishes the relation between the capitalist state and the precise forms of the political struggle of the dominant classes in a formation dominated by the CMP. Thus, he sees 'Bourgeois rule as the outcome and result of universal suffrage, as the express act of the sovereign will of the people . . .';[12] and he says 'the nation made its general will the law, that is to say, it made the law of the ruling class its general will'.[13] How then, in this complicated context, does state power organize itself into its own unity, *into a unity of class power*, while presenting (and precisely in the sense that it does present) a relative autonomy vis-à-vis the dominant class or classes? It is only because Marx's analyses are unclear on this point that they seem contradictory.

Let us see what Marx means in these texts by 'opposition between the state and society'. First of all, it is clear that it is not a contradictory dislocation between the state and the economic, i.e. it is not for example a particular dislocation between the base and the juridico-political superstructure. On the other hand, Bonapartism (as a type of state – 'the religion of the bourgeoisie') is grasped precisely as a specific form of correspondence between the juridico-political superstructure and the relations of production either in the CMP or in a formation dominated by the CMP. When we look at all the preceding analyses as a whole, it is clear that where Marx understands a process of antagonism between state and society, the public and the private, etc., he is (as I have pointed out[14]) grasping the effects of the autonomy of the instances of the CMP in the field of the class struggle. In the relation of the structures to the field of the class struggle, this is reflected by a specific dislocation between the state and the economic class struggle. The form taken by this dislocation is precisely the relation between the state (representative of 'unity') and the isolation of the socio-economic relations, by means of popular sovereignty and of the political body of 'people-citizens'. Antagonism between the state and society means the dislocation and respective autonomy of the political from the economic and the dislocation of the state from the 'isolated' economic class struggle.

But this 'antagonism between the state and society' indicates something

12. 'The Class Struggles in France', *MESW*, 1958, Vol. I, p. 226.
13. 'The Eighteenth Brumaire', *MESW*, 1970, p. 168.
14. See p. 134 ff. above.

more than the problem so far stressed, namely a relative autonomy of the state from the politically dominant classes. The relation between the state and the political interests of these classes, which Marx frequently distinguished from their 'private', 'economic', 'selfish', etc., interests, *establishes itself only by a relative autonomy between the state and these classes,* whose secret is revealed by Bonapartism: its essential characteristic is precisely that particular independence of the state from the dominant classes. The capitalist state is not directly linked to the economic interest of the dominant classes, in the sense that the economic struggle is absent from its institutions or that the agents of production distributed in classes are present in the form of 'people-citizens'; rather it is linked to their strictly political interests by being relatively autonomous from these classes. We can thus already state that the mature Marx's phrase 'antagonism between the state and society' indicates *not only the autonomy* of the respective structures of the political and of the economic reflected in the relation between the state and the economic class struggle, *but also the relative autonomy* of the state from the politically dominant classes. Granted that this term 'autonomy' should not be given the same meaning in its various applications, and that it is merely serving to locate the problems, it does nonetheless establish the relation between these two phenomena.

Thus, in this context, Marx clearly sees the relation between the unity of class power peculiar to the capitalist state and the fact that that state represents the political unity of the agents, whose economic relations manifest the effect of isolation: *this unity is the condition of the possibility of the state's relative autonomy vis-à-vis the dominant classes.* This state claims as its function the creation of 'the civil unity of the nation'.[15] On the Paris Commune, Marx says in *The Civil War in France*: 'The unity of the nation was not to be broken, but on the contrary, to be organized by the Communal Constitution and to become a reality by the destruction of the state power which claimed to be the embodiment of that unity, independent of, and superior to the nation itself, from which it was but a parasitic excrescence.'[16] This is the strictly political unity which the state represents vis-à-vis the 'isolated agents' of the economic class struggle: these agents Marx sees as the 'incoherent shapelessness of the social body' of which the state claims to provide the political unity. Marx gives some *indications* about the relation between this phenomenon and the unity

15. 'The Eighteenth Brumaire', *MESW*, 1970, p. 169.
16. 'The Civil War in France', ibid., p. 288.

peculiar to institutionalized political power, in his analyses of Bonapartism concerning the *centralist* character of the capitalist state: for he does not use his notion in the simple 'administrative' sense, but precisely to indicate the characteristic unity of the power of the capitalist state. Engels's remarks on the 'unitary state' and the 'unitary republic' in the *Critique of the Erfurt Programme* follow the same line.

This characteristic unity of institutionalized power *corresponds precisely to the fact that it constitutes an unambiguous power for the dominant classes or fractions*. Marx returns to this point time and time again. This state is related in this way to the political interests of the dominant classes or fractions (to their strictly political organization) in their political class struggle with the dominated classes.

Bonapartism, which is seen here as a type of capitalist state, as 'the religion of the bourgeoisie', corresponds to its political interests, to its unambiguous political class power. Moreover, this is true of the *historical* phenomenon of French Bonapartism which served the exclusive interests of the bourgeoisie; while the small-holding peasantry, represented by Louis Bonaparte, were in fact only a supporting class with no hold on political power. It is a question, then, of a relation between the capitalist state and the interests of the dominant classes and fractions, i.e. their political interests. In fact, that hegemonic class or fraction which finally holds the political power of a capitalist formation autonomous from the economic and political struggles, can dominate effectively only if it sets up its economic interests as political interests. In holding state power it can perpetuate existing social relations only through a whole series of compromises which maintain the unstable equilibrium of the classes present, and through a whole range of political organization and particular ideological functioning, by which it manages to present itself as the representative of the general interest of the people and the embodiment of the unity of the nation. It is a question of the role of the capitalist state vis-à-vis the dominated classes; and it is this which establishes the specific relation between this state and the political interests of the dominant classes or fractions.

But why can *this relation* (i.e. the unity peculiar to institutionalized power as the unambiguous power of these classes) establish itself only through that relative autonomy of the capitalist state to which Bonapartism as religion of the bourgeoisie gives us the key?

Marx and Engels give us the answer: owing to its constitution and its position in the class struggle, the bourgeoisie was (except in exceptional cirumstances) apparently *incapable* of raising itself through its own *political parties* to the hegemonic level of organization. Marx often speaks of: 'This bourgeoisie, which every moment sacrificed its general class interests, that is, its political interests, to the narrowest and most sordid private interests',[17] of this bourgeoisie 'which proved that the struggle to maintain its public interests, its own class interests, its political power, only troubled and upset it, as it was a disturbance of private business'.[18] But we should note the two following points:

a. The bourgeoisie's incapacity to raise itself to the strictly political level stems from its inability to achieve its own internal unity: it sinks into fractional struggles and is unable to realize its political unity on the basis of a politically conceived common interest.

b. Most importantly, this incapacity also stems at the same time from the bourgeoisie's struggle against the dominated classes and from the fact that it finds it particularly difficult to realize its political hegemony vis-à-vis these classes. Discussing the fractions of the bourgeoisie, Marx says of the parliamentary republic that it was 'the unavoidable condition of their *common* rule, the sole form of state in which their general class interest subjected to itself at the same time both the claims of their particular factions and all the remaining classes of society'.[19] And yet 'present-day France [namely Bonapartism] was contained in a finished state within the parliamentary Republic'.[20]

Marx and Engels also explain the reasons why bourgeoisie experiences this difficulty in the realization of its hegemony *over the dominated classes*. These are: the internal fractioning of the bourgeois class; the continued existence of the classes of the small producers in capitalist formations and their complex reflection at the political level; the rise and organized political struggle of the working class; the institutions of the capitalist state (for example, universal suffrage), which hurl all the classes or fractions of society on to the political scene, etc. *In short, everything happens as if the specific co-ordinates of the struggle of the dominant classes contribute to prevent their political organization.*

What then is the role of the capitalist class state in this context? It can be stated as follows: it takes charge, as it were, of the bourgeoisie's political interests and realizes the function of political hegemony which the bourgeoisie is unable to achieve. But *in order to do this, the capitalist state*

17. 'The Eighteenth Brumaire', ibid., p. 159.   18. ibid., p. 157.
19. ibid., pp. 151–2.   20. ibid., p. 167.

assumes a relative autonomy with regard to the bourgeoisie. This is why Marx's analyses of Bonapartism as a capitalist type of state are so significant. For this relative autonomy allows the state to intervene not only in order to arrange compromises vis-à-vis the dominated classes, which, in the long run, are useful for the actual economic interests of the dominant classes or fractions; but also (depending on the concrete conjuncture) to intervene against the long-term economic interests of *one or other* fraction of the dominant class: for such compromises and sacrifices are sometimes necessary for the realization of their political class interests. A good example are the state's so-called 'social functions' which have nowadays assumed an increased importance. While it is true that these social functions at the moment conform to the policy of state investment (i.e. they are intended to absorb the surplus of monopoly production) and so conform to the economic interests of the monopolies, it is equally true that they have been *imposed* on the dominant classes by the state, through the pressure of the dominated classes: this is often revealed by a hostility between the state and the dominant classes. Such functions have even sometimes been imposed by *social democratic* governments; but, strictly speaking, this does not alter the situation. These governments used the state and its relative autonomy to function as the political organisers of the dominant classes.

However, in order concretely to take on this relative autonomy which, inscribed in the play of its institutions, is what is precisely necessary for hegemonic class domination, the state *is supported by* certain dominated classes of the society, in that it presents itself, through a complex ideological process, as their representative: it encourages them in various ways, to work against the dominant class or classes, but to the political advantage of these latter. In this way it succeeds precisely in *making* the dominated classes *accept* a whole series of compromises which appear to be to *their* political interest. In the concrete historical case of French Bonapartism, Marx reveals this complicated functioning of the capitalist state in relation to the small-holding peasantry, and the petty bourgeoisie: 'As against the bourgeoisie, Bonaparte looks on himself, at the same time, as the representative of the peasants and of the people in general, who wants to make the lower classes of the people happy within the frame of bourgeois society. New decrees that cheat the "True Socialists" of their statecraft in advance.'[21] For, in spite of the differences established by Marx between

21. ibid., p. 176.

the parliamentary power of the republic and the executive power of the Bonapartist state (relating to differences between the historical forms of the state), Bonapartism, inasmuch as it is a capitalist type of state, manages to present itself as precisely emanating from the general interest and as the representative of the unity of people-nation. In the concrete case of French Bonapartism, since Bonaparte was elected by the universal suffrage which he had himself re-established, he is more 'representative' than the republic which had suppressed it: 'If by its motion to restore universal suffrage the executive power appealed from the National Assembly to the people, the legislative power appealed by its Questors Bill from the people to the army.'[22]

Thus, in fulfilling its political function, the capitalist state comes to rely on dominated classes and sometimes to play them off against the dominant classes. It does this by concretely realizing the relative autonomy which it has vis-à-vis the dominant classes inscribed within its institutions: this autonomy allows it to remain in constant liaison with their political interests. In fact, within these precise limits, the capitalist state does not take even one step away from the political interests of the bourgeoisie; in the case of French Bonapartism, Marx clearly demonstrates how Louis Bonaparte, the 'official' representative of the petty bourgeoisie and the small-holding peasantry, never took a single political measure which was to their advantage. Within the *limits* imposed by the relation between the structures and the field of the class struggle, this relative autonomy of the state can *vary* according to (i) the modalities taken on by its function vis-à-vis the dominant classes, and (ii) the concrete relation between the forces present. For example, the state may function as the *factor of the political organization* of these classes, a function which manifests itself in the complex relation of the state to the parties of these classes. In this case, the state's relative autonomy is to be deciphered in its relation to these parties, which continue to take on their own organizational function. Or else the state may *substitute* itself for these parties by continuing to function as the factor of hegemonic organization of these classes. Or again in certain situations it may even *take total control of the political interests of these classes*: this is the situation in the concrete historical phenomenon of French Bonapartism. In this last case, the relative autonomy of the state is such that the dominant classes or fractions appear to renounce their political power, just as Marx said in his analyses of the Second Empire.

22. ibid., p. 163.

However, all these variations occur within the limits of the relative autonomy constitutive of the capitalist type of state; these limits are related to the characteristics peculiar to the class struggle in capitalist formations: *they are clearly distinguished from those classes of state autonomy which arise from an equilibrium between the forces present in the class struggle.* The difference lies principally in the fact that in the latter case politically organized or politically disorganized 'equivalent' forces are generally present. In both cases, it is characteristically difficult during that period to decipher the direct relation between the state and the dominant classes' political interests in the field of the class struggle. The state continually plays the forces present off, one against the other; and it therefore contributes to the effective domination of certain classes (since it is never a neutral arbitrator) only through its role as cohesive factor and maintainer of the structures of a given formation. In that case the structures and the field of the class practices are a particular dislocation. However, in the case of the relative autonomy of the capitalist state, it is always possible, within the framework of a political periodization, to establish the direct relation of the state to the dominant classes' political interests, whether it functions as the factor of political organization of these classes, or whether it takes direct charge of these interests.

Hence, this relative autonomy of the capitalist state follows from its strictly political function vis-à-vis the various classes of a formation dominated by the CMP. To be more precise it follows from:

a. Its function as factor of *political organization* of the dominant classes; for because of the isolation of socio-economic relations and because of the break-up of the bourgeois class into fractions, etc., the dominant classes are more often than not unable to raise themselves by their own efforts to a hegemonic level vis-à-vis the dominated classes. This is precisely how we should understand Marx's, Engels's and Lenin's frequent characterizations of the capitalist state as '*the organization* of the dominant class' or again '*the organization* of class domination'.

b. Its function as the factor of *political disorganization; i.e.* its function of preventing the working class from organizing itself into an 'autonomous' political party. The political organization of the working class (its political struggle) is a factor which necessitates, and at the same time prevents, the hegemonic organization of the dominant classes. In this case, the state politically organizes the dominant classes and ensures at the same time the political disorganization of the working class. The effect of constant isolation presented by the working class's economic struggle necessitates the political organization of this class into an autonomous party which will realize its unity. But the state's function is to maintain it in this isolation (which is its own effect) by presenting itself as the representative of the political unity of the people-nation: this contributes to its relative autonomy vis-à-vis the dominant classes.

c. Its particular and often all-important function vis-à-vis certain classes of the non-dominant modes of production in the capitalist formation, which are affected by the over-determining isolation of the dominant CMP; see for instance the peasantry, in particular the small-holding peasantry, and the petty bourgeoisie, what Lenin called the ocean of small-scale producers. These classes, thrown on to the political scene by the institutions of the capitalist state, often constitute *supporting classes*. By a complex ideological process, the state benefits from these classes' incapacity to affirm themselves politically, because of their place in the process of production, as opposed to the working class who benefit from the socialization of the labour process: the state often makes a direct claim to be the political representative of the interests of the small producers.

In this way it is possible to decipher the *relation* between the unitary character of institutionalized power in the capitalist state and its relative autonomy vis-à-vis the dominant classes. The *paradoxical* character of this relation lies in the fact that this state assumes a relative autonomy with regard to these classes, precisely in so far as it constitutes their *unambiguous* and *exclusive* political power. In other words, this autonomy vis-à-vis the politically dominant classes, inscribed in the institutional play of the capitalist state, neither authorizes the dominated classes *effectively to participate* in political power nor cedes 'parcels' of institutionalized power to them. State power is not a machine or an instrument, a simple object coveted by the various classes; nor is it divided into parts which, if not in the hands of some, must automatically be in the hands of others: rather it is an ensemble of structures. Within the framework of a state autonomy resulting from an equilibrium of the forces present, it is sometimes possible to note a certain *distribution* of institutionalized political power, but this is impossible within the limits of the relative autonomy constitutive of the capitalist type of state. Its political unity as representative of the unity of the people-nation is, in the last analysis, only its unity in so far as it is the unambiguous political power of the dominant classes. Its relative autonomy, which is a function of its unifying feature as national-popular-state is, in the last analysis, only that autonomy necessary for the hegemonic organization of the dominant classes; i.e. it is only that relative autonomy which is indispensable for the unambiguous power of these classes.

Thus, in its relations to the field of the class struggle, the capitalist state's relative autonomy depends on the characteristics peculiar to the economic and political class struggle in the CMP and in a capitalist formation. This must be understood in the general sense of the relations between the structures and the field of the class struggle. In this sense, the state sets the *limits* within which the class struggle affects it; *the play of its institutions allows and makes possible* this relative autonomy from the dominant classes and fractions. The *variations and modalities* of this relative autonomy depend upon the concrete relation between social forces in the field of the political class struggle; in particular, they depend on the *political struggle of the dominated classes*. It is at this point that the problem of the *equilibrium of social forces* present in the political struggle comes in. This equilibrium is not the necessary condition of the relative autonomy of the capitalist state vis-à-vis the dominant classes and fractions, in the sense that this autonomy, within these limits, depends on the very characteristics of the field of the class struggle in the CMP and in a capitalist formation. It is, however, evident that this equilibrium intervenes decisively in the modalities and variations of this autonomy. These considerations therefore indicate the two following points:

a. That equilibrium, in the general sense or in the sense of catastrophic equilibrium, is not (as in other types of states) the only form which allows the political struggle of the dominated classes to act on the relative autonomy of the capitalist state. In so far as this autonomy is inscribed in the play of its institutions, the political struggles of the dominated classes can be expressed there, even without having attained the threshold of an equilibrium of social forces;

b. That this autonomy, which appears here as the effect of the political struggle of the dominated classes, should not be conceived as resulting from an equilibrium of forces. In particular, although it is real in the sense that it is inscribed within the limits set by institutional play, it completely fails to function in the same way as an autonomy resulting from an equilibrium of the forces present.[23]

23. These two cases of state autonomy can be in contradiction, in the sense that their concrete co-existence is often impossible. Significantly, it is in the case of an autonomy

(iii) THE SO-CALLED PHENOMENON OF TOTALITARIANISM

Contemporary political theory has tackled these characteristics of the capitalist state in a distorted fashion, using the ideological theme of 'totalitarianism'. As the subject is so vast I shall only give some brief indications concerning it.[24]

Although some attempts have been made to solve the so-called phenomenon of totalitarianism by subsuming it under the general theory of 'dictatorship', the more general line has been to attempt to conceive it as a specific political form applicable to contemporary transformations of the capitalist state, thus to contrast it radically with the liberal form of the state. This theory is as follows: the problematic of totalitarianism is intimately linked to the perspective of 'individuals', subjects of society and producers of the state, and the totalitarian state depends on a form of institutionalized power whose legitimacy is founded in a 'mass' society. The state, the alienated essence of the 'massified atoms' of an industrialized society, nowadays appears in its full antagonism towards society. In the liberal society and the liberal state, individuals possess a sphere of private autonomy, which results from their participation in the political and which is promoted by the class differences preventing this global massification. In contrast to this, we are now witnessing radical transformations: total destruction of the individual essence in the technological process; disappearance of the class struggle in favour of a homogenized society of reified atoms, identical and disparate (the mass), creation of a new alienation, the totalitarian state, which totally monopolizes the individual essence in its antagonistic opposition to society; total acquisition by state power of all the spheres of individual activity, absorption of the

---

resulting from the equilibrium of the forces present that the state ceases to function as political organizer of the dominant classes; this is clearly seen in state-party relations: it is in this case, then, that a *profound crisis* of political domination may occur, *a crisis of hegemony*: and this is not by any means true of the relative autonomy of the capitalist type of state. On the other hand, when this equilibrium of forces does not experience a crisis (i.e. a modification of the ensemble of the relations of a formation or of one of its phases or stages) but limits itself to the political domain alone, these two kinds of autonomy may combine in forms which vary with the concrete situations.

24. The literature on 'totalitarianism' in general is enormous. See in particular: H. Arendt, *The Origins of Totalitarianism*, 1951; W. Kornhauser, *The Politics of Mass Society*, 1965; Adorno, *The Authoritarian Personality*, 1950; C. Friedrich (ed.), *Totalitarianism*, 1944. The only attempt to approach the phenomenon from a Marxist viewpoint is found in F. Neumann, *Behemoth: The Structure and Practice of National Socialism*, 1944, and *The Democratic and Authoritarian State*, 1957.

private domain into the womb of the state Behemoth; a complete non-participation of the individual in the political, the individual becoming a mere cog in this monstrous new mechanical Leviathan.

I will go no further with this apocalyptic mythology although it is true that it sometimes furnishes interesting descriptions of the modern juridico-political instance. Although these analyses are governed by the ideological problematic of the individual-subject, and although the current transformations which it hypothesizes are derived more from phantasmagoria than from science, it is still possible to decipher in them real problems concealed beneath the mask of the ideological.

In particular, the capitalist state derives its *principle of legitimacy* from the fact that it presents itself as the unity of the people-nation, understood as an ensemble of homogeneous entities, identical and disparate, which it establishes as political individuals-citizens. As certain theorists of totalitarianism have correctly remarked, it is here that it differs radically from other forms of 'despotism', for example from 'absolute' political power, which is formally similar, but which is carried on by forms of tyranny founded on divine-sacred legitimacy.[25] Yet these forms, as found in slave or feudal states, certainly bound power within *strictly defined* limits. In other words, it is exactly that type of legitimacy of the capitalist state (representing the unity of people-nation), which allows the specific functioning of the state encapsulated by the term 'totalitarianism'. This 'people' is merely the politico-ideological expression of the ideological and political structures' effect of isolation on the agents, an effect which is manifested in the socio-economic relations. It is thus easy to discern the real phenomena encapsulated ideologically by the term 'mass'.[26]

So too, that functioning of the capitalist state encapsulated by the term totalitarianism, and which in fact concerns this state's relation to the classes, is made possible by the relation between its principle of legitimacy and the isolation of the economic; for this isolation both conceals from the agents the class character of their relations and allows the direct expression of the class struggle to be absent from this state's institutions. It is precisely this which has led the theorists of totalitarianism to admit (very revealingly) a correlation between the political form of totalitarianism and

25. See Arendt, op. cit.; also Talmon, op. cit.

26. For guide-lines on posing this problem in rigorous Marxist terms, see R. Banfi, 'Abozzo di una ricerca attorno al valore d'uso nel pensiero di Marx' in *Critica Marxista*, January/February 1966, pp. 137 ff.

what they call an absence or decline of the class struggle. According to them a society in which the class struggle is present, in which opposing class interests are politically organized to act as a 'mediation' between the individual and political power, is a society with a 'pluralist' political form of power. The totalitarian state emerges only in a mass society where class membership no longer functions and the individual is thus directly given over to political power.[27]

This is an ideological answer to the real problem which it masks: what is true is that that functioning of the capitalist state grasped as 'totalitarian' is correlated, not with some kind of lack of opposing class interests or lack of 'mediating' associations between the 'individual' and the state, but rather with a lack of direct expression of the class struggle in the institutions of political power. What was an impossibility when the classes were fixed as castes or estates within the institutional organization becomes possible in the popular-class-state; i.e. it is possible, in a state which functions as a class state in so far as the political class struggle is absent from its institutions and in so far as it presents itself as the unity of the people-nation. In other words, to put it in a descriptive manner, the concentration of political class power has nowhere been so intense and reinforced (i.e. totalitarian) as when it has succeeded in excluding its institutional class character from its ideological principle of legitimacy.

Moreover, this becomes even more important when we look at the impact of the effect of the isolation of socio-economic relations of capitalist formations on the other levels of the class struggle. This has been grasped as a correlation between the totalitarian phenomenon and an absence of class struggle; but in fact, it is also concerned with the impact of this isolation of the economic class struggle on *political class organization*. Thus, the nazi and fascist states which are often considered to be particularly intense forms of totalitarianism, concern the fact that certain classes lack their own political organization; and this is (amongst other things) the result of the retroactive effect of the isolation of the economic

27. See Arendt, op. cit., pp. 305 ff.; Kornhauser, op. cit., pp. 33 ff., 48 ff., 76 ff. Making all due allowances, we can compare this conception with Durkheim's critique of despotic authoritarianism which he claims to be founded on an absence of 'mediating' organizations between the individuals and the state. In the last analysis, the ideological problem of a relation state-alienation/social-individual, posed by these theories of totalitarianism, is the same as that posed by Rubel and Nora (see p. 280 above, notes 10 and 11) in their accounts of Marx's analyses of Bonapartism: they thought that they had discovered in them two contradictory conceptions – (i) of the relation state-alienation/individuals, (ii) of the relation state/classes.

struggle on the political struggle. This, therefore, is by no means a dissolution of the class struggle amongst the 'massified' individuals, but a complete absence of political class organization because of the isolation of the economic struggle. This has affected above all those classes which, in addition to their isolation resulting from their intrinsic conditions of economic life, have suffered the effect of isolation which the capitalist mode of production imposed on other modes of production, namely the petty bourgeoisie and certain fractions of the peasantry, such as the small-holding peasantry. For example, the nazi state in Germany went hand in hand with their failure to have their own political organization and with the support which they gave the state through the ideological mechanism of power fetishism; they considered the state as *their* political representative, since it incarnated the unity of the people-nation. But we should also not forget that the nazi state, while being at the service of the monopolies, coincided *with a period of particularly intense crisis in the strictly political organization of the bourgeois class itself.*[28]

I shall leave aside the problem of the fascist state. The fascist state is a very complex phenomenon which cannot be absorbed into the general phenomenon of totalitarianism: it can be studied only by examining the relation between the social forces in the concrete conjuncture.[29]

28. Gramsci, in particular, brought this to light in his texts on 'Caesarism' and fascism, where he tried to define a specific phenomenon of 'Caesarism' which would take different forms according to the various social formations. Caesarism, on this theory, results not from a simple equilibrium between the social forces present, but from a *catastrophe-equilibrium*, from a situation in which these social forces 'balance each other in such a way that a continuation of the conflict can only terminate in their reciprocal destruction' (*Prison Notebooks*, p. 219). This situation attributes to political power forms different from those which it takes on in the case of a general equilibrium: in the capitalist formation, this situation occurs as a *political crisis* of the social forces present, as the particular political disorganization of the social forces (particularly the bourgeois class) on which this catastrophe-equilibrium plays. *Gramsci takes fascism to be the form of Caesarism proper to developed capitalist formations* (see, in particular, *Prison Notebooks*, pp. 219–23).

29. I do not intend to discuss this complex problem here. I shall note only the following. If, as is normal, we attribute a very vague sense of 'authoritarianism' or 'totalitarianism' to the term fascist state, it loses all its specificity: in this sense, every concrete form of the capitalist state is more or less 'fascist'. Moreover, if we follow the theoretical line of the Third International before the Seventh Congress and see fascism simply as that form of the capitalist state which corresponds to monopoly capitalism and imperialism, we end up with this same result: in this sense, every contemporary form of state should be 'fascist' in varying degrees. These conceptions are obviously insufficient, especially as they fail to allow a scientific study of specific political forms.

Thus, the term *totalitarianism* cannot refer to any precise political phenomenon. Although we have tried to distinguish it from '*authoritarianism*', it denotes simply a particularly 'strong' character of state power. The phenomena attributed to it are in fact related to the characteristics of unity and relative autonomy peculiar to the capitalist state in general. Use of the notion of totalitarianism debars us from analysing these phenomena scientifically. What is ideologically grasped as the state's 'totalitarian' character vis-à-vis the masses, in fact concerns the concentration and specific unity of political power, a particular reinforcement of the *exclusive and unambiguous class power in the capitalist state*, i.e. in the popular-class-state which represents the unity of the people-nation. Similarly, the so-called antagonistic opposition of the totalitarian state to society is, in the last analysis, only the relative autonomy of the capitalist state vis-à-vis the dominant classes. Finally, the so-called relation between the totalitarian phenomenon and the absence of class struggle is merely the particular relation of the capitalist state to political class organization in capitalist formations. In the last analysis, we should recognize that the main contri-

---

We must attribute to the term 'fascist state' *a precise meaning* which denotes those specific state forms which appeared in Nazi Germany and (to a different degree) in Fascist Italy. We are here concerned with specific forms of state, specific in that they cannot be inserted into the typological framework of the capitalist state because they are characterized precisely by an articulation of the economic and the political, different from that specifying the capitalist type of state. As will become clear, this is by no means the case in the authoritarian framework of the 'typical' capitalist state which allows us to conceive of Bonapartism as the 'religion of the bourgeoisie'. I note also the following two points: (i) This divergence of the fascist state (conceived in this way) from the capitalist state poses no *theoretical impossibilities*, in the same sense that war capitalism poses no theoretical impossibilities for the analysis of the CMP or even of monopoly capitalism: these are *marginal historical divergences*. (ii) The fascist state as it appears in a capitalist formation, unlike other 'dictatorial' or 'absolutist' forms, of course presents numerous characteristics of the capitalist type of state, although it is situated on the margin of its typological framework. This is a theoretical problem which, *mutatis mutandis*, is formally related to that of the Bismarckian state: see above II, 4 (iii). It is exactly this which has led to the absorption of the fascist state into the capitalist type of state, by connecting it with 'Bonapartism': see, for example, the Bonapartism/national-socialism parallel drawn by A. Thalheimer, *Über den Faschismus*, reproduced in *Faschismus und Kapitalismus*, 1967, pp. 19 ff.; and H. Berl, *Napoléon III: Demokratie und Diktatur*, 1948. *When we have said this, we have still given no reply to the following question: what, in the concrete conjuncture of a capitalist formation, are the concrete factors (i.e. the political class relations) which produce the specific political phenomenon of the fascist state?* And this problem is too complex to be discussed within the scope of this book.

bution of theories of totalitarianism is as follows: that they insisted on the relation between (i) political institutions as representing the political unity of agents whose class relations exhibit the effect of isolation, and (ii) the particular unifying character of political power and its consequent characteristic relative autonomy. And this relation can be explained only by the Marxist analysis of political power. Further, it is certain that the present transformations of the CMP correspond to transformations of the capitalist state in its present form. It is equally true that it is impossible to decipher them within the problematic of totalitarianism and to specify them, for example, by describing them as totalitarian. In fact, the real characteristics, implicitly included by this term, *are by no means in opposition with the form of the liberal state in the strict sense of the term*: the real phenomena masked by this political ideology are found in the form of the liberal state, precisely in so far as they are related to the capitalist type of state. We have already encountered this problem in relation to political ideologies, when we stated that the real characteristics of present-day political ideologies, covered by the term totalitarian political ideologies, are, in fact, to be found in liberal political ideologies, and are constitutive traits of bourgeois political ideologies. Thus it is not surprising to see numerous ideological theorists of the totalitarian phenomenon explicitly admitting that the characteristics of this phenomenon are present in the liberal state itself, whilst discovering their source in the modern state in general.[30]

30. See, for example, Talmon, op. cit.

4. The Capitalist State and the Dominant Classes

(i) THE POWER BLOC

Up to now, we have examined the unity and relative autonomy of the capitalist type of state from the particular viewpoint of their relation to the general field of the class struggle; we must now also examine them from the viewpoint of their specific function in the *relation between the dominant classes and fractions* within a capitalist formation. In what follows we shall concentrate on this political function. And, once again, we shall use Marx's analyses, in so far as they concern the concept of the capitalist state. In doing this, we must remember our remarks on the power bloc, and, in particular, the following points:

1. At the level of political domination in a capitalist formation, we can establish the characteristic coexistence of several classes, and most importantly of fractions of classes, constituting a power bloc. This derives from:

  a. the capitalist relations of production. For example, it derives from the particular coexistence of the large-scale owners of ground-rent with the bourgeoisie, as the dominant classes of the capitalist formation. (In the beginning, the large-scale owners of ground-rent are the class of the landed nobility or a fraction of the nobility; later they become an autonomous fraction of the bourgeoisie.) And it derives from the particular fractioning of the bourgeoisie into commercial, industrial and financial fractions;

  b. the type of dominance of the CMP over the non-dominant modes, and from the consequent presence of these classes in the power bloc;

  c. the structures of the capitalist state which make it possible for several classes, fractions of classes, etc. to be present in the political scene.

2. The type of relations between the classes or fractions of classes which make up the power bloc have been determined. Contrary to some of Marx's notions (e.g. fusion or synthesis) the power bloc constitutes a contradictory unity of *dominant* classes or fractions, a unity dominated by

the *hegemonic* class or fraction. This unity of the power bloc is constituted under the protection of the hegemonic class or fraction which politically *polarizes* the interests of the other classes or fractions which are part of it. This reveals an important characteristic of the power bloc; despite certain ambiguous expressions, Marx's analyses explicitly rely on one basic principle: the relations between the various classes or fractions of this power bloc cannot consist of a *sharing out* of institutionalized political power, such that the hegemonic class or fraction simply possesses a more important share than the others. In other words, if the conception of state power divided into shares does not hold for the relations between dominant and dominated classes nor for those between dominant classes and supporting or allied classes, no more does it hold for relations between the classes and fractions which make up the power bloc. To this extent it is true that underlying Marx's analyses is the representation of the correspondence between the state and the *specific interests* of the hegemonic class or fraction, inasmuch as they polarize those of the other classes or fractions in the power bloc. In the last analysis, it is always the hegemonic class or fraction which appears to hold *state power in its unity*; and it does this so explicitly that it often appears in Marx as the 'exclusively dominant' class or fraction.

Thus political unity of the power bloc under the protection of the hegemonic class or fraction means unity of state power, in so far as it corresponds to the specific interests of this class or fraction. This characteristic is related, amongst other things, to the internal play of the institutions of the capitalist state, to the unity and relative autonomy peculiar to it, here considered from the point of view of the state's function vis-à-vis the power bloc. For, from another point of view, this particular relation between the state and the hegemonic class or fraction in no way derives from a direct dependence of the state 'machine' on this class or fraction. On the contrary, it goes hand in hand with a relative autonomy both from the latter, and even from the power bloc in its ensemble.

3. In fact, along with the coexistence on the terrain of political domination of the several classes and fractions which make up the power bloc, we find their characteristic incapacity to raise themselves to political unity under the protection of the hegemonic class or fraction. In other words, we find that the bourgeois class or fractions of that class are incapable of raising themselves to the hegemonic level through their own parties on the political scene. They are incapable (*through their own organizational means*)

of transforming their specific interest into the political interest which would polarize the interests of the other classes and fractions of the power bloc. Thus, they cannot provide the unity of the classes and fractions of this bloc. This is principally due to the profound division of the bourgeois class into antagonistic fractions, a division which starts from the level of the actual relations of production: 'This bourgeoisie which every moment sacrificed its general class interests, that is, its political interests, to the narrowest and most sordid private interests. . . .'[1] It is also due to the fact that on the side of the capitalist class of 'private capitalists' the effect of isolation on socio-economic relations is not compensated by anything, as it is by 'collective labour' on the side of the wage-earning workers of the working class. Left to themselves the classes and fractions at the level of political domination are not only exhausted by internal conflicts but, more often than not, founder in contradictions which make them incapable of governing politically. Even if, in the ensemble of class relations in a capitalist formation, these are secondary contradictions or (more rarely) secondary aspects of the principal contradiction, their impact is all-important. Coupled with the principal contradiction, or with its principal aspect, they create by their class functioning a permanently unstable situation of domination at the political level.

4. This, in fact, is what Gramsci insisted on in his text on 'Caesarism', even though he ascribed a theoretical specificity to the 'Caesarist' phenomenon and did not consider it characteristic of the capitalist type of state: he did this by relating it to a 'catastrophe equilibrium' between the fundamental social forces. However, he marks the limits of this explanation, while providing useful indications for the interpretation of this type of state.

It would be an error of method (an aspect of sociological mechanism) to believe that in Caesarism . . . the entire new historical phenomenon is due to the 'equilibrium' of the 'fundamental' forces. It is also necessary to see the interplay of relations between the principal groups . . . of the fundamental classes and the auxiliary forces directed by, or subjected to, their hegemonic influence.[2]

It is precisely these contradictory relations between the social forces of the bourgeois class, which is constitutively divided into fractions, which

1. 'The Eighteenth Brumaire', *MESW*, 1970, p. 159.
2. *Prison Notebooks*, p. 222.

reveal the immanent Caesarist tendencies of the capitalist type of state in, for instance, Bonapartism as the religion of the bourgeoisie.

It is clear how important these remarks are, when we consider that most contemporary political theories deny the existence of a dominant class and propound the conception of *political élites* between which power is *shared*; these theories are based on the notion that today's bourgeoisie no longer constitutes the monolithic and coherent class which it once did.[3] But in fact, the bourgeoisie has *never* constituted a class-subject of this kind, though this, of course, does not alter its characteristic class dominance or the unity of its institutionalized power: this unity is relatively autonomous from the bourgeois class, maintaining an unambiguous correspondence to the specific interests of the hegemonic fraction of that class.

What is the role of the state in this case? In fact, it is *the factor of the political unity of the power bloc under the protection of the hegemonic class or fraction. In other words, it is the factor of hegemonic organization of this class or fraction* since its specific interests are able to polarize those of the other classes or fractions in the power bloc. Marxist theory has often accentuated this role of the state vis-à-vis the *classes or fractions in power*: but it has normally described it as the state's *role of arbitration*. This latter myth stems from a misunderstanding of the over-determining role played by the secondary contradictions in a formation; and we must therefore destroy it. In this case, we are not, strictly speaking, concerned with the state's function vis-à-vis classes or fractions already politically organized by means of their own parties: i.e. we are not concerned with arbitration between already constituted social forces. Everything happens precisely as if the state permanently played the role of political organizer of the power bloc, something which will become clearer when we study the capitalist state's relations to the parties of the classes and fractions of this bloc. The state plays this role only because the political parties of the bourgeois class and of its fractions are unable to play an autonomous organizational role, let alone one analogous to the role of the working class's parties. Hence the state's essential role emerges more clearly as the factor of the political unity of the power bloc under the protection of the hegemonic class or fraction (this is its role with regard to the non-hege-

3. See T. Bottomore, *Classes in Modern Society*, 1966, pp. 28 ff.; *Elites and Society*, 1966 pp. 24 ff.

monic classes and fractions of the power bloc) and as the organizing factor of the interests of the hegemonic class or fraction (this is its specific role vis-à-vis the latter).[4]

With regard to the dominant classes and fractions, the capitalist state *presents an intrinsic unity*, combined with its relative autonomy, not because it is the tool of an already politically unified class, but precisely because it is the *unifying factor* of the power bloc.

Social forces, therefore, do not *share* institutionalized power; what we have here is a case of several classes and fractions present on the terrain of political domination, which are able to assure this domination only to the extent that they are politically unified. The state derives its own unity from this plurality of dominant classes and fractions, in so far as their relation is incapable of functioning by means of a share-out of power and needs the state as the organizational factor of their strictly political unity. This unity is realized under the protection of the hegemonic class or fraction and thus corresponds to the unity of the state as the organizational factor of this class or fraction. In this sense the unity of state power is, in the last analysis, to be found in the state's particular relation to the

4. This is particularly clear in the state's relations with *the parties of the dominant classes and fractions*. These parties have rarely been able to take on an organizational role in relation to these classes and fractions, let alone a role analogous to that of the socialist and (later) the communist parties. They have generally assumed the function of *representing these classes and fractions to the state*, and have constituted themselves as 'parliamentary fractions'. It therefore seems correct to conclude that they have in general functioned *especially* as the *transmission belt* of state power. But this is too general: we can be more precise and establish that the more these parties decline, the more autonomy the state takes on with regard to the dominant classes and fractions, by taking control of this organizational role. *The decline of these parties does not mean a political disorganization of the power bloc*, in so far as the state itself takes over this role: this is often so in the case of a state autonomy in which the executive is characteristically predominant, when this latter is combined with the decline of the parties and their replacement by pressure groups. It is also important to point out that the theoretical analyses of the parties of the bourgeois class and those of the working class can *by no means proceed from the same principles*. This mistake is made in most of the analyses carried out by contemporary political scientists, and even by most Marxist theorists: see, for example, the important article of U. Cerroni, 'Per una teoria del partito politico', *Critica Marxista*, September/December 1963, pp. 15 ff. The difference is not merely that 'the new type of party' looks to a revolutionary transformation of social relations; nor does the bourgeois parties' organizational incapacity stem merely from the fact that the bourgeois class looks to maintain existing social relations. In fact, the bourgeois parties, in general, utterly fail to fulfil that autonomous role as organizer of these classes which is precisely necessary for the maintenance of existing social relations: this role falls to the state.

hegemonic class or fraction, i.e. in the fact of the *univocal correspondence of the state to the specific interests of that class or fraction.* This is precisely what Marx meant in his analyses of France during the period 1848–52: he demonstrates over and over again (i) the coexistence of this relation between the state and the power bloc and (ii) the unitary functioning of institutionalized power to the benefit of the hegemonic class or fraction. Using these facts, we can destroy another fairly widespread contemporary myth, according to which the bourgeois state of the past was the representative of the bourgeois class, whilst the present-day monopoly capitalist state is the representative only of the monopolist fraction.

Strictly speaking, this is doubly incorrect: although the capitalist state represents the interests of the power bloc as a whole, it has always functioned in a specific relation with the hegemonic class or fraction of this bloc, and it has always been at the service of the specific interests of this class or fraction. This, of course, did not prevent the political domination of other classes and fractions of the power bloc. From another point of view, the present-day relation between the state and the hegemonic monopolist fraction in no way prevents other fractions of the bourgeoisie from belonging to the power bloc: I cannot·here go into this problem since discussion of it would take us too far afield. I shall simply point out that although the development of *imperialism* gave rise to *new cleavages* and to *displacements of contradictions* (imperialist and comprador bourgeoisies, national bourgeoisie, middle bourgeoisie), it did not abolish the fundamental co-ordinates of the power bloc. (This is a view completely opposed to that which locates the present line of demarcation of political domination between a handful of dirty monopolists on the one hand, and the rest of the nation on the other.)

Moreover, this function of the capitalist state also determines its *relative autonomy* vis-à-vis the power bloc and to the hegemonic class or fraction, an autonomy which may take on several concrete forms. The state may, for example, present itself as the political guarantor of the interests of various classes and fractions of the power bloc against the interests of the hegemonic class or fraction, and it may sometimes play off those classes and fractions against the latter. But it does this in its function of political organizer of the hegemonic class or fraction and forces it to admit the sacrifices necessary for its hegemony. To say, therefore, as in the *Communist Manifesto*, that the state is the managing committee for the common affairs of the bourgeoisie in its ensemble is both correct and insufficient: it is insufficient if it makes us lose sight of the state's complex role vis-à-vis the power bloc, and its particular relation to the hegemonic class or fraction.

It is this relative autonomy of the state which is to be found particularly in the case of Bonapartism. In fact, Marx shows that the concrete historical case of French Bonapartism originates from the contradictions of the classes and fractions in power, and from the inability of any one of these to raise itself to be the hegemonic class or fraction and thus to take the unification of the power bloc under its protection. From this point of view, the Second Empire is related to the dissolution of the power bloc under the protection of finance capital:

The Party of Order was a combination of heterogeneous social substances. The question of revision of the constitution generated a political temperature at which the product again decomposed into its original constituents. . . . The disintegration of the Party of Order did not stop at its original elements. Each of the two great factions, in its turn, underwent decomposition anew.[5]

Parallel to this in the same context, Marx insists on the point that the hegemony of financial capital is threatened at the moment when it breaks with its political party (with the 'politicians which represented it') and becomes 'Bonapartist'.[6] The state of the Second Empire is thus relatively autonomous from the power bloc and from this financial fraction, even though it serves the interests of the bourgeoisie in its ensemble and *in particular* the interests of financial capital, a point to which Marx returns in *The Civil War in France*.[7] Constantly throughout their concrete political analyses, Marx and Engels relate Bonapartism (the religion of the bourgeoisie), as characteristic of the capitalist type of state, to its intrinsic unity and to the relative autonomy which it derives from its function vis-à-vis the power bloc and the hegemonic class or fraction.

But here too it is necessary to be wary of the notion of equilibrium: this relative autonomy of the state from the power bloc and the hegemonic class or fraction does not depend on an equilibrium of the force *of the*

5. 'The Eighteenth Brumaire', *MESW*, 1970, pp. 151 and 154.
6. ibid., p. 156.
7. Recent studies have confirmed Marx's analyses. Although Louis Bonaparte took *very important* measures for the benefit of the industrial bourgeoisie, this did not mean that the financial bourgeoisie did not retain hegemony. Rather, it was under Louis Bonaparte that the financial bourgeoisie began to take an interest in the industrialization process. See G. Dupeux, *La société française, 1789–1960*, 1964, pp. 132 ff.

dominant classes and fractions, amongst which institutionalized power operates as arbitrator. In fact, as a general rule, it is precisely that hegemonic class or fraction whose political organization is constituted by the state, which is preponderant amongst the other forces of the power bloc: but this privileged position which it occupies does not prevent the relative autonomy of the state from it.

In this case, too, it is clear that the state's unity and relative autonomy take on particular forms (i.e. different degrees) in the various concrete forms of the state and of the régime. These are variations within the limits fixed by its structures.

(ii) THE SEPARATION OF POWERS

In order to clarify further the intrinsic unity of the capitalist state, we shall consider the institutions proper to that state: in particular we shall examine the famous theory of separation of powers. In fact, despite the declaration of a *separation* of powers (of legislative, parliamentary power from executive power) the capitalist state functions as a *centralized unity*, organized as a result of the dominance of one of these powers over the others. But this distinction between the legislative and the executive is not a simple juridical distinction: it corresponds both to the precise relations of political forces and to real differences in the functioning of state institutions. However, the important point at the moment is to emphasize that, contrary to a conception of a multi-centred, balanced share-out of the state's internal power, we can always decipher the characteristic dominance of one of these powers, i.e. of that one which constitutes the principal instance of state unity. This instance (generally the legislative or the executive) constitutes the nodal point where unitary institutionalized power is concentrated within the complex state organization. It reflects the index of the internal relations of *subordination* by the delegation of power, of the various state 'powers', to this dominant 'power', which constitutes the principle of the unity of state power.

How can we decipher this central place of institutionalized power? The unity of the capitalist state stems from the fact both that it represents the political unity of the people-nation and that it constitutes the political unity of the power bloc under the protection of the hegemonic class or fraction. The principal instance of the internal unity of the state *is the place where the relation between these two principles of state unity are concentrated*, the place where the legitimacy of institutionalized political power is expressed.

In the relation between the state and the 'isolated' socio-economic relations (to which the state's relation to the dominated classes is, in the state institutions, ultimately reducible), that instance constitutes the place where popular sovereignty is reflected.

In the relation between the state and the dominant classes or fractions, that instance denotes the place where the hegemonic class or fraction is constituted inside the state: the state being the factor which unifies the power bloc under the protection of the hegemonic class or fraction.

As a general rule that place remains the same. And this is so precisely to the extent that, in this institutional place and through the intermediary of the state, this class or fraction manages to set itself up as the representative of the people's general interest, as the materialization of popular sovereignty; it thus manages to establish its specific interests as the interests of the power bloc and under its protection to realize the unity of this bloc. In short, that instance of the internal unity of the capitalist state concentrates the relation between the two principles of unity of institutionalized power. Through the intermediary of the state, it is the place where the political organization of the hegemonic class or fraction is constituted vis-à-vis 'society' and the power bloc.

These remarks allow us to decipher how the state functions in a unificatory manner, despite the apparent separation of powers: we should also go yet more deeply into the state's relation to the power bloc. I must repeat that the legislative/executive distinction in fact encompasses a whole series of heterogeneous factors. The important point here is to see why and how these factors, reflected in the relation between the state and the power bloc, have been *precisely* institutionalized as executive/legislative relations, and what is more, have been conceived as a separation of powers.

In the terrain of political domination, the presence of several classes and fractions (which underpins the formation of the power bloc) is fundamental. We can in fact establish that the distinction between powers is due to the complex relations of the classes and fractions of this bloc, and it was instituted in case the different classes and fractions of this bloc should gain a hold either over the executive or over the legislative, i.e. in case these different classes or fractions should crystallize in different institutional places. In this sense, the distinction between institutional powers is a typical characteristic of a state functioning over and against the power bloc. Marx gives us some indications of this in *The Eighteenth*

Brumaire and in *The Class Struggles in France* where he studies the relation between the executive and the legislative, before Louis Bonaparte's coup d'état, as reflecting the relations between the financial fraction (the executive) and the industrial fraction (the legislative).

In what sense does this distribution of powers really function? In the case where the executive and the legislative are controlled by the same hegemonic class or fraction, the distinction of powers is *non-existent* in its functioning: this is too obvious to need stressing. We need only mention the classic case of Britain, where, *despite appearances*, the legislative/ executive distinction has, until recently, never really functioned: this results from the particular configuration and functioning of the power bloc in Britain, which we have noted frequently above.

It is more interesting to see what happens when the executive and the legislative reflect different classes or fractions of the power bloc. Is there, in this case, a real 'separation' of state powers, in short, an *effective sharing* of the political power to the advantage of these different classes or fractions? This is by no means so. In this case, in fact, the unity of institutionalized power is maintained by being concentrated around the dominant place where the hegemonic class or fraction is reflected. The other powers function more especially as *resistances* to the dominant power: inserted into the unitary function of the state, they contribute to the organization of the hegemony of the class or fraction which is reflected a̠ ̠ political force in the dominant power.[8]

This can be noted both in the formation of the state resulting from the French Revolution (as well as in that of the Third Republic) and also on the level of political theory, in particular in the work of Montesquieu who was certainly the most important and influential theorist of political democracy. Both Eisenmann and Althusser[9] have shown that Montesquieu in no way established the separation of powers, as he is claimed to have done, and that his theory of the *distribution* of powers, which presupposes

8. It is important to note that in the 'neo-liberal' school mentioned above, the revived conception of institutional 'checks and balances' covers the integrationist conception of power with a multi-centred equilibrium in a society: for example, R. Dahl, op. cit., pp. 83 ff. On terminology, I think it is worth repeating my remarks about the concept of power: the concept of power is related to class power, and therefore, when we designate institutional structures by the term 'power', we must mean *power centres*.

9. C. Eisenmann, op. cit., and L. Althusser, *Montesquieu, la politique et l'histoire,* Paris, 1964, especially Chapter 5 (cf. English translation, *Politics and History*, London, 1972).

a state unity, does not refer to a constitutional/juridical conception of a separation of the various spheres of legality. It refers to a certain conception of the relations of social classes in struggle, within the framework of the transition period considered by Montesquieu. The relations between the executive and the legislative (separated into lower and upper chambers) are related to a certain conception of the relations between social forces, i.e. relations between royalty, with its seat in the executive power, nobility, with its seat in the upper chamber, and the 'people', the bourgeoisie, with its seat in the lower chamber.

But Montesquieu says something more: his conception of the distribution of powers presupposes a conception of *the unity of institutional power*, in the sense that this distribution is not conceived as a separation-*sharing* which threatens the unity. The unity is itself related to the dominance of one of these powers over the others, which constitutes the nodal point of state power. Althusser poses the problem correctly, although he retains the term 'sharing': 'If we are satisfied with revealing, beneath the mythical cover of the separation of powers, the real operation of a share-out of power between different political forces, it seems to me that we run the risk of entertaining the delusion of a natural, *prima facie* equitable share-out. We have passed from power to might (*puissance*) but have the terms really changed? It is never merely a question of equilibrium and sharing. This is the last myth which I want to denounce . . . For this clarification itself poses a question: *to whose advantage is this share-out made?*' And Althusser clearly shows that, in Montesquieu's theory, the dominant institutionalized power, the organizational centre of state unity is provided by the upper chamber, the seat of the nobility.

Let us take as our example the distribution of powers as set up in the state resulting from the French Revolution.[10] The separation of the executive (the king and his ministers) from the legislative (the National Assembly) in the framework of the Constituent Assembly of 1789 corresponds to the conflict between the nobility and the bourgeoisie, which held, respectively, the executive and the legislative. In the framework of this distribution, and within the framework of this newly created bourgeois state based on popular sovereignty, the distribution is carried out to the advantage of the executive and the nobility. The Convention overturns this stage of affairs and redistributes the executive (at first to the Executive Council and then to the Committee of Public Safety) and the legislative

10. See A. Soboul, *Précis d'histoire de la Révolution Française*, op. cit.

(to the Assembly or the Convention). The executive is here in the hands of the commercial fraction of the bourgeoisie, later represented by the Montagnards, while the legislature is in the hands of the financial and industrial fraction, represented by the Gironde. Within the unity of this bourgeois state, it is, in the long run, the financial bourgeoisie and the legislative power which assume the dominant role; and this ends in the permanent eviction of the Montagnards from power.

The case is even clearer in the framework of the Constitution of the Third Republic.[11] The Bordeaux Assembly endowed France with the Republican régime as it was to function for a long time through the so-called 'Loi des Trente', which regulated ministerial repsonsibility and the relations between the President (the head of government) and the Assembly; but it did not in any way propose to institute the dominance of parliament which the functioning of this form of state raised. In fact, the financial bourgeoisie and the big landed proprietors, represented by the Monarchists and the Bonapartists, aimed at instituting the primacy of the executive over the legislative for two reasons: because (i) their seats in parliament appeared weak in the face of the Radicals and the Republicans, and (ii) under Thiers and MacMahon, they were able to establish themselves within the administrative body of the executive. It is moreover just this dominance of the executive which characterizes MacMahon's presidency. However, in the course of the evolution of the Third Republic, by a complex process whereby these classes and fractions were able to establish their control over parliament (the financial fraction) and over the Senate (the landed proprietors), the distribution of powers no longer assumed more than a formal importance, since legislative power remained the central instance of the state.

11. See G. Hanotaux, *Histoire de la France contemporaine*, 1908, Vol I; R. Dreyfus, *La République de M. Thiers*, 1930; D. Thompson, *Democracy in France since 1870*, 4th edn, 1964, Chapter 3; D. Halévy, *La République des Ducs*, 1937.

5. The Problem in the Forms of State and the Forms of Régime: the Legislative and the Executive

(i) FORMS OF STATE, FORMS OF LEGITIMACY

This relation between the legislative and the executive provides us with an excellent example for the concrete analysis of the problem of *forms of state* and the degrees of unity and relative autonomy characterizing each form. In the light of the preceding analyses, this will help us to establish the exact *relevance* of the criterion of legislative/executive relations for distinguishing between forms of state. I shall have to make two preliminary remarks:

1. Apart from its political significance in the relations of class power, and leaving aside its constitutional-juridical expression which is most often an ideological product, this legislative/executive distinction covers several heterogeneous factors. First of all, it covers factors of a *technical* order which concern the functioning of the state, in so far as the executive, in the broad sense of the term, encompasses in particular what has been called the *state apparatus*, i.e. the bureaucracy, administration, police, army. Its functioning within the capitalist state cannot be absorbed into the functions peculiar to the directly elective assemblies, i.e. the representatives in the strict sense. As a result, the distinction between these powers and the dominance of one of them over the other undoubtedly cover differential forms of the articulation of the economic and the political and indeed of the intervention/non-intervention of one in the other: for example a predominance of the executive often implies a specific intervention of the political in the economic.[1]

1. The very object of the notions of the legislative and the executive varies, of course, according to the different forms of state. In what follows, we shall give them a more precise sense, by distinguishing the particular institutions and functions which these notions cover, according to the different forms of state. I shall waste no time on the *constitutional-juridical* sense of this distinction (i.e. the power to make and carry out decisions, political and administrative power, governmental and consultative power) since this merely masks class power relations. In fact, it is relevant here only to point out the class power relations, which *institutionally fix* technical divisions as a *distinction* between political functions. *It is precisely in this sense that the term 'executive' is not identical with that of state apparatus.* It covers a political power centre by denoting a

2. The distinction between the forms of state is, of course, related to variations of the articulation of the economic and the political within the limits set by the dominance of the CMP in the *periodization into phases* of a capitalist formation: it concerns a whole series of transformations of state functions, of displacements of dominance between these functions, of differentiations of forms of the intervention of the political in the economic and of the economic in the political.[2] But, as we have noted, although these variations concerning the forms of state cover the differential forms of the intervention and non-intervention of the economic and the political in the structures, *they are not directly determined by it.* In other words, they are reflected in differential state forms only by being concentrated in the relations between the state and the field of the class struggle: i.e. in (a) the relations between the state and isolation of socio-economic relations, and (b) the relations between the state and the power bloc, in the framework of the political class struggle, and (c) according to the forms of combination of these two relations.[3]

The relevance of the criterion of the legislative/executive distinction as a distinctive feature of the typology of state forms can thus be established. While that distinction covers differential functions of the state, which are related to variations in the forms of intervention/non-intervention of the economic and political, this distinction *is not in itself relevant as a criterion of forms of state*: this is because the *correlation* between forms of state and

---

particular functioning of the state apparatus. This must be emphasized since some of the statements made by Marx (in *The Eighteenth Brumaire*) and by Lenin (in *The State and Revolution*) *are ambiguous* in this respect: they sometimes seem to identify the terms 'executive' and 'government' with that of 'state apparatus', in the sense that the executive does not indicate a centre of particular political power, but only the state's technical apparatus, 'the personnel of the state'. This would obviously prevent us from seeing the political reasons for the executive/legislative distinction and the complex class relations tied together in their relation. Moreover, a careful reading of Marx shows that for him the predominance of the executive in a form of state indicates the particular political function of the state apparatus in relation to the transformations of legitimacy and to the class relations of the power bloc. It must also be noted that several contemporary political science theorists both retain various *non-juridical* criteria for classifying the structures and functions of the political system and maintain the typological schema of the executive/legislative distinction: see, for example, Almond and Coleman (ed.), *The Politics of the Developing Areas*, Princeton, 1960, Introduction, pp. 3–64, which contains general remarks on the typological systems; R. Dahl, *A Preface to Democratic Theory*, 1964, pp. 63 ff.; S. W. Eisenstadt, *The Political Systems of Empires*, Glencoe, 1963. In France, Duverger, Vedel and Lavau are among the more important of such theorists.

2. See p. 125 above.   3. See p. 137 above.

the legislative/executive distinction is itself *over-determined*. The relevance of the criterion of legislative/executive relations is based on the fact that the state's relation to the economic and political class struggle is concentrated in it. Moreover it is that which allows us to understand *why* and *how* the differential forms of articulation of the economic and the political characteristic forms of state are reflected in a relevant way in the legislative/executive relation.[4]

A. In the state's relation to the isolation of the economic class struggle (to which its relation to the dominated classes is ultimately reduced, *in the form in which it is present* in its very institutions), this distinction appears relevant because it corresponds to differentiations between the forms of legitimacy of the capitalist state.[5] Thus, it corresponds to differentiations between the complex ideological processes through which this state presents itself as the representative of the unity of the people-nation and through which it acts to produce the political disorganization of the dominated classes. This results from the fact that the very isolation of socio-economic relations (i.e. the relations whose unity the state claims is embodied in itself) is merely the effect of the juridico-political and of the *ideological*. In fact, whether the hegemonic class or fraction is reflected in the legislative or in the executive, since that place will be the dominant instance of the state, it must also (in principle) concentrate the state's relation to the economic class struggle. However, the forms in which the executive or the legislative present themselves as the unity of the people-nation are different. The characteristic predominance of the legislative or of the executive thus specifies the forms of the state in the relation state/isolation-of-socio-economic-relations, since that predominance corresponds to differentiations between the forms of bourgeois legitimacy. The specific transformations of articulation, of intervention and non-intervention of the economic and of the political which characterize the stages of a

4. The *'technologist'* deformation is so wrong that it can never be over-criticized. It sees in the present-day predominance of the executive the direct effect of the intervention of the political in the economic and of the enlarged 'technical' role of the bureacratic administration. But in fact this functioning of the state apparatus in the so-called 'planned' economy can easily occur in the framework of a predominance of the legislative. Evidence for this is to be found in the present relative differences between the state structures of (a) France and (b) Italy and Germany; for despite appearances, state intervention is as strong in the latter two cases as in the former. *The problem is clearly above all a political problem.*

5. See p. 223 above.

capitalist formation are reflected in the state by differentiations in legitimacy.

In fact, although in the framework in which parliament predominates, *legitimacy* tends to be conflated with *legality*, that is to say with a specific normative system of rule-making, which presents itself as the general will decreed by the people's representatives, the ideological processes function in a different way as regards the legitimacy of the executive: the role of parliamentary publicity decreases and this produces a masking of real knowledge about the bureaucracy (i.e. about the preponderant role of the state apparatus indicated by the predominance of the executive); 'charismatic' elements inserted, of course, in the type of bourgeois legitimacy, become important since they concentrate hierarchical legitimacy by delegating the power of the state apparatus to the person of a 'leader' (*chef*). This 'leader' presents himself as the representative of the unity of the people-nation, through a whole gamut of ideological weapons,[6] grasped today by the ideological phrase 'personalization of power'. Thus, the state's relation as 'representative' to the social classes is short-circuited and operates here by embezzling the role of parties and by the state apparatus's direct manipulating of public opinion, etc.

Marx's analyses (and in particular those of *The Eighteenth Brumaire*) in which he points to the displacement of dominance from the legislative to the executive as the relevant criterion for forms of state must be interpreted in this sense. The bourgeois forms of legitimacy are transformed: and this, it seems to me, is exactly what Marx wished to stress when he said that 'the executive power, as opposed to the legislative power, expresses the nation's heteronomy as opposed to its autonomy'. This point must be stressed, for a whole parliamentary tradition of the working-class movement has expressed its distrust of the executive power (a distrust due in particular to its idyllic illusions of the legislative) by interpreting these analyses as a challenge to the executive's legitimacy. This has allowed them to make a cheap critique of the executive's predominance and to refuse to make an adequate critique of the capitalist state as such.

In short, this tradition sees parliamentary legitimacy as the only 'authentic' legitimacy of bourgeois *political democracy* (i.e. the sole legitimate expression of the 'people'); and it sees in the predominance of the

6. Marx and Engels analysed these ideological weapons brilliantly with regard to Louis Bonaparte and Boulanger. See, in particular, what Engels says on 'Boulangism' in Friedrich Engels/Paul and Laura Lafargue, *Correspondence*, 3 vols, London, 1959-63.

executive an *illegitimate* power, a kind of deformation of the national-popular-class-state.[7] It could not be more false: in the framework of the capitalist class state, parliamentary legitimacy is no 'closer to the people' than that legitimacy which corresponds to the predominance of the executive. In fact, these are always *ideological* processes in both cases. In the case of a predominance of the executive, legitimacy can perfectly well be inserted in the framework of the popular sovereignty of the capitalist type of state: unlike other types of legitimacy (e.g., charismatic legitimacy through divine right) which it resembles only in a very superficial way, this legitimacy is only a differential form of the type of bourgeois legitimacy. In his analyses of the Second Empire, Marx demonstrates quite clearly how Louis Bonaparte managed to get his executive power to pass as the representative of the unity of the people-nation, as the incarnation of popular sovereignty, by even actually re-establishing the universal suffrage previously abolished by the parliamentary Republic.

Thus the executive's legitimacy is often characterized as a series of ruses, whereby the predominance of the executive attempts to mask its illegitimacy by borrowing features from the one possible kind of popular sovereignty, that of parliament. In fact the situation is not at all like this: rather their common characteristics are based on the fact that they are merely differential forms of the popular sovereignty of the people-nation. The ideological processes which govern classical parliamentary legitimacy, and therefore the legitimacy of French Bonapartism, are in fact only differential forms of the same type. The proof, as history has shown, is that the popular sovereignty of political democracy finds its expression equally well in a classical parliamentarism and in a Bonapartist semi-dictatorship. Even Max Weber (admittedly within his own perspective) noted the deep typological kinship between the legitimacy of parliamentary supremacy and what he described as that of 'authoritarian' political forms.[8] This legislative/executive distinction, concerning the relation between the state and the dominated classes, is a relation between the state and the isolation of the socio-economic relations; it concerns forms of legitimacy and, *as a general rule, it is not directly determined by the political struggle of the dominated classes*. Let me explain. In the 'parliamentarist' deformation

7. This tradition has been especially strong in the French working-class movement. It is partly explicable by historical reasons which go back to the French Revolution (the prestige of elected assemblies is established at this time) and to Jacobinism's impact on the movement.

8. cf. M. Duverger, *Institutions politiques*, Paris, 1966, pp. 162 ff.

it is often held that parliament presents itself to the dominant classes as a place of danger, since it may be conquered at any time by the dominated classes as a result of universal suffrage. And so, in this sense, the legislative/ executive distinction is a guarantee for the dominant classes, since, in case of the dominated classes taking parliament by storm, it allows the centre of gravity of the unity of power to move. From Kautsky[9] onwards, many authors have interpreted progressions towards a predominance of the executive on the basis of a parliamentary advance of the dominated classes. Marx and Engels, with no experience of such situations, sometimes appear to slide towards this interpretation: but it is, generally speaking, *a myth*. In fact, as far as the conquest of parliament by the dominated classes is concerned, class domination has at its disposal a whole gamut of defences to protect itself from such misadventures.[10] Besides, the dominant classes have never in the long run been mistaken on this point. It is only in very rare cases that a predominance of the executive characteristic of a form of state has corresponded to any risk that the dominated classes might conquer parliament. This is proved by the numerous western countries in which the predominance of the executive is nowadays asserted, but which, for the most part, are far from running this risk: a risk which has for a long time been defused in the classical parliamentary framework. This is not to say that the dominant classes did not believe in this danger at a certain time; and in this respect, this belief of theirs was exactly parallel to illusions suffered by a fraction of the working-class movement. But the behaviour of the social democrats soon stifled such fears on the part of the dominant classes. The contemporary predominance of the executive corresponds effectively to the difficulties met by the monopolist fraction in organizing its political hegemony with regard to the dominated classes in parliament (i.e. with regard to transformations of legitimacy); but these difficulties are no evidence of a real danger of parliament being taken over by the dominated classes: that would be something quite different.[11] In any case, even if this danger proved to be

9. Kautsky, *The Social Revolution*, Chicago, 1902.

10. e.g. the electoral systems, which are in this respect only new forms of suffrage based on property-ownership, in the class sense of this term.

11. When I say that this move towards the dominance of the executive does not *as a general rule* directly coincide with the political struggle of the dominated classes, I mean that *it is not directly determined by it*. The decline of parliamentarianism is undoubtedly *indirectly related (i.e. within a margin of indeterminacy) to the political rise of the working-class movement*. But this, of course, is not the same as the risk of a conquest of parliament by the working classes: it is related, amongst other things, to the above-mentioned

justified, it would be impossible to interpret it as a conquest of political power by the dominated classes, not only because state power would in this case be concentrated in the executive but also because of the whole range of functioning of the state's power and apparatus in a capitalist formation.

B. In the state's relation to the power bloc, the displacement of dominance from the legislative to the executive is a relevant criterion for differentiating between forms of state, in that it concerns the modifications of the hegemonic fraction of the power bloc according to the stages of a formation and the displacement of those places in which the political power of this fraction with regard to the power bloc is reflected: cf. the displacements of hegemony from the industrial fraction to the financial fraction, and then the monopolist fraction. For example, the characteristic predominance of the executive where the monopolies are hegemonic is a direct response to a particular incapacity to organize this hegemony, with regard to the *power bloc*, in the parliamentary framework. The particularly acute contradictions between the various fractions of the power bloc in the monopolist stage, geared and reflected in parliament through a particular dislocation between these fractions and the parties due to traditional 'survivals' of party representation account for this organizational incapacity. Henceforth hegemony is organized through different processes, *inside the executive*.

This becomes clearer in this *form of state* when we look at the relation implied by that form between the state and the parties of the power bloc.

---

difficulty of the monopolist fraction in organizing its hegemony in parliament; i.e. it is related to the problem of *legitimacy*. It is precisely in this sense that we must not confuse the executive's predominance in the framework of a form of state with the repressive role of the state which increases with the political rise of the dominated classes: *in this case, the predominance of the executive is by no means necessary for the state to assume this role*. Contrary to certain idyllic opinions on this subject, the parliamentarianist framework, with the legislative predominant, *facilitates to a large extent* this repressive role. In short, the political rise of the dominated classes does not, in this case, directly call for a predominance of the executive but for a recrudescence of forcible repression, and it is (as experience has shown) perfectly compatible with the classic parliamentary system. On the other hand, Lenin, of course, designated the 'democratic republic' as the 'best régime possible' for the working class in a capitalist formation. But even if we suppose that this indicates a supremacy of parliament, we cannot possibly delude ourselves into considering that this is the only 'popular' capitalist form of state, the only one 'close to the masses', while criticizing the present supremacy of the executive as illegitimate.

It is true that the concrete modalities of party representation are inserted into the *political scene*, according to the strictly political periodization into *forms of régime*. But for all that, the relation between the forms of state and the functioning of parties is not unimportant. The forms of state fix the limits for the parties' functioning in the political scene; they circumscribe the *general framework* of the parties' *role* vis-à-vis the power bloc and its political class organization. In other words, the forms of state (the predominance of the executive or of the legislative) are related to the role of the parties of the power bloc, in that they are linked to the *class* relations of the power bloc, to the modalities of political organization of this bloc; these forms of state thus set the limits to the space occupied by the political scene: so, in a very general way, that predominance of the executive which is characteristic of a *form of state* corresponds, as far as the power bloc is concerned, to a characteristic decline of the specific organizational role of the parties of this bloc. This can have numerous consequences, for example the substitution of *pressure groups* for parties, etc.[12] This is a case in which the state takes direct control of the political organization of the hegemonic fraction and of its hegemony vis-à-vis the power bloc.

Thus, as a general rule, the predominance of the executive, which is characteristic of a form of state, signifies today a particularly sharp failure of the monopolist fraction to organize through its own parties its hegemony vis-à-vis the people-nation (i.e. transformations of legitimacy) and hegemony vis-à-vis the power bloc. There is, in short, a recrudescence of organizational political practice by the state apparatus.[13]

This broad distinction between the legislative and the executive is no substitute for a specific study of the various *centres of political power*, in the various forms of state. These centres comprise a variety of institutional places such as the assemblies, the administration, the army, the police,

12. It is true that even in a period of predominance of the legislative, pressure groups have played an important role; but this was a role which was combined with that proper to the parties. Today they function *totally differently*, in that they appear to *take over themselves* the parties' 'demand-cum-professional' role, while the state apparatus takes over the political role of the parties in the power bloc. See J. Meynaud, *Les groupes de pression en France*, 1958, and *Nouvelles études sur les groupes de pression*, 1962; G. Lavau, 'Note sur un "pressure group" français: la Conféderation Générale des Petites et Moyennes Entreprises' in *Revue française de science politique*, 1955.

13. A. Gorz makes some remarkable analyses of·this in *Le Socialisme difficile*, 1967, Chapter I, 'Syndicalisme et politique: crise de la démocracie représentative'.

the magistracy, the municipalities, the political parties themselves, the various present-day 'commissions' such as the planning commission and economic and social council in France, etc. What is necessary then is to distinguish these places from *centres of economic power* and *those of ideological power*.

When we look at the state's concrete functioning and at the various forms of legitimacy, the distribution of these institutional positions appears as a general rule to coincide with the executive/legislative distinction. This is particularly evident when we study the contemporary political system, which exhibits a polycentrism of these places, i.e. a multiplicity of political power centres (and not, of course, a pluralism of class power), which are concentrated in the currently predominant executive. This predominance corresponds to the hegemony of monopolies, and to their incapacity to organize this hegemony over the power bloc and over the people-nation by means of their own political parties in parliament. Hence there is a decline of the parties in the power bloc, a recrudescence of the political role of the state apparatus, and an organization of this hegemony of the monopolies by means of the state in the executive itself. This polycentrism of the executive merely reflects in its functioning the current relations of the power bloc to the monopolies, since the executive in its ensemble satisfies the interests of the monopolies. Given that particular hierarchical organization of delegated functions which specifies the executive, this hegemony of the monopolies is today assured by the conquest of the 'heights' of the executive, not only of the top state personnel but also, and in particular, *the higher echelons* of the executive; none of which, however, prevents the relative autonomy of the state apparatus, the bureaucracy's own political role, etc. In short, the class relations of the power bloc, which used to be reflected either in the legislative or in the legislative/executive relations, now tend increasingly to be transposed to the centres of the executive itself and to opt for the executive's particular functioning.

It is now necessary to consider the problem of the unity of the capitalist state in the case in which the legislative and executive are differentiated, in the manner established above. The predominance of one of these powers represents the central instance of the unity of the state in that it concentrates within it the two following principles of state unity: (i) it reflects the political legitimacy of a formation and (ii) it is the seat of the hegemonic fraction's organization. In a given period, however, certain dislocations may occur: parliament may continue to present itself as the representative place of popular sovereignty, of the unity of the people-nation, whilst the hegemonic fraction is reflected in the executive. The correspondence between the form of state legitimacy and the dominance of elected assemblies is then clear, although the hegemonic fraction does not succeed in imposing its hegemony within the parliamentary framework and retreats to the executive. In this case, there is clearly no kind of disarticulation of state power; i.e. there is no kind of *double power* of institutionalized 'separate' powers. The unity of institutionalized power is organized under the dominance of that power which is the seat of the hegemonic class or fraction of the power bloc.

In fact, there is here a dislocation between the double hegemonic function of this class or fraction: for while, through the intermediary of the state, it continues to hold its hegemony over the power bloc, it loses its hegemony vis-à-vis the ensemble of the social formation. This is reflected in a distortion between the institutional seat of its power and the form of the state's legitimacy. In such a situation, which may actually go as far as a *political crisis*, there is (again as a general rule) a brief period of recrudescence in the activity of the state repressive apparatus; and it is during this period that the state falls under the direct control of this class or fraction. However, the state finishes by regaining its relative autonomy vis-à-vis this class or fraction, by operating with a view to coinciding with the form of legitimacy; and it does this, whether by re-establishing the old state of affairs (i.e. by organizing the hegemony of this class or fraction in parliament) through a whole series of modifications of electoral régimes, of interventions in party relations, etc. or by modifying the legitimacy itself through various means.

(ii) FORMS OF RÉGIME, POLITICAL PARTIES

It is self-evident that these forms of state can be studied concretely only in their combination with *forms of régime*, taking in the *political scene*, by circumscribing the general framework for the role of the parties vis-à-vis the power bloc. The political scene concerns the concrete modalities of party representation in relation to the open or declared action of the social forces. The combination of forms of state with the configuration of the political scene produces political régimes.

I shall avoid a study in depth of the problem of a typology of political régimes, by referring only to Duverger's particularly important remarks on this subject in his various books. He was the first author to demonstrate the relations in this typology between (i) the predominance or equilibrium of the executive or legislative (using the terms legislative and executive not in their constitutional and juridical sense, but in a sense close to that adopted here) and (ii) the concrete configuration of the political scene. In this way he demonstrates the importance of factors like the number of parties (two-party or multi-party régimes) and the structure peculiar to these parties (*loose* or *rigid* two-party or multi-party systems).[14] His analyses can give us very useful indications, provided that emphasis is laid on the fact that Duverger, like most political scientists, fails to operate the distinction between the two periodizations and the two cases in question, which are here those of *forms of state* and *forms of régime*. His typology of forms of régime absorbs the distinction with forms of state.

In my analyses of the power bloc I pointed out[15] that the lack of a distinction between the two cases and the two periodizations leads to a confusion between the class configuration of the power bloc and the party relations in the political scene. Thus, it becomes difficult to localize the various dislocations and exactly to decipher the class frame of the political scene. In this case, the lack of such a distinction also produces its own effects. Because of it, we cannot see that the distinction into régimes takes on a totally different sense according to the various forms of state in which these régimes are situated: we can divide up these régimes only if we start from the forms of state circumscribing their space. It is only in this way that what appears as a correlation (e.g. the predominance of the executive with a loose two-party or multi-party system) can be made into an explanation, by reference to the ensemble of the co-ordinates of a stage of a formation and to political class practice; and what appears to be a combinatory (*combinatoire*) is revealed to be a precise combination (*combinaison*).[16]

The unity and relative autonomy peculiar to the capitalist state vis-à-vis the dominant classes and fractions and their *degrees* and *concrete forms*

14. M. Duverger, *Sociologie politique*, 1967, pp. 116 ff.; *Les Partis politiques*, 1964, pp. 387 ff. He suggests a distinction between (i) presidential régimes of the 'pseudo-two-party' (i.e. loosely two-party) kind or of the 'multi-party' kind, (ii) parliamentary two-party régimes and (iii) parliamentary multi-party régimes. Cf. A. Haurion, *Régimes politiques et structures économico-sociales* for the important analyses contained in this stencilled course for doctoral students.

15. See p. 248 above.

16. For the distinction between these two terms, see note 9 in the Introduction above. [Trans.]

can therefore be studied only in this combination of forms of state and régime: and this is so, in so far as they are closely tied to the concrete modalities of party representation, to the forms of political organization of the power bloc. If we take as our example only the separation of powers and the unity of institutionalized power, we see that the 'separation' functions quite differently when the legislative predominates in either a multi-party or a two-party system, or again when the executive predominates in either a loose or a rigid two-party or multi-party system.[17] However, the distinction between forms of state and forms of régime is absolutely vital for us when we study the relation between unity of the state and the unity of the hegemonic class or fraction of the power bloc, as it appears in the political scene in the framework of régimes. In short, it is vital for distinguishing the real effects on the unity of state power of the combination between forms of state and forms of régime, effects which often misleadingly appear to be effects of the régime alone.

Let us consider as an example a form of state with predominance of the legislative and a multi-party régime: this is the typical case in which governing party-coalitions appear to threaten the unity of state power by sharing it out amongst the various parties of this coalition. In fact, most often the unity of state power is faced by the unity of the power bloc under the protection of the hegemonic class or fraction, i.e. there is an *unambiguous* relation between state power and this class or fraction. We can show this by examining the form of state and the class configuration of the power bloc: and by this means, we shall also make clear the exact arrangement of the masked actors on the political scene. In fact, in such a case, the unity of state power is revealed by the parliamentary organization of the hegemony of this class or fraction over the others, whether by the complex dominance of the hegemonic class's or fraction's party over the other parties (e.g. the 'dominant party' in the governmental coalition) or by a complex mediation of representation in the political scene, by means of which this class or fraction is represented inside the various parties of this coalition, or else it is revealed by the fact that the party, or parties, of this class or fraction hold the key sectors of government.

Moreover, it is through this combination of forms of state and forms of régime that we can also evaluate the degrees of the state's relative autonomy vis-à-vis the dominant classes or fractions. For example, the

17. See Duverger, the chapter entitled 'Les partis et la séparation des pouvoirs', in *Les Partis politiques.*

autonomy of a form of state in which the executive predominates depends on the concrete class configuration of the power bloc, on the parties' general role, as delimited by this form of state and on the parties' particular behaviour in the political scene in the framework of forms of régime. In other words, the predominance of the executive implies an increased state autonomy vis-à-vis these classes and fractions only when it is combined with a characteristic decline of the parties' organizational role *reflected right in the political scene*; a correlation which occurs quite often and is particularly clear in the case of the historical phenomenon of French Bonapartism. As Gramsci pointed out, following Marx, it is manifested in a situation of *crisis of party representation*, i.e. by a rupture between the various classes or fractions and their representatives.[18]

It is, however, often possible to decipher variations within this correlation: for example, the relative autonomy of the state may be more important in a multi-party régime in which the legislative predominates (something which is particularly apparent in the role of the bureaucracy given governmental instability) than in a two-party régime in which the executive predominates and where the structures are strong and these parties' internal discipline is rigid (e.g. contemporary Britain); or it may be more important still in a multi-party régime where the executive predominates (e.g. contemporary France).

The combination which I have already pointed out may provide us with an explanation: in the case of a two-party system where the parties' internal discipline is strong (e.g. Britain) the monopolies apparently exhibit a particular capacity for their own political organization of their hegemony; and this reduces the importance of the autonomy of the state apparatus with regard to them. The relations between the open action of the hegemonic fraction and the power bloc, as well as the organization of their hegemony vis-à-vis the people-nation, *are already knit together inside one single party*, or inside two parties which alternate in occupying the forefront of the political scene. The hegemonic fraction becomes the *ruling* fraction by occupying the 'heights' of this or these parties by means of its 'agents'; this is a political concept and not a mere word designating interpersonal relations. This is clearly the case in the USA where the parties' weaker organization has sometimes allowed a

18. 'These situations of conflict between "represented and representatives" reverberate out from the terrain of the parties . . . throughout the state organism, reinforcing the relative power of the bureaucracy' (*Prison Notebooks*, p. 210).

relative autonomy to the state, which came into play in Roosevelt's 'New Deal'. This autonomy has also come into play (as it were despite the system) in the particular case of the 1945 Labour Government in Britain.[19]

19. On British Labour Governments, R. Miliband, *Parliamentary Socialism*, London 1964, is the most illuminating work.

V
Bureaucracy and Elites

1. The Problem and Theory of Elites

We can now make a rigorous examination of the state apparatus. In Marxist theory, of course, this discussion has always centred around the problem of bureaucracy, although this is in fact only one, if the most important, of the aspects of the state apparatus. Moreover, theoretical research has been widely distorted because of the errors of Trotsky's analyses and in particular because of the ideological rubbish churned out by his successors. I shall therefore try to avoid the ideological terrain of this discussion by staying close to the scientific analyses provided by Marx, Engels, Gramsci and Lenin on this subject. The only other analyses which I shall use will be Max Weber's since, although he is open to many criticisms, it can be stated with certainty that he has made the most successful attempt at elucidating this problem.

I shall begin with a short examination of the theories of '*political élites*', since such theories have been considerably influential in contemporary political theory and since they are explicitly offered as critiques of the Marxist theory of the political. But without any doubt they are addressed to misinterpretations of Marxism; though Marxist theory has laid itself open to these critiques by frequently allowing its scientific concepts to be distorted. In short, most of the theories of political élites pose problems which can no more be solved by Marxism distorted in this way than by the ideological perspectives proposed by them themselves. Such problems can be resolved only within the scientific problematic of Marxism.

In fact these theories of political élites tackle two relatively distinct problems and pose the question of the relation between them. These problems are:

A. That of the 'politically dominant class' sometimes covered in the conception of political élites by the specific term of 'political class'. In this respect, the principal complaint against Marxist theory is that it supposedly claims a necessary identity between the economically dominant class and the politically dominant class. Against that, these theories claim that this identity is not always present, and starting from there undertake various attempts to elaborate a conception of political power differing radically from the Marxist conception. Grafted on to this critique is the current which posits the so-called 'transformations' of the capitalist system: according to it, we cannot nowadays talk of an economically dominant class in the Marxist sense of the term, since the separation of ownership from control, the circulation and mobility among social groups, etc., make it necessary for us to have recourse to other explanations of the formation of political power.

B. That of the state apparatus and the bureaucracy.

a. In the Marxist conception these theories see an empirical concentration of all political functions in the hands of the economically-politically dominant class and their practical exercise by the members of that class themselves. For instance, the feudal class exercised control over the functions of political government, of public administration, of the military, etc., but this is effectively not the case for the bourgeoisie. And so, on this theory, it is necessary theoretically to explain this dislocation by recourse to a conception which locates the basis of political power in the very existence of the state apparatus and which, by confusing *state power* with *state apparatus*, attributes to the bureaucracy its own political power.

b. In Marxist theory, these theories see the conception of a state functioning as a mere tool for the domination of the dominant class: Marxist theory would thus deny even the possibility of examining the relative autonomy of the bureaucracy vis-à-vis the dominant class. Those who hold this view are forced to have recourse to attributing to the bureaucracy an autonomous political power, *parallel* to economic or political 'class' domination. For according to these theories, this is the only way to explain the particular functioning of the bureaucracy.

Wright Mills expresses these critiques of distorted Marxist theory in an extremely clear form, when he explains why he rejects the term 'ruling class' in favour of 'power élite'.

'Ruling class' is a badly loaded phrase: 'class' is an economic term; 'rule' a political one. The phrase 'ruling class' thus contains the theory that an economic class rules politically. That short-cut theory may or may not at times be true, but we do not want to carry that one rather simple theory about in the terms that we use to define our problems. . . . Specifically, the phrase 'ruling class', in its common political connotations, does not allow enough autonomy to the political order and its agents, and it says nothing about the military as such. . . . We hold that such a simple view of 'economic determinism' must be elaborated by 'political determinism' and 'military determinism'; that the higher agents of each of these three domains now often have a noticeable degree of autonomy. . . .[1]

Before examining the relations established by these theories between the state apparatus in the strict sense and what is designated as the politically dominant class, we shall take a quick look at the solutions suggested by these theories. As a general rule, they are concerned to find a basis for political power other than that acknowledged by Marxist theory; i.e. other than the complex relation between the political and the relations of production. There are several variants of this: for instance, they may follow Pareto (schematically speaking) and see a quasi-ontological relation between governors and governed: this is akin to Schmitt's Hegelian master/slave schema; or they may follow Mannheim's schema of the '*freischwebende Intelligenz*', starting from the élites' intellectual monopoly vis-à-vis the masses; or, following a more important current originating with Max Weber, they may start from the question of the control of the state apparatus, considering the state itself either as the exclusive foundation of political power, independent of the economic, or as the foundation of political power, independent from, but parallel to, economic power. This latter formulation is especially interesting for us. It deciphers the bureaucracy's functioning by starting from the bureaucracy's own political power, derived simply from its control of the state apparatus which is the autonomous foundation of political power.

What relations are admitted to exist between that social group which controls the state apparatus, especially the bureaucracy, and the other political élites? Or in Marxist terms, what are the relations between the bureaucracy and the dominant class? This question is all the more interesting in that it reveals an internal dispute between these theories, with some affirming *the unity of political élites* and others *the plurality of political élites or governing categories*. Moreover, this question also touches on a problem belonging to authentic Marxist theory, the problem of the unity and specific cohesion of the social category, the bureaucracy.

A. The conception of the plurality of political élites or governing categories is unimportant, since it is merely a typical ideological reaction

1. C. W. Mills, *The Power Elite*, New York, 1956, p. 277. T. B. Bottomore gives a very good and clear exposé of these critiques addressed by the theories of élites to Marxist theory, in *Elites and Society*, 1966, Chapters I and II and in *Classes in Modern Society*, Chapter I. In my chapter on power (above) I analysed the conception of power underlying most of the analyses of political élites.

to the Marxist theory of the political: it is the reaction of the functionalist school.[2] Performing its ideological function this denial of all unity amongst the so-called political élites or governing categories aims with the most perfect clarity at cutting off any route which might surreptitiously be taken towards an even minimal evocation of the class struggle. As soon as you admit the unity of these élites or categories, you run the risk of danger-ous contact with those who still admit the existence of a dominant class and, as if by chance, it is again Aron who has perceived this most clearly. Under the protection of functionalism, which de-specifies the concept and reality of the political, by considering it as the diffuse and indistinct function of the 'leadership' of the various 'elements-domains' of an 'integrated' social 'totality', the result is as follows: political élites are defined according to their place of leadership in the various domains of the social reality (including the political in its institutionalized form, the state): they are, therefore, political élites by virtue of being governing categories (*categories dirigeantes*). They are a *plurality* both because (i) these various domains (including the state in the strict sense) have no other relations with them than that of being integrated in a circular fashion in the social ensemble and because (ii) these '*high social strata*' of the various social groups represent divergent interests plurally integrated. Is it possible to maintain that the 'top trade unionists', the 'top personnel' of *all* the important political parties, the 'top managers' of the monopolies, the 'top state bureaucrats' (who would make up the governing categories on this theory) constitute a political unity? To say the least this would be an overstatement! In this context the state apparatus (the bureaucracy and more specifically its 'heights') is supposed to possess its own political power; and the relation of this to the others is governed by the general conception of the 'parcelling out' of political power which is characteristic of the functionalist theory.

B. The most interesting school for us is that which accepts the unity of political élites and sometimes expresses it by the notion of 'political class'.[3] Although this school criticizes the Marxist conception of the

---

2. See T. Parsons, 'The Distribution of Power in American Society' in *World Politics*, X, no. 1, where he gives a critique of C. W. Mills, op. cit., and where the functionalist principles of this conception are made very clear. For supporters of the pluralist conception, see R. Aron, 'Classe sociale, classe politique, classe dirigeante' in *Revue Européenne de sociologie*, 1, (2), 1960; 'Classe politique ou catégories dirigeantes?' in *Revue française de sciences politiques*.

3. See especially G. Mosca, *The Ruling Class*, 1939, pp. 12 ff.; R. Michels and his

dominant class – on the grounds that it (i) fails to take account of the modern decentration of political functions and the role peculiar to the bureaucracy and (ii) presupposes a political unity of the bourgeois class which no longer exists today – it nevertheless clearly intends to retain the general schema of *political domination*. This too contains several variants: the unity of these various élites is sometimes based (as is Mosca's 'political class') on the mere fact of their relation (in terms of influence or participation) with institutionalized political power. This power, without any possible foundation, is considered as a simple place whose very existence unifies the various élites, with the heights of the bureaucracy constituting simply one élite among others. Subsequently, this school attempts to discover *parallel* sources of political power, considering the economic itself as one source of power and the state as another. The élites, including the bureaucracy, though they are reduced to their relations to these various sources, are nonetheless unified, according to Wright Mills, by the fact that the 'heads of economic corporations', the 'political leaders' (including the heights of the bureaucracy) and the 'military leaders', that is to say all the élites, belong to what he calls the 'corporate rich'. In this case, this conception, which wanted to supersede so-called Marxist economic determinism and examine the autonomous functioning of the bureaucracy, appears to reduce the problem precisely to an economic over-determinism. The political functioning of the state apparatus is absorbed into the fact that its members, along with other élites, belong to the unifying centre of the high income group. This unity is also occasionally related to the dominance over the other élites either (i) of that élite which holds power based on the relations of production (see Meynaud) or (ii) of that élite which holds power based on the actual control of the state apparatus, which is the parallel basis of political power (see Michels and certain other disciples of Weber's theory of bureaucracy). Moreover, this dominance is in fact totally inexplicable in the context of these conceptions. Finally, as in Burnham, this unity is sometimes explained by the fact that the various élites belong to the new technico-bureaucratic 'class' of managers, which controls production in large enterprises through the so-called separation of ownership from control and in the nationalized sector through its membership of the state apparatus.

---

bureaucracy/political class in *Political Parties*, 1966, pp. 43 ff., 188 ff.; C. W. Mills, op. cit; J. Meynaud, *Les Élites politiques*, 1960. See also Burnham et al. on the 'managerial class'. The supporters of the conception of the unity of élites are those persons most influenced by the Marxist conception.

Since others have already made sufficiently exhaustive critiques of the theoretical presuppositions of these theories, I shall not undertake one.[4] The major defect of these theories consists in the fact that they do not provide any *explanation* of the foundation of political power. In addition, they acknowledge a plurality of sources for political power but can offer no explanation of their relations. They thus end in conclusions diametrically opposed to those which they originally envisaged: whilst giving a critique of the distorted Marxist conception of the dominant class, and whilst hoping in particular to examine the functioning peculiar to the bureaucracy, they end up by acknowledging the unity of the political élites. But in their case, this unity remains ideological. As far as the bureaucracy is concerned, since they recognize its own political power, they end up either by reducing its functioning to membership of an imaginary economic group (Mills) or by considering it as the exclusive 'subject' of political power in a narrow sense (the Weberian school) or in a broad sense (Burnham).

4. See especially the critique of Mills by Sweezy in 'Power Elite or Ruling Class?' in *Monthly Review*, September 1956.

2. The Marxist Position and the Question of the Class Affiliation of the State Apparatus

The problem posed by the theories of élites can now be resolved within the Marxist theory of the political. In fact, it is quite clear that such critiques of Marxist theory are aimed only at its distortions.

In the first place, I shall examine the critique of the concept of the *dominant class*. This theory holds that the concept of class applies to the economic level alone, that of domination to the political level alone: inevitably, therefore, by an improper extension, the concept of the dominant class implies that the economically dominant class is the politically dominant class. In fact, I demonstrated above (pp. 57 ff.) in what sense it is entirely incorrect to say that the concept of class covers only the relation between the agents and the relations of production: rather it indicates the effects of the ensemble of the structure on the field of social relations. I also showed (pp. 99 ff.) that the concepts of power and domination, in their relation to the concept of class, by no means cover *only* the level of political *structures*, but also the *ensemble of the field of social relations*, i.e. economic, political and ideological class practices.

Starting from these considerations, we explained the possibility of decentration and dislocation between the various positions of economic, political and ideological domination held by the various classes. While the economic level of relations of production determines in the last instance the places of power and domination in the field of the class struggle, it does this only through its reflection in the complex ensemble of a formation. We also came across numerous examples of dislocation between the economically and the politically dominant classes. In addition, having shown the complex structure and relative autonomy of the political, as well as the different spaces which it comprises, we showed the possibility of a decentration of the various political functions held by the various classes: for instance, differentiation between politically dominant classes which are part of the power bloc and the hegemonic class of this bloc, which ultimately holds political power and has the role of politically organizing the power bloc; or a differentiation between these and the ruling class (*classe régnante*) which has the role of representation in the political scene. In short, the rigorous Marxist conception of the dominant class in no way implies an empirical concentration of the various political functions in the hands of the actual members of a class, but explains this possibility of decentration according to the concrete forms of the class struggle and according to the political structures, i.e. the types and forms of state, and the forms of régime.[1] But this is only a matter of the relations between various classes and it completely fails to solve the problem posed by *the state apparatus* as a social group. I shall continue to use the term 'bureaucracy' because of the importance it has assumed, although along with the army, the police, etc., it is only a part of that group commonly described by the Marxist classics as the 'state administration'. In making the distinction between fraction, stratum and category, I indicated that the bureaucracy constitutes a specific *category*.[2] When the complex whole of a mode of production and the specific efficacy of its various instances is taken into consideration, it is clear that the bureaucracy is the *specific effect* of the state's regional structure on the agents in a *social formation*: this same mechanism is noticeable in the case of the 'intellectuals' in their relation to the region of ideology. Although it is true that this regional structure of the political also has effects on the agents distributed into social classes or fractions of classes (in so far as these concepts do not cover the effects on the agents of the economic alone), the production of this category of bureaucracy constitutes its specific effect. From the point of view of the bureaucracy, this is made clear first of all by the fact that it belongs to the state apparatus, in that, in some way, it sets the institutions of political power in operation.

The bureaucracy as a social category of the state apparatus is however only one aspect of the problem. In fact, it is very important to distinguish the two senses which the term bureaucracy may assume, which are indeed the two senses bestowed on it by Marx, Engels, Lenin and Gramsci. Strictly speaking, the second sense does not directly designate this social category but *a specific system of organization and internal functioning of the state apparatus*, which expresses above all the political impact of bourgeois *ideology* on the state, a phenomenon often expressed in the particular term of *bureaucratism* or *bureaucratization*.[3] This distinction

1. See pp. 249 ff. above. 2. See p. 84 above.
3. This distinction can also be found in Weber (*Wirtschaft und Gesellschaft*, Part III, Chapter 6) and Michels. In ensuing discussions, it was mainly seen as one between (i) bureaucracy as a 'system of transmission and execution' (bureaucratism), and (ii)

takes on a double importance: (i) it poses the question of the relations between bureaucracy and bureaucratism, between the location of this
category and the functioning of this system of organization, in particular
the functioning of the state apparatus, in a determinate social formation;
(ii) it poses the question of the possibility of the permanent existence of
bureaucratism, independent of the existence or non-existence of the
bureaucracy as a social category. This is Lenin's whole problematic in his
texts on the transition state in the USSR and on the permanence of
bureaucratism, which he designates as 'the tendency towards bureaucratization', without the existence of the 'bureaucracy' as a distinct
category.

In any case, these two aspects of the bureaucratic phenomenon *always
concern the state apparatus and not state power*. In particular, the bureaucracy, as a specific social category, depends on the concrete functioning
of the state apparatus and not on its own state power.

The importance of this problem has undoubtedly been exaggerated; to
start with, we can say that in itself the bureaucracy cannot constitute a
particular class nor even a fraction of a class (whether autonomous or not).
Engels used the term 'class' to designate it, but this was in exceptional
circumstances and the term obviously cannot be retained. For what
specifies the bureaucracy is precisely its peculiar relation to institutionalized power and the fact that it belongs to the state apparatus; thus it can
be only the effect of the state's relation to (a) the economic structures and
(b) the social classes and fractions. In this context, to say that the bureaucracy has no specific place in the relations which define the classes at the
level of the relations of production in the strict sense is not enough. Even
if it were enough in order to reject the notion of the bureaucracy as a class
already existing at the level of the relations of production, it would not be
enough to reject the conception of it as a *fraction* of a class: in fact,
autonomous fractions of classes can be defined at the level of political
relations alone. Since the functioning of the bureaucracy is specified by
its particular relation to the state, and by the fact that it belongs to the

bureaucracy in terms of power (the bureaucracy in the strict sense). This is the case for
A. Touraine, 'L'aliénation bureaucratique' in *Arguments*, No. 17, 1960; G. Lefort,
'Qu'est-ce que la bureaucratie?', ibid.; G. Lapassade, *Groupes, organizations, institutions*, 1967, pp. 57 ff.; as well as for the analyses in *Socialisme ou Barbarie*, influenced
by Trotskyism. This whole current sees *bureaucratism* as a *general* problem of organization and relates the existence of the *bureaucracy* to its *own power*. Neither conception is
valid according to the Marxist distinction between bureaucratism and bureaucracy.

state apparatus, it can be strictly determined at the political level only by the class functioning of this state. In other words, what has sometimes been considered as a privileged characteristic of the bureaucracy (namely, its particular relation to the state) not only does not constitute it as a social class or fraction of a class but, whilst specifying it as a category, precisely excludes it from being an autonomous fraction of a class at the political level, by circumscribing its functioning within the class power of this state.

In other respects, the discussion which has sometimes led to falsifying this characteristic of the bureaucracy has borne upon the state's role in the process of production, i.e. on its various economic functions. These economic functions have sometimes appeared capable of attributing to the bureaucracy (in certain cases) a specific place in the relations of production in the strict sense. But the state's functions are precisely circumscribed by its political class power. A good example is the case of the *state bourgeoisie* in certain developing countries: the bureaucracy may, through the state, establish a specific place for itself in the existing relations of production, or even in the not-yet-existing relations of production. But in that case it does not constitute a class by virtue of being the bureaucracy, but by virtue of being an effective class.

This résumé was essential in order to pose the problem of the relation between the bureaucracy and the classes and fractions of classes. The bureaucracy constitutes a specific category in that it has itself a *class-affiliation*. This is a matter of the classes or fractions of social classes from which the various strata of the bureaucracy originate, from which the members of the administration are recruited. Marx, Engels and Lenin insisted on the fact that the bureaucracy must, from this point of view, be regarded as distinguished into certain distinct strata, with differing recruitment and class affiliation. For example, in the case of the German and French bureaucracy, Marx and Engels distinguish what Lenin calls 'the heights' of the bureaucracy, which belong respectively to the landed nobility and the bourgeoisie, and the subordinate strata belonging to the petty bourgeoisie. Moreover, concerning the class recruitment for the heights of the bureaucracy, Marx and Engels often distinguish between the various fractions of the bourgeois class, and in particular between the industrial and financial fractions.[4]

4. K. Marx, 'The Eighteenth Brumaire', *MESW*, 1970, pp. 166 ff. and 173 ff.; 'The Civil War in France', ibid., pp. 271–309; *On Britain*; F. Engels, 'Der Status quo in

Marx and Engels wanted *to mark* the importance of this class or fraction from which the 'heights' of the bureaucracy are recruited by the specific concept of the *class in charge* of the state. This concept seemed indispensable to them, in order to indicate that this class or fraction might or might not identify itself with the hegemonic class or fraction of the power bloc, i.e. with what is normally but incorrectly designated as the politically dominant class or fraction. In short, the heights of the bureaucracy may depend on a politically dominant class or fraction which is part of the power bloc but which is not the hegemonic class or fraction of this bloc. Typical cases are the British state apparatus after 1830, and that of Germany after Bismarck, where these heights were recruited from the landowning class, although the bourgeoisie held the hegemonic place. Moreover, this class or fraction in charge of the state may or may not identify itself with the ruling class or fraction in the political scene. Throughout the examples which I have given, there has clearly been a whole series of dislocations between the hegemonic classes or fractions and those ruling or in charge of the state from which the heights of the bureaucracy are recruited.

These remarks are important, since the whole problem of the bureaucracy is that it constitutes a *specific category*. This means that its particular functioning (what specifies it as a category) *is not directly determined by its class membership*, by the political functioning of those classes or fractions from which it originates: it depends on the concrete functioning of the state apparatus, i.e. on the place of the state in the ensemble of a formation and on its complex relations with the various classes and fractions. This is precisely why the bureaucracy, as a social category, is able to possess its own unity and coherence, despite the diversity of recruitment and class affiliation of its various strata: this political unity of the bureaucratic category cannot therefore be related to the class in charge of the state.

Neither can it be related to that of the hegemonic class or fraction which, in the last analysis, holds *state power*. I shall concentrate on this point. When Marx and Engels distinguished between *state power* and *state apparatus*, they insisted on the fact that the bureaucracy was not an autonomous class or fraction and so could not have its own political power.

Deutschland', *Werke*, Vol. 4, pp. 40 ff.; *The Housing Question*, *MESW*, 1958, Vol. 1, pp. 546–635; Preface to 'The Peasant War in Germany', *MESW*, 1970, pp. 235–241; Preface to the first English edition of *Socialism, Utopian and Scientific*, ibid., pp. 375–93.

So-called 'bureaucratic power' is in fact the mere exercise of the state's functions (this is the second sense given by Marx and Lenin to the term 'state apparatus'), since the state is not the foundation of political power but the *centre of political power* belonging to determinate classes, and so, in this case, to the hegemonic class or fraction.[5] In other words, in the last analysis, the functioning of the bureaucracy corresponds to the political interest of this class or fraction: this, however, is due to the intermediary of the state's complex relations with this class's or fraction's political power and not to that of the bureaucracy's class affiliation or recruitment. So while the bureaucracy has no class power of its own, nor does it directly exercise the power of the classes to which it belongs; furthermore, it fails to do this precisely *because* it belongs to these classes. This is clear in the case of a dislocation between the class or fraction in charge of the state and the hegemonic class or fraction. In such a case, as Marx and Engels show in their writings on Britain, the bureaucracy does not exercise a power of the class in charge, but a power of the hegemonic class or fraction. It is the more important to point this out, since frequent attempts are made to found this relation between the bureaucracy and the political power of the hegemonic class or fraction by trying to establish the identity of this latter with the class from which the heights of the bureaucracy originate: whether in the fantastical sense of Wright Mills or by the even more fantastical method of investigating mysterious and various hidden relations of near or distant kinship between these heights and the members of the hegemonic class or fraction.

Thus we come to the second aspect of the problem. *Even in the case where* the hegemonic class or fraction is that from which the heights of the bureaucracy are effectively recruited and where there is thus an identity between the hegemonic classes or fractions and those in charge of the state, the relation between the bureaucracy and the political power of the latter is not always directly determined by its class affiliation: it passes through the intermediary of the state. The characteristics of unity and cohesion peculiar to the bureaucracy as a specific category cannot be reduced by its class affiliation to the unity and cohesion of the class in charge which is, in this case, also the hegemonic class: they depend on the bureaucracy's specific relation with the state and on the fact that it belongs to the state apparatus. It is precisely this which allows it to func-

5. Marx's and Engels's general theme is that the bureaucracy is the 'agent' or 'representative' of the hegemonic classes.

tion politically with relative autonomy vis-à-vis the hegemonic class or fraction whose power it exercises.

In fact, then, the bureaucracy poses a particular problem. Because of its specific relation with the state, in the case of an identity between the hegemonic class and the class in charge, the bureaucracy accedes to a relative autonomy with regard to the latter; and in the case of a dislocation between these classes, it puts itself at the service of the political interests of the hegemonic class, in spite of its class affiliation to the class in charge. In this latter case, it nevertheless still possesses a relative autonomy with regard to the hegemonic class, not by virtue of its affiliation to a different class (i.e. the class in charge) but by its character as a specific category through the intermediary of its relation with the state. I therefore point out that in order to justify the relative autonomy of the bureaucracy's political functioning, there is no theoretical need to concede it its own political power, any more than it is necessary to attribute its own power to the state (since the state is simply the centre of class power) in order to justify the state's relative autonomy vis-à-vis the power bloc and the hegemonic class.

While the bureaucracy's class affiliation does not directly determine its own political functioning, it does affect that functioning to some extent. Marx and Engels provide certain examples in which this is clearly the case, though generally within the *limits* set by the state's relation to the hegemonic classes. This is particularly striking in the case in which the hegemonic classes or fractions are different from the classes from which the bureaucracy is recruited, including the class in charge. But both in this case and as a general rule, the fact that the bureaucracy's class affiliation is to the class in charge has an impact which does not manifest itself in that class's own political power – and this is *because* the heights of the bureaucracy are recruited from within it: this is a political power *other* than that which it holds through its position in the class struggle. It is not a direct manifestation of power, but is reflected rather in the additional limits and barriers posed by the class affiliation of the heights of the bureaucracy to the hegemonic class or fraction. This, in fact, is the general conclusion to be drawn from Marx's analyses of the state apparatus in Britain (the capitalist ground-rent aristocracy versus the bourgeoisie) and from Engels's analyses of the Prussian state apparatus (big feudal land-owners versus the bourgeoisie).[6]

6. In my critique of the conception of 'zero-sum power' (pp. 117 ff. above), it

Although in a much subtler way, this is what emerges in the periods of *transition* in the strict sense. In this case, because of the dominant role devolving upon the political instance, because of the particular instability of state power and because of the unstable and precarious equilibrium of the classes in struggle, the state apparatus's class affiliation can play a determinant role to the advantage of the non-hegemonic classes in charge: it is not that this affiliation in itself confers political power on them, *but it creates the conditions for their accession to this power*. It is precisely from this angle that Marx views the state apparatus in France. 'But under the absolute Monarchy, during the first Revolution, under Napoleon, bureaucracy was only the means of preparing the class rule of the bourgeoisie (the bourgeoisie being, as we know, here and now the tenant class). Under the restoration, under Louis Philippe, under the parliamentary Republic, it was the instrument of the ruling class.'[7] But the French case is a particular one. During the transition in Britain, the especially clear and successful establishment of the dominance of the CMP operated as it were despite the class affiliation of the state apparatus (landed nobility). In the transition in Germany, the bourgeois class established its hegemony *by means of* the state apparatus, although the class affiliation of the latter was to the landed nobility. It is possible for the bureaucracy concretely to function in these ways, in so far as their operations depend strictly on the relation between the social forces and the state's role during the transition period. However, this class affiliation of the apparatuses of the transition state also continues to make itself felt, in this case too, in the form of *hindrances* and *resistances* to the establishment of the dominance of the CMP, within the limits posed by the general process of transition: they vary according to the state's precise role in this process and are particularly clear in Germany where the state's role is very important. Moreover, as we shall see, this is the theoretical line governing Lenin's analyses of the bureaucratic problem in the USSR (the bourgeois specialists in the state apparatus) in the initial stage of the transition.

The state apparatus's class affiliation is important not only in connection with the relations between the heights of the bureaucracy and the class in charge. While the particular hierarchical functioning characteristic of the bureaucracy has allowed these heights to have a decisive impact, the

---

became clear that these limits to a class's power do not in themselves mean that the class setting the limits experiences a gain in its own power; i.e. there is, in this case, no increase in the power of the class in charge by means of the bureaucracy.

7. 'The Eighteenth Brumaire', *MESW*, 1970, pp. 169–70.

petty-bourgeois class affiliation of the apparatus's *subordinate strata*, coupled with the particular place occupied by the petty bourgeoisie in France and Germany (unlike Britain), has taken on a characteristic importance in those countries.

This class affiliation of the state apparatus's subordinate strata is worth examining. It is, in fact, one of the causes of the *particular extension of the state's bureaucratic apparatus*. Marx, Engels and Gramsci stressed this relation between the extension of the state bureaucratic apparatus and the existence of the classes or fractions of small-scale producers (whether the petty bourgeoisie, the small-holding peasantry, etc.) in a formation on the road to establishing the dominance of the CMP. Gramsci, for example, posed the question in the following way: 'Does there exist, in a given country, a widespread social stratum in whose economic life and political self-assertion . . . the bureaucratic career, either civil or military, is a very important element?'[8] The reasons for this relation are (i) of an *economic order*: the coexistence of the modes of small-scale and capitalist production 'create an unemployed surplus population for which there is no place either in the land or in the towns, and which accordingly reaches out for the State offices as a sort of respectable alms and provokes the creation of State posts';[9] (ii) of a *political order*: the extension of the bureaucratic apparatus allows the dominant classes to conquer these subordinate strata by transforming them into supporting classes; (iii) of an *ideological order*: in particular, the ideology of power fetishism held by these supporting classes, in addition to the particular lack of their own political organization, which makes its members particularly suited to serve as the subordinate strata of the bureaucratic apparatus.

However, the reasons for the extension of the bureaucratic apparatus resulting from the class affiliation of its subordinate strata are not identical with the reasons for its existence and functioning. These depend rather on the position of the classes of small-scale producers in the field of the class struggle. In short, they are not identical with the reasons depending on the bureaucracy's own political action vis-à-vis these classes. For example, because of the economic conditions of life (e.g. isolation, etc.) and the incapacity of the classes of small-scale producers politically to organize themselves, their position necessitates and makes possible

8. Marx, 'The Eighteenth Brumaire' and 'The Civil War in France', both in *MESW* 1970; also his texts on Spain; Engels, 'Der Status quo in Deutschland', op. cit.; Gramsci, *Prison Notebooks*, p. 212. For Lenin, see below.

9. Marx, 'The Eighteenth Brumaire', *MESW*, 1970, p. 174.

a bureaucratic apparatus which represents them in a particular way. Thus their support for the dominant power is conditioned by the apparatus's own action; it is not conditioned by the fact that the subordinate strata belong to these classes. Moreover, the functioning of this subordinate petty-bourgeois state apparatus in its relation of unity with the 'heights' varies according to the state structures and therefore according to the state power of the dominant classes.

Finally, the relation between the bureaucracy as a social category and the classes of small-scale producers results from the fact that the bureaucracy is the effect of the regional instance of the state on a *social formation.* The bureaucracy expresses the concrete coupling in this formation of the CMP with the other modes which engender the classes of small-scale production. This relation thus depends on the over-determination of these classes (a) by the classes of the capitalist mode and (b) by their relation to the capitalist state.

3. The Capitalist State – Bureaucratism – Bureaucracy

The analysis of the bureaucratic problem thus presupposes the rigorous establishment of the relations between (a) the specific category of the *bureaucracy*, (b) *bureaucratism* as the particular system of organization of the state apparatus and (c) *the structures of a type of state*. It is therefore necessary to examine (i) the bureaucracy in the framework of a determinate mode of production and of a formation dominated by that mode (here the capitalist mode) and (ii) its insertion in the framework of the class struggle of this formation, which is a different problem from that of its class membership.

I shall merely give a few indications about bureaucracy and bureaucratism in the framework of the CMP and a capitalist formation. For this, I shall both follow Marx's, Engels's, Lenin's and Gramsci's indications and also consider Weber's analyses, since he contributed a great deal in elaborating the position of the particular relations of bureaucracy and bureaucratism to (a) the capitalist system and (b) political democracy. The only valuable analyses of subsequent political science concerning the bureaucratic phenomenon merely extend his remarks. Weber's analyses provide valuable guidelines for us, especially if we take into account the critiques which can be made of them.

I shall firstly recapitulate the critiques which I made above. On bureaucracy, Weber's general problematic leads both to bureaucratism being given an inadequate and vague status and to bureaucracy being given a false one.

(i) *Bureaucratism*: he establishes its relation to the capitalist system under the vague notion of 'formal rationality', an ensemble of normative models which governs the organization of the various sectors of the capitalist system.

(ii) *Bureaucracy*: for him this social group ends in being the subject/creator of modern political power and the subject of political development, precisely in so far as he makes it into the subject/creator of these behavioural norms at the political level.[1] Hence we witness a systematic masking of the relation between the bureaucracy and the social classes, and indeed of the political class struggle, Weber's conception of bureaucracy being, of course, formulated explicitly to combat that of the class struggle.

Nevertheless, we must remember that he, along with the Marxist classics, establishes a necessary relation between bureaucratism/bureaucracy and the capitalist mode of production. Although he situates the bureaucratic phenomenon *without any distinction* in the *various sectors* of a capitalist formation, he stresses in particular its relation to the political form of the modern state, i.e. the capitalist state. This relation is necessary but has two aspects: schematically, the bureaucratic phenomenon (bureaucracy and bureaucratism) seems to him both (i) to be indispensable for the functioning of the ensemble of a capitalist formation and of its political forms and (ii) to carry within itself the seeds of important contradictions, exhibited especially on the political level.

Since the analyses of Merton, a representative figure of functionalism, contemporary political science has followed Weber in examining the bureaucratic problem according to the notion of *dysfunction*.[2] According to this school, the functioning of the bureaucracy does not constitute a specific political problem or phenomenon except in those exceptional (indeed 'pathological') cases where its functioning in the capitalist system goes beyond the integrationalist frames of reference of this system. More or less all of American sociology's analyses of bureaucracy can be fitted into this perspective: according to them a distinction must be drawn between a functional bureaucracy (i.e. one useful for the system) and a dysfunctional bureaucracy; the task being to readjust 'human relations' within the framework of this system. Weber, therefore, appears as the black sheep: although he established a relation between (a) the existence of the bureaucracy and bureaucratism and (b) what he calls the rationality of the system (i.e. although he saw bureaucracy and bureaucratism as the most efficient framework for action in the system), he also stressed the necessary contradiction between the bureaucratic phenomenon and political democracy.

1. Here and in what follows I am referring to *Wirtschaft und Gesellschaft*, Part III, Chapter 6.
2. R. Merton, 'Bureaucratic Structure and Personality' in *Social Forces*, XVIII, 1940, pp. 560 ff. M. Crozier is the typical French representative of this school: see *Le Phénomène bureaucratique*, 1963, pp. 233 ff.

But this contradiction is badly located and leads to Michels's conception of 'bureaucracy/political class' in its relation to political democracy. In the Weberian schema in general, the fault is already apparent in the relation of bureaucratism to capitalism expressed in the notion of 'rationality'. For Weber this notion has two senses. In its first, very precise sense, it relates to the system of budgetary accountancy in the capitalist firm and state. In this case, it is too narrow, designating only a partial and secondary effect of the structures of this mode of production. It is also used in the extremely vague sense of 'rationality' in general. In this sense, as Marcuse has shown in taking this representation to its ultimate conclusions,[3] the bureaucratism/capitalism contradiction appears in Weber's theory as the conversion of the formal rationality of bureaucratic functioning into 'irrationality' weighing down upon the system. Moreover, it is worthwhile recalling that in his early works Marx himself makes his critique of bureaucracy and of its relation to the modern state and bourgeois society according to the theme of 'rationality/irrationality' which belongs to his problematic of alienation.

In fact, Engels, Gramsci, Lenin and the mature Marx establish both the necessary relation between the 'bureaucratic phenomenon' (bureaucracy and bureaucratism) and the capitalist state and a capitalist formation, and also the contradictory nature of this relation. In particular, *bureaucracy*, as the specific object of theoretical research, in no way depends on an *exceptional* and *pathological* functioning of the capitalist state apparatus: it expresses a character constitutive of the state apparatus relative to the theoretical type of the capitalist state. Thus, when the mature Marx, Engels and Lenin make their critique of the bureaucracy of the capitalist state apparatus as a 'parasitic body', a 'foreign body' in society,[4] it is not in order to mark out an exceptional character which this apparatus takes on in a concrete situation in a capitalist formation. In fact, they intend to mark a whole series of contradictions between this specific category of state apparatus and the capitalist formation (a 'parasitic body') which is absolutely vital for that apparatus's functioning, and whose existence depends on the capitalist type of state. These contradictions are located in the relations between the functioning of the bureaucracy and the *social classes*. They derive (i) from the CMP in a formation, i.e. from the relations between the bureaucracy and the classes of this mode, including

3. H. Marcuse, *One Dimensional Man*, op. cit.
4. e.g. Marx, 'The Eighteenth Brumaire', *MESW*, 1970, p. 169; Lenin, *The State and Revolution*, where he comments on capitalist formations.

the bourgeois class and the bureaucracy's relative autonomy from it; and (ii) from the relations between the bureaucracy and the classes of the other modes of production of a capitalist formation, namely the classes of small-scale producers. In its necessity and in its relations to the classes, the bureaucracy thus appears as the effect of the capitalist type of state in a capitalist social formation, according to the forms in which the capitalist mode of production is coupled to the other modes and according to the resulting political relations.

I shall follow the same theoretical line on bureaucratism. We must mark out the necessity and the contradictions of a certain system of organization of state apparatus, in its relations to the ideological models of the capitalist mode and the modes of small-scale production, i.e. to *bourgeois and petty-bourgeois ideology*. The contradictions will here be located at one and the same time in the very heart of the capitalist political ideology, between the legitimacy of political democracy and the forms assumed by capitalist ideology in the functioning of the bureaucracy, and between this latter and the petty-bourgeois aspect of ideology which preside over that functioning.

To say therefore that bureaucracy and bureaucratism are related to a type of state (the capitalist state) and to the concrete forms of this state, is already to possess the perspectives of the Marxist classics vis-à-vis the bureaucratic phenomenon: *the bureaucratic phenomenon is a specifically political phenomenon*. When it is located in the ensemble of a capitalist formation, under its aspect of bureaucratism as the normative ideological model of organization, it presents *homologies* with the organization in the *various sectors* of this formation: e.g. firms (organization of work), the cultural domain ('bureaucratization' of culture), etc. In this case, these homologies are the result of the dominance of an ideological model over the ensemble of a formation. However, the bureaucracy, in the strict sense, designating a specific social category, is related to its membership of the state apparatus.

It is in this way that we can locate the economic factors of bureaucracy. These factors, related to the capitalist relations of production along with those of the other modes in the capitalist formation, *have no direct impact* on the generation of the bureaucracy. *Only in so far as they are reflected in the state's structures and functions* do they have an impact on the bureaucracy itself and its relation to the social classes: e.g. when the 'surplus-population' of the classes of small-scale producers forces them to find employment in the bureaucracy as a source of income. The principal aspect of the problem here is, as Marx says, *the characteristic extension* of the state's 'attributes and functions' in a capitalist formation, and in particular, an extension of those functions which concern its specific intervention in the economic with regard to other types of state.[5] More-over these functions are spread over a whole range of activities, from tax collection and extension of the state's budget (the importance of both of which is stressed both by Weber and by the Marxist classics) to its more direct intervention in the economic, as witnessed in the stage of state monopoly capitalism. It is here also that the problem of nationalized state property comes up. This is a problem which it is worth stressing, especi-ally because of the misinterpretations to which it has given rise. These include the 'managerial' tendency, based either (i) on a confusion of the relations of production with the technical division of labour within the firm, and on the so-called modern 'separation of private property and control', or (ii) on a general conception of 'organizations'. This tendency has seen in the economic, ideologically conceived (organization of business, etc.) the foundations of the 'class' of bureaucrats.

The extension of the capitalist state's 'attributes and functions' does not bear only on economic functions, but also on its political and ideo-logical functions. It is an important extension for the bureaucracy, mainly because it determines the increase in the numbers of the state personnel. While it is true that, for various reasons, this bureaucracy can be extended into 'surplus numbers', i.e. beyond the number necessary to accomplish these functions, it is no less true that the relation between the extension of the state apparatus as social category and that of the state apparatus in its functions is crucial here.

This extension of the state's functions takes on increased importance when, as often occurs, it corresponds to the displacement of dominance from one instance to another in a formation. In such a situation, the state assumes the dominant role in a capitalist formation. This affects the bureaucracy's political functioning and the role of this functioning, which increases with the state's dominant role. Within this relation, we must, therefore, distinguish between the impact of the extension of the state's functions on the numerical growth of the bureaucratic category, and the

5. See *The Eighteenth Brumaire* and *The Civil War in France*. Weber also stressed this aspect of the problem.

impact of the state's role of dominance on the bureaucracy's political functioning, since these two factors do not necessarily exactly overlap. Marx and Engels make this distinction when they analyse the state apparatus and the bureaucracy in France, Germany and Britain. In France and in Germany the bureaucracy has a particular and important political role, because of the dominant role which often devolves on the state instance. The impact of the extension of the state's functions on the extension of the bureaucratic category is, however, particularly marked in France, because of the extension of the small-holding peasantry: over-determined by capitalist production, its 'surplus population' is found a place in the state apparatus. In Britain, on the other hand, the particularly successful dominance of the CMP over the other modes leads both to a disintegration of the classes of small-scale producers and also to the economic's holding the dominant role, i.e. to the establishment in the British social formation of the matrix typical of the CMP. The role of the bureaucracy is less important, which means that in Britain this specific category has almost never established itself as a social force. It is, of course, possible to speak at greater length by analysing the subsequent and different evolution of the bureaucracy in these various countries, and the political role played by it, but I shall leave this to the reader.

The study of the bureaucratic category in a capitalist formation cannot be limited to the problems of the functions devolving on the capitalist state. It depends in the first place on the structures of this state and on its place in the ensemble of the instances of the CMP. The essential element here is that relative autonomy of the political from the economic which characterizes the CMP in contrast to the other modes, e.g. to the feudal mode. The effect of this particular feature on the conditions which make possible the bureaucracy's existence as a *specific category* has been pointed out both by Marx and Weber.

In the feudal mode of production and in the relation between the economic and the political characteristic of it, the exercise of public functions depends on personal, economico-political links between those in possession of these functions and the monarch who represents state sovereignty. The exercise of these functions is identical, particularly with the classes' place in this mode, with their 'public status' as 'castes' and with the functioning of feudal rights. This is what Weber called 'administration by notables'; the dominant feudal class here concentrates in its own hands the exercise of political functions. In this case, it is precisely *class affiliation*, under the form of caste or estates, which directly determines that administration of the state which excludes the possibility of a bureaucracy functioning as a specific category. Moreover, this is equally clear as far as the functioning of the ideological in a feudal formation is concerned: this functioning prevents the formation of a specific category of 'intellectuals'; see the problem of the clergy as a class, indeed as a caste.

We studied the passage from this situation to the modern bureaucracy more fully in our analyses of the absolutist state. This passage presupposes the capitalist type of state, i.e. a juridico-political instance which is relatively autonomous from the economic and which establishes the concrete characteristics of bureaucratism. It is to this capitalist 'type' of state that Marx refers when he describes the constitution of the French bureaucracy.

This executive power with its enormous bureaucratic and military organization . . . sprang up in the days of the absolute monarchy . . . the seignorial privileges of the landowners and towns became transformed into so many attributes of State power, the feudal dignitaries into paid officials and the motley pattern of conflicting medieval plenary powers into the regulated plan of a state authority. . . . The first French Revolution, with its task of breaking all separate local, territorial, urban and provincial powers in order to create the civil unity of the nation, was bound to develop what the absolute monarchy had begun: centralization, but at the same time the extent, the attributes and the agents of the governmental power.[6]

Before examining the impact of the capitalist state on the functioning of the bureaucracy, we must study the second aspect of the problem, the aspect of bureaucratism. By bureaucratism we mean a particular mode of organization and functioning of the state apparatus, which *in the case of the capitalist state is coextensive with the specific bureaucratic category*. Bureaucratism is due *both to the structures of the capitalist state and to the impact of the dominant capitalist ideology on the normative rules of organization of the state apparatus*. These are two relatively distinct factors in bureaucratism. The impact of the dominant capitalist ideology on bureaucratism assumes several forms:

a. Either a general form, concerning the very constitutive characteristic of every ideology; e.g. the specific masking of knowledge, manifested in bureaucratic 'secrecy';

b. Or the particular forms of capitalist ideology (studied by Marx in the fetishism of commodities) which range from the impersonal character

6. 'The Eighteenth Brumaire', *MESW*, 1970, p. 169.

of bureaucratic functions (e.g. ideological constitution of the 'individual-person') to the normative models of the division of labour;

c. Or juridico-political forms, the dominant region of the dominant capitalist ideology. In this case, we are dealing in particular with the impact of bourgeois legitimacy on bureaucratism; both Marx, in his mature works, and Weber (the 'rational-legal' legitimacy) have stressed this. Within the framework of this legitimacy, bureaucracy seems to represent the political unity of the people-nation; it is both able to and does present itself as a 'neutral body' embodying the general interest; and its political functioning vis-à-vis the classes is thus systematically masked.

d. The impact of the dominant capitalist ideology and even of the petty-bourgeois ideology on bureaucratism is manifested finally by their effects on the masses' lack of culture and knowledge. It is precisely this which allows the bureaucratic monopoly of knowledge.

It is thus clear, precisely by means of its relations to the dominant ideology in the ensemble of the capitalist formation, that the bureaucratism of the state apparatus presents homologies with the normative models governing the organization and division of labour in the various sectors of this formation: i.e. in factories, cultural institutions, etc.[7] Nevertheless, bureaucratism is a *specific effect* of this ideology only for the state apparatus, precisely in so far as it is related to the existence of the bureaucracy as a social category within capitalist formations. A further reason for this is that in this domain ideology is coupled with the state's structures so as to produce bureaucratism in its relations to the political phenomenon of bureaucracy; in short, *bureaucracy in its relations to the political class struggle*.

But if bureaucracy is a *specific* social category, it is because of (a) the *specific unity* presented in its functioning as a social group, and (b) its *relative autonomy* from the social classes, both from the classes to which it belongs and from the dominant classes. In a capitalist formation, these characteristics depend mainly on bureaucratism as resulting from the dominant ideology and from the state: and secondarily, they depend on the relations of the class struggle to this state.

Bureaucratism has been analysed so often that there is no need to

7. Marx indicated these *homologies* in his analyses both of the technical division of labour in large firms (see *Capital*, Vol. I) and of the state apparatus whose work is divided and centralized as in a factory (see 'The Eighteenth Brumaire', *MESW*, 1970, p. 169).

labour it again. So I shall briefly recall certain of its features; I shall leave aside those which derive from distinctive features of the state and those which derive from ideology, and I shall not attempt to classify them in order of importance. Marx, Engels, Gramsci and Lenin[8] have studied them; as has Weber, whose analyses are useful here. We may give the following general definition: *bureaucratism represents a hierarchical organization of the state apparatus, by means of delegation of power, having particular effects on the functioning of that apparatus.* As a general rule it is correlative with:

1. The axiomatization of the juridical system into rules/laws, which are abstract, general, formal and strictly regulated and which distribute the domains of activities and competences (Engels, Weber);

2. The concentration of functions and the administrative centralization of the apparatus (Marx, Engels, Gramsci);

3. The impersonal character of the functions of the state apparatus (Marx, Weber);

8. Lenin's most important analyses on this subject are to be found in his post-1918 analyses of the socialist state in transition: see, in particular, *Collected Works*, Vols. 29–33, 36, 42, 45. The problem is that in these texts by the term 'bureaucracy' Lenin means 'bureaucratism'; indeed he generally uses 'bureaucratism', along with 'bureaucratization' (meaning 'tendencies towards bureaucratization'). The following is the general theoretical line which emerges from these texts: because of various characteristics of the transition (e.g. absence of an exploiting class, the proletariat's political organization, etc.), *it is possible* in this period of transition *that a 'bureaucratism' may exist which is not linked to the existence of the 'bureaucracy' as a specific category.* The permanent existence of 'bureaucratism' without a 'bureaucracy' is related to (i) *the ideological legacy* of the preceding social formation (especially the capitalist ideology) and *the permanent existence in the socialist state of characteristics belonging to the preceding state,* including the existence of 'specialists' in the ranks of the administration who are bourgeois 'in their way of life and in their ideology'; see *Complete Works*, Vols. 30, 31 and 33; and (ii) the economic, political and ideological consequences of the presence in the Russian formation of *state capitalism* and the classes of *small-scale producers*, notably the small-scale peasant producers. However if we take this into account, Lenin's analyses can be useful for the capitalist formation, especially for the impact of the capitalist and petty bourgeois ideologies on 'bureaucratism'. They are equally useful concerning the general theoretical line for examining the bureaucratic phenomenon: and here it is vital to note that in so far as the permanent existence of 'bureaucratism' in the USSR concerns the 'bourgeois' specialists of the state apparatus, Lenin does not relate it to these persons' 'bourgeois' class affiliation in the relations of production but to their bourgeois ideology: the bourgeoisie in the USSR was almost liquidated at this time. This problematic must be extended to the existence of the bureaucracy in capitalist formations, where it is also not related to its class affiliation but to the state's structures (since it is *bureaucracy* which is in question here) and to the impact of ideology.

4. The mode of payment of these functions by fixed salaries (Marx, Weber);

5. The mode of recruitment of civil servants by co-optation or nomination by the 'heights' or again by a particular system of competition (Marx, Weber);

6. The separation between the civil servant's private life and public function; separation between 'home' and 'office' (Marx, Weber);

7. A systematic masking of knowledge of the apparatus, i.e. bureaucratic secrecy, vis-à-vis the classes (Marx, Engels, Lenin, Weber);

8. A masking of knowledge within the apparatus itself, with the 'top civil servants' holding the keys of science (Lenin);

9. A characteristic disparity between the scientific education of the 'heights' and the subordinate strata's lack of culture (Marx, Lenin); etc.

This bureaucratism of the organization of the state apparatus entails a strictly hierarchical functioning by the delegation of power and of sectors of functions, a particular internal form of distributing authority and legitimation from above, a perpetual referring of responsibilities to the upper echelons, all of which characteristics were often described by Marx, Engels and Lenin as well as by numerous other authors. It is bureaucratism precisely which, in the functioning of the state apparatus, primarily attributes to bureaucracy its character of unity, and which thus constitutes it as a specific category: it is this fusion of the dominant ideology with the structures of the capitalist state which, despite the divergences in the class affiliation of its various strata, allows the bureaucracy to function as a social category. It is true that this social group has its own interests (e.g. access to the administrative functions as sources of income, frameworks for careers, etc.) but these are not enough to constitute it as a specific category, because of the disparity of these interests among the bureaucracy's diverse strata; and because, although these interests explain, to a certain extent, the close relation between the bureaucracy and the dominant classes, they do not explain the relative autonomy of the bureaucracy from them, an autonomy which contributes to the formation of the bureaucracy as a specific category.

4. Bureaucracy and the Class Struggle

The relation of bureaucratism and bureaucracy to the capitalist state leads us back to the problem of relations between the bureaucracy and the *class struggle* in a capitalist formation. This relation alone can reveal to us the relative autonomy of the bureaucracy from the dominant class in this formation; and this autonomy, together with the unity peculiar to it, constitutes the bureaucracy as a specific category.

Marx and Engels adopt an unvarying theoretical line on this problem: this relative autonomy of the bureaucracy from the dominant classes is absolutely and exhaustively determined by the relations between the capitalist state and the class struggle. Since the bureaucracy has no power of its own, its relative autonomy is none other than that which devolves on this state in the power relations of the class struggle; state power is held by classes, since the state is in fact only a power centre.

The problem of the capitalist state's relative autonomy in Marx and Engels is, however, explicitly related (according to the one conception theoretically elaborated by them) only to the equilibrium between the social forces present. Consequently, although for them the bureaucracy's relative autonomy is strictly determined by the state's autonomy from the classes, it is located only in those situations realizable by this equilibrium. It is in this sense especially that Marx examines the problem of bureaucracy with respect to the concrete historical phenomenon of French Bonapartism' and wrongly reduces this phenomenon to the model of an equilibrium of forces. He says: 'bureaucracy ... under the Restoration, under Louis Philippe, under the parliamentary Republic ... was the instrument of the ruling class, however much it strove for power of its own. Only under the Second Bonaparte does the State seem to have made itself completely independent':[1] (the question here is that of the relative autonomy of the Bonapartist bureaucracy from the dominant classes). Engels puts the case even more clearly:

In reality however the state as it exists in Germany is likewise the necessary

[1]. 'The Eighteenth Brumaire', *MESW*, 1970, pp. 169-70.

product of the social basis out of which it has developed. In Prussia – and Prussia is now decisive – there exists side by side with a landowning aristocracy which is still powerful, a comparatively young and extremely cowardly bourgeoisie, which up to the present has won neither direct political domination, as in France, or more or less indirect domination as in England. Side by side with these two classes, however, there exists a rapidly increasing proletariat which is intellectually highly developed and which is becoming more and more organized every day. We therefore find here, alongside of the basic condition of the old absolute monarchy – an equilibrium between the landed aristocracy and the bourgeoisie – the basic condition of modern Bonapartism – an equilibrium between the bourgeoisie and the proletariat. But both in the old absolute monarchy and in the modern Bonapartist monarchy the real governmental authority lies in the hands of a special caste of army officers and state officials which in Prussia is replenished from its own ranks. The independence of this caste, which appears to occupy a position outside, and so to speak, above society, gives the state the semblance of independence in relation to society.[2]

Engels here clearly attributes to the bureaucracy its own power: he even occasionally goes so far as to consider it a class; but both of these expressions are obviously false. What is important is the position he gives to the relative autonomy of the bureaucracy. Sometimes, again, he locates it in the particular situation of equilibrium which is that of *catastrophe-equilibrium*; e.g. in his text, 'Der Status quo in Deutschland':[3] 'This régime, represented by the bureaucracy, is the political synthesis of general impotence. . . . The poverty of the German *status quo* consists principally in this, that no class has so far been strong enough . . . to make itself the representative of the interests of the whole nation.' This catastrophe-equilibrium is close to another of Marx's interpretations of the relative autonomy of the bureaucracy in French Bonapartism, that it is due to the fact that: '. . . the bourgeoisie had already lost, and the working class had not yet acquired, the faculty of governing the nation.'

But these models of equilibrium are as insufficient for explaining the relative autonomy of the capitalist state from the dominant classes, as they are for explaining the relative autonomy of the specific category of the state apparatus from these classes. This relative autonomy is a constitutive feature of the capitalist type of state (and therefore of its concrete forms) even in the case where there is no equilibrium of forces. So, while we find

2. 'The Housing Question', *MESW*, 1958, Vol. I, p. 605.
3. op. cit., p. 26.

in Marx an examination (on a *practical level*) of the relative autonomy of the capitalist type of state from the dominant classes, we also find a further examination, *directly determined* by the first, of the bureaucracy's relative autonomy from those classes, even in the concrete case of a non-equilibrium of forces. The reader should refer to the previous chapter which deals with the factors in the relative autonomy of this type of state and of its concrete forms in capitalist formations. Marx's analyses of the bureaucracy overlap very exactly his analyses of the capitalist state in its relations to the classes; he stresses the bureaucracy's own unity vis-à-vis these classes, which is caused by the combination of the state's structures with the dominant ideology, in particular the juridico-political ideology.

Refracted in this way, the bureaucracy's unity is related to the ensemble of levels of the struggle between the classes in a capitalist formation, both the classes of the capitalist mode and those of the non-dominant modes of production of this formation. It is related, in the first place, to the effect of isolation which is characteristic of the economic struggle between the bourgeoisie and the working class, and with the particular isolation of the small-holding peasantry and petty bourgeoisie. This isolation enables the state bureaucracy to present itself as a political unity, representing the unity of the people-nation. Marx insists on this point in his analyses of the particular relation between the bureaucracy and the small-holding peasantry: 'By its very nature, small property-holding forms a suitable basis for an all powerful and innumerable bureaucracy. It creates a uniform level of relationships and persons over the whole surface of the land. Hence, it also permits of uniform action from a supreme centre on all points of this uniform mass.'[4] Engels lays equal stress on this point in his analyses of the relation between the bureaucracy and the German petty bourgeoisie with its 'petty local interests, its local organization in the various towns, its local struggles and local progress'.[5] The bureaucracy/bourgeoisie relation is in fact twofold: it is the relation between the bureaucracy and (a) the 'ordinary bourgeois' who are prepared to sacrifice their private interests to their general class interests (isolation effect) and (b) a bourgeoisie deeply split into class fractions.

4. 'The Eighteenth Brumaire', *MESW*, 1970, p. 174.
5. 'Der status quo in Deutschland', op. cit., p. 22. Cf. also Lenin, 'The Tax in Kind', *Collected Works*, Vol. 32, p. 351: 'In our country bureaucratic practices have different economic roots, namely, the atomised and scattered state of the small producer with his poverty, illiteracy, lack of culture, the absence of roads and *exchange* between agriculture and industry, the absence of connection and interaction between them.'

At the level of the political class struggle, it is a question of the relation between the bureaucracy and the struggle of the dominant classes and their fractions: this leads to the problem of their *political organization*, since the bureaucracy becomes a representative factor of their political unity, by means of the state which plays the role of producer of this organization. In the relation between the bureaucracy and the classes of small-scale producers, it is a question of their constitutive incapacity to organize themselves politically: this entails their power fetishism and the bureaucracy's role of representing their unity. At the political level, the small-holding peasantry and the petty bourgeoisie are 'typically' represented by the bureaucratic body, which maintains them in their political disorganization, by means of the state.[6]

In short, the relative autonomy of the bureaucratic category from the dominant classes is related to that of the capitalist type of state and to that of its forms in the capitalist formations. By rigorously following through our conclusions on the relative autonomy of the state, we can say that the bureaucracy itself, as a social category, assumes this autonomy, in that it accurately reflects the political power of the dominant classes and represents their interests in the particular economic, political and ideological conditions of the class struggle in these formations.

These remarks allow us to clear up a certain number of questions.

A. The question of certain aspects of the relation between bureaucratism as the system of organization of the state apparatus and the forms of the bourgeoisie's political domination: in ideological discussion, this question has centred around the theme of the 'dysfunctionalism' of the bureaucratic apparatus. In fact, (i) this question is not of a technical order (one of technical efficacity or non-efficacity) but completely political; and (ii) it cannot be grasped by the notion of dysfunction. What Marx's and Engels's analyses make clear is that, although bureaucratism is a necessary political effect of the dominance of the CMP in a formation, it presents a whole series of contradictions with its forms of political domination.

6. These analyses are to be found especially in Marx's texts on France. We should note that, according to the social formations considered, this typical relation of 'representation' of the classes of small-scale producers by the state apparatus may crystallize into a 'state body' other than that of the bureaucracy in the strict sense: one example is the army. This is the case for several countries in Latin America: see José Nun, 'Amérique Latine: la crise hégémonique et le coup d'état militaire' in *Sociologie du travail*, no. 3, 1967.

Strictly speaking, these are *the contradictions inherent both in the dominant political ideology and in the structures of the capitalist state.* Examples are, as Engels showed, the contradictions between the bureaucratic secrecy necessary for the apparatus of this state and the principle of publicity which characterizes both bourgeois political ideology (e.g. public opinion, etc.) and the 'representative' state;[7] or, as Marx showed, between the functioning of the executive power (including the bureaucracy) and the functioning of parliamentary representation.

There is, however, one aspect which is often dealt with too cursorily: *these contradictions are also derived from the relations between bureaucratism and the classes of the small-scale producers,* in so far as this effect (bureaucracy and bureaucratism) of a type of state on the class struggle is reflected in a social formation. This relation, which produces these contradictions, is so obvious that Engels went so far as to base the whole of 'Der status quo in Deutschland' on the 'incompatibility' of the bourgeoisie's political domination with the 'bureaucratized' political forms.[8] Moreover, Lenin, too, sees in the bureaucratism of the socialist state in transition both the ideological legacy of capitalism and the impact of petty-bourgeois ideology. This aspect of the relation between bureaucratism and the political forms of bourgeois domination refers to:

1. The contradictions *between the dominant capitalist ideology and the petty-bourgeois ideology in the capitalist state apparatus.* This petty-bourgeois ideology is necessary for the functioning of bureaucratism in the capitalist state apparatus. Power fetishism, which is characteristic of this ideology, contributes to the establishment of normative rules which bring into operation hierarchical subordination in the subordinate strata of the state apparatus. However, this fetishism threatens the ensemble of the apparatus and thus comes into contradiction with the capitalist ideology dominant there. Examples would be personalization of offices through privileges (in contradiction with their impersonal character), fatalism and lack of action (in contradiction with the ideology of efficacity), etc.

2. The contradictions *between the type of capitalist state and the characteristics which are imposed upon it in a formation by the existence of the classes of small-scale producers.* Such is the case with the 'hypertrophy' of the state apparatus in France because of the existence of the small-holding peasantry and the petty bourgeoisie which is at the origin of,

7. 'Der status quo in Deutschland', op. cit.
8. 'The bureaucracy was established in order to govern the petty bourgeoisie and the peasantry', ibid., p. 30.

amongst other things, the contradictions between executive power and the system of parliamentary representation in this country.

These considerations allow us to clear up a 'paradoxical' problem concerning the bureaucratic phenomenon, a typically capitalist phenomenon: the less clear and obvious is the dominance of the CMP over the other modes in a formation, the more important is the impact of bureaucracy, and the greater the chances of the bureaucracy raising itself into a social force. As proof, we have only to compare the French and German cases with that of Britain.

B. Several authors, including Weber and Michels, have pointed to what they call the contradiction between bureaucratism and the forms of 'democracy'. Such authors belong with the tendency which establishes a relation between bureaucratism and 'totalitarian' political forms, conceived as radically distinct from 'democracy' in general. Furthermore, the bureaucracy is in this context often considered as the subject/creator of bureaucratism, of the norms of bureaucratized functioning and of institutionalized power, and hence, as the foundation of totalitarian institutionalized forms. To analyse the real phenomena masked by this ideological problematic, we must separate out a series of distinct problems; and we must even leave aside the problem of the contradictions between bureaucratism and the socialist democracy of the dictatorship of the proletariat as posed by Marx, in his texts on the Paris Commune, and by Lenin, when dealing with the socialist state in transition, since this is posed in a context totally different from that which we are considering here.

What can be said about the problem of the relations between bureaucratism and *bourgeois democracy*, i.e. the institutionalized forms of the bourgeoisie's political domination? From the point of view of *legitimacy*, which is essential for the analysis of bureaucratism, *the legitimacy proper to the bureaucracy* (i.e. the impact of the dominant political ideology on the functioning of the state apparatus) clearly belongs to *the type of bourgeois legitimacy*. In this sense, bureaucratism is a characteristic feature of the type of this legitimacy, just as much as bureaucracy is a characteristic of the capitalist type of state. There is in fact a legitimacy proper to the state apparatus which is none other than the characteristic features of bureaucratism. Because of its hierarchical functioning resulting from the delegation of power and power fetishism, the legitimacy of this state apparatus contains, for example, charismatic elements bearing on the supreme authority of a 'leader' who is the top of the state pyramid, tendencies towards the isolation of the state apparatus from popular representation, etc. This legitimacy proper to the bureaucracy is however only *a particular form of bourgeois legitimacy*, i.e. that form which characterizes the dominance of the executive. Bureaucratic legitimacy is by no means contrary to the typical legitimacy of the capitalist state, any more than forms of state dominated by the executive (including the various Bonapartist-Caesarist forms) are contrary to the typical forms of bourgeois domination, i.e. to the institutions of political democracy. We can, however, witness a whole series of contradictions and dislocations between the legitimacy of the state apparatus and that of a form of state with parliamentary dominance; or between the legitimacy of a state form with executive dominance and that of the social formation, in which the form of legitimacy dominating it is parliamentary legitimacy.

C. In the case of a form of capitalist state dominated by the executive which is in agreement with the form of dominant legitimacy in a formation, the internal legitimacy of the bureaucratic apparatus coincides with the legitimacy in the ensemble of the formation. This poses in a particularly acute form the question of the *bureaucracy's own role* in a concrete form of a state dominated by the executive. In fact, if it has such a role, it is to be found in the impact of the politico-ideological phenomenon of bureaucratism rather than in a bureaucracy defending its own economic interests and supporting the executive. I cannot repeat too often that bureaucracy is constituted as a specific category by its relation to the political and the ideological.

This depends on whether or not the bureaucracy constitutes *a social force* in the concrete conjuncture. Two preliminary remarks must be made:

1. The first is quite obvious: since the bureaucracy is neither a class nor a fraction of a class, it can in no way play a principal role in the constitution of a form of state. In the case of a state dominated by the executive and corresponding to the dominant legitimacy of a formation, this form is established from the ensemble of factors in the class struggle. The same is true in the case of a dislocation between this form of state and the dominant legitimacy in formation, this dislocation being reducible neither exclusively nor even principally to the existence of the bureaucracy.

2. The second remark is less obvious: although the bureaucracy as such (from the moment that it can constitute a theoretical object) is a specific category, although it possesses a relative autonomy and unity peculiar to it, *it is not for that reason a social force*, any more than the classes or autonomous fractions of classes are. As a specific category *it can* in a concrete conjuncture become one, as Lenin stressed in the case of the capitalist

state. When it constitutes a social force, it possesses a role of its own in political action: *but this does not confer on it a power of its own.* This can also be the case for the classes/social forces (e.g. the working class or, in extreme cases, the supporting classes) which can constitute social forces without thereby possessing power of their own.

Constituting the bureaucracy into a social force depends on the conjuncture, e.g. on the state's role (dominant or not) in the ensemble of instances. This was the case for instance in Germany in particular, and to a lesser extent, in France, at the time when the bureaucracy was a social force in the general framework of the dominant role which has often devolved on the state. It also depends on the concrete situation of the class struggle: e.g. the above-mentioned situations of a general equilibrium of forces, and especially those of a catastrophe-equilibrium, operating in the framework of a capitalist state, create conditions favourable for the constitution of the bureaucracy as a social force. The same is true for the case of the particular political disorganization of the dominant classes (e.g. crisis of party representation in the political scene) whether or not combined with situations of equilibrium, or for the case of the constitution of the classes of the small-scale producers, of the peasants, and in particular the small-holding peasants, and of the petty bourgeoisie into social forces: in this latter case, the bureaucracy raises itself into a social force by functioning as the political 'representative' of these classes; and the same again is true for the case of the general crisis of legitimacy in a formation. In short, there is an ensemble of factors which, in their always original combination within a formation, may allow the bureaucracy to function not merely as a specific category possessing its own unity and relative autonomy, but as an effective social force.

This existence of the bureaucracy as a social force can be deciphered within the framework of a correlation with the forms of the capitalist state. It is particularly clear in those particular historical forms of the capitalist state known as Caesarist, such as the Empires of both Bonapartes in France. In these cases, the bureaucracy exercises its function as a social force, which it holds by reason of the conjuncture itself, by contributing effectively to the constitution and support of these forms of state. The bureaucracy as a social force certainly possesses its *own particular role*: namely to support these particular forms of state, by means of the bureaucratism which characterizes its internal legitimacy.

In *The Eighteenth Brumaire*, Marx clearly demonstrates the particular support which the state apparatus in France gave Louis Bonaparte by means of bureaucratism. This support is mainly conditioned not by the simple material interests of the members of the state apparatus, but by bureaucratism.

Index

abstract, abstract-formal, 13, 15, 17, 22; real, real-concrete, 12–13, 22, 145–6, 196
Adler, Max, 179
agriculture, 74, 161, 168–72, 174, 182, 231
alienation, 124, 195–7, 280, 343
alliance, 83, 97, 165n, 167, 175, 234n, 236, 240–5, 251–2
Althusser, Louis, 14n, 18n, 40–1, 87, 305–06
America, 153, 272, 320–1
American path, 170n, 231
anarcho-syndicalism, 206
Anderson, Perry, 82n, 200
anthropologism, 12, 64–6, 109, 221
apparatus(es), 43, 115–17, 164, 165n, 171–3, 177–8, 182–3, 191–2, 216, 249–250, 271, 272, 308–09, 311, 325–30, 332–59
Apter, David, 47n, 224n
Aristotle, 217
army, 164
articulation, 15–17, 29, 49, 50, 69–70, 71, 87–93, 129, 150, 157, 209, 234, 273, 274
authoritarianism, 290–4, 312
authority, 105–06, 146–7, 165, 222
autonomy, relative, 29, 161n, 163, 193, 217, 256, 259, 261–2, 263–74, 282, 284–5, 286, 294–303, 319–20, 348; specific, 41, 46–7, 57, 72, 127, 129, 135, 136, 139, 143, 148, 150, 151–2, 203, 214, 227, 237

Babeuf, François-Noël, 179n
Balandier, Georges, 52n, 224n
Balibar, Étienne, 87–9
base, 17, 50, 156n, 196, 281
Bettelheim, Charles, 149–50
Bismarckism, 80–1, 144–5, 155, 167n, 170, 172, 174, 180–1, 249, 260, 271–2, 294n

Blanc, Louis, 180, 271
Blanqui, Auguste, 179n
bloc, historical, 197, 200–01; of parties, 251–2; power see power bloc
Bonapartism, 22, 79–81, 107–08, 118, 167n, 180, 183, 243–4, 258–62, 279–86, 294n, 302–03, 320, 351
Bourdieu, Pierre, 61, 65n, 223n
bourgeois individualism, 219
bourgeois revolution, 168–84
bourgeois state, 158, 306–07
bourgeoisie, 80, 81, 82, 85, 90–1, 157–67, 173, 176–7, 181–4, 189, 203–04, 211–12, 232–4, 236–40, 250, 252, 284–9, 293, 297–300, 320, 334, 351–9; commercial, 84, 169–172, 173–7, 233, 307; financial, 84, 170–1, 233, 251, 307; industrial, 84, 169–71, 173–7, 233, 251; land-owning, 169–70; petty, 170, 174, 175–7, 179, 182, 210, 243, 251, 276, 285–6, 288, 293, 334, 338–40; state, 334
Britain, 81, 90, 113n, 114, 153–4, 155, 161–2, 165n, 168–73, 176, 177, 180, 181, 182, 203–04, 232, 250, 252, 320, 321, 335, 336, 337, 338, 346
Bukharin, Nicolai, 50, 91
bureaucracy, 84, 85, 94, 164–5, 199, 216, 269, 278–9, 311, 325–30, 332–40, 341–359
bureaucratism, 22, 332–5, 341–4, 347–50, 354, 355–6, 359
Burnham, James, 329, 330

Caesarism, 260–1, 293n, 298–9
capital, 32, 66, 159; concentration, 127, 128, 176
caste, 70, 71
category(ies), 84–5, 94, 332–4, 335, 337, 346, 348–50, 357–8
civil society, 124–5, 127–8, 134–5, 139–40, 151–2, 196, 226, 279–82